A DEATHLESS STORY
OR
THE "BIRKENHEAD" AND ITS HEROES

"I can fancy a future Author taking for his story the glorious action off Cape Danger, when, striking only to the Powers above, the *Birkenhead* went down; and when, with heroic courage and endurance, the men kept to their duty on deck."

WM. MAKEPEACE THACKERAY, *May*, 1852.

A DEATHLESS STORY

OR

THE "BIRKENHEAD" AND ITS HEROES

BEING THE ONLY FULL AND AUTHENTIC ACCOUNT OF THE FAMOUS SHIPWRECK EXTANT, FOUNDED ON COLLECTED OFFICIAL, DOCUMENTARY, AND PERSONAL EVIDENCE, AND CONTAINING THE NARRATIVES AND LIVES OF ACTORS IN THE MOST GLORIOUS OCEAN TRAGEDY IN HISTORY

BY

A. C. ADDISON

AUTHOR OF "THE STORY OF THE *BIRKENHEAD*," HEREWITH INCORPORATED

AND

W. H. MATTHEWS

SON OF A LATE NAVAL SURVIVOR

WITH MAP, FACSIMILES OF LETTERS
AND OVER SIXTY ILLUSTRATIONS

London : HUTCHINSON & CO.
Paternoster Row   1906

PREFACE

AT the close of 1902, the 50th anniversary year of the shipwreck, appeared *The Story of the "Birkenhead,"* a work which received everywhere a warm and patriotic welcome as commemorating an event the memory and moral of which will never die. The circulation of the book naturally led to further discoveries in connection with a subject of such attractive and worldwide interest. Each additional piece of information or clue, as it came to hand, was carefully sifted or followed up. For more than two years this process of ingathering and investigating went steadily on. It involved an immense correspondence. It extended to all parts of the United Kingdom, to the Cape, and to districts of South Africa. Not only did Military materials accumulate, but on the Naval side also new matter of value to the subject and its associations began early to collect. It was then that W. H. Matthews, the son of a late Naval survivor, with whom the story, more particularly in its maritime aspects, had been a lifelong study, joined forces with the author of the first book, and the work of research and absorption was continued in unison with the happiest results. Fresh ground has been broken in many directions, and paths are now trod the existence of which was not before suspected. The joint authors feel they can safely say that the subject is at last exhausted, and that all that is to be learnt, or can with advantage be stated, about the *Birkenhead* and its heroes is contained within the covers of this book. They have, at any rate, striven to achieve that desirable end, and they believe they have succeeded.

The pioneer work is incorporated in the present volume, and the whole record, with its numerous additions, has been much improved in form and arrangement. The aim has been to avoid all needless repetition of the main circumstances of the story, which is presented as far as practicable in consecutive shape and orderly sequence. The personal experiences of survivors of course remain, as they should do. It is, indeed, only by means of them that we get the full story. At such a time everybody would see things which nobody else saw, and would probably estimate the things that were commonly seen from different standpoints. And their escapes, trials, and sufferings were severally their own concern, described best in their own language. Their testimony is therefore important, and nothing in the history of the wreck is more interesting or informing than these pulsating individual narratives.

From South Africa itself come additions to the story of deep and pathetic, and, it must also be added, tragic interest. The book is especially indebted to Mr. O. Leigh-Clare, M.P., afterwards Vice-Chancellor of the Duchy of Lancaster, the late Colonel Wright's executor, and to Major A. D. Seton, nephew of the heroic Colonel who commanded the troops on the *Birkenhead*, for their kindly and ready help in furnishing materials of great importance to the subject. To many others also, survivors themselves and their relatives, the War Office, the Admiralty, the Commissioners of Chelsea

PREFACE

Hospital, the Council of the United Service Institution, and the officials of the British and South Kensington Museums, the thanks of authors and readers are due for valued assistance rendered.

Included in the work is a unique series of portraits, presented for the purpose in honour of the subject, of the five last Commanders-in-Chief of the British Army, whose names are more or less associated with the *Birkenhead*, together with the letters on the subject of two of their number. First we have the Duke of Wellington, who, in the closing days of his great career, was brought closely into touch with the *Birkenhead*, and whose last official act almost was to sign the document reproduced in these pages conferring a Distinguished Service pension on the senior surviving officer. Next in order is Viscount Hardinge, who backed up the efforts of Sir Wm. Napier to obtain the *Birkenhead* Monument. Then follows the Duke of Cambridge, who in his early Army days was second Lieutenant-Colonel of the 12th Lancers, with which regiment he served in Ireland, and in later life was a personal friend of Captain Bond-Shelton, of the same corps, a surviving officer; and who, as Commander-in-Chief, specially thanked Colonel Wright, then Assistant-Quartermaster-General, for his satisfactory supervision of the disembarkation of troops from the Crimea. Then come Lord Wolseley and Earl Roberts, who took up the subject so earnestly at the 50th anniversary.

The list of those thus honouring the *Birkenhead* is continued by King Edward VII., whose portrait was specially signed for this book on a date that will ever be memorable, October 21st, 1905, Trafalgar Centenary day; the Duke of Connaught, our first Inspector-General of the Forces, as

Colonel-in-Chief of the Highland Light Infantry, of which Colonel Seton's regiment, the 74th, is now the 2nd Battalion; and the King of Italy and the King of Portugal, monarchs proudly claimed by this country as friends and allies, King Carlos being also Colonel-in-Chief of a *Birkenhead* regiment, the Oxfordshire Light Infantry, formerly the 43rd. Copies of the earlier book were, in recognition of the subject, accepted cordially by the Royal personages named, the Emperor of Japan and the Prince of Wales.

The completed work in the hands of the reader is dedicated to the British people, and especially to our Army and Navy, to whose glorious traditions belongs the Deathless Story.

A word has to be added touching a discovery of a remarkable and quite romantic kind which was made when the work for the book was almost finished, and this Preface had been written. By a happy chance the fact transpired that the fathers of the joint authors actually served as shipmates in the *Castor*, the flagship stationed at the Cape when the *Birkenhead* was wrecked, on board which many of the survivors were conveyed, and in the cabin of which Commodore Wyvill wrote his Naval report on the disaster. Their service together in the *Castor* was during the three years' commission of the frigate, 1855-58, referred to in Chapters XI. and XIV. Mr. Daniel Addison, of Brixton Hill, S.W., formerly in the Royal Navy, well remembered Chief Officer of Coastguards W. H. Matthews, as he afterwards became, as a *Birkenhead* survivor serving in the *Castor* at the same time as himself, and he had many pleasant recollections both of his old shipmate and the voyage. It was, of course, known that Mr. Addison belonged to the *Castor* early in his interesting career; but until the truth was ascertained it was not suspected that he sailed in the frigate throughout this commission with Mr. Matthews.

A third shipmate of the cruise was found to be still living in the person of Mr. Wm. Griffiths, of Brighton. All Her Majesty's ships in those days carried a fiddler. Mr. Griffiths discharged that blithesome duty on the *Castor*, and he was also remembered for an extraordinary misadventure which befell him on board. He was heaving the lead on entering St. Augustine's Bay, Madagascar, when a mischievous pet monkey, kept by a gunroom officer, untied the rope supporting him and he pitched headlong into the sea. The frigate, a fast sailer, was put about, and the victim of the prank, who luckily was a strong swimmer, was picked up more dead than alive after a long immersion in the shark-infested waters. The cause of all the trouble was then a voluntary exile at the masthead, whither it had fled in alarm on realising the seriousness of its action.

The beautiful picture of the flagship which appears in the book was prepared with the assistance of the *Castor* survivors named.

    A. C. ADDISON } JOINT AUTHORS.
    W. H. MATTHEWS

March, 1906.

CONTENTS

                                  PAGE

I
INTRODUCTION 1

II
THE WRECK 12

III
THE OFFICIAL STORY 36
    (*Military and Naval reports, and statements by survivors.*)

IV
THE DEATH ROLL 62
    And the Muster Roll.

V
TRIBUTES TO THE BRAVE 68

VI
A HERO'S WORK FOR HEROES 81
    (*The action and letters of Sir Wm. Napier.*)

VII
THE IRON DUKE AND THE "BIRKENHEAD" . . . 97

VIII
MORE PERILOUS ADVENTURES 101
    The *Castor's* Launch.
    The Corvette *Amazon* with Survivors on board.

CONTENTS

IX
NAVAL SURVIVORS COURT-MARTIALLED 104

X
FROM THE CRADLE TO THE GRAVE 110
(*History and voyages of the* Birkenhead.)

XI
SISTER SHIPS AT THE CAPE 119
The *Castor*—Commodore Wyvill, Commander Bunce.
The *Rhadamanthus*.
Schooner *Lioness* and the *Megæra*.

XII
GALLANT AND GIFTED COLONEL SETON 126

XIII
THE CAREER OF COLONEL WRIGHT, C.B. 143

XIV
CAPTAIN SALMOND'S PATHETIC END 158
Other *Birkenhead* Officers—Mr. Wm. Brodie, Mr. R. B. Richards, Dr. Culhane, Mr. C. K. Renwick, Mr. Benjamin Barber.
Chief Officer of Coastguards W. H. Matthews.
Thomas Drackford.
Surgeon-General Bowen.

XV
GRAPHIC NARRATIVE OF AN OFFICER 179
(*Written by Ensign Lucas.*)

XVI
FIFTY YEARS AFTER 185

XVII
"ALL THAT WAS LEFT OF THEM" 196
(*The* Birkenhead *Survivors,*)

CONTENTS

XVIII

FATE OF SOUTH AFRICAN SURVIVORS 231
    Mr. Charles Daly.
    Sergeant W. H. McCluskey.
    (*Memoir by Captain Blackbeard, Mayor of Beaconsfield.*)
    Colonel R. A. Nesbitt, C.B.
    Corporal Wm. Butler.

XIX

A DAUGHTER OF THE REGIMENT 248
    (*Mrs. Parkinson, one of the children saved.*)
    The 2nd Queen's and the Wreck.

XX

DANGER POINT 255
    ("*Lest we forget.*")

XXI

THE TRAGIC DEATH OF A SURVIVOR 261
    (*Trial of McCluskey's Murderer.*)

XXII

THE POETIC PICTURE OF THE "BIRKENHEAD" 270
    By Sir Francis Hastings Doyle.
    By Dr. John A. Goodchild.

XXIII

REMARKABLE PASSAGES IN THE LIFE OF JOHN DRAKE, MARINE 281

XXIV

RECOLLECTIONS OF A RAMBLING LIFE 296
    (*Written by Corporal Wm. Smith, 12th Regiment,
    a* Birkenhead *Survivor.*)

LIST OF ILLUSTRATIONS

The Scene on board the Sinking Troopship, by Mr. Thos. M. Hemy . . . . *Frontispiece*	
(*Copyright Picture of Messrs. Hy. Graves & Co.*)	
H.M. King Edward VII. . . . . *Facing p.*	2
H.M. The King of Italy . . . . „	6
H.M. The King of Portugal . . . . . . „	10
Nearing the Sunken Rock . . . . *Page*	15
Striking the Rock . . . . „	19
Breaking . . . . „	23
The Wreck . . . . „	27
Picture of the Wreck by Mr. Chas. Dixon, R.I. . . *Facing p.*	30
(*From "Britannia's Bulwarks."*)	
Photograph of Entries in Port Book at Capetown, including Statement of Arrival and Departure of the "Birkenhead," with Description and Details of Passengers . . . „	40
Photograph of Entries in Port Book at Capetown, stating Arrival of Schooner "Lioness" in tow of the "Rhadamanthus," with Survivors from the Wreck of the "Birkenhead" . . . . „	48
Photograph of Entries in Port Book at Capetown, stating Arrival of the "Rhadamanthus" with "Birkenhead" Survivors on Board . . . . „	58
The "Birkenhead" Monument at Chelsea Hospital . . „	66
The Loss of the "Birkenhead" . . . . . . „	80
(*From the Picture by Captain Bond-Shelton, 12th Royal Lancers.*)	
"Birkenhead" Letter written by General Sir Wm. Napier to Major Wright . . . . „	86
(*Facsimile reproduction.*)	
The Clipper Ship "James Baines" with Troops for India . „	92
(*Inspected before leaving Portsmouth by Queen Victoria and Royal children, when Colonel Wright explained to them the Birkenhead disaster.*)	
Field-Marshal the Duke of Wellington, K.G., Commander-in-Chief at date of the Wreck . . . . . . „	96
(*With portion of letter and signature.*)	
Extreme Peril of "Castor's" Launch, sent to Survey the "Birkenhead" Rock . . . . „	100

LIST OF ILLUSTRATIONS

PERIL OF H.M. CORVETTE "AMAZON" WITH "BIRKENHEAD" SURVIVORS ON BOARD	*Facing p.* 102
FIELD-MARSHAL H.R.H. THE DUKE OF CAMBRIDGE, K.G.	,, 106
THE "BIRKENHEAD" TROOPSHIP	,, 112
(*The only known Picture of the Ship as she actually existed. Owned by the late Mr. Barber, Chief Engineer, R.N., a survivor, and the work of a brother officer.*)	
H.M.S. "CASTOR," FLYING THE COMMODORE'S PENNANT AS FLAGSHIP AT THE CAPE	,, 118
(*The only existing Picture of this noted frigate in full rig.*)	
THE "CASTOR'S" FIGUREHEAD	,, 122
ADMIRAL WYVILL	,, 122
MODELS OF H.M. PADDLE SLOOP "RHADAMANTHUS," SHOWING (1) DECK DETAILS AND ARTISTIC FIGUREHEAD, (2) BROADSIDE OF VESSEL	,, 124
(*One of the first steamships built for the British Navy. Photographed by permission of Council of the Royal United Service Institution, Whitehall.*)	
EARLY PORTRAIT OF COLONEL SETON IN UNIFORM OF ROYAL NORTH BRITISH FUSILIERS	,, 126
(*From a Miniature in the possession of the family.*)	
FIELD-MARSHAL H.R.H. THE DUKE OF CONNAUGHT, K.G., INSPECTOR-GENERAL OF THE FORCES	,, 132
(*As Colonel-in-Chief of the Highland Light Infantry, of which the 74th Regiment is now the 2nd Battalion.*)	
MONUMENT TO THE 74TH HIGHLANDERS IN ST. GILES' CATHEDRAL, EDINBURGH	,, 138
(*Commemorating Colonel Seton and Birkenhead heroes.*)	
COLONEL E. W. C. WRIGHT, C.B.	,, 142
COPY IN CAPTAIN WRIGHT'S HANDWRITING OF QUESTION CONCERNING THE WRECK WHICH HE ADDRESSED TO LIEUTENANT GIRARDOT; AND LIEUTENANT GIRARDOT'S REPLY	,, 146
OFFICIAL COMMUNICATION CONFERRING DISTINGUISHED SERVICE PENSION ON CAPTAIN WRIGHT. ONE OF THE LAST DOCUMENTS SIGNED BY THE DUKE OF WELLINGTON	,, 148
(*Facsimile reproduction.*)	
BATTALION ORDER CONVEYING TO CAPTAIN WRIGHT THE QUEEN'S APPROBATION OF HIS SERVICE AT THE WRECK	,, 150
(*Facsimile reproduction.*)	
COLONEL WRIGHT'S RECORD OF SERVICE IN HIS OWN HANDWRITING	*Pages* 154, 155
INVITATION TO OSBORNE, INSCRIBED WITH THE RECORD OF AN INTERESTING EVENT IN CAPTAIN WRIGHT'S HANDWRITING	*Facing p.* 156
CAPTAIN ROBERT SALMOND, R.N.	,, 158
(*Portrait painted some years before the wreck.*)	
LETTER WRITTEN BY CAPTAIN SALMOND ON EVE OF THE WRECK	,, 160
(*Facsimile reproduction.*)	
SURGEON WM. CULHANE, R.N.	,, 162
MR. B. BARBER, R.N.	,, 164
CHIEF OFFICER OF COASTGUARDS W. H. MATTHEWS	,, 166

xvi   LIST OF ILLUSTRATIONS

Thomas Drackford	Facing p. 174
Surgeon-General Robt. Bowen, F.R.C.S.	,, 176
Captain G. A. Lucas, late 73rd Regiment	,, 180
"Roll Call" of Survivors	,, 186
(Duplicate of Document presented to the King.)	
Field-Marshal Viscount Wolseley, K.P.	,, 188
Field-Marshal Earl Roberts, V.C., K.G., Commander-in-Chief at Date of Fiftieth Anniversary	,, 190
Lieut.-Colonel J. F. Girardot, late 43rd Light Infantry	,, 196
Letter written by Colonel Girardot at Date of Fiftieth Anniversary	,, 198
(Facsimile reproduction.)	
Captain R. M. Bond-Shelton, late 12th Royal Lancers	,, 202
Captain G. A. Lucas, late 73rd Regiment	,, 204
(In his robes as Chief Magistrate of Durban.)	
Mr. J. T. Archbold, the Gunner of the "Birkenhead"	,, 206
(With portion of letter written shortly before his death.)	
Colour-Sergeant John Drake, R.M.L.I.	,, 208
Colour-Sergeant John O'Neil, 91st Regiment	,, 210
Colour-Sergeant Bernard Kilkeary, 73rd Regiment	,, 214
Sergeant Francis Ginn, 43rd Light Infantry	,, 216
Corporal Wm. Smith, 12th Foot	,, 218
Private John Smith, 2nd Queen's Regiment	,, 222
Thomas Coffin	,, 224
("The Man at the Wheel.")	
Private Wm. Tuck, R.M.L.I.	,, 226
Benjamin Turner	,, 228
Thomas Kelly	,, 230
Mr. Charles Daly	,, 232
Sergeant W. H. McCluskey	,, 236
Portions of Letter written by Colonel Nesbitt, C.B., in the Year of his Death, concerning the "Birkenhead" and Surviving Officers	Page 243
(Facsimile reproduction.)	
Colonel R. A. Nesbitt, C.B.	Facing p. 244
Mrs. Parkinson, née Marian Darkin	,, 248
Danger Point Lighthouse and Keepers' Quarters	,, 254
Danger Point Lighthouse	Page 255
Views of Danger Point and Vicinity	Facing p. 256
David Faro	,, 258
Map Sections showing Points named in the Story	,, 260
Portrait of Colour-Sergeant John Drake, R.M.L.I., in Uniform	,, 282
General Viscount Hardinge, G.C.B.	,, 300

A DEATHLESS STORY

CHAPTER I

INTRODUCTION

TIME has not dimmed nor have events o'ershadowed the lustrous memory of the *Birkenhead*. The story of that shipwreck is as dear to the hearts of Britons everywhere to-day as it was when first its facts and true significance were known to the world. And why? Not merely because it was a great shipwreck. Unhappily we have had hundreds of them, and they have always been tragic and costly in human lives—some more so than others, in proportion to their magnitude and circumstances. Not alone because it was an instance of the display of high and determined courage and laudable self-sacrifice. Happily we have known many such. Gallantry and intrepidity, daring in its divers forms, and fortitude even, that "guard and support" of the other virtues, are peculiar to the vocation of our soldiers and sailors. Does not our national history teem with the best illustrations of these things? There is no call or need to label the *Birkenhead* as an exalted specimen of anything of the kind. What, then, does it pre-eminently represent? The answer is that it affords us the most striking example of heroism and discipline, combined and triumphant, under appalling conditions, that has ever been known or recorded. Some hundreds of soldiers and seamen, officers and men, went to a sure and a shocking death rather than jeopardise the safety of women and children who had been placed in the only boats which pulled from the wreck. That accounts for the heroism. The discipline which made its action possible was marvellous because the troops on board the sinking ship were mere drafts composed for the most part of young soldiers going out to reinforce their several regiments on the South African frontier. Well might the conduct of these heroes wring from an admiring world applause the echoes of which will resound for all time. It was well deserved. The courageous man defies the presence of danger, and exhibits his spirit in doughty deeds; the valorous shine in battle and the intrepid throw themselves headlong where peril most appals, just as gallant men dash into the thickest of the fight; while the passive courage we call fortitude bears up nobly through it all, let come what will. But heroism crowns these splendid qualities with a radiance of its own, partakes of the best of them all; and it is heroism, steadfast and resolute, and discipline, unbroken and steady, which mark so surely the men of the *Birkenhead*. In them the "perfume of heroic deeds" has been wafted down to us, and will be borne onward to future generations with undiminished fragrance. To them apply with peculiar force and fitness the thrilling lines of Swinburne on "Grace Darling":

> Stars and moon and sun may wax and wane, subside and rise,
>   Age on age, as flake on flake of showering snows be shed;
> Not till earth be sunless, not till death strike blind the skies,
>   May the deathless love that waits on deathless deeds be dead.

No wonder the *Birkenhead* lives in the affections of a people and is cherished there. It is an abiding memory. It might in substance be stronger than it is—less shadowy, truer historically, and more real. The popular fictions associated with the *Birkenhead* and accretions which have gathered to the subject are astonishing. Some of them are noted towards the end of this book, where it will be seen that a responsible scholar, writing as late as 1903, out-errors them all by declaring, not that these heroes went to their death singing "God save the Queen," but that they quitted the world saluting it with a parting musketry volley! When *The Windsor Magazine* spoke about the *Birkenhead*, some time before this melodramatic outburst, it was content to assert that "the whole force—officers and men—stood at the salute" while the doomed ship, in the poet's words, "sank low." But the magazine made amends for its modesty in this matter by

H.M. KING EDWARD VII.

(Photo by W. & D. Downey, Ebury Street, S.W. Signed specially for this book on the Centenary Day of Trafalgar, October 21st, 1905, in honour of the *Birkenhead*)

INTRODUCTION 3

telling a wonderful story of a boy hero "just out of school, a mere lad of seventeen, who yet was an officer in the 74th Highlanders, now the Highland Light Infantry." Young Russell, according to this account of him,

was ordered into one of the boats carrying the women and children, for the purpose of commanding it, and he sat with dimmed eyes in the stern, some way off the doomed ship, watching the forms of his beloved comrades and fellows standing upright there. He saw the ship go down, carrying with it the hundreds of brave hearts. He saw those fearful creatures of the deep seizing their prey, and heard the screams of scores of human beings torn to pieces by sharks.

Amid torments such as these the lad's heroism has its setting.

Then, when all for him was safe, when to him was given (with honour) life, ambition, and glory, he saw a sailor's form rise close to the boat, and a hand strive to grasp the side. There was not room in the craft for a single person more without great risk of upsetting the boat, and this sailor was a married man with a dependent family.

By this time the reader will have been sufficiently worked up for the climax. He will possess a dim foreboding of it, and pausing, will brace himself resolutely to know the end. It is worse than he anticipated:

Alexander Cumine Russell rose in the stern of the boat. With a bold plunge he jumped clear of it, and helped that sailor into what had been his own place—and safety. Then, amid a chorus of "God bless you!" from every soul in the boat, the young officer—a lad of seventeen, mind!—turned round to meet his death. And those in the boat shut their eyes and prayed. When they opened them again, Alexander Cumine Russell was nowhere to be seen!

How poetic! The tale is artistically told, but it has no other merit. It has no value, because it is not true. In no single particular does it border even upon the truth. In short, it is a pure invention. Ensign Russell's fate was a glorious one: he died doing his duty, but not at all in the manner here described. The self-sacrifice actually displayed at the time needs no such exaggeration; but like other features of the wreck, it has been more or less distorted. Early in 1905 it was publicly stated, in a reference to the death of a former wife of a *Birkenhead* soldier, that "the soldiers and crew to the number of 454 formed into line on the deck and went down with the vessel twenty minutes after the collision," and that "by this devotion 184 of the women and children"—a number exceeding that of the writer already quoted, whose moderate estimate is 166—"were saved to record the gallant sacrifice—heroism which has inspired poets, including Mr. Rudyard Kipling." Now Kipling does say emphatically of "the *Birken'ead* drill" that it is a "tough bullet to chew." Applied to certain *Birkenhead* "facts," the operation is scarcely less arduous. There appeared in a second pictorial print, *The Royal Magazine* for August, 1905, what purported to be a personal account of his experience at the wreck of a worthy old survivor, Corporal Wm. Smith of the 12th, who, although he was below at the chain pumps all the time, is made to describe circumstantially what took place on deck,* and one of his most curious observations is the statement put into his mouth that certain officers were superintending the removal of the women and children to the boat and "handing some of them to the gangway with a politeness and attention which is so wonderful that, sore as my own strait is, I cannot help smiling." Captain Lucas would smile too when he read this absurd parody, so contrary to the actual scene portrayed by himself, which shows us the terrified women being torn from their husbands and dragged to the gangway by main force. When at the last moment Corporal Smith sprang on deck, after performing the "hardest twenty minutes' work I ever did in my life," he was, as he declares in his authentic narratives in this book, "stark naked." † He is depicted by the imaginative magazine artist struggling for life in the water, encumbered as he clings to a floating spar by a heavy Military overcoat, with the number of his regiment conspicuous on the shoulder-strap! So in detail is the truth assailed. At a survivor's death a few months before, a writer recalled how—

when the ship struck, the captain ordered the boats to be lowered, crying that all was lost, and Major Wright, in command of the troops, ordered them to fall in, and threatened to shoot the first man who stepped towards

---

* "I remained below the whole time. I know very little about what happened on deck."—See statement by Corporal Smith, Chapter XVII.

† "When the vessel went to pieces I found myself in the water, stark naked, having taken the precaution to tear off my shirt, as I could not swim."—Corporal Smith, Chapter XXIV.

the boats. Up to their waists in water, the drowning men maintained discipline.

It is not a humorous subject by any means, yet here and there have been unconscious attempts to make it so. The "Royal Marine Guards" on board had already been spoken of, and allusion was at the same time made to what befel a gallant surviving officer.

When he came up from the pumps he found two children on the floor of the saloon cabin. These he transferred to one of the boats. Going down with the vessel, he succeeded in swimming ashore, there to find his charges on the beach in the water.

The surprise of Cornet Bond, had this been the case, could only have been measured by his responsibilities. Happily he made no such discovery. Not castaway innocent children, but his own trusty steed, was what he found in the water on the beach. The poor charger had swum ashore. It was quite content to be a horse and nothing more—was glad, no doubt, that it still was one. Comes now a force to be reckoned with, a printer's error, and a touch as with a magician's wand transforms the equine shape. So that its treatment is, after all, capable of a satisfactory explanation.

The graver misrepresentations are more to be regretted. They are evidence of the fallacies which for long years have survived the wreck of the *Birkenhead*. We may now hope they will be dispersed. The study of the story should accomplish that. We would none of us care for it to descend to posterity in the character of a fairy tale, built largely upon ignorance as to the facts, and upon imagination as to the deductions to be drawn from them. There is a powerful fascination about the *Birkenhead*; but it is not a chapter of romance. The scene upon the decks that memorable February morning yielded no ostentatious displays of anything. There were no stage effects. There was no spectacle, save that of men overtaken by sudden disaster and aroused to a fearful danger calmly giving and obeying orders, and resolutely doing their duty in the face of prospective death. The spell of the story lies in its collective heroism. We have in it the observance of perfect discipline and control under conditions calculated to cause panic—not by seasoned troops, but by young soldiers for the most part fresh from home, who had been but a short time in the ranks; not by one regiment under its familiar leader, but by details of several different regiments under strange command. We have also shown here the existence of a spirit and an influence which restrained men under a great temptation and enabled women and children to be saved. The maintenance of this discipline and the presence of this self-sacrifice were in a large measure due to the officers of the regiments, who were indeed shining lights in that dark and terrible hour, directing the men, cheering and encouraging them, and by their conduct and example inspiring confidence in the rank and file. It was a grand display of discipline under the severest test, an object-lesson for all time of what discipline can effect, worthy of all emulation. So thought the King of Prussia, who, military monarch that he was, yet saw in the *Birkenhead* a high example which his own disciplined soldiers might with advantage take to heart; for he ordered the record of duty nobly done in the very jaws of Death by these brave Britons to be read at the head of all his regiments.

The subject was not honoured in the same way by our own country, but as a legacy of which any nation would be proud it received grateful if tardy recognition. In the colonnade of Chelsea Hospital there stands a Monument to the officers, non-commissioned officers and men who perished so nobly in the historic shipwreck. It was placed there by command of Queen Victoria, whose gracious act in ordering it to be raised had the seal of the approval of all her subjects. Not only has the *Birkenhead* this well-earned memorial on a spot consecrated to the preservation of our best Military traditions: poet and painter have vied in doing it honour, if sometimes at the cost of strict historical truth, with a popular success that cannot be questioned. There are the beautiful but fanciful lines of Sir Francis Hastings Doyle, and the noble if less musical verses of Dr. John A. Goodchild. The best of all the pictures are those reproduced in this book, the truest the tragic representation by Captain Bond-Shelton, done from a vivid recollection of the actual scene in which he was one of the actors.

H.M. THE KING OF ITALY

(Photo by Cav. L. Lamarra, Naples. Specially presented in honour of the *Birkenhead*)

INTRODUCTION

While, however, the *Birkenhead* has not been forgotten or neglected, the story itself has never until now been fully told. Not that it is not well worth the telling. Nothing in our Military and Naval annals is more interesting and valuable in its way, and therefore more deserving of preservation. Nothing in the proud history of our Arms affords a higher and brighter example or stimulates more to worthy deeds. Why, then, have the erroneous notions existing upon this subject been allowed to continue uncorrected? Why has not the whole story been put before the public in available permanent form? Not because it would not repay the labour of doing it. That assuredly is not the explanation. The reason probably has been that the subject was one difficult of comprehensive literary treatment. Its materials were scattered and fragmentary, entailing a vast amount of search to collect and bring together in acceptable shape.

For as will be seen, there is a great deal in the subject that is instructive and entertaining apart from the central feature of the story comprised in the tragedy and heroism of the wreck. Here and there the *Birkenhead* has occupied a short chapter in a book of shipwrecks and disasters at sea, often defective and unreliable. It has been dealt with once at least in recent years within the narrow limits of a magazine article. That was in 1897, when the incidents of the historic shipwreck were ably and critically reviewed, and the great moral to be derived from it was emphasised by Major-General Maurice in an Anniversary Study in *The Cornhill*. Such a recital would serve, if a passing, a useful and a welcome purpose. What, however, is desired for the general reader is that he should have the whole of the facts and circumstances before him and the actual testimony of the actors in the scene. He can then be left to study the story for himself and form his own judgment with regard to it. That opportunity has hitherto been denied him. It is the purpose of this volume to supply the deficiency—to fill the gap thus left in the line of our national literature—and at the same time to present a sufficient contemporary picture of men and things as they existed at the time of the shipwreck; to illustrate as well as to narrate; and later on to introduce the reader to those gallant men of the *Birkenhead* who survived fifty years after the disaster, so that, within the covers of this book, he may make their personal acquaintance and come to know and understand both them and their story. This is precisely what has been lacking in the past. People have loved to hear and to talk about the *Birkenhead*—for is it not a tradition of theirs? —and at a respectful distance they have admired its heroes. But they have not known the full story. Their knowledge of it has been scanty and superficial; their interest in it keen but unrequited. Is it to be wondered, then, that upon many points of the story they should have been woefully misinformed?

The very presence of a *Birkenhead* memorial in England has hitherto escaped the knowledge of many who ought to have been well aware of its existence. A case in point came prominently to notice only in January, 1905, when the Lord Mayor of a provincial city innocently proclaimed his ignorance of the fact. The occasion was the anniversary of the wreck of the *Warren Hastings* in 1897, celebrated by the York and Lancaster Regiment by a dinner in the Sheffield Cutlers' Hall. The Lord Mayor in a speech paid a deserved tribute to the excellent discipline maintained on the *Warren Hastings*, which enabled every man of a detachment of the 2nd Battalion of this Regiment to be saved.

That episode, said the Lord Mayor, reminded him of another—namely, the sinking of the *Birkenhead* in 1852. This vessel went down with 500 officers and men, standing in the presence of death as calmly as on a parade ground, whilst the women and children were saved. The then King of Prussia was so impressed by the event that he caused that splendid story of iron discipline and perfect duty to be read aloud at the head of every regiment in his kingdom. Why had no national monument been erected in memory of those heroes? A country which could produce such men capable of such discipline would hold its own in safety if properly led.

A Military audience cheered this speech to the echo, but none present corrected the assertion that no national monument has been raised to the *Birkenhead* heroes. The speaker had a just appreciation of the *Birkenhead*, and what he said about it so admirably does him honour. The oversight which he committed would doubtless have caused him real regret could he have been made conscious of it. The incident simply strengthens what has been urged with regard to the public and the *Birkenhead*. The subject itself is splendidly esteemed, but its circumstances and associations have become obscured or forgotten.

Let us look ahead. This Introduction to the story should not close without a special reference to the great object-lesson we have in the *Birkenhead*, and the inestimable value of it to our young folk to-day. And here the finely phrased eulogy of the Lord Mayor who has spoken presents itself opportunely. The practical worth of a method or rule may sometimes be as well gauged by a small thing as by a great one. It is the same thing in either case. What made it possible for those men to be kept together, orderly and steadily, on the deck of the *Birkenhead*, was first of all discipline. Discipline prevented confusion or panic, calmed first fears, and led to the saving of some lives by the heroic sacrifice of many others.

Over twelve hundred scholars were safely marched out of a Glasgow school on December 18th, 1903, while the building was fast being destroyed by fire. Coolness and discipline effected this dramatic rescue. The infants prattled their way out to the tune of a march played by a pupil teacher in order to drown any affrighting sounds that might reach the ears of the little ones. It was all a triumph of discipline and of quiet, intense presence of mind.

The event recalled a scene at the Shaftesbury Road School in East Ham, when a month before two thousand children were marched out and saved from a fire.

On January 5th, 1904, there was an outbreak in a public school at Toronto, which claims to be the first city to have adopted fire drills, and the six hundred children in the classrooms, under the orders of the teachers, " marched out in line as steadily as soldiers," the building being cleared in less than two minutes. Within five minutes the whole structure was a mass of flames.

On the morning of January 26th, 1905, dense volumes of smoke awoke inmates of the house of Mr. Tatham, where about fifty Eton boys were sleeping. The lads were aroused. Some dressed, others in their night attire, they bravely set to their fire-drill, and observing discipline and self-control, marshalled in the corridors. They were all able to file out of the burning building in safety.

The same year, on the afternoon of August 29th, Lansdowne Road School at Cardiff was struck by lightning, "the noise resembling the firing of a cannon." The boys' classroom was filled with smoke and soot, and chimney-bricks crashing into the girls' school caused a scene of wild confusion. Children shrieked and ran about panic-stricken; but the teachers soon got them under control by fire-drill, and marched them unharmed into the playground.

Finally, to shift the scene but to continue the lesson in a situation of imminent deadly danger, may be cited that grand display of "'*Birken'ead* drill' heroism," as it was called, in the Solent on October 16th, 1905, as a result of which a court-martial assembled at Portsmouth to try a lieutenant charged with hazarding the safety of Submarine A4. According to the evidence given, immediately the vessel was submerged water began to pour in through a ventilator, improperly closed. The boat sank rapidly to a depth of ninety feet, and water flooded the fore part and extinguished the lights. But the crew remained coolly at their posts, and the vessel was raised to the surface after three and a half minutes. All were happily saved. A tragedy was averted by the narrowest margin—and the deciding factor was discipline. The gallant officer in charge of the boat warmly praised the crew's conduct. He himself was found guilty of default, but in consideration of his coolness and presence of mind under exceptionally trying conditions, was simply reprimanded.

Well-wishers of their race and kin cannot insist too strongly on the supreme importance of discipline wherever any numbers are present, be the need and the scene of its action the deck of a sinking ship, the walls of a blazing school, or the bowels of a submarine; let the enemy which has to be fought be devouring fire, noxious fumes, engulfing water or lurking voracious sharks. We have seen what

H.M. THE KING OF PORTUGAL

(As Colonel-in-Chief of the Oxfordshire Light Infantry, formerly the 43rd Light Infantry
Photo by Vidal & Fonseca, Lisbon. Specially presented in honour of the *Birkenhead*)

discipline can do on occasions of sudden emergency, in the hands even of the very young. We shall see what it achieved as practised by soldiers and sailors at the wreck of the *Birkenhead.* It would accomplish almost anything, anywhere. "The schoolmaster is abroad," once declaimed Lord Brougham, "and I trust to him, armed with his primer, against the soldier in full military array." The disciplinarian, it is cheering to know, is abroad also: he deserves as high and as sure a place in the scheme of our material well-being.

CHAPTER II

THE WRECK

> Like ships that have gone down at sea
> When heaven was all tranquillity.—THOMAS MOORE.

IN January, 1852, when this eventful history opens, we were at war with the Kaffirs in South Africa and more troops were being sent out to the aid of Sir Harry Smith at the Cape of Good Hope. On the 2nd of the month the service companies of the 1st Battalion Rifle Brigade, under the command of Colonel Buller, embarked at Dover in the *Megæra* screw steamer; and drafts from the depôts of ten other regiments were received on board the *Birkenhead*. These reinforcements numbered together about 1,200 men of all ranks. The *Megæra* put into Plymouth disabled, and her passage was delayed. The *Birkenhead*, a fine iron paddle-wheel steamer in those days, one of the best of her type in the Royal Navy, used as a troopship and carrying four guns, sailed from Cork Harbour on January 17th. Below were the drafts taken out in the *Birkenhead* for the different regiments serving on the frontier.

2ND (QUEEN'S) FOOT.—Ensign Boylan, one sergeant and 50 men.

6TH REGIMENT.—Ensign Metford, one sergeant and 60 men.

12TH (ROYAL) LANCERS.—Cornet Bond, Cornet Rolt, one sergeant and five men.

12TH REGIMENT.—Lieut. S. Fairclough, one sergeant and 68 men.

43RD LIGHT INFANTRY.—Lieut. Girardot, one sergeant and 40 men.

45TH REGIMENT.—One officer,* one sergeant and 15 men.

60TH RIFLES, 2ND BATTALION.—One sergeant and 40 men, attached to 91st Regiment.

73RD REGIMENT.—Lieut Robinson, Lieut. Booth, Ensign Lucas, one sergeant and 70 men.

74TH REGIMENT.—Lieut.-Colonel A. Seton, Ensign Russell, one warrant officer and 60 men.

* Unnamed. Probably a warrant officer.

THE WRECK

91ST REGIMENT.—Captain Wright, one sergeant and 60 men.
STAFF.—Two surgeons and one assistant surgeon.
WOMEN AND CHILDREN.—56.

TOTAL.

Officers	12
Warrant officers	2
Sergeants	9
Rank and file	468
Surgeons and assistant	3
Women	25
Children	31
	550

It was blowing heavily when the ship left port, and the gale continued till she had passed the Bay of Biscay. The steamer called at Madeira, Sierra Leone, and St. Helena for coals and provisions, and after what, in spite of the rough weather encountered at the outset, was considered a good passage, arrived at Simon's Bay, in the neighbourhood of Capetown, on February 23rd. Three women had died of child-birth and one of consumption on the voyage, leaving their number 21, and three births had taken place, raising the number of children to 34. This variation made the total of the drafts on board on reaching the Cape 549. The women and children were landed forthwith, except those taking passage to Algoa Bay, about 20 in number, who were afterwards saved from the wreck.* Lieutenant Fairclough, of the 12th, Mr. Freshfield, clerk of the vessel, and a few men were also landed, and left behind sick at Simon's Bay. Before the ship proceeded on her voyage she took in 350 tons of coal, some provisions, and the officers' horses.

Besides those of the original roll left on board, Mrs. Nesbitt, wife of Quartermaster Nesbitt, who was engaged on the frontier, one Andrew White a servant of Colonel Cloete, and two or three Colonial troopers went as passengers in the steamer, which also embarked Corporal O'Neil and two men of the 91st returning from Robben Island to their headquarters. The ship's company, all told, officers and men, including a file of Royal Marines, numbered about 130.

* According to the official return, this is the correct number of women and children saved, although in some places a higher figure is given.

Captain Robert Salmond was the officer commanding, and Mr. William Brodie the master. There were two second masters, Mr. R. D. Speer and Mr. Jeremiah O'D. Davis; and two master's assistants, Mr. R. B. Richards and Mr. C. W. Hare. Mr. John Thomas Archbold was master gunner of the ship, and Mr. William Culhane the surgeon. *The Times* estimated the total number of souls on board, "as accurately as can be ascertained," to have been 638. *The Annual Register* placed it at 630, allowing 130 officers and seamen for the crew. This is as near as the figures can be determined in the incomplete state of the official record. Probably the *Times'* estimate was the more correct of the two. A careful balancing of numbers inclines us to believe that it rather understates than exaggerates the grand total.

On the afternoon of February 25th, Commander Salmond received the Government despatches for Sir Harry Smith, together with the orders of Commodore Wyvill of *H.M.S. Castor*, in naval command at the Cape, to at once put to sea. Accordingly at 6 p.m. the *Birkenhead* resumed her voyage and proceeded on her way to Algoa Bay (Port Elizabeth) and the mouth of the Buffalo River (East London), points on the south-east coast of Africa, to land her drafts. The evening was fine when the vessel steamed out of Simon's Bay on the final stage of her outward-bound trip. The troops were in high spirits, anticipating as they did a speedy landing at their journey's end. The ship was duly picked off on the chart at eight o'clock within False Bay by the Master, Mr. Brodie, and the officer of the watch, Mr. Speer; the course was shaped S.S.E. ½ E., and Cape Hanglip, which was rounded at 9.30, was given a berth of about four miles. The man at the wheel, John Haines, A.B., from ten o'clock till twelve of the first watch, steered that course, with directions not to go to the eastward of it. The weather continued favourable and the sea was smooth as the good ship ploughed leisurely through it at a speed of eight knots or thereabouts. Midnight had turned; all but the watch were below; the scene around was one of calm repose. Only the throbbing of the engines disturbed the silence of the night as the noble vessel rolled gently in the swell setting in towards the shore some two miles away. Lights could be observed twinkling there, like answering signals to the sparkling stars in the gloomy firmament above, and now and again could be heard faintly the distant beating of the surf as it fell sullenly upon that rock-bound coast. Mr. Davis, one of the second masters, was in charge of the deck. The Commander and the Master were below. Thomas Coffin was at the wheel. A good lookout was kept by two men stationed at the bows; and a leadsman, heaving his line from the paddle-box, took soundings in that last middle watch, for the ship was near the land, the loom of which had all the night been visible from three to four points on the port bow. At about ten minutes before two o'clock the leadsman, Abel Stone, ordinary seaman, got

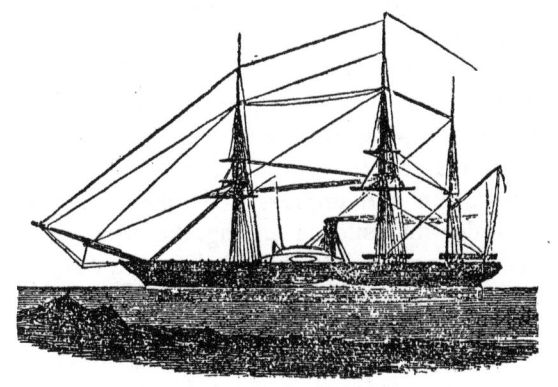

NEARING THE SUNKEN ROCK

soundings in twelve or thirteen fathoms, of which he gave notice to the officer of the watch. He threw the line again; but before he could get another cast of the lead the ship struck!

Suddenly, and without any warning of the presence of such a danger—if we except that conveyed by the leadsman a short time before *—she crashed on to the reef of rocks off Danger Point, some fifty miles from the anchorage she

---

* It has been said that had the helm at once been ported on the leadsman giving notice of his last sounding, the ship would have been saved. It must, however, be remembered that survivors rescued from the maintopmast-yard saw breakers to seaward of the wreck, showing that the point where the vessel struck was not the extreme end of the reef or chain of rocks.

had left eight hours earlier. Then the leadsman found seven fathoms of water alongside; there were two fathoms only under the bows, and eleven by the stern. A submerged pinnacle rock had penetrated the ship's bottom just abaft the foremast. It must soon have been realised that the vessel was doomed. Through the torn hole the water poured, and the inrush was so great that most of the men on the lower troop-deck were drowned as they lay in their hammocks. The rest of the men and all the officers hurried upon deck.

Commander Salmond, who was roused by the shock, hastened from his cabin and inquired the time, a few minutes past two o'clock, and the course steered. It was reported to be S.S.E. ½ E., which he stated was quite correct. He immediately ordered the engines to be stopped, the small bower anchor to be let go, the quarter-boats to be lowered and lie off alongside the ship, the paddle-box boats to be got out and a turn astern to be given to the engines.

Meanwhile Lieut.-Colonel Seton,* of the 74th Highlanders, who commanded the troops on board, called the Military officers about him and impressed on them the necessity of preserving order and silence among the men, at the same time directing Captain Wright, of the 91st, to see that the orders given by Commander Salmond were executed. This Captain Wright did. Thirty file, or sixty men, were at once told off in reliefs to the pumps on the lower after-deck, and sixty more were sent to haul on the tackles of the paddle-box boats. Officers went to direct them. The rest of the troops, with a view to easing the fore part of the ship, were assembled on the poop, where the terror-stricken women and children had been collected under the awning, and there the men remained drawn up in charge of non-commissioned officers. There was no confusion, no murmuring. All orders issued were promptly obeyed, and perfect discipline and steadiness prevailed among the men on the sinking ship.

* Although he appears to have been addressed as "Major" Seton, the senior military officer on board held the rank of Lieut.-Colonel. His promotion to be Lieut.-Colonel of the 74th, *vice* Lieut.-Colonel John Fordyce, killed in action, was published in the *Gazette* on January 16th, 1852, and bore date November 7th, 1851. It had not, however, been officially notified when the *Birkenhead* sailed.

THE WRECK

The scene on board at this time was not the less terrible because men faced the situation bravely. Blue lights, burnt by Gunner Archbold by the Captain's direction, flared at the stern, throwing into ghostly relief the heaving decks and swaying masts of the sinking steamer. Rockets were also fired, but alas! there was no help at hand.

Commander Salmond, on rushing from below on the vessel striking, shouted orders energetically and did all that man could do to retrieve the mistakes which had brought about the disaster. But it was too late. The "turn astern" given to the engines had made matters worse than they were. In ten minutes after the first concussion the ship struck again under the engine-room, bulging the side in several feet and tearing open the bottom. The water rushed in, drowning the fires and stopping the engines, and those in charge of them with difficulty made their escape to the upper deck.

The crisis of the wreck was thus materially hastened.* Misfortune dogged the ill-fated vessel to the end, and baffled at every turn the despairing efforts of the gallant soldiers and seamen. Only three boats of the number on board—and they were at the best all too inadequate—could be lowered and got away. The pinnace or large boom boat in the centre of the ship could not be got at at all, owing probably to the upheaval of the deck and the accumulation of wreckage. The port paddle-box boat had almost been hoisted out when the tackle broke and it was rendered useless. With the fall of this boat Cornet Rolt of the 12th Lancers and others were drowned.† In the case of the other paddle-box boat, it was found that the pin of the davits was rusted in and could not be released. That valuable means of saving life had in consequence also to be abandoned. As a gig on the starboard side was being lowered one of the ropes broke and the boat was swamped, drowning most of the men in her. What a commentary on the system which prevailed

---

* The engines were of 556 horse-power, and they made sixteen or twenty revolutions in going astern. The ship was perceptibly moved on the rock before she struck a second time.

† A gallant but ineffectual attempt to save the life of Cornet Rolt was made by Colour-Sergeant Drake, Royal Marines.

on board ship—on Her Majesty's ships—in those days, and how different to that which obtains in our Navy to-day. Rotten tackle, pins and bolts actually rusted in from sheer neglect and want of overhauling—a state of things particularly reprehensible in a troopship carrying not only large numbers of men, but wives and families also. Still, under God's providence, all these women and children were saved. On seeing that the ship must sink, the Commander ordered them to be got into a cutter. This was done, under the direction of Colonel Seton, by Ensign Lucas of the 73rd and Sergeant Kilkeary of the same regiment. It was a work of much difficulty. The ship was now rolling heavily. Terrified women, with babes in arms, clung in a last embrace to husbands they were leaving to their fate, and in their agony would have preferred to perish with them; but firmly, and as expeditiously as possible, this sad task was accomplished. Simultaneously with his call for the cutter, Captain Salmond ordered the horses to be pitched out of the port gangway. This was effected by Cornet Bond, whose humanity and bravery were conspicuous, and his men of the 12th Lancers.

Meanwhile the *Birkenhead* was grinding and breaking on the rocks. The second cutter, with the women and children, in charge of Mr. Richards, master's assistant, had scarcely got clear, with the first cutter and the gig containing men, when the ship's prow broke off at the foremast, the bowsprit leaping into the air towards the foretopmast, while the funnel crashed down on the side to starboard, carrying away the paddle-box and boat and crushing and killing the unfortunate men pulling on the tackles. Less than a quarter-of-an-hour had then elapsed since the vessel ran on the rocks. Work at the chain pumps below had been proceeding all this time, officers and men exerting themselves to the utmost in the impossible endeavour to lessen the water in the ship's hold, in the faint hope they had that by this means she might be kept afloat. Ensign Lucas, on being relieved by Lieutenant Girardot of the 43rd, had gone on deck to superintend the disposal of the women and children in the second cutter, and was working with a party at the paddle-box boat-tackle when

THE WRECK

the funnel fell. This indefatigable young officer then returned to the pumps, relieving Lieutenant Girardot and being himself relieved by Lieutenant Booth of the 73rd, who, poor fellow, perished there with his fifty men. Lieutenant Girardot and a number of others, in response to a call for all hands to go aft, as the ship was sinking by the head and it was thought her stern might be brought into the water, went on to the poop deck, where Colonel Seton, Ensign Lucas, and other officers were gathered. Here they stood clustered together calmly awaiting their fate. The stern was now high in the air. At this moment the Commander called out, "All those that can swim, jump overboard, and make for the

STRIKING THE ROCK

boats," which were standing off at some short distance from the wreck. Captain Wright and Lieutenant Girardot, upon hearing this, " begged the men not to do as the Commander had said, as the boat with the women must be swamped." *
In response to this chivalrous appeal the soldiers grouped upon the sinking poop almost to a man "stood fast." To their eternal honour be it said, "Not more than three made the attempt," and the cutter with the women and children pulled safely away. Shortly afterwards the ship parted in the middle and the poop went down, and all who had stayed on board her were struggling in the water.

* There is abundant evidence that this request was first made by Colonel Seton. Captain Wright and Lieutenant Girardot, with equal credit to themselves, reiterated it.

All was over with the *Birkenhead* five-and-twenty minutes after striking. Only the maintopmast and topsail-yard remained above the surface where she sank. Awful was the sight she left behind her. Many who went down with the vessel rose again to join in the struggle for life, desperate, despairing, in many cases brief, on the dark and rolling bosom of the deep. Drowning was not the only fate that these poor wretches had to fear. There were other horrors. Sharks abounded in those waters, and it was their knowledge of the presence of these monsters, waiting hungrily for helpless prey, that made the greater heroes of the men upon the poop when, for the sake of the women and children, they sacrificed their last apparent chance of salvation. The shore, rugged and surf-beaten, was also known to be bordered, for some distance out, with a growth of deadly kelpweed, so dense that the strongest swimmer was powerless when caught in its sinuous folds.

Terrible indeed was the scene that followed the final plunge of the shattered and broken steamer. It is described in vivid language by Ensign Lucas, and Cornet Bond and others of the survivors tell of some of the horrors encountered in the water. Many were the lives that were lost through the destroying agencies existing there which combined to lend tragedy to the wreck. The gallant Seton had already gone.* His last words were addressed to Ensign Lucas on the poop just before the end came. Gone also was the brave Commander, Mr. Salmond, who is spoken of as having done his duty, like a Briton and a sailor, to the last.† Gone too was Mr. Brodie, the Master, washed off the bridge and drowned.‡ When the poop sank, many seized

---

* Mr. C. K. Renwick, who was thrown with Colonel Seton from the poop-deck when the ship sank, afterwards declared that the Colonel was seized and dragged down by some of the men who were struggling in the water.

† "Captain Salmond might have saved himself easily, but he remained giving orders until the after-part of the vessel surged and threw him overboard."—Statement from *Narrative of a Non-Commissioned Officer*.

‡ According to the same narrative, "Mr. Brodie, the Master, was in the act of clearing the paddle-box boat when the ship parted in two, and he was killed at once." On the other hand, Mr. Archbold, the gunner, says that he and Mr. Brodie were washed overboard together, and that he afterwards found Mr. Brodie upon a truss of hay.

upon the fragments of wreckage that strewed the sea—portions of masts, timber from the decks, furniture from the cabins, trusses of hay, overturned boats, and what not. It was the irony of fate that the two paddle-box boats should have been washed and tumbled ashore. One was full of water and the other keel uppermost; but they saved some lives, even in that condition. On the flotsam and jetsam cast up from the wreck, several contrived to get to land. Some reached there by swimming, and escaping through the kelpweed. Of these was Cornet Bond, who had put on a lifebelt before taking to the water. Five of the horses gained the beach, of which his was one; the rest were drowned in the weed, eaten by sharks, or swam out to sea on being thrown overboard and so were lost. Among those who luckily got to shore was Captain Wright of the 91st, who afterwards did so much to help his fellow-survivors. Lieutenant Girardot, Ensign Lucas, Gunner Archbold, and Quartermaster Maxwell were also of the fortunate number. Both the second masters of the ship were drowned; so was one of the master's assistants, Mr. Hare. The death-roll of officers of the ship was a heavy one, and so was that of the Military officers on board, fourteen in all, of whom only five were saved:

Captain Wright	91st Regiment.
Lieutenant Girardot	43rd ,,
Ensign Lucas	73rd ,,
Cornet Bond	12th Lancers.
Dr. Bowen	Staff Surgeon.

Fifty or more men, wretched and ill-clad, found refuge on the ship's mast and yard, which remained standing out of the water. There the majority of them clung throughout the night and the succeeding forenoon, until taken off, more dead than alive, by the *Lioness* schooner, which went to their assistance. Some of their number had dropped into the sea, too cold and exhausted to maintain their feeble hold longer; others attempted at daybreak, with but little success, to get ashore on portions of wreckage that washed by them. With these men on the maintopsail-yard was Mr. Hire, the Commander's clerk, who thus survived the disaster. The rescuing schooner had already fallen in with the two cutters which pulled away from the wreck. In the first of these was Mr. Renwick, chief assistant engineer, Dr. Bowen, and thirty-four men. The second cutter, as we have already seen, contained the women and children, in charge of Mr. Richards, master's assistant, who had command of the boats. There was also the gig, which had only a crew of eight men on board when Dr. Culhane, the assistant surgeon, swam to her from the wreck and she pulled away with him. The gig picked up Mr. Renwick, but afterwards transferred him to the first cutter to take charge of that boat.

The three boats, on leaving the scene of the wreck, made for the shore in close company, but on nearing there found it too risky to attempt to effect a landing through the heavy ceaseless surf. At daylight they sighted the schooner in the offing, and put out to sea again in the hope of falling in with her. The second cutter with the women and children, having only six oars at work, was left behind by the other two boats. Dr. Culhane closed with the first cutter, and selected eight of her best men to pull the gig towards the schooner, which so far had been chased to no purpose. It was then that Mr. Renwick was transferred to the first cutter. With her selected crew the gig started energetically in pursuit of the schooner, but was foiled by a freshening breeze and abandoned the chase. The schooner meanwhile had sighted the first cutter, and at ten o'clock took her survivors on board. Less than an hour later the *Lioness* picked up the second cutter, which had rigged up a woman's shawl as a sail. The gig, whose experience was unfortunate throughout, pulled fifty miles before finding a safe landing. She reached Port D'Urban, a point fifteen miles from the wreck where a Mr. Phillipson had a store, at three in the afternoon, her men completely done up, and Dr. Culhane rode over a hundred miles across country to Capetown with the news of the disaster, which involved the loss of 445 lives. Of all on board, only 193 were saved.

Great was the consternation caused at Capetown when Dr. Culhane, worn out and exhausted by his long rough ride,

THE WRECK

faltered into the township on a jaded horse on February 27th,* with the melancholy tidings of the loss of the fine ship † which, forty hours previously, had left Simon's Bay with her gallant company on what gave every promise of being a short and safe passage round the coast. How tragic in its significance that first news, and the character of its bringing. The tale would half tell itself before the distressed bearer opened his lips to speak it!

Just ten years before a similar messenger of misfortune arrived before the gates of Jellalabad. It was a surgeon then, Dr. Brydon, the "remnant of an army," who brought the mournful story of the fatal retreat from Cabul. Happily

BREAKING

Dr. Culhane was not a sole survivor, nor was the disaster he had to describe of the same magnitude; but it was awful enough, and its suddenness was overwhelming. It was related officially to Commodore Christopher Wyvill, who transmitted it forthwith to General Sir Harry Smith, as Governor and Commander at the Cape. Dr. Culhane stated the fact of the wreck, adding that

* Commodore Wyvill says at 2 p.m. Dr. Culhane himself says, in one place, at 9 a.m.; but as he arrived at Port D'Urban at 3 p.m. the day before, and left an hour later, and as he rode, he says, for twenty hours, he probably arrived at Capetown about the time the Commodore states. It is not surprising, under the harassing circumstances, that Dr. Culhane should make minor errors of observation as to time and distance, of which this is apparently one.

† The impression at first given was that only about seventy persons were saved " out of 690 souls, nine of whom have landed " in the gig.

the quarter-boats were lowered, and about 65 persons got into them; the gig was also down. While getting the paddle-box boats out the heave of the ship in sinking washed them away.* Many were drowned below before they could effect their escape to the upper deck.

And further, that nothing had been heard of the cutters "except that they pulled out to sea to get picked up by a sailing vessel." He gave a list of persons saved from the ship by the three boats which got away, and stated the belief that they were the only survivors.

The Commodore enclosed these particulars, at the same time informing the Governor that he had despatched Commander Bunce, of the *Castor*, with twenty-five men to form boats' crews, in the *Rhadamanthus*, the only steamer in port, to the scene of "this fearful disaster," to afford all possible relief and to search for the missing boats.

As it is possible they may be compelled to effect a landing, I would be glad if your Excellency gave instructions to the resident magistrates and field-cornets on the coast to keep a look-out for them, and render every possible assistance.

That evening Commander Bunce fell in with the schooner *Lioness* of Algoa Bay, Mr. Ramsden master. This vessel had on board the persons who were in the cutters, and forty others, whom they had succeeded in taking off the maintopsail-yard of the ship, which was the only part of the vessel visible above water; altogether 116 in number. It being calm, and the schooner some distance from Simon's Bay, the *Rhadamanthus* towed her in, and proceeded afterwards to Point Danger in search of any people who might yet be clinging to the spars and pieces of wreck floating about; also for any who might have landed. An examination of the coast having been made for upwards of twenty miles by land and sea, and no other persons being found except those who had landed during the night and day of the wreck on the coast near Point Danger, the *Rhadamanthus* received them on board, and returned to her anchorage on the morning of March 1st. The persons so saved were sixty-eight in number, of whom six were officers (four Military and two Naval). They

* One paddle-box boat could not be lowered because the pin of the davits was rusted in. The tackle of the other boat broke when it was being hoisted out.

THE WRECK

reached the land by swimming and on pieces of wreck. These, with nine others who escaped in the gig, and those who were rescued by the schooner, made the total saved 193.

Commodore Wyvill, in reporting further to the Governor, gave the list of these survivors, adding that from Captain Wright's statement he found that no others had been saved. The coast had been examined for upwards of twenty miles by a whaleboat, by people on shore, and by the boats of the *Rhadamanthus*. Dyer Islands had also been searched.

> All the sufferers of this unfortunate wreck are on board Her Majesty's ships *Castor* and *Rhadamanthus*, and the soldiers are very thinly clothed. I have to request your instructions as to the disposal of the troops, and beg that directions may be given for the necessary clothing to be furnished.

By the Governor's direction this information was published without delay " as affording some further relief " to public anxiety at the Cape, which was naturally acute at the time. Subscriptions were raised to relieve the distress of the unfortunate widows and children of the soldiers, who were comfortably housed in the barracks at Capetown.

Let us now follow the fortunes of the men who, after the wreck, managed to gain the shore. Many of them were naked, and almost all were without shoes. Thus unprotected, and after long immersion in salt water, they were exposed for many hours to a burning sun, and as, stiff, sore, and faint, they plodded painfully onward, their feet and limbs were torn by thorns.

Captain Wright, 91st Regiment, who reached the land in company with others on some wreckage,* exerted himself manfully in doing what he could for his comrades in distress. Some such guiding spirit was a vital necessity at the time. The men who providentially got ashore escaped grave dangers; but they were not yet " out of the wood." Perils and hardships confronted them; the fear of starvation itself menaced them for awhile. They were castaways in a wild and desolate country, and, as we have seen, the trials they had already had to combat had left them in anything but a fit condition to grapple with those which still lay ahead.

---

* And, according to Corporal William Smith, 12th Regiment, cheered his companions with a stave of " The Bay of Biscay, O."

But Captain Wright knew something of the coast and country—he had been in those parts before—and he put his knowledge to the full use. With indomitable spirit and rare resource he took affairs in hand and pulled his people through their difficulties. It was about noon on February 26th when the majority of them landed. As soon as Captain Wright stepped ashore with the party whose chances he had shared on the driftwood, he made his way to a little fishing station some six or seven miles from Danger Point. Owing to the country being covered with thick thorny bushes, their progress was slow; but after walking till about 3 p.m. they came to where a waggon was outspanned, and the driver of it directed them to a small bay, where was the hut of a fisherman.

The bay was Stanford Cove. They arrived there about sunset; and as the men had nothing to eat, Captain Wright went on to a farmhouse eight or nine miles from the cove and sent back provisions for that day. Next morning he sent another day's provisions, and the men were removed to a farm belonging to Captain Smales, an old officer of Dragoons, twelve or fourteen miles further up country. Lieutenant Girardot of the 43rd, Ensign Lucas of the 73rd, and Cornet Bond of the 12th Lancers accompanied this party, which amounted to sixty-eight men, including eighteen sailors. Captain Wright then went down to the coast and put up in a hut, and was occupied during Friday, Saturday, and Sunday in examining every part of the rocks for at least twenty miles, in the hope of finding some men who might have drifted in. He fortunately fell in with the crew of a whaleboat employed in sealing on Dyer Islands, and he got them to take the boat outside the seaweed, about a quarter-of-a-mile from the shore, while he and James Jeffery, the purser's steward of the *Birkenhead*, who accompanied him, searched carefully among the rocks. The seaweed on the coast is very thick,* and of immense length, so that it would have caught most of the driftwood. Happily the boat picked up two men, and the

---

* An old sailor, who was on the gunboat *Wasp* when she ran ashore near the scene of the wreck a few years afterwards, told us that the seaweed which grows so thickly on this coast is known as "bottle weed," from the close resemblance it bears to bottles floating in the water. It is a very large species.

searchers on shore also found two. Although they were all much exhausted, two of them having been in the water as long as thirty-eight hours, after a night's rest in the hut they were all right next day except for a few bruises.

On Saturday Captain Wright luckily encountered a pair of good Samaritans in the persons of Mr. Mackay, the Civil Commissioner of Caledon, and Field-Cornet Villiers. Mr. Mackay told him that he had ordered the men at Captain Smales' farm to be clothed from a store which the Commissioner had there. Forty soldiers, it was afterwards found, received clothing in this way. Mr. Mackay, the Field-Cornet, and Captain Wright, accompanied by a party of men brought

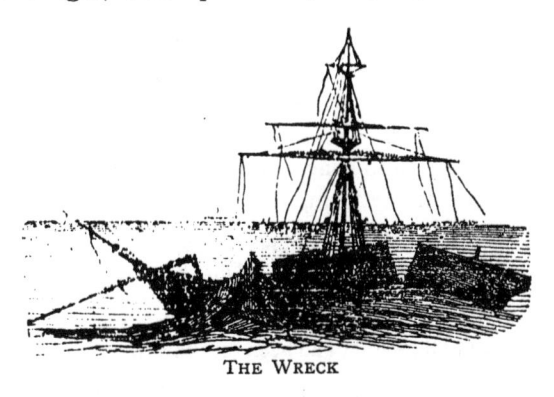

THE WRECK

down by Mr. Villiers, proceeded along the coast as far as the point running out to Dyer Islands to assist in burying the dead and collecting what things were washed ashore. All the bodies met with were at once interred. "There were not many, however," Captain Wright afterwards reported; "and I regret to say it could be easily accounted for," he grimly added. Five of the horses thrown overboard reached the shore, were caught there, and brought to Captain Wright. One of them belonged to himself, another to Cornet Bond, a third to Colonel Seton, and the other two to Dr. Laing, staff surgeon, and Lieutenant Booth, 73rd Regiment. It was considered probable that other horses got ashore at different points on the coast; but only these five were seen and captured. Captain Wright handed the horses over to Mr. Mackay, with instructions to send them to him at Capetown so that they might be sold and the proceeds accounted for.

On February 28th the *Rhadamanthus* was seen off Stanford Cove. Captain Wright went down there, and found that Commander Bunce, of the *Castor* frigate, had landed and gone up to Captain Smales to order the men down to the cove, so as to embark in the steamer to be conveyed to Simon's Bay. When down on the coast on the Sunday, the Field-Cornet told Captain Wright that at a part where he and his men had been a few bodies were washed up and buried; also that a few boxes had come ashore, which were broken in pieces and the contents strewn about the rocks. Captain Wright then ceased to hope that any more persons were living, and proceeded to the cove to join the other men. Soon afterwards he left, in charge of forty-six soldiers and two officers, for Simon's Bay. Ensign Lucas, who on landing from the wreck had been much cut and bruised by the rocks, was still unable to travel, and had to be left with the hospitable Captain Smales at the farm.

> It was [wrote Captain Wright] eighty-six hours on the Sunday afternoon I left the coast, since the wreck had taken place; and as I had carefully examined every part of the rocks, and also sent the whaleboat over to Dyer Islands, I can safely assert that when I left there was not a living soul on the coast of those that had been on board the ill-fated *Birkenhead*.

The castaways were embarked in boats and taken on board the *Rhadamanthus*, and arrived in Simon's Bay at 3 a.m. on Monday, March 1st. Eighteen of the men were bruised and burnt by the sun, and the Commodore ordered them into the Naval Hospital. The rest were all right, but seventy required to be clothed, every shred belonging to them having been lost.

It will be seen in these pages that Dr. Culhane does not escape obloquy for the part he played after the wreck. The censure was no doubt honestly meant, but as will be shown later on, it was undeserved. The Commander of the vessel is blamed with more reason for "hugging the land too closely." In compliance with his orders, Captain Salmond was endeavouring to make a quick passage round the coast so as to disembark his reinforcements, which were urgently needed, at the earliest moment. But it was not desired that he should so shorten the voyage as to imperil the safety of the ship, nor ought he to have done so. Commodore Wyvill, from whom his orders were received, would certainly not have advised it, and moreover he condemns the course adopted.

In the same passage of his report the Commodore charges both the Commander and the Master with neglect of duty in not attending on deck after ten o'clock. There is here, however, a good deal to be said for these unfortunate officers, who had both been very hard worked during the brief stay in Simon's Bay. "I'm as busy now as Old Nick, coaling, watering, provisioning, and getting all ready to be off to-night." So wrote Captain Salmond in his last letter home, penned on the day of departure from the Cape only a few hours before his death. His labours and anxieties would be shared by Mr. Brodie, and both would, without doubt, be thoroughly tired out that night and in need of rest. So they left the deck in charge of junior officers, first Mr. Speer and then Mr. Davis. The very deliberateness with which these risks were taken shows the security that was felt in what was done. Neither of these superior officers, able and vigilant as they usually were, could have suspected the presence of any danger. Otherwise they would have remained on deck. There was a deadly peril, but it was concealed. It lay like a stealthy serpent ready to spring on its hapless victim in a path which prudence should have shunned. The elements of a disaster were there in waiting, none the less real because not realised—till too late. The immediate cause of the wreck may have been the mistaking of a fire burning on shore for Cape Agulha lighthouse, which there is reason to believe misled the officer of the watch. Captain Wright, in his memorandum to Commodore Wyvill, makes a statement tending to this conclusion, and the same opinion is expressed by Ensign Lucas.

All mistakes and blame, however, recede and are forgotten in the contemplation of the heroism displayed on board the doomed ship. It was a triumph of duty unflinchingly done under the most trying conditions, of orders steadily given and patiently obeyed at a time when discipline less perfect and courage less determined would have yielded to fatal disorder. These things never have been and never will be questioned. Not a little doubt has existed as to the outward shape which this discipline assumed—the form in which it manifested itself. Erroneous notions have prevailed upon this subject which may here and now be rectified by the only reliable and satisfactory process, that of an examination of the evidence. It may at once be declared that the result of this investigation does not appear to rob the actual deck scene of the *Birkenhead* of its picturesqueness. All the available information is before the authors, who will sift it carefully and impartially and leave the reader to decide the truth for himself.

It has been asserted, sometimes with quite unnecessary vehemence, that there was no "falling in" of the soldiers. Let us see. Colour-Sergeant Drake, of the Royal Marines, who saw Colonel Seton make his appearance on deck, says he heard the Colonel distinctly tell the officers who surrounded him "to order the troops to fall in, which they immediately did on both sides of the quarter-deck." * A similar statement may be found in a chapter on the *Birkenhead* in Gilly's *Narratives of Shipwrecks in the Royal Navy between* 1793 *and* 1857, a responsible work. Here the writer, after speaking of Captain Salmond's appearance on deck, quotes Captain Wright as to Colonel Seton calling the Military officers together and directing them to preserve order and silence amongst the men, and adds:

He [Colonel Seton] then ordered the soldiers to fall in, which they did, with the utmost order and alacrity, on both sides of the quarter-deck.

The statement has from time to time been repeated with variations in other places, and upon it is based the generally accepted view of what really occurred. The contrary assertion of Colonel Girardot, that "the men were never fallen into ranks," cannot be held to dispose of it. The men were evidently fallen in, if they were not kept standing strictly in rank. There was some sort of orderly formation, and as recorded on another page, the troops on the poop were probably there in charge of non-commissioned officers, the

* See statement quoted in account of Colonel Seton.

THE WRECK OF THE "BIRKENHEAD"

(By Mr. Charles Dixon, R.I. From *Britannia's Bulwarks*, by permission of George Newnes, Limited)

officers themselves being otherwise employed. There was no "call to arms" by beat of drum—no time for it, in fact; nor was it necessary. The soldiers did nothing theatrical—why should they? Their bearing was steady and dignified, and so remained throughout the crisis.

Colonel Girardot's denial of the falling into ranks was one of several which he made at the 50th anniversary of the wreck respecting certain fables and fictions which, like barnacles on a ship's hull, have fastened themselves to the story of the *Birkenhead*—the allegations, for instance, that "the troops stood on deck with arms presented," that they went down "firing a last salute with a volley in the air," and notions scarcely less extravagant traceable to the poem of Sir Francis Doyle.

There is one statement which has been designated a picturesque untruth but which has, nevertheless, some foundation in fact. It emanates at any rate from a source the good faith of which will not be questioned. Writing to a gentleman at Edinburgh* soon after the wreck, the Hon. William Hope, then Auditor-General at the Cape of Good Hope, told how—

> a sergeant of the 60th who was saved says that Colonel Seton was at the gangway with a drawn sword in his hand, keeping the way clear for the women to get into the boats, and preserving order, and when he had done this he gave the sergeant the sword and went on the poop to give some orders, when the vessel broke in two pieces, and Colonel Seton went down with all on the poop.

The non-commissioned officer alluded to was Sergeant (afterwards Staff-Sergeant-Major) David Andrews. He also made a statement at the time which will be found in these pages. It contains no reference to the sword incident, though the omission proves nothing; but in Gilly's *Narratives of Shipwrecks*, already quoted, we have the story repeated in these words:

> Colonel Seton took upon himself the charge of seeing the women and children safely placed in this boat [the second cutter], himself standing in the gangway with a drawn sword in his hand to see them passed down, and to prevent by his authority, if necessary, any of the men from crowding into the boat so as to endanger it.

* Mr. John Cook, writer to the Signet.

And the writer adds:

> This duty being satisfactorily effected, the boat was pushed off with orders to lie on their oars at about a hundred and fifty yards' distance from the wreck.

Again, the story is substantially repeated, with some slight additions, presumably founded on statements gathered from other sources, in a Memoir of Colonel Seton published in *The Biographical Dictionary of Eminent Scotsmen*. This account speaks of the getting out of the only boats available at the wreck, and goes on to say:

> An instant rush to these sole hopes of safety might have been expected—it would have been nothing more than the instinctive impulse of self-preservation, which so often gets the start of more generous considerations—and apprehensive of some such event, Colonel Seton stood on the gangway with his sword drawn to prevent it; but, to the honour of the soldiers be it said, no such attempt was offered; on the contrary, they received his orders as coolly, and obeyed them as punctually, as if they had been drawn up on the parade ground and put through a few manœuvres. His first care was for the women and the children; and though the vessel was every moment sinking, they were all conveyed safely into one of the cutters, himself superintending their removal. Being still apprehensive of a reaction and a sudden rush into the cutter, by which it would be swamped, he ordered a young cornet to bring him a table-knife from the cabin to cut the rope, and cast the boat loose should the attempt be made; but still it was not offered, and the knife was useless.

It would be the cornet who was to cut the rope and cast off the laden boat had that been necessary; but it was not. These interesting details are neither confirmed nor denied anywhere else.* They may be strictly true; it is impossible to discover any reason why they should not be so. They accord with the strong personal character of Colonel Seton, whose courage was of the resolute kind, and they detract in no way from that of the soldiers.

Then doubt has been cast upon the statement that the officers, before the end came, shook hands on the deck in

---

* After the above was written we saw a memorandum in the handwriting of Mr. David Seton, brother of Colonel Seton, of a conversation he had with Cornet Bond, 12th Royal Lancers, four years after the wreck, substantiating the statement about the table-knife. This is included in the chapter dealing with Colonel Seton.

THE WRECK

a silent leave-taking. The chapter in Gilly's *Narratives* says:

> The officers now shook hands and took leave of one another; when, on a sudden, the vessel broke again crosswise abaft the mainmast, and the poop, heeling over with a lurch, plunged beneath the water.

The officers are shown in the act of handshaking in the famous picture reproduced in this book. The idea may have been taken from Gilly's work, or, what we think is more probable, the artist received it from Captain Bond-Shelton, from whom the whole suggestion of the picture was derived. Well, this handshaking was a very natural and proper thing under the circumstances. The officers may not have done it precisely in the manner shown; but they evidently did it, quietly and unostentatiously, because we have the personal testimony of Captain Lucas that before the poop sank he shook hands with Colonel Seton and hoped they would meet on shore; and that of Mr. C. K. Renwick that Colonel Seton, himself, " and all the other officers still standing there, shook hands and took leave of one another." *

We further find in Gilly's *Narratives* an incident not mentioned in any report or statement officially respecting Captain Salmond's orders to the gunner.

> The Captain had ordered Mr. Archbold, the gunner, to fire some guns; but on getting the keys of the magazine out of the cabin, the latter found the lower deck full of water. He ran aft and related this circumstance to the Captain, telling him at the same time that he had some blue lights and rockets in the passage leading to his (the Captain's) cabin. Mr. Salmond ordered him to fire them off, which he did.

There is nothing improbable about this. Mr. Archbold in his statement makes no mention of it. He only says " I was ordered by the Captain to fire the rockets and burn the blue lights, which I did." Whatever else may have transpired in the way of preliminaries, that is a truthful and sufficient report. The Master Gunner, we may take it, confines himself to what he did, and omits from his record that which did not happen. So that there is no apparent reason

---

* See narrative of Captain Lucas, and letters of that officer and Mr. Renwick in notice of Colonel Seton.

why this statement,* and the others cited also, should not be accepted, if not as faithful in every detail, as correct in the main. On the evidence forthcoming the authors believe, on these essential points of difference, that the troops fell in, and that those who were not employed on the work going forward remained fallen in on the poop-deck; that Colonel Seton, in his anxiety for the safety of the women and children and his determination at all hazards to ensure it, stood at the gangway with a drawn sword; and that the officers shook hands when the end approached.

On the point which, without going so far as to say it is improbable, is perhaps the least probable, but which cannot be disputed on any evidence—that of the display of a sword—we have the statement of Sergeant O'Neil that Captain Wright of his regiment threatened to shoot any man who attempted to enter the boats. There is not much to choose as a deterrent between a pistol and a naked sword. If the use of the one could be threatened, why should there not have been the warning presence of the other? Happily neither—the *morale* of the troops being what it proved to be—was needed.

The accompanying sketches of the doomed ship were afterwards made by Captain Wright, 91st Regiment. They illustrate the several stages of the catastrophe. First we have the ill-fated vessel nearing the sunken rocks; in the next sketch she is striking; and the two following sketches show the mode of her destruction. The fore-part of the vessel fell on the on-side of the rock, and the machinery, being heavy, kept that part down, leaving the stern, which was buoyant, above water. It had, however, a rocking motion, and in a little time the ship broke in two at the second water-tight compartment, when the sea rushed in and drew down the whole stern, and those upon it, below water, leaving out only the maintopmast and topsail-yard, to which many of them clung.

The picture here reproduced by permission of Messrs.

---

* Corporal William Smith, 12th Regiment, says a few Congreve rockets were thrown up, but that "a gun could not be fired, as the magazine was almost instantly under water."

Henry Graves & Co., showing the scene on board the sinking troopship, was done by Mr. Thomas M. Hemy, the painter of popular dramatic sea subjects (a brother of C. Napier Hemy, A.R.A.), from his own idea after seeing Captain Bond-Shelton's picture of the wreck at the Military and Naval Exhibitions in 1890-91. The picture was inspected by Queen Victoria at Osborne and has been exhibited all over the world, not the least successfully at the Naval and Fisheries Exhibition of 1905. It possesses great artistic merit.

The fine picture of the "Wreck of the *Birkenhead*" also reproduced in these pages by special arrangement is by Mr. Charles Dixon, R.I., and is one of a beautiful series of water-colours prepared by this eminent marine painter for *Britannia's Bulwarks*, a work edited by Commander Charles Robinson, R.N., and published at the offices of *Navy and Army Illustrated* and by George Newnes, Ltd.

CHAPTER III

THE OFFICIAL STORY

> Were doomed at last
> To tell as true a tale of danger past
> As ever the dark annals of the deep
> Disclosed, for man to dread or woman weep.—*Sea Poem*.

THE reader will gather fully in what follows the story of the wreck in all its details. He has seen already what befell the survivors who got ashore, and he will now learn the perils through which many of them passed before they reached the land. There is the report of Captain Wright, as senior Military officer; also the despatch of Commodore Wyvill, together with the statements of surviving officers saved by the boats and those of Captain Wright, supplementing his report; Mr. Archbold, the gunner; Mr. Ramsden, Master of the schooner *Lioness*; and Commander Bunce, who proceeded in the *Rhadamanthus* to the scene of the wreck to afford relief. This despatch and these statements were sent home by the Commodore of the station for the consideration of the Board of Admiralty. There is the account furnished by Cornet Bond, and later we shall come to the graphic narrative of Ensign Lucas, who also got ashore by his own exertions and helped others to reach there at the imminent risk of his life. In addition to these sources of information we shall have the personal statements of survivors, officers and men, Military and Naval, made at the 50th anniversary of the wreck. It is a moving story which they all tell, and one that deserves to be known and remembered wherever our native tongue is spoken and our history and traditions are studied and cherished.

We have first the report of Captain Ed. W. C. Wright, 91st Regiment, giving the official Military account of the disaster by the senior officer surviving. It is addressed to

THE OFFICIAL STORY

Lieut.-Colonel Ingleby, R.A., the Commandant of Capetown, and is dated Simon's Bay, March 1st, 1852. Captain Wright commences by announcing "with feelings of the deepest regret" the loss of the *Birkenhead*. He narrates the circumstances of the disaster, telling how, when the ship struck, Colonel Seton—

> called all the officers about him, and impressed on them the necessity of preserving order and silence among the men. He directed me to take and have executed whatever orders the Commander might give me.*

The report proceeds:

> It was about twelve or fifteen minutes after she struck that the bow broke off. The men then all went up on the poop, and in about five minutes more the vessel broke in two, crosswise, just abaft the engine-room, and the stern part immediately filled and went down. A few men jumped off just before she did so, but the greater number remained to the last, and so did every officer belonging to the troops. All the men I put on the tackles, I fear, were crushed when the funnel fell; and the men and officers below at the pumps could not, I think, have reached the deck before the vessel broke up and went down. The survivors clung, some to the rigging of the mainmast, part of which was out of the water, and others got hold of floating pieces of wood. I think there must have been about 200 on the driftwood. I was on a large piece along with five others, and we picked up nine or ten more. The swell carried the wood in the direction of Danger Point. As soon as it got to the weeds and breakers, finding that it would not support all that were on it, I jumped off and swam on shore; and when the others, and also those that were on the other pieces of wood, reached

---

* We have before us the printed copy of his report which Captain Wright afterwards cut from the press for preservation. One or two slight errors of reproduction are corrected, and at the point indicated occurs the following marginal note written in pencil: "Unfortunately, shortly after giving these orders, Major Seton was drowned." In a letter which he afterwards wrote to Mr. David Seton, Captain Wright also says that he did not see Colonel Seton again after the commencement of the wreck. This is important. It shows that in the events which rapidly followed Captain Wright must have lost sight of Colonel Seton, and it acquits the Captain of any intentional withholding of the credit due to Colonel Seton, who was on board to the last, for the heroic efforts we now know he made, by personal exertion and appeals to others, to save the women and children. At the same time, it proves that the appeal of Captain Wright, and presumably that of Lieutenant Girardot, on behalf of the women and children, was spontaneous—not merely a repetition of something they had apparently never heard, but independent of it. At the foot of the copy of his printed report the Captain writes in ink: "About 80 or 90 of the crew drowned, besides 358 troops."

the shore, we proceeded into the country, to try to find a habitation of any sort where we could obtain shelter.

Captain Wright modestly states what was done for the men washed ashore, and the steps taken to secure the bodies and articles from the wreck which were cast up by the sea. Then he bears his valuable testimony as to the conduct of the men on board the troopship. His words will live for all time.

The order and regularity that prevailed on board, from the time the ship struck till she totally disappeared, far exceeded anything that I thought could be effected by the best discipline; * and it is the more to be wondered at, seeing that most of the soldiers had been but a short time in the service. Every one did as he was directed; and there was not a murmur or a cry among them until the vessel made her final plunge. I could not name any individual officer who did more than another. All received their orders, and had them carried out, as if the men were embarking instead of going to the bottom. There was only this difference, that I never saw an embarkation conducted with so little noise or confusion.

He encloses a list of the people embarked, distinguishing those saved.

I think it is correct except one man of the 91st, whose name I cannot find out.† The only means I had of ascertaining the names of the men of the different drafts was by getting them from their comrades who are saved. You will see by the list enclosed that the loss amounts to nine officers and 349 men, besides those of the crew; the total number embarking being 15 officers and 476 men (one officer and 18 men were disembarked in Simon's Bay).

The report next speaks of the women and children, and expresses an opinion with reference to the gig.

I am happy to say [observes Captain Wright] that all the women and children were put safely on board a schooner that was about seven miles off when the steamer was wrecked. This vessel returned to the wreck at about 3 p.m., and took off 40 or 50 men that were clinging to the rigging, and then proceeded to Simon's Bay. One of the ship's boats, with the assistant-surgeon of the vessel and eight men, went off, and landed about 15 miles from the wreck. Had the boat remained about

---

* Italics ours.

† The name is probably that of Corporal John O'Neil, 91st Regiment, who embarked with two men at Simon's Bay a few hours before the vessel struck. He swam ashore, but was not included in the list given of those saved.

the wreck, or returned after landing the assistant-surgeon on Danger Point—about which there was no difficulty—I am quite confident that nearly every man of the 200 who were on the driftwood might have been saved, for they might have been picked up here and there, where they had got in among the weeds, and landed as soon as eight or nine were got into the boat. Where most of the driftwood stuck in the weeds the distance to the shore was not more than 400 yards, and as, by taking a somewhat serpentine course, I managed to swim in without getting foul of the rocks, or being tumbled over by a breaker, there is no doubt the boat might have done so also.

At this point Captain Wright reverts to the last scene on board the troopship.

One fact [he says] I cannot omit mentioning. When the vessel was just about going down, the Commander called out, "All those that can swim, jump overboard and make for the boats." Lieutenant Girardot and myself were standing on the stern part of the poop. We begged the men not to do as the Commander said, as the boats with the women must be swamped. Not more than three made the attempt.

As already pointed out in these pages, this noble request emanated in the first instance from Colonel Seton. Captain Wright and Lieutenant Girardot, equally to their credit, repeated it at this critical juncture, with a result that reflects lasting honour alike on the officers who made the call and the troops who heard and obeyed it. It must have given Captain Wright keen satisfaction to be able to record the incident. He refers in a postscript to the extreme kindness and attention shown by Captain Smales to the men at his house; and by Captain Ramsden, of the *Lioness* schooner, and his wife, to those taken on board that vessel.

Next we have an important despatch of twelve paragraphs written by Commodore Wyvill on board the *Castor* frigate and dated March 3rd, 1852, describing, "with much pain," the occurrence of the disaster, and stating conclusions deliberately formed with regard to it on the evidence forthcoming. This despatch, with enclosures, reached the Board of Admiralty in London on April 7th. Commodore Wyvill recounts the ascertained circumstances preceding the wreck, and coming to the directions of Commander Salmond to the Military officers in attendance to send troops to the chain pumps, says "*The orders were implicitly obeyed and perfect discipline* *maintained."* * Speaking of what followed the drowning of the engine fires, and the escape of the engineers and stokers to the upper deck—

Instantly [says the Commodore] the ship broke in two abaft the mainmast and sank, leaving the maintopmast and topsail-yard only visible above water. *Up to this awful moment the resolution and coolness of all hands were remarkable.** Mr. Salmond gave his orders with much presence of mind to the last. The three boats which had stayed by the ship now left her to seek a landing or to save themselves, and at daylight they were out of sight of the wreck.

Having called upon the surviving officers for their statements of the circumstances attending the loss of this ill-fated ship—

I have now [he goes on] the honour to lay them before their Lordships for their information, together with lists of the people saved, but I regret I cannot furnish the names of the unfortunate individuals who have been drowned on this most melancholy occasion, as the muster books and rolls have been lost. There is no doubt that the course of the ship was shaped to hug the land too closely, and as it does not appear that Mr. Salmond or the Master had attended on deck from ten o'clock in the first watch until the accident occurred, it would infer much inattention and extreme neglect of duty on their parts; and when soundings were first struck, had the helm been put to port, this ill-fated ship might have escaped the danger. It is much to be lamented that not an officer has been saved who can give any satisfactory information on these points. It is also deeply to be deplored that a young officer, Mr. Richards, master's assistant, should have been the only executive officer in command of the boats; and but for the circumstance of their leaving the scene of the wreck before daylight, the landing-place discovered on Point Danger by those who reached the shore on rafts would have shown itself, and the hapless individuals who were clinging to the pieces of the wreck and spars might have been picked off and carried to the shore by the boats, and thus many more lives would have been saved. Also, when the schooner visited the wreck, had the cutters examined the coast in the locality, it is probable they might have found a few others. I can only attribute this fatal error to want of judgment, and to the excited state of the people in the boats under such appalling circumstances.

What follows would give the Commodore more pleasure in writing.

Captain Wright, of the 91st Regiment, who landed on a piece of the wreck, lost no time in procuring and sending assistance to his

* Italics ours.

PHOTOGRAPH OF ENTRIES IN PORT BOOK AT CAPETOWN, INCLUDING STATEMENT OF ARRIVAL AND DEPARTURE OF THE "BIRKENHEAD," WITH DESCRIPTION AND DETAILS OF PASSENGERS.

fellow-sufferers. He walked several miles along the coast, obtained the use of a whaleboat, and returned again to give all relief in his power, taking charge of all who landed. The Civil Commissioner, Mr. Mackay, and a Captain Smales, residing near Stanford Cove, were most hospitable and active in clothing and feeding the poor fellows as they reached that place. To Mr. Ramsden, the Master, I have expressed my thanks for his humane kindness and exertions in proceeding in his schooner to the wreck and saving the people who were clinging to the topsail-yard. Commander Bunce, with the boats, though too late to save life, by his activity prevented a long and painful journey to the sufferers, and succeeded in embarking and bringing them to this port in the *Rhadamanthus*. From the deep water and the dangerous position in which the wreck has sunk, I do not entertain any hopes of recovering anything of value; but I have sent Commander Bunce by land to the vicinity to recover and dispose of the property as he may think best, an account of which I will send to their Lordships by the next mail. The soldiers will shortly join their respective Regiments; and I purpose sending the remaining officers and crew of the late *Birkenhead* to England by the first opportunity (Her Majesty's ship *Amazon*, which arrived here last night and will sail about the 12th inst.), to be dealt with as their Lordships may see fit.

Commodore Wyvill adds:

I have deemed it advisable to entrust this despatch to Mr. Freshfield, the late clerk of Her Majesty's steamship *Birkenhead*, who from his knowledge of the circumstances, though not present at the wreck, having been left behind at my residence sick, will be able to give their Lordships every information, and particularly as to the names of the drowned officers, &c. It will also enable the accounts of this unfortunate ship to be closed.

The reader will learn more of Mr. Freshfield and his mission later on.

To take the enclosures accompanying Commodore Wyvill's despatch in the order in which he presented them, we have first that of Thomas Ramsden, master and owner of the schooner *Lioness*, dated Simon's Bay, February 27th.

I beg to report to you [wrote Captain Ramsden] that when the *Lioness* was off Walker's Bay I observed a boat inshore pulling towards me on the morning of the 26th inst. at about ten o'clock, which I picked up, and found her to contain 37 survivors from the wreck of the *Birkenhead*. On hearing that there were two other boats I proceeded in search of them, and three-quarters of an hour afterwards I succeeded in picking up the other cutter with the women and children; but after cruising about for the third boat I made for the wreck, which I reached about two o'clock in the afternoon of the same day, and sent the cutters away to pick up the men hanging to the spars, by which we rescued 35 soldiers and sailors in a nearly naked state. The wreck had disappeared all but a piece of the maintopmast and topsail-yard, to which the men were clinging. Nothing else could be saved. I observed that some had succeeded in landing on the Point, but only to the number of about ten. Finding that I could do no more at the wreck, I made for this anchorage, and was towed by Her Majesty's steam vessel *Rhadamanthus* when about nine miles from the anchorage. I was glad to have it in my power to relieve the sufferers of this unfortunate ship, who were on board with me about 36 hours. The women and children were provided with suitable clothing by my wife, and all that I and my ship's company could spare we supplied to the men.

Captain Ramsden was a practical man.

As I am desirous of prosecuting my voyage to the West Coast of Africa without delay [he adds], I beg you will be pleased to order the provisions to be replaced and the defects of the ship made good, my boat and gunwale being injured by getting in the cutters. The unfortunate people have been put on board the *Castor* at nine o'clock.

No doubt his very moderate request would be readily complied with.

Dr. Robert Bowen, second staff-surgeon, who was saved by the first cutter, in his report of March 1st, speaks at the outset in terms of commendation of the conduct of officers and men at the wreck:

I remained in the vessel till she parted in two just before the paddle-boxes, as it seemed to me, and then seeing no hope of the ship floating, and Mr. Salmond saying that those who could swim had better try and save their lives, I lowered myself from the poop and swam. The ship went down in three or four minutes after I left her, so far as I can judge. I was picked up by the first cutter. During the time I was on deck the officers and men, both Naval and Military, *displayed the greatest coolness and the perfection of discipline.** Mr. Salmond's orders were given, answered, and carried into effect with as much quietness as if it had been only an ordinary occasion. I spoke to Mr. Salmond only a short time before the ship parted, and he was as cool and self-possessed as possible.

Dr. Bowen found one man in the boats deserving of blame, and others worthy of all the praise he bestows on them.

After I got into the cutter we took in as many men as she could with safety carry, and the crew behaved with the greatest courage and pro-

* Italics ours.

priety with the exception of one marine, whose conduct was disrespectful to Mr. Renwick, and who appeared to grumble rather than assist. The first and second cutters and gig pulled in company for Cape Hanglip, under the orders of Mr. Richards, as when we neared the shore we found the surf breaking heavily. At daylight we all pulled seaward for a sail which was in sight, but after a long pull, as there seemed no chance of reaching her, we again pulled for Hanglip. A north-westerly breeze now sprang up and freshened, with a sea that was rather too much for our deeply-laden boat, and after hailing the gig that was ahead of us, and waving hats for some time without being able to attract the attention of her crew, we put the boat before the wind and pulled for a schooner that appeared to be standing in. This proved to be the schooner *Lioness*, and she took us up about half-past 11 a.m. The master of this schooner then stood in shore for the second cutter with Mr. Richards, the women and children, and some soldiers. We picked them up. They were, like ourselves, pulling for the schooner. When we first made them out they appeared to be under sail, which proved to be a woman's shawl spread on a boathook. We could see nothing of the gig, but as she had a picked crew from the first cutter for the purpose of chasing the schooner in the morning, we were not in much apprehension on her account. The schooner then visited the wreck and took many men from it. This was done by Mr. Renwick and Mr. Richards and the cutters' crews. These two gentlemen displayed the greatest courage, determination, and intelligence in getting the men away from the wreck, as well as during the whole affair. Their conduct was that of brave men. Mr. Richards' duty in the boat with the woman and children was arduous in the extreme, and well performed. Mr. Hire, who was on the wreck about thirteen hours, displayed the greatest courage and coolness. Mr. Renwick was nearly exhausted and much bruised when we in the first cutter took him out of the gig, for the purpose of lightening her to chase the schooner, but after sunrise he soon rallied and behaved nobly. Nothing could exceed the kindness and attention of Mr. Ramsden and his wife on board the *Lioness*: nothing was too good for us, and he made every effort to save as many souls as possible. He deserves the highest praise.

The criticism of Commodore Wyvill, with reference to the boats and the executive officer in charge of them, was certainly not based upon Dr. Bowen's interesting statement.

But Mr. R. B. Richards, master's assistant, the young officer who had command of the boat, speaks for himself. In his report, dated from the *Rhadamanthus*, Simon's Bay, March 1st, he first tells of the scene on board the *Birkenhead* and the getting away of the cutters and gig.

At the time the vessel struck [he says], I was in my hammock in the fore cockpit. I immediately ran on deck in my shirt, and on looking down the fore hatchway I saw the cockpit was half-full of water. It rising very fast, I went aft and heard the Captain give orders to rig the chain-pumps. I went below in the after cockpit, and with the purser's steward and carpenter shipped the pump-handles. I then went on deck and assisted in clearing away the first cutter and starboard paddle-box boat falls. The vessel was rolling heavily, and settling down by the head very fast. The Captain ordered the soldiers on the poop, which was done in a quiet manner. He then called me and ordered me to get the women and children into the second cutter and save them if possible. The boat was lowered with a quantity of water in her, and nearly swamped alongside. The women and children were then passed into her, and some of the soldiers also jumped in off the gangway, in all thirty-five persons. I got clear of the vessel, which immediately parted in two just before the paddle-boxes. I then heard the Captain calling for a boat to save Mr. Brodie, the master. I pulled to the wreck, but could not see him. I was obliged to get clear of the wreck again almost immediately, as the boat was nearly swamped and a great number of men swimming towards her. I then saw the first cutter and second gig astern of the wreck. I hailed and asked if they were full, and told them to take in as many as they could carry with safety. They then pulled up towards me. I heard Mr. Renwick call to me to pick him up. I told him we were nearly sinking and full of people, and to go on a little further to the gig, which picked him up shortly afterwards. We stayed by the wreck about an hour.

About an hour! It may have seemed so to Mr. Richards, but the mistake is plain as the narrative resumes.

After she parted in two, and having as many in the boats as we could carry, I stood in towards the shore to see if I could land those that were in the boats. We got in as far as the breakers, and I found the surf was running too high to land without staving the boats and endangering the lives of those that were already saved, especially those of the women and children. I then hailed the boats to keep further out, as I was nearly in the breakers and should be swamped; we, however, succeeded in getting out of them, and then proceeded along the shore to the north-west six or seven miles, but could not see any place we could land at. At daylight we observed a schooner in the offing five or six miles off. I consulted with the other officers, and we considered it the best way to try and come up with the schooner. After chasing her between two and three hours a breeze sprang up from the westward and she stood off the land. The first cutter and gig were then very nearly out of sight ahead of me, as we could not keep up with them, only being able to pull six oars. I found it was useless my proceeding any further in chase, so I stood in towards the land. We were then in sight of the wreck, but could not distinguish any men on it. We made very little way towards the land, and the breeze freshening we were obliged to keep the boat before it to prevent her sinking. We were within two or three miles of the land when we again saw the schooner standing towards us. We pulled the boat round, and with a woman's shawl for a sail succeeded in making a little way towards her. She hove to and picked us up at about two o'clock p.m., when I found the first cutter on board with Mr. Renwick, Dr. Bowen, and 34 men. We could not see the gig, and therefore made all sail towards the wreck, off which we hove to at half-past three. Mr. Renwick and myself then proceeded in the cutters and succeeded in saving 45 men off the topmast and topsail-yard. We could not see anything between the wreck and the shore, and thinking all that were saved had reached the shore we proceeded in the schooner to Simon's Bay, having on board 116 people.

A young officer, with an immense responsibility, Mr. Richards appears to have acted very well. Riper judgment might have served in ways which have been pointed out—had they suggested themselves to it at the time; but what he did do could not have been done better.

Mr. G. W. S. Hire was clerk on board the *Birkenhead*, acting for Mr. Freshfield, whose illness detained him at the Cape. Mr. Hire was one of those rescued from the main-topsail-yard of the wreck, and his story of what befel him was written for the Commodore on the *Rhadamanthus* on March 1st.

I slept in the fore cockpit, and between two and three in the morning of the 26th of February I was awoke by the ship striking against something. I got on deck and went aft to the Commander, who told me to get the books ready to go in the boat, as he did not think there was any immediate danger. I did so, and went again on the poop. I had hardly got there when she went in halves amidships. I stopped by the Commander and Mr. Speer, second master, at the wheel until the poop went down, taking us with it. I came up again close to the main-yard, and went thence to the topsail-yard as she settled down, where I remained. I did not see any officer or the boats. There were, I think, about fifty men on the yard with me; some of whom dropped off during the rest of the night, and at daylight some went on shore on parts of the wreck. I saw a vessel about five or six miles to windward, which afterwards proved to be the schooner *Lioness*. I tried to get one of the gigs, which appeared above water, but could not. At about half-past 3 p.m. the next day the schooner came down close to us, and the two cutters, with Mr. Richards, master's assistant, and Mr. Renwick, engineer, came and took us off to the schooner, where we received the greatest kindness both from the master and his wife, who did everything in their power to assist and make us comfortable.

The clerk's was a strange experience, to go down with the poop and come up again close to the main-yard, then nearer the surface of the water than the yard shown in the sketch of the submerged ship made by Captain Wright. Mr. Hire's was a lucky escape.

The statement of Mr. Charles Kerr Renwick, chief assistant engineer, also supplied from the *Rhadamanthus* on March 1st, pictures for us in bare and striking outline the scene in the engine-room of the doomed ship.

I was awoke by the vessel going ashore and water rushing from the main deck into the fore cockpit. I ran into the engine-room in my shirt only, and found there Mr. Whyham, Mr. Kitchingham, and Mr. Barber. The engines were stopped, and water pouring from the main deck through the door over the starboard cylinder, I shut the door, and about a minute afterwards orders were given to go astern. The engines, after making from sixteen to twenty revolutions, stopped, the water rising so high as to extinguish the fires. While opening the starboard injection cock I observed a large portion of the starboard bilge buckled upwards, plates and ribs both started and water rushing in. Mr. Whyham having reported to the Commander that the water had risen above the level of the air-pump lids, ordered all hands out of the engine-room. I then went aft and remained on the poop until she broke in two.

Mr. Renwick escaped death by only a hair's breadth. He shared the fortunes of Dr. Culhane and his men in the gig, afterwards exchanging to the first cutter, of which he took charge.

On rising in the water I swam towards the shore for about fifteen minutes, but observing what appeared to be two boats about a hundred yards to my left, I proceeded in that direction. On nearing the first one I hailed, and was answered by Mr. Richards, who told me to go ahead to the other boat, as his was full. At this time I was seized by a boy, who took me down; after struggling I rose, and was picked up insensible by the second gig. On recovering I found Dr. Culhane and six or seven others in the boat. The three boats being full, closed and pulled in towards the shore to pick out a landing-place, the surf breaking very heavily, as far as we could see. At break of day we saw a sail standing towards us, distance about five miles, we being then about four or five miles from the wreck and three or four from the shore. We consulted together and decided to pull towards her, as we were unsuccessful in finding a place to land without smashing the boat. We

THE OFFICIAL STORY

pulled two hours or so after her, and made very little progress in nearing her. Dr. Culhane then proposed to close with the first cutter, select eight good men, and to continue the chase, the second cutter being at this time distant about a mile astern. We did so, and no officer being in the first cutter I took charge of her and continued to follow the gig. A breeze sprang up, when the vessel quickly left us. Both gig and first cutter pulled in towards land; obliged to pull before the sea to prevent the boat swamping, there being in her 36 men. About 11 a.m. observed the vessel standing towards us on the port tack to leeward. At twelve were picked up by her, which turned out to be the schooner *Lioness* of Capetown, Captain Ramsden. I pointed out to him the position, as I supposed, of the other boats. He immediately made sail in that direction, and at 2 p.m. succeeded in picking up the second cutter, with men, women, and children, in charge of Mr. Richards. A man at the masthead being unable to see the gig, we made all sail towards the wreck, and arrived off the reef about 3.30 p.m. Mr. Richards and myself, in the two cutters, proceeded to the wreck and succeeded in rescuing Mr. Hire, clerk, and 36 men who were clinging to the maintopmast and topsail-yard. Having closely examined the whole coast without perceiving any other persons afloat, made sail for Simon's Bay, having on board in all 116 persons.

These people were placed on board the *Castor*, while the *Rhadamanthus*, which had towed the schooner in, again proceeded to the scene of the wreck.

The story is taken up by Dr. William Culhane, assistant surgeon, and carried to the stage at which, after his hard ride across country, the steamer is despatched to afford relief. The report, bearing date March 1st, is from the Naval Hospital at Simon's Bay, of which Dr. Culhane was an inmate.

I have the honour to inform you that I was the last person to leave the wreck * of Her Majesty's steam vessel *Birkenhead* when she got on the rocks off Danger Point. The poop was on a level with the sea when I swam from her, and at that time I could not see any of the boats. I succeeded, after swimming about a mile or more, in reaching the second gig, and when I got into her we mustered ten. I remained there for some time. Could not see the wreck, it being dark, and did not see any men near. The two cutters were near, and they left and we followed, thinking to make the shore; but at daylight Mr. Richards saw a sail,

---

* "Every officer was on board when she sank except Mr. Richards, who was on board the cutter, and Dr. Culhane, of the ship."—*Vide* Captain Wright's second statement. Dr. Culhane quitted the wreck when it was on the point of sinking. So did other officers.

and we all determined to pull for it, but after chasing the schooner for at least twenty miles in the gig, as I had eight men who volunteered from the cutter to pull for the schooner, she got ahead of us, and we did not give up until she was out of sight, and then thought it the most expedient way to reach you in order to let you know the melancholy loss of the men and officers who were on board, except those who were on the mast. When I left the wreck we pulled for ten hours before we reached the shore, and were six miles ahead of the cutter when we gave up all hopes of reaching the schooner.

Dr. Culhane has his grievances, as well as those who railed at himself.

The people in the cutter say that they made signals to us, but the eight men and myself can assure you that we did not see any signal to us. I reached Port D'Urban about three o'clock p.m. The day after the wreck I rode on horseback from there to Capetown, and arrived at Simon's Bay in about twenty hours from the time I started; and after pulling a space of about 50 miles and riding about 110 miles across the country, I am sorry to hear that it has been said that I left the boats. We saw the schooner tack and come in the direction of where we last saw the cutters, and she hove to as if to take them on board, and afterwards steered towards the wreck. We should have been very glad to be there at the time, as we dreaded that we could not get a landing place. I assure you that I tried every effort to reach you in order that you might be able to send a steamer to the wreck, and that was the object of the other eight of the boat's crew.

This report must command sympathy. Poor Dr. Culhane! On the one hand he is blamed for quitting the scene of the wreck. Here he has to defend a charge of disregarding signals made to the gig, and he seems also to have been censured by somebody for leaving the boats. Absurd! No wonder he felt aggrieved. Nobody in authority did anything but praise him for that strenuous and successful effort of his to obtain relief for those who stood in such dire need of it.

Commander B. H. Bunce made his report from his ship, the *Castor* frigate, and it is dated February 29th. He states that in obedience to the Commodore's orders he proceeded in the *Rhadamanthus* to Danger Point, arriving off there on the morning of the 28th, and after examining the wreck with her maintopmast alone above water, he continued in the boats to Stanford Cove, where he found four of the men who had reached the shore from the wreck, from whom he received information that many more were at a farm called "Klyne

Photograph of Entries in Port Book at Capetown, stating Arrival of Schooner "Lioness" in tow of the "Rhadamanthus" with Survivors from the Wreck of the "Birkenhead"

River," about fifteen miles distant. He rode out to the farm and found sixty more, "all of whom had been clothed, fed, and housed most hospitably by Captain Smales, the proprietor," with whom he made arrangements for sending them down to Stanford Cove in the morning to embark them in the *Rhadamanthus*—the sick to come in waggons. Next morning he proceeded with Captain Wright and Mr. Mackay to the neighbourhood of the wreck, and travelling the beach for some distance—

found it strewn with small spars, pieces of deck, etc., and the paddle-box boats, both of which were rendered unserviceable when the vessel broke in two pieces. Numbers of dead bodies had been found and buried, and great numbers must have perished by getting entangled in the large kelp weed which fringes the coast about Danger Point.

Reporting from information he had been able to collect as to the wreck, Commander Bunce says:

The two cutters and one gig had been lowered and manned, and ordered to be off. All the women and children were put into one cutter under the charge of Mr. Richards, the master's assistant, the senior surviving Naval officer. Some 30 or 40 of the men clung to the maintopmast and rigging; some swam to the boats, and getting heavily laden, the boats pulled out clear of the wreck. Many were below when the vessel broke, and went down in her, and the rest, on bundles of hay, spars, stools, doors, tables, and the paddle-box boats bottom up, were driven about between the shore and the wreck. The 68 officers and men whom I brought down in the *Rhadamanthus* are the only survivors out of those who were on those rafts, paddle-box boats, &c. Many must have been drowned from exhaustion, and many have been knocked to pieces on the ledges of rocks over which the sea was breaking.

He goes on to speak emphatically as to the boats.

In communicating to you this disastrous occurrence, I cannot but express my opinion that if the boats had kept by the wreck until good daylight, landed the extra hands in one of the small creeks about, and then given their attention and assistance to the poor fellows floating and struggling in the water, a great many more might have been saved, for the weather was fine, the sea quite smooth, and not a breath of wind.

As to this, we have something to say in another place. Commander Bunce describes the removal of those hanging to the mast and yard of the troopship by the rescuing schooner, these—

making in all on board her saved from the wreck 117, which, with the nine landed in the gig and the 68 in the *Rhadamanthus*, makes a total of 194 of all denominations saved out of the 630 she left Simon's Bay with on board.

He enclosed a list of the officers, soldiers, seamen, women and children saved.

We come now to the second statement of Captain Wright, 91st Regiment, dated Simon's Bay, March 1st, and furnished to Commodore Wyvill. In some respects this document is more important and more interesting even than that sent by Captain Wright to the Military authorities. At the outset Captain Wright recalls incidents which demand close consideration as possibly explaining the cause of the wreck.

> About half-past ten I was on deck, and the officer of the watch, Mr. Speer, observed to me that he had passed the light, at the same time pointing out to me a light on the port side of the vessel. I made the remark at the time, " Surely that is not Cape Agulha's light, for if so the cape must have moved nearer the Cape (meaning Cape Point) than it was when I was here five years ago." From the appearance of the light I was satisfied that it was from a lighthouse, and not from a fire on the hills, many of which were burning, and therefore I concluded that another lighthouse had been built since I was here in 1847. I then went to bed. About two o'clock a.m. on Thursday, I was awoke by a severe shock, and on getting up found that the vessel had struck. I came up on deck and found the Commander, Mr. Salmond, and Mr. Davis, second master, on the poop. I was standing alongside them. The Commander asked Mr. Davis how the light was bearing when he last saw it. Mr. Davis replied by naming some point of the compass. When the Commander turned away, Mr. Davis remarked to me that it was odd where that light was, and he gave me distinctly to understand that he alluded to a lighthouse light, and not a fire on the hills. I have now every reason to suppose that the light which was seen was a fire lighted of dry wood on Cape Mudge to act as a signal fire to the fishing boats which go out from that point. I saw the light for a long time myself, and certainly considered it a lighthouse light, as I have before stated.

This confusing of lights may, as is pointed out elsewhere, have had an important bearing on the immediate cause of the wreck. Captain Wright reiterates the remarks in his first report as to the order and discipline maintained on board.

> After the vessel struck the Commander remained on the poop and gave his orders to Major Seton and myself. The utmost order was observed by all on board, and until the vessel totally disappeared there was not a cry or murmur from soldiers or sailors. *It struck me as being one of the*

most perfect instances of what discipline can effect,* and almost led me to believe that not a man on board knew the vessel was likely to go down. About ten minutes after the vessel struck the Commander sent me to Mr. Brodie, who was on the bridge, to know what assistance he required to get the paddle-box boats out. He told me to get 30 men put on to each tackle so as to get the boats off. I did so, and then went to the Commander on the poop to see if he had any more orders; he told me to get 20 men more to the chain-pumps. I directed Lieutenant Girardot, 43rd, to do this, and it was done. Almost immediately the vessel's bows snapped off, the bow part going up in the air towards the foremast; the funnel fell over to starboard at the same time, almost carrying away the paddle-box and boat. The other paddle-box boat was being canted over just at this time, and Mr. Brodie disappeared from the bridge, having been knocked over somehow or another. Just before the vessel broke at the bows, the Commander had ordered the horses to be pushed overboard, and directed Mr. Richards to get into the cutter to receive the women and children. All this was done with the utmost regularity, and the boats stood off about one hundred yards from the ship. The Commander also ordered out the large boat in the centre of the ship, but it could not be moved as the ship was breaking up at the bows.

Reference is again made to the successful appeal addressed to the men at a critical moment not to jump overboard and endanger the boats.

Just before the vessel broke a second time, which was in about twenty minutes after first striking, the Commander called out for all officers and men who could swim to jump overboard and make for the boats. Lieutenant Girardot was standing alongside of me by the poop rail at the time. We called out to the men not to go overboard to the boats, as we feared their being swamped, they being full of women and children (at least one of them we knew was). Very few men went, and the rest remained on the poop until that part sank, and then down we all went together.

Again, also, Captain Wright speaks in strong terms about the boats.

Every officer was on board the vessel when she sank except Mr. Richards, who was on board the cutter, and Dr. Culhane, of the ship, who got into one of the gigs and then made the best of his way to Bot River, some fifteen or twenty miles from the wreck, rowed there by eight of his crew. I cannot express how much the loss of this boat was felt, and had it returned after landing Dr. Culhane I have no hesitation in saying that nearly every man of the two hundred (about) who were on the driftwood between the wreck and the shore must have been saved,

* Italics ours.

as they could have been picked off the spars and wood on which they were when they were outside the seaweed, which prevented them from coming in to shore. The boat could have made forty or fifty trips to shore between daylight and dark and landed the persons in the boat in a cove just to eastward of Danger Point.

Captain Wright reviews briefly what was done ashore for the men saved from the wreck by himself, Field-Cornet Villiers, and Civil Commissioner Mackay, and the embarking on the *Rhadamanthus*. It cannot be said that Captain Wright is forgetful of the deserts of others.

I cannot conclude this memorandum [he says] without alluding to Mr. Archbold, the master gunner, who was on the same raft with me for some time. While there he was as usual active to a degree, and encouraged the other 15 men who were also on it; but this was no more than his daily custom when on board the ship, for there he was perpetually at work, and to some purpose too. The ship's steward, James Jeffery, although much exhausted after having been in the water so long a time, accompanied me in my search round the rocks on the coast, and did his best to give me all the assistance in his power.

Captain Wright some time after received an interesting letter from Jeffery on the subject. This is quoted on another page.

Mr. Archbold, the gunner of the *Birkenhead*, whose activity at the wreck we have seen is commended by Captain Wright, also made a statement which formed one of Commodore Wyvill's enclosures. This supports the opinion of Captain Wright with regard to the boats, but recognises the value of the help they brought to the wreck in the schooner *Lioness*. The statement is included in the sketch of the veteran seaman which appears in another part of the book where it is supplemented by a few notes made by Mr. Archbold in 1902, a year before he died, the only surviving Naval officer.

In an independent narrative some further interesting particulars of the wreck and what followed are furnished by Cornet Bond, of the 12th Lancers, who says he was awakened by the vessel striking the rock, and immediately dressed and went on deck, where he found all in confusion.

I heard the Captain give orders to "back her," which I hardly think was carried into effect, as the fires were almost immediately extinguished.

Unfortunately this order was carried into effect with unforeseen consequences.

The Captain [says Cornet Bond] then ordered Major Seton [meaning Colonel Seton] to get the horses up and throw them overboard, and I with a sergeant and some men belonging to the 12th Lancers succeeded in doing so. I then went on the poop, where the Captain was standing. He told me to go and get the women and children up, which I did by carrying up two of the latter. The others followed and were immediately lowered into the boats. At this time the greatest order and regularity prevailed. All the officers were then employed with gangs of men at the pumps, and a number of soldiers, under command of Mr. Brodie, the master, were endeavouring to haul out the paddle-box boat on the port side, which was nearly hoisted out when the tackle broke, and it remained fixed in the air. The fore part of the ship now broke off at the foremast, and soon after she cracked in the middle and filled with water. A great many of the men on the troop-deck were drowned in their hammocks, not being able to effect an escape. All those who could succeed in reaching the poop now crowded there, and the Captain sung out to those that could swim "to make for the boats," of which there were three, at a distance of 150 yards. They did not come nearer for fear of being swamped. A gig on the starboard side was then ordered to be lowered, in which Mr. Rolt, of the 12th Lancers, who was unable to swim, and several seamen, were seen to enter; but in lowering it one of the ropes broke, and she was swamped. Poor Rolt rose, but was unable to reach the shore, and was drowned. The poop immediately afterwards, owing to the force of the water rushing up, went down, drawing all those who were on it, as well as myself, under water.

Then began the struggle for life.

I rose to the surface almost immediately. I had one of Mackintosh's life-preservers on, which may be filled in the water, which I did. The sea at this time was covered with struggling forms, while the cries, piercing shrieks, and shoutings for the boats were awful. I swam astern in hopes of being picked up by one of them. I hailed one sixty yards off, but could not reach it, as they pulled away, I suppose, for fear of too many attempting to get in. I then turned round and made for the shore, about two miles distant, which I finally succeeded in reaching at a little after 5 a.m. by swimming only. Two men who were swimming close to me I saw disappear with a shriek, most probably bitten by sharks.

How often we find the same terrible incident recorded in the statements of survivors; the remembrance of—

> A solitary shriek, the bubbling cry
> Of some strong swimmer in his agony.

Cornet Bond reached the shore at last by a great effort, and when there guided others who were afloat to a safe point of landing. The first thing he saw on gaining *terra firma* was his own horse, which had got there before him.

> I fortunately hit on a landing-place, but owing to the great quantity of seaweed I had to struggle through, and being quite exhausted, I almost failed in reaching it. I then walked up a sort of beaten track from the beach in hopes of finding some habitation. In doing so I perceived my horse at a short distance standing in the water on the beach. I got him out and then returned to the place at which I landed, when I saw a raft with about nine men on it endeavouring to land, but they did not succeed in doing so until they saw me on the rocks standing opposite to the proper spot; they then steered straight for me, and finally landed at 7 a.m. Lieutenant Girardot, of the 43rd Light Infantry, was one of them.[*] At the same time two or three other men were thrown on the rocks off a spar, and landed very much cut and bruised and entirely naked. We all then proceeded up this track, and after two hours' march we saw a waggon up the shore, to which we went and obtained some bread and water. The driver directed us to proceed further up the beach and at five miles' distance we should find some fishing cottages belonging to Captain Smales, where we arrived very much fatigued at noon. Here we obtained some more bread, and then marched on to Captain Smales' residence, about twelve miles off, over the sands. On our way thither we met a bullock waggon, which took some of our men, who were too much knocked up to proceed, back to the cottages we had just left. At seven o'clock p.m. our party, consisting of 2 officers and 4 men, arrived at Captain Smales', where we were most kindly received, the men being provided with both clothes and victuals.

Next morning, with the Field-Cornet and District Magistrate (Mr. Mackay), they walked back to the beach.

> On our way thither we met numbers of men who had landed. Some came ashore in the paddle-box boats, which had floated up; the one was full of water and the other keel uppermost. One of the ship's quartermasters told me that there were seven others in the boat with him, which was full of water. They, however, all died from cold, having been many hours in the boat and quite naked. He had his clothes on. We also met Captain Wright, 91st, who had landed on the sponson: he had been along the shore and had picked up several men. Some rafts reached the shore with bodies lashed on them quite dead; other bodies washed up, some of them dreadfully mangled by sharks.

[*] Lieutenant Girardot speaks of this meeting in a letter printed on a later page.

THE OFFICIAL STORY

Cornet Bond speaks of the party being taken off by the *Rhadamanthus*, and in conclusion confirms the evidence of others that—

the time from when the ship struck, to the period at which the poop sank and those on it were precipitated into the water, did not occupy more than twenty minutes.

Finally, there is the narrative drawn up by a non-commissioned officer,* one of the survivors of the wreck. Some of the incidents herein described will be new to the reader. The writer comes at once to the striking on the rock—

which made a hole in the port side, under water, just before the paddle-wheel. She began to fill immediately [he says]. Hands were turned up to get the boats out; lowered two cutters down and one gig; then turned to get the paddle-box boats out, but the pin of the davits was rusted in and would not come out. At this time the vessel was swinging, grinding, and grating against the rocks very much. Some set to work at the chain-pumps in the after cockpit. The next thing was to throw the horses overboard and get all the women and children in the second cutter, which Mr. Richards took charge of, with orders to land them at the nearest place; but they could not land on account of the breakers, so her head was put out to sea. Just at this time, the *Birkenhead* parting in two just before the engine, the fore part of the deck sank with several people on it. Captain Salmond then gave orders to do the best they could to save their lives. The other cutter and the gig were lying off, manned. Several men jumped overboard and swam to the boats, the Captain standing on the poop giving orders.

Up to this time perfect order and discipline were observed—all the men quiet and steady, and obedient to orders.

At this time the Captain was standing on the poop with several others; the after-part of the ship then lurched forward and all were thrown into the water. Some swam to the boats and some to the wreck. The maintopmast and maintopsail-yard were out of the water, and all who could made for the topsail-yard. Part of the forecastle deck was then floating at about twenty yards' distance. Captain Salmond swam for the wreck that was floating, and as he was swimming something that was washed off the poop struck him on the head and he never rose again. All were clinging to the raft till it broke up, and then some swam back to the wreck and some to the maintopsail-yard. About 45 people were on the yard, where they remained about twelve hours

* Name not stated. Believed to be a Naval petty officer.

till the *Lioness* schooner came and took them off about two o'clock on the Thursday afternoon. About 100 of the soldiers were drowned below. The vessel filled so fast that they had no time to get up. From the time we first struck, which was about two o'clock on the morning of Thursday, until the vessel was all to pieces, was about half an hour.

In the opinion of this shrewd observer—

Captain Salmond might have saved himself easily, but he remained giving orders until the after-part of the vessel surged and threw him overboard; he might still have been saved if it had not been for this accident.

Young Mr. Rolt, of the Lancers, asked the sergeant of Marines to try and save him; he did try, and got him on the raft, but as it surged against the rocks it parted, and he sank.

About 117 men, women, and children, came into Simon's Bay on board the schooner, and 30 or 40 landed on another raft. That number could be counted on the beach. Of the 45 that remained on the yard were Mr. Hire, the clerk; John Drake, sergeant of Marines; John Cooper, private, Marines; John King, a stoker; and 42 soldiers, and all, with one exception, behaved most admirably. They were rather in a hurry to get into the schooner's boat when she came to take them off, which nearly caused an accident, but all were saved.

The behaviour of the crew was admirable—all obedient to orders.

There is no chance of Captain Salmond being alive. Mr. Brodie, the Master, was in the act of clearing the paddle-box boat when the ship parted in two, and he was killed at once.

The narrative concludes with a tribute to Captain Ramsden. "He clothed and fed us as well as he could, and we shall always remember his kindness." A tribute well deserved and well expressed. The treatment of survivors by Captain and Mrs. Ramsay appears to have won the gratitude of them all.

In a letter received from him by his uncle, Dr. Morgan Culhane, of 7, Steyne, Worthing, six weeks after the wreck, on April 7th, Dr. Culhane states more circumstantially his method of quitting the ship.

I was one of the last who left the wreck [he here says]. When the poop was on a level with the sea the Captain said, " Now all you that

THE OFFICIAL STORY

can swim, leave the ship." I saw the Captain in the mizzen rigging about that time. I then determined to have a tug for it, took off my clothes, except my flannel jacket and my cap, and stood on the aftermost part of the poop and remained on board about five minutes. I swam about for some time before I reached a small boat (the second gig). I hailed it; the men in the boat knew my voice and took me in. It was then dark. We remained there for a short time to see if we could pick up any of the sufferers. The two cutters had then left; we followed, came up to them, and intended to try for a landing-place as soon as light should appear. The first thing we saw was a schooner in the distance, to which we gave chase, but she went on at a smacking pace. We had no sails. We then turned back and tried to make the shore. When we reached it the men had been pulling for ten hours, and had pulled 50 or 60 miles since we had left the wreck. I thought the most expeditious way to render assistance would be to get here (Simon's Bay) as soon as possible to send a steamer down, as the boat I was in was of little use on that coast. I rode as far as Capetown (95 miles), leaving Port D'Urban at four o'clock p.m. the day of the wreck, and arriving at Capetown at nine o'clock the following morning.

Happily we now have this matter of the conduct of Dr. Culhane in its proper perspective, and in view of all the circumstances it may, we think, be fairly and safely said that he was not seriously to blame, if to blame at all, for anything which he did at the wreck or after it. No reasonable exception whatever can be taken to his action in riding to Capetown for assistance. On the contrary, it was an arduous duty well performed, and good results sprang from it. The criticisms of Captain Wright, Commodore Wyvill, and Commander Bunce, as to the boats, no doubt appeared to them to be well justified at the time. But we can now see that the only things apparently possible were done. To have remained longer near the wreck would have meant the inevitable swamping of the boats by the poor fellows who would have clambered into them. They all seem to have accommodated as many as they could safely carry. The boats tried to land forthwith, and had they been able to they would, no doubt, after putting their occupants ashore, have returned to the assistance of the men still struggling in the water. But they found it impossible to land because of the breakers, and were not foolish enough to attempt it.

Viewing things calmly, as we are now able to, with a

proper adjustment of the whole of the circumstances, it is easy to excuse the reproachful language used officially on this subject. The writers were evidently burning with indignation at what they considered, we may think erroneously, a needless waste of human life. They only saw one side of the picture plainly, and not so clearly the side which is now as distinctly turned to us. Taking their cue from the official reports, critics at home lashed out more vigorously, and in the records of the time may be found denunciations which were as bitter as they were unjustifiable. To take an example—we may hope it is an extreme one—a public print[*] girds fiercely at one who, it declares, "has achieved notoriety by taking good care of himself," and indulges at the poor surgeon's expense in sarcasm of a particularly biting kind.

> His object in trotting to Capetown, he tells the Commodore, was that he might be able to send a steamer to the wreck, and that such also was the object of the other eight of the boat's crew. That is, his shipmates were to struggle in the water, floating on driftwood, knocked on the head by spars, bitten by sharks, or sinking from sheer exhaustion, though some hundred and fifty of them might have been picked up and rescued by half-dozens at a time with the gig of which this doctor had deprived them. And these men were in their death-struggle, while the zealous doctor was trotting a hundred miles across the country to inform the Commodore that there were Englishmen a-drowning, and that it would be well for him to send a steamer out.

The sting of the whole, as is usually the case, lies in the tail.

> England having thus paid the lives of more than a hundred of her bravest sons for the preservation of Mr. Culhane, will no doubt feel bound in honour to take care of a gentleman whose retention in her service cost so large a sum in death and widowhood and orphanage.

We can only regret that before such an un-English libel was penned the result of the Court Martial, which sat the following month, was not awaited. That inquiry was not only as to the loss of the ship, but was also directed to an investigation of the subsequent conduct of the officers arraigned. The trial on the third day was understood to have special reference to Dr. Culhane, and what was the

---

[*] *The Examiner*, April 10th, 1852.

PHOTOGRAPH OF ENTRIES IN PORT BOOK AT CAPETOWN, STATING ARRIVAL OF THE "RHADAMANTHUS" WITH "BIRKENHEAD" SURVIVORS ON BOARD.

THE OFFICIAL STORY

outcome of it? It was not only found that no blame was imputable to him or to any other survivor—

> but on the contrary the Court see reason to admire and applaud the steadiness shown by all in the most trying circumstances, and the conduct of those who were first in the boats, and who, to the best of their judgment, made every exertion for the rescue of the portion of the crew and passengers who remained upon the wreck.

That should finally dispose of the matter, and in favour of Dr. Culhane, who, it will be seen, for some years after the wreck continued to perform honourable service in the Navy. The mistake really committed by Dr. Culhane was made on his return to England, when, stung apparently by what was stated, he seems to have brought counter-allegations against others which were shown to be as groundless as those levelled at himself. But the controversy was a "storm in a teacup," and was speedily forgotten by the public, as it deserved to be.

The courage and devotion of the soldiers at the wreck received fitting recognition from Sir Harry Smith in a General Order issued on March 11th.

> Under the appalling and distressing circumstances of the wreck of H.M.S. *Birkenhead* [ran the Order], by which nine officers and 349 soldiers perished, it is a source of no small satisfaction to the Commander-in-Chief to find, from Captain Wright's report, that the strictest order and regularity were observed amongst the troops from the time the vessel struck until she went down, and that by a noble self-devotion no attempt was made by the men to save themselves at the risk of swamping the boat which contained the women and children. Captain Wright himself merits every encomium, and the true valour of men was never better exemplified than on similar awful occasions, and bravely have the lost human beings met their fate. This soldier-like and gallant conduct will be reported to Her Majesty the Queen and Commander-in-Chief.

The report was made, and in July Sir Harry Smith, having heard from the Horse Guards, had the satisfaction of announcing that—

> Her Majesty has been graciously pleased to express her high admiration of the discipline, fortitude, and devotion displayed by the officers and troops on that trying occasion, and I am to request [he adds] that you will be pleased to make the same known to Captain Wright and the other survivors, as well as to the other troops under your command.

Later on we shall see how sincere and whole-hearted this admiration was.

Accompanying this chapter are beautiful photographic reproductions of interesting entries in the Port Book at Capetown, written at the time of the wreck. The photographs were obtained for this work by Mr. Herbert Penny, secretary to the Capetown branch of the Navy League, with the kind assistance of Mr. A. Walsh. The first noteworthy entry is that of the *Birkenhead* itself.

Arrived Simon's [Bay] February 23rd, departed February 25th, 1852, H.M.Str. *Birkenhead*, 4 guns, Captain Salmond, from Cork, January 7th; Madeira, January 20th; Sierra Leone, January 30th; St. Helena, February 11th; bound to Simon's Bay. Passengers: Major Seton and Ensign Russell (74th Highlanders), Captain Wright (91st), Ensigns Boylan (2nd) and Metford (6th), Lieutenant Fairclough (12th), Lieutenant Girardot (43rd), Lieutenants Robinson and Booth and Ensign Lucas (73rd), Cornets Bond and Rolt (12th Lancers), Mrs. Metford, Drs. Bowen and Robertson, and 491 men, 25 women, and 31 children (Drafts of the above Regts.). Brings a few letters.

Next we have the entry relating to the schooner *Lioness* towed in by the *Rhadamanthus* with survivors from the wreck. Also on this page are particulars of the mail steamer *Propontis*, in which Mr. Freshfield, the clerk of the *Birkenhead*, returned to England, bearing Commodore Wyvill's despatch enclosing statements made by survivors.

Arrived Simon's [Bay] February 27th, departed March 2nd, 1852, schooner *Lioness*, tonnage 132, towed in by H.M.Str. *Rhadamanthus*; Captain T. Ramsden, from Algoa Bay, February 23rd, bound to Table Bay. Agents, Thomson and Co. In ballast. On the 26th instant, fell in with two cutters belonging to H.M.Str. *Birkenhead* at 9 a.m., about 15 miles west of Danger Point. The *Lioness* then stood in for the Wreck and succeeded in Saving altogether **116 souls**—viz. 4 Officers, 63 soldiers, 29 seamen, Marines & Boys, 7 Women & 13 children.

The remaining entry to be noted concerns the *Rhadamanthus* and the rest of the survivors.

Arrived Simon's [Bay] March 1st, 3 a.m., departed March 9th, 1852, H.M.Str. *Rhadamanthus*, Comr. Belam, from Danger Point, 29th February, 8 p.m., bound to Simon's Bay. **With 68 men**, being the

THE OFFICIAL STORY

remainder of the Survivors of the Wreck of H.M.Str. *Birkenhead*, who had managed to reach the Shore on driftwood and by swimming.

These entries are finely written in the Port Register, but there was a little of the carelessness characteristic of the period in the rendering of names. "Mitfred," "Fanthough," "Guendot," "Boot," and "Rold" are included among the *Birkenhead's* passengers; the names are corrected in the copy given above. The entries are useful for the comparison of numbers, and they form a valuable record.

CHAPTER IV

THE DEATH ROLL

How sleep the brave who sink to rest
By all their country's wishes bless'd !—WM. COLLINS.

THE death roll of the *Birkenhead* was a heavy one, and far exceeded the muster roll called when all was over and the stragglers who had gained the shore, and those mercifully preserved in the boats or on the mast of the sunken wreck, were collected together. It is set out in as complete a state as possible in the lists which follow of the soldiers and Naval and Military officers who perished :

DRAFT 2ND OR QUEEN'S REGIMENT.—Ensign Boylan, Corporal M'Manus, Privates H. Cull, T. McKenzie, Geo. Marsh, James Rowley, Joseph Burke, Charles Cornell, James Coe, Richard Coleman, Wm. Clay, Wm. Forbes, J. Green, John Greenleaf, John Howard, George Knight, Patrick Lavery, John Martin, Charles Mooney, James Nason, Michael O'Connell, James Oxley, George Price, John Quinn, Timothy Simmons, G. Shaughnessy, Nathaniel Thomas, Samuel Vesse, B. Webster, J. Walker, Thomas Woolfall, George Weller, W. H. Wheeler, Zwyker (bandmaster), A. Mills, Wm. Day.

DRAFT 6TH ROYAL REGIMENT.—Ensign Metford, Abraham Bark, Michael Beckett, Wm. Brown, John Bryan, Patrick Bryan, Wm. Bryan, Joseph Bromley, Dennis Caulfield, Patrick Carrigan, Hugh Dickson, R. Finn, Wm. Fletcher, John Grady, Joseph Hudson, Henry Keane, M. Kelly, Wm. Kitching, Henry Lombrest, John Mayn, Hugh Meara, Cornelius Maloney, Patrick Maloney, Thomas Maloney, Michael Morgan, John Oolrenshaw, Charles Prince, Patrick Ryan, John Rider, John Rennington, Thomas Spicer, Mark Summerton, Michael Starr, Thomas Smith, Edward Torpy, George Tully, John Tierney, George Worth, J. West, Thomas White, James Millham, Henry Jacobs, John Lewis, Patrick McCann, Joseph Harris, Alfred Clifford, John Croker, James Handley.

DRAFT 12TH ROYAL LANCERS.—Cornet Rolt, Sergeant John Straw, G. Hutchings, I. Englison, Coalborn.

DRAFT 12TH REGIMENT.—Privates Thomas Archer, J. Armstrong, Barrett, T. Bellingham, W. Boswell, George Bradley, J. Byrne,

THE DEATH ROLL

M. Carrington, M. Cellars, M. Clince, B. Cummins, J. Costello, J. Cragg, W. Demmack, J. Durkin, J. England, J. Field, T. Fitzgerald, P. Flanagan, T. Flanley, O. Freeman, W. Fynn, A. Grimshaw, F. Hart, S. Hayward, Samuel Johnston, J. Wootton, T. Kelcher, J. Kelly, C. Lambden, M. Lawler, E. Lee, J. McDermott, J. McDonnel, T. McMorrow, W. Matravis, A. Meally, J. Mullany, T. Moran, R. Morrison, R. Munns, D. O'Connor, J. Owen, W. Palmer, J. Pettifer, T. Purcell, C. Reynolds, J. Roche, R. Sheppard, W. Smith, W. Spriggs, J. Thompson, W. Tigne, T. Wales, W. Wilson.

DRAFT 43RD LIGHT INFANTRY.—Sergeant Wm. Hicks, Corporal Joseph Harrison, Corporal Benjamin Cousins, John Anderson, John Butler, John Byrne, Wm. Bullen, Daniel Brennan, Thomas Cave, John Cosgrove, George Gilham, William de Bank, Thomas Dews, Wm. Donnel, Joseph Penning, Kelly, J. Houghton, John Riddlesden, D. Riordan, T. Sullivan, Vickerey, Edward Quin, Maurice Welch, Charles Ranshaw, G. Sheppard, John M'Quade, Michael M. Parklin, Timothy Sheehan, H. Tucker.

DRAFT 45TH REGIMENT.—G. Cocker, Wm. Connel, M. Dockery.

DRAFT 60TH RIFLES.—Corporal Francis Curtis, James Brown, James Brookland, James Callaghan, Wm. Chapman, Eli Elliot, Thomas Frost, Arthur Hamilton, Michael Kelcher, Wm. Kelly, Charles Lucas, James Maher, James Moore, John McAcy, Daniel McQuade, Patrick O'Brien, Thomas Peacock, John Rees, Wm. Russell, H. Scutts, James Story, Patrick Stokes, James Thompson, Wm. Wilkins, Wm. Wilkinson, James Wilson, Wm. Woolward, John Wallis, Simon Jacobs, Joseph Ladd.

DRAFT 73RD REGIMENT.—Lieutenant G. W. Robinson, Lieutenant A. H. Booth, H. Birmingham, James Bernard, James Biggam, Wm. Brennan, Daniel Buckley, John Byrne, Wm. Barton, E. Bryan, Michael Caffrey, Matthew Collins, Patrick Cooney, John Clements, Charles Dawson, Hugh Deegan, J. Dudley, Patrick Doyle, Hugh Feeley, Matthew Fitzpatrick, Michael Flanagan, Michael French, Malachi Gavin, Michael Gavin, L. Giles, John Grant, Wm. H. Hall, John Hannen, Patrick Hanley, Robert Houchin, Michael Hurley, Wm. Kearns, Timothy Kelly, George Lawrence, Thomas Larkin, Michael Maber, John Haher, John Murphy, Thomas Murray, Patrick O'Brien, Wm. O'Connel, Michael Ronen, George Randall, George Darsey, Wm. Flynn, Philip Scott, P. Sheehan, Daniel Shea, James Sullivan, Robert Shephard, George Smith, James Wilson, H. Holmes, James McMurray, W. Buckley, C. Wells.

DRAFT 74TH HIGHLANDERS.—Major Seton, Ensign Russell, Corporal M. Mathison, Corporal Wm. Laird, George Anderson, Archibald Baxter, John Bennie, Robert Blackie, Walter Bruce, John Cataneech, John Cowan, David Cousin, Wm. Donald, David Donaldson, James Gibson, Charles Gowan, D. R. Goman, J. H. Graham, Thomas Harrison, Alexander Hendry, David Hunter, James Kirkwood, John Lowrie, James Morton, Alexander Murdock, Alexander Mathison, Thomas Maxwell, Alexander Miller, David Miller, George Miller, Wm. McAnley,

James Mackinnon, Edward McLeod, John McElarney, Thomas Robertson, Ebenezer Rutherford, John Sharp, Duncan Shaw, Robert Smith, Wm. Smith, Robert Steward, Wm. Steward, John Thompson, Adam Thompson, Francis Turner, Robert Walker, George Watson, Peter Hamilton, John Nelson, Thomas Pride.

DRAFT 91ST REGIMENT.—Sergeant Wm. Butler, Corporal Alexander Webber, Corporal Smith, Joseph Birt, James Brian, James Buckingham, Wm. Wybrow, James Cavanagh, Daniel Daley, James Drury, Hugh Ford, Patrick Gaffey, John Harpey, Stephen Haggan, Patrick Haggan, Thomas Jays, George Kemp, Francis Hackenley, James Evans, A. Montgomery, Wm. Mathieson, John Smith, W. S. Smith, Patrick Smith, Wm. Clark, James Tarney, Christopher Wyer, Alexander Winnington, Joseph Grant, John Moore, Wm. Woodman, George Justice, James Moon, Wm. Foster, Wm. Measures, Wm. Sedgwood, Patrick Kelly, James Delaney, Alexander McFadden, Henry Hayward, Patrick Hussey, John Sweeny, David Pratt, T. Walsh.

Andrew White (a servant).

Staff-Surgeon Laing, Staff-Assistant-Surgeon Robertson.

OFFICERS OF THE "BIRKENHEAD" DROWNED.—Mr. R. Salmond, master commanding; Mr. W. Brodie, master; Mr. R. D. Speer, second master; Mr. J. O'D. Davis, second master; Mr. W. Whyham, chief engineer; Mr. C. W. Hare, master's assistant; Mr. James M'Clymont, assistant engineer; Mr. Deeley, assistant engineer; Mr. Kitchingham, assistant engineer; Mr. T. Harris, boatswain; Mr. James Roberts, carpenter.

THE MUSTER ROLL

The soldiers, women, and children saved by the ship's boats were as stated in the accompanying list.

2ND REGIMENT.—John Moore, Michael Maley, P. Peters, John Peters, Thomas Chadwick, Robert Page, Henry Double, Henry Vernon, James Gildea, Benjamin Worill, Patrick M'Crery.

6TH REGIMENT.—Sergeant Teile, W. Bushe, William Clark, Thomas Coa, James Goldin, John Herrich, James Wade, William Welch.

12TH REGIMENT.—Daniel Waters, Thomas Sangaw, John Irvin, James Johnson, Robert Dolan, John Yale, John Simon, P. Ward.

43RD REGIMENT.—John Herin, Edward Ambrose, James West.

45TH REGIMENT.—Adam Keating.

60TH RIFLES.—William Burlow, Thomas Nuttall, Thomas Smith, William Sooter.

73RD REGIMENT.—Sergeant B. Kilkeary, William Bushe, Thomas Cash, James Fitzpatrick, William Halfpenny, Patrick May, Michael O'Brien, Patrick Lynch, John Sullivan, William Wood.

74TH REGIMENT.—Sergeant Harold, Wm. Boyce, C. Ferguson, James Henderson, D. Kirkford, Walter Taylor, John Smith, Charles Walker, Daniel Shaw.

THE DEATH ROLL

91ST REGIMENT.—John Stanley, David Carey, P. Mullins, P. Cunnynham, John Cougham, John Lamb, John Walmsley, Frederick Winterbottom.

WOMEN.—Mrs. Darkin, Mrs. Nesbitt, Mrs. Mullins, Mrs. Hudson, Mrs. Zwyker, Mrs. Spruce, Mrs. Montgomery.

Thirteen children.

Mr. Bowen, staff-surgeon.

TOTAL: One officer and 62 soldiers, 7 women, and 13 children.

When the *Rhadamanthus* reached the scene of the wreck she found on the shore near Danger Point sixty-eight survivors who had succeeded in landing there. It appeared (as mentioned by Captain Wright in his report), from search of the coast for twenty miles, that no others had been saved or were likely to be found. Following is the list of the Military persons recovered, in addition to those saved by the boats:

OFFICERS.—Captain Wright, 91st Regiment; Lieutenant Girardot, 43rd Regiment; Ensign Lucas, 73rd Regiment; Cornet Bond, 12th Lancers.

12TH LANCERS.—J. Dodd, W. Butler.

2ND REGIMENT.—A. Auther, W. Babb, J. White, J. Boyden, John Smith.

6TH REGIMENT.—J. Kitson, R. Hunt, M. Hartey, J. Hobdy.

12TH REGIMENT.—G. Bridges, G. Wells, W. Smith, L. Higgins, J. M'Donnell.

43RD REGIMENT.—F. Ginn, G. Peters, G. Lyons, G. Brachley, M. Hornett, P. Allan, J. Woodward.

60TH RIFLES.—Sergeant D. Andrews, A. Lackie, H. Voss, J. Hanlon, H. Maltier, J. Stanfield.

73RD REGIMENT.—D. Sullivan, J. O'Reilly, W. Dopson, P. Taylor.

74TH REGIMENT.—G. Taylor, J. M'Mullin, R. Hartle, J. Keath, D. Munroe, J. M'Gregor, J. M'Kee.

91ST REGIMENT.—Corporal O'Neil, J. Holden, P. Flynn, J. Cordey, A. M'Kay, A. Hutson, J. Laucey, J. Haggard.

TOTAL: Forty-seven soldiers, 4 officers.

The members of the ship's company saved by the boats are named below:

William Culhane, assistant surgeon; C. R. Renwick, assistant engineer, 1st class; Benjamin Barber, ditto, 3rd class; R. B. Richards, master's assistant; G. W. S. Hire, clerk.

SEAMEN, ETC.—John Bowen, A.B.; Thomas Dunn, A.B.; George Till, A.B.; John Smith, A.B.; Charles Noble, A.B.; John Haines, A.B.; Thomas Daley, A.B.; Wm. Langmaid, A.B.; John Ashbolt, stoker; George Randall, stoker; John King, stoker; Thomas Dew, stoker;

Henry Maxwell, quartermaster; Edward Wilson, boatswain's mate; James Lacey, captain maintop; James Wessum, sailmaker's mate; Wm. Neale, carpenter's mate; J. Dobson, carpenter's mate; Thomas Handrain, leading stoker; James Jeffery, paymaster and purser's steward; Edward Gardner, stoker; John Hoskins, stoker; E. Crocker, A.B.; Sam. Harris, A.B.; Richard Tiggle, A.B.; H. Cheesman, A.B.; Abel Stone, Ord., 2nd class; John M'Cabe, stoker; Wm. Chase, stoker; George Kelly, stoker; Martin Rush, A.B.; Robert Phinn, A.B.; George Windsor, A.B.; Thomas Harris, A.B.; John Lewis, A.B.; Thomas Woods, stoker; John Thalen, A.B.; John Dyke, A.B.; James M'Carthy, A.B.; Thomas Forbes, A.B.; Henry Bewhill, A.B.; Wm. Woodward, seaman; Thomas Drackford, seaman; Thomas Coffin, seaman; Wm. Gale, boy, 1st class; William Henry Matthews, boy, 2nd class; George Wyndham, boy, 2nd class; Benjamin Turner, boy, 2nd class; J. R. Howard, not on ship's books.

MARINES.—John Drake, colour-sergeant; William Northover, private; Thomas Daniels, private; John Cooper, private; William Tuck, private; Thomas Kearns, private.

Some of the above-named are included in the following list of two officers and sixteen seamen and others of the ship's company taken off Danger Point.

OFFICERS.—Mr. Barber, assistant engineer; Mr. John T. Archbold, gunner.

Edward Crosser, A.B.; Samuel Harris, ditto; Thomas Handrain, stoker; Edward Wilson, boatswain's mate; James Wessum, sailmaker's mate; James Lacey, captain maintop; James M'Neal, cooper's mate; Henry Maxwell, quartermaster; James Jeffery, paymaster and purser's steward; Edward Gardner, stoker; Richard Tiggle, A.B.; John Hoskins, stoker; Wm. Tuck, private, R.M.; Thomas Kearns, ditto; George Wyndham, boy, 2nd class; Benjamin Turner, boy, 2nd class.

All the muster rolls and books on board were of course lost with the ship.

The Military loss, as shown by the returns, was 358, or 9 officers, 11 non-commissioned officers, and 338 privates, of a total of 508 on board. The Naval loss, including many officers, was 87. This gives the number of lives altogether sacrificed as 445, compared with only 193 saved of the total of 638 persons on board. Mrs. Nesbitt, wife of Captain and Quartermaster Nesbitt of the 12th Regiment, had two young sons, Richard and Henry, with her on the *Birkenhead*. They were among those saved. Richard Nesbitt afterwards entered the Imperial service and distinguished himself in the Colonial

THE "BIRKENHEAD" MONUMENT AT CHELSEA HOSPITAL

(Special photo by the Portrait and Picture Co., Chelsea)

wars. He obtained celebrity as the commander of Nesbitt's Horse in the Tembu and Basuto rebellions of 1880-82, and again in the South African War of 1899-1902, when for his services in the field he was made a C.B. An account of the career of Colonel Nesbitt, written by himself, and of his sudden death near Port Elizabeth towards the close of 1905, is included in a later chapter.

Cornet John Rolt, 12th Royal Lancers, one of the officers drowned at the wreck, was the youngest son of Mr. Peter Rolt, of Hyde Park Gardens, London. He was in his 20th year, and had only joined his regiment a short time when the *Birkenhead* sailed. His still surviving sister, Mrs. Collier, was residing at Ascot, Berks, in 1905. A cousin of this gallant youth, Lieut.-Colonel J. Rolt Triscott, an officer on the retired list, writing from Southsea in this year, said of his kinsman, quoting from a record in his possession: " His calmness at the dreadful wreck in Simon's Bay is reported to have been beyond all praise." His fate, it will have been seen, was peculiarly distressing.

CHAPTER V

TRIBUTES TO THE BRAVE

Good things should be praised.—SHAKESPEARE.

IT was not until April 7th that *The Times* announced the "Total loss of Her Majesty's steamer *Birkenhead*," and gave particulars of the "fearful disaster which has thrown a gloom over the whole of the community at the Cape." The fateful news had reached London the day previous, although questions asked in both Houses of Parliament elicited the reply that no official intelligence of the affair had at that time come to hand. When the report received confirmation and details of the disaster became known, deep commiseration succeeded the first sensation of dismay which the ominous news awakened, and there was a desire manifested to fix the responsibility and blame for an occurrence so appalling; but the predominant feeling, as we gather from contemporary prints, was one of intense admiration of the conduct of the heroic troops.

There is no mystery about the calamity [commented *The Times*]. We are not left, as in the case of the *Amazon*, to conjecture the origin of the disaster. Just what happened to the *Orion* off the Scottish coast, and to the *Great Liverpool* off Finisterre, has happened now. Captain Salmond, the officer in command, anxious to shorten the run to Algoa Bay as much as was possible, and more than was prudent, hugged the shore too closely; 454 persons have lost their lives in consequence of his temerity. As soon as the vessel struck upon the rocks the rush of water was so great that the men on the lower troop-deck were drowned in their hammocks. Theirs was the happier fate: at least they were spared the terrible agony of the next 20 minutes. At least the manner of their death was less painful than that of others who were first crushed beneath the falling spars and funnel, and then swept away to be devoured by the sharks that were prowling round the wreck. From the moment the ship struck all appears to have been done that human courage and coolness could effect. The soldiers were mustered on the after deck. *The instinct of discipline was stronger even than the instinct of life.** The men fell into place as coolly as on the parade ground.

There follows a quotation from Captain Wright's report, with the comment:

> Poor fellows! Had they died in battlefield and in their country's cause their fate would have excited less poignant regret; but there is something inexpressibly touching in the quiet, unflinching resolution of so many brave hearts struggling manfully to the last against an inevitable disaster. It is gratifying also to find that the women and children were all saved.

Other incidents are cited in their order. It is noted that "Captain Salmond, who appears to have done his duty after the vessel struck," had not survived the wreck, and *The Times* adds:

> It certainly cannot be imputed as a fault to the Admiralty or the Government that a Naval officer of good repute for skill and competency should, in an unhappy moment of temerity, have navigated his ship in so reckless a manner.

On the same date *The Morning Herald* drew a doleful picture which reflects the state of the public mind with regard to the disaster.

> By this distressing accident, seven Military officers and 350 soldiers were lost, and with them perished eight Naval officers and 60 seamen. The crises of some of our most severe and bloody actions have been determined at a smaller amount of sacrifice than what we have now to record as the result of this awful and tremendous calamity. The heart sickens as we contemplate a scene so dreadful. It is bootless now to ask whether it might have been avoided. The commander of the unfortunate vessel is no more, and the bulk of his officers and crew have perished with him.

There is the brighter side of the story, and the paper hastens to voice the public sentiment as to that.

> But it is due to the memory of the brave men who perished to hold up their conduct to that admiration which their heroism and devotion so richly merit. We venture to assert that the whole annals of Naval disaster afford no nobler instance of coolness, true courage, and steady discipline than was exhibited by the ill-fated Major Seton, and the officers and soldiers under his command. We defy the whole history of our race to produce a more striking instance of bravery and coolness

---

* Italics ours.

than is here exhibited ; and it only adds to our regret when we reflect that such heroic self-devotion did not suffice to preserve lives so justly valuable to their afflicted country.

Much the same views are expressed by the London *Globe* of the same day. The feeling was overwhelming, for this journal says :

There are moments when the public mind is so full that it loses all capacity of retaining aught else, and it were perfectly idle to solicit attention to any political topic, in presence of the catastrophe at the Cape. The melancholy lists of the drowned, including contingents from no less than nine regiments, forming a truly formidable total of lives suddenly destroyed, bring us back to the war gazettes of the Peninsular struggle, without the national excitement that bore up against the calamities of the battlefield.

But there are more comforting reflections.

One of the most characteristic incidents of the late fearful tragedy at Point Danger was the preservation of all the women and children, without exception ; while the cool courage of the men, as detailed in the official report, speaks for itself. When the narrative of this sorrowful, but far from discreditable occurrence, is perused by foreigners, we have no fear for the national chivalry when tested as thus in the hour of trial. We cannot too highly admire the intrepid attitude and cool conduct of the commanding officer, whom the official report styles *Major* Seton.

Returning to the subject in a subsequent issue, *The Morning Herald* observes with force and eloquence that—

in proof of the promptitude with which the people of these islands can adopt not merely the outer discipline of the soldier, but enter into the loftiest feelings and most chivalrous self-devotedness of the profession, the circumstances attending the catastrophe which so lately befel the *Birkenhead* in Simon's Bay cannot be too often referred to, and never can exhaust the most sustained and profound reflection.

And it recalls that—

the men who, within a quarter-of-an-hour of certain death, obeyed the orders of their heroic officer ; who calmly "*disembarked*" the women and children ; who refrained at the word of command from taking the desperate leap from the wreck—their last sole chance of escape—lest they might capsize the boats freighted with females and infants : these men were all young soldiers, who had never seen an enemy in the field ; they were men not confined to any part of the country ; they were English, Irish and Scotch. Most mournful [the writer concludes] is the loss of these heroic men ; but it is in so dying that they became translated into heroes.

Yes, they were English, Irish and Scotch, and their countries were equally proud of them. *The Scotch Press* of April 10th speaks of the death roll of the *Birkenhead* as—

affording the best of all evidence of the cool heroism manifested by the gallant but unfortunate men in deliberately preferring a watery grave, while they sent away in safety every woman and child on board the ill-fated vessel. Indeed, the instance is one, almost without a parallel, of the courage and training of British soldiers, inasmuch as while death in one of its most appalling forms stared them in the face, the men received and obeyed their orders as quietly and readily as if they had been on parade. The catastrophe occurred eight thousand miles away, but it has created a sensation as if it had happened yesterday and on our coasts. Many a Scotsman has found in that wreck a watery grave. The tragedy cannot be recalled, but surely we may provide against its repetition.

This journal, while praising the conduct of the troops, does not forget the cause and the occasion for it. In a strongly worded passage, which is interesting now as showing the reasons which, on general grounds, at that time appear to have justified it, the *Press* laments that—

neither punishing with severity, nor risk of life or property, nor public opinion seems to have any effect on seafaring men. A man may be sent to prison, like the captain of the *Orion*, or to the bottom, like the captain of the *Amazon*, and the next week we will find other commanders of vessels "hugging the shore" to shorten a voyage by a few hours, or proceeding to sea with a ship nearly in a state of ignition. Habituated to danger, accustomed to hairbreadth escapes, and removed a great portion of their lives from that healthful communion of thought and feeling which operates so powerfully on other men, the officers in charge of ships are, many of them, reckless to a degree which surprises and (too often by the catastrophes which ensue) appals us. Of this last description is the loss of the Government steamer *Birkenhead*.

There is a demand for some stronger controlling measure to ensure more care on the part of commanders, "since nothing short of this will prevent the recklessness of men who, apart from this, may be both skilful and humane."

The Scotsman of the same date, in an article on the subject, says that in one respect the *Birkenhead* catastrophe—

contrasts favourably with almost all similar shipwrecks of recent occurrence—namely, in the perfect order and discipline maintained on board ;

and declares that—

> to the admirable self-possession and promptitude of the officers, and the not less praiseworthy obedience and subordination of the men, even in that hour of horror and peril, the salvation of so many lives on board is mainly to be attributed.

A Dublin paper,* dealing with the question of national character, says with generous warmth:

> Now an exemplification of British character has just occurred which is highly, we will say beautifully, national, and we hope that even the most prejudiced of our journalists will show that they know what is right and noble by applauding it. We allude to the scene on board the *Birkenhead*, near Simon's Bay. Could anything be more manly, more generous, more truly—we had almost said more exclusively, but we are admonished that it was not so—English, than the whole conduct of the officers and men in that trying moment? If we want to find the *morale* of a people, it is in such critical situations we should look for it; and what people in the world could have furnished anything to equal the heroism of that occasion?

The paper gives extracts from Captain Wright's report, which, it observes,

> will be read with a melancholy pleasure as evincing the patience, the order, the intrepidity, gallantry, and tenderness, which go to make up the genuine English character.

The value and sincerity of this testimony will be the better appreciated when the reader knows that earlier in the same article the confession had to be made that "they brand us"—Ireland, that is—"as a nation of assassins; we retort, and pronounce England to be a vast Circæan sty." This perverted state of popular feeling on both sides of the Channel is, however, deplored, and people in their views of national character are asked to distinguish between individual offenders and the mass of the community. Then we have the argument that—

> national character is not to be inferred from individual acts, either of extreme viciousness or of high virtue, unless the public sympathy goes along with them in a marked and almost spontaneous manner,

and this leads up to the tribute to the *Birkenhead*.

> It was [the writer also says] a solemn occasion, and the noble fellows had "bent up" their minds and faculties to meet it as men and British

---

* Preserved among Colonel Wright's papers. Name not given, but evidently a leading organ—*Mail* or *Express*.

soldiers. It seems as if the words of Wellington at Waterloo, at the turning point of the day, "What will they say in England?" were at that anxious moment in all their thoughts—not, however, we trust and believe, to the exclusion of a far more ennobling and tranquillising contemplation.

Turning then to the share of Ireland in the honour of the occasion, and duly claiming it, this Dublin paper still displays its admiration for the English.

Captain Wright says that many of the soldiers were young recruits; and as the vessel had sailed from an Irish port, no inconsiderable proportion of them must have been Irishmen. Our country, then, claims her share in the passive heroism (the most trying and difficult kind of heroism) of that day; but the spirit which overruled and guided it was essentially British, and we doubt if, under any other flag, a similar amount of self-control could have been produced, and sustained up to the very moment when the deep gaped to receive them.

There is a magnanimous candour about what follows.

Amongst the topics of depreciation upon which writers and talkers among us are apt to expatiate, to the prejudice of the English character, is that of excessive selfishness. The English are a provident and cautious people, and therefore we—who seldom think into the next half-hour—pronounce them selfish. But see John Bull in the prow of this doomed ship; behold him standing within 150 yards of an asylum, where, doubtless, many a fond arm was stretched out, reckless of its own peril, to receive him; and mark with what a generous abnegation of his own life he folds his arms and renounces the proffered help.

The writer cites the appeal made to the men not to make for the boats, and its result. "All honour to their memory," he exclaims. "It will surely be embalmed in the tears of every woman, from fifteen to sixty, who reads this simple statement."

Let us return now to the English press. *The Illustrated London News,* in describing at the week-end the "Fatal Wreck of Her Majesty's steamer *Birkenhead,* and Large Loss of Life," tells with pride how—

the coolness and steady obedience to orders which the troops manifested on that awful and trying occasion present an instance of the noblest results of discipline.*

These are words to be remembered.

"A catastrophe like this cannot easily be made real to the understanding of us dwellers on the land," says *The Examiner*

---

* Italics ours.

of April 10th. "The fate of the *Pegasus*, of the *Great Liverpool*, of the *Orion*, has been warning insufficient against a perpetual recurrence of the same disaster." But—

the long annals of shipwreck furnish no picture more impressive than that which is conveyed to us of this large body of men labouring calmly in the face of death.

They "died true heroes," and the way in which they delivered to safety the women and children, "themselves finally dying with grand tranquillity, is not to be read without the deepest emotion."

The Examiner turns with a shudder—

from the indescribable horror of the final effort, when there was no ship upon the sea, to swim ashore through the thick seaweed, under which sharks habitually lurk.

Some of the survivors, it notes, "describe their companions in this last struggle suddenly disappearing beneath the water with loud shrieks," which unhappily they did.

The Examiner is wrathful, and casts about for a victim. It finds one in Dr. Culhane, and acting on imperfect knowledge of the circumstances, proceeds to chastise the unfortunate surgeon.

As in the case of the *Amazon*, the officers stood by the vessel to the last. Every officer, except the surgeon, was on board when she finally sank. All had calmly awaited death in the performance of their duty to provide help as they could for those committed to their care.

But for the injustice it does the surgeon, this passage might well be left undisturbed. There is warrant for the assertion that the wreck was caused by "a manifest want of prudence," and for what is said about useless boats and broken tackle. Not so for what follows.

Here, as in a recent case, one minor officer (it was a midshipman on that occasion, now it is a surgeon) has achieved notoriety by taking good care of himself. Mr. Vincent was lauded as something little short of a hero for escaping from the *Amazon*, and now that Mr. Culhane has shown equal skill in rowing away from the *Birkenhead*, it will be only fair that he should be dubbed hero too. Mr. Culhane defends himself by saying that the cry of *sauve qui peut* had gone forth before he took to his own preservation. This also was the precise defence of the friends of Mr. Vincent; but in neither case does it appear that any other officer had proceeded to act upon the cry which these gentlemen so alertly

TRIBUTES TO THE BRAVE 75

obeyed. The latter case differs from the earlier in a more certain measure of the mischief occasioned by so marked an exception to the discipline which generally prevailed.

This passage is quoted merely as an interesting curiosity. These charges against Dr. Culhane have already been dealt with, it is hoped successfully, in the earlier pages of this work.

The Service journals of the time, it need scarcely be said, made themselves heard on a subject which so intimately concerned the Forces they represented.

When [remarked *The Naval and Military Gazette* on April 10th] we have to announce to our readers this week a loss of brave men far exceeding that in many a glorious victory, we feel unmitigated sorrow; for the loss of life by the wreck of H.M. steamship *Birkenhead*, like that on the sinking of the *Royal George*, might, by even the most ordinary caution, have been spared. It is said that in the deepest sorrows for the dead some consolation for the survivors may be found; and if the reflection that the soldiers on board the *Birkenhead* died bravely, doing their duty to the last, and remembering that, as obedience to their officers is their *first* duty, so also it should be their *last*, be consoling to the relatives and friends and comrades, then most assuredly they must feel comfort.

The *Gazette* speaks of the "admirable coolness, true courage, and steady discipline" of "these gallant soldiers and sailors," whose—

heroic and devoted conduct merits all praise, and is proved by the fact that while the officers, and soldiers, and sailors perished, *all* the women and children, as we have learned, have been saved.

It reviews the loss entailed, and asks its readers—

to dwell upon the heroic devotion of these *young* soldiers, for they were almost all *very young* soldiers: and when [it goes on] they hear soldiers called "the scum of society" * by Peacemongers and the Cobdenites, let them ask if the "cream of England's society" would have acted more gallantly, more bravely, more unselfishly!

The *Gazette* passes on to insist upon the severity of the test of courage which the men of the *Birkenhead* withstood.

The whole letter of Captain Wright, 91st Regiment, must be read with deep interest by all, from the Queen herself to her humblest subject; and while the Queen must feel a Royal pride that she has such soldiers and subjects, her subjects must also feel pride that they can claim such heroic men for their comrades and countrymen. The pomp and circumstance of glorious war stir the spirits of the least daring, and the wonder

* See extract from *The Spectator* of a later date, further on in the book.

is great that courage should in fight ever fail ; but the sterner and nobler courage that with moral resoluteness can face danger and death, and unselfishly abstain from self-preservation at the command of discipline, for the purpose of the general safety, is that courage which shipwreck tests most especially ; and this severe test the courage of *British* soldiers and sailors—we say it not invidiously—has pre-eminently been found to stand. Can any other nation of Europe afford such instances as our history affords ? To the long list of noble and devoted acts of courage in shipwreck we may now add that of the soldiers and crew of the *Birkenhead*.

A high tribute is paid by another Service journal * of the same date to the Military discipline displayed, and the supreme value of discipline at all seasons of crisis is at the same time emphasised.

Amidst the deep and widespread lamentations and sympathy which the frightful wreck of the *Birkenhead* has occasioned in Great Britain, it is beyond all measure consolatory to find—even in the crisis of such a calamity—so magnificent an illustration of the power of discipline among our brave soldiery as that described in the affecting letter of Captain Wright.

The passage describing the order and regularity prevailing on board is extracted.

Is not this beautiful ? [asks the journal]. Ought not every Englishman's heart to throb with intense gratitude that the English Military system creates such men ? Can *any* Englishman refuse the tribute of a tear to the noble spirits who, in the last minutes of their existence, acknowledge the duty and the force of obedience ? Shame on the men who can suffer the current of generosity to be checked when the question before the public is the recompense of her soldiers ! For ourselves, grateful as we feel that the discipline of our admirable Army has been so superbly vindicated, we cannot say that we are by any means astonished at the circumstances detailed. Since the hour when the struggle commenced at Roleia—we might even go back to the operations in the Low Countries—British troops have learnt that their personal honour and the interests of their country are dependent entirely upon their rigid fidelity to their commanders in the hour of peril. It is no vulgar sense of personal safety which influences them. They know that the security of a whole body is dependent upon the steadiness, attention, and fortitude of each individual, and in this fine spirit they endure the visitations of Heaven and the assaults of man. What we now hear of the troops in the unfortunate steamer is what all the world heard nearly thirty-seven years ago, when British squares of infantry

* Preserved among Colonel Wright's papers.   *United Service Gazette.*

stood to be "pounded," nor moved from their stern and invincible attitude, though cannon-balls rushed through their ranks and cuirassiers and lancers hovered around them, until the voice of the immortal Chief sent them in one impetuous line upon the hitherto invincible Guards of the oppressor. The earth trembled beneath their terrific charge, the proudest soldiers of Europe fled, scared as they advanced, and the struggles of a quarter of a century were brought to a glorious issue in less than half-an-hour. And this was Fortune's tribute to British discipline. May nothing ever happen, either through the incompetency and indifference of commanders or the slavish deference of ministers to vulgar demagogues, to destroy so mighty a bulwark of our liberties, so firm a protection to our possessions!

The journal recalls that when upon a similar occasion a vessel with troops was wrecked near the Cape, the Government hastened to reward Captain Bertie Gordon, of the 91st, for his conduct in securing the safety of the men under his command, and says that so good a precedent, were precedent needed, would surely be the guide of the Commander-in-Chief on the present occasion. We may suppose that precedent was not forgotten in what followed, although the service involved was in this instance of a higher character.

The Naval and Military Gazette reverts to the subject on April 17th with some striking thoughts on the makings of true heroism.

In the abstract there is a vast difference between valour and heroism; between the spirit which actuates the man first on the scaling-ladder and the man last on the wreck. A man may be pre-eminently fearless in danger, even a mighty conqueror, without having a spark of heroism in him. Valour, a quality superior to mere bravery, is, at least, more or less of animal instinct, of self-seeking. Heroism is more than a sense of moral duty bravely carried out; something exceeding even a generous impulse. It is the most exalted of human virtues, not confined to any one department of life. God-like! Ay, advisedly we say God-like; for the spirit which leads a man to crucify the thoughts of self, to sacrifice his very life to save others, is surely an emanation of something beyond human will—an influence superhuman.

Observing that vessels foundering at sea afford, perhaps, more conspicuous instances of the effects of discipline, and have drawn forth more acts of heroism in its highest sense than any other incidents of life, the writer states some examples of "this exhibition of the divinity that stirs within him, an earnest of man's 'partaking of the divine nature' in a hereafter perfect state of existence." And he speaks first of the tale of devoted loyalty and heroism of "Rio, of the *Guardian*."

Five hundred miles from the Cape of Good Hope, when the ship under his command was fast settling down in the water—her doom, beyond the reach of help, appearing inevitable—this heroic fellow, after dispatching the ship's boats with all the people they were capable of holding, and consigning to an officer a letter recommending his mother and sisters to the commiseration of the Lords of the Admiralty, with the few noble-hearted men whom the boats would not contain and in whom he had kindled that spirit which moved himself, calmly awaited his fate in the sinking ship, which had been entrusted to his command by his Sovereign. How mysterious are the ways of Providence! The boats never more were heard of; while the *Guardian* was, as it were by accident, barely kept afloat, with her decks scarcely out of water, by the empty water-casks bearing her up until she just reached Table Bay, when she sank at her anchors.

We have next cited the case of the *Kent*, East Indiaman, having on board the 31st Regiment. The vessel was wrapped in flames, and there seemed scarce a possibility of all on board being saved by the boats, which amidst a high sea slowly passed to and from the *Cambrian*, by good fortune brought to the spot. What heroism, it is asked, was that which could have dictated the directions to quit the ship in "funeral order," a command given by Major MacGregor and instantly confirmed by Colonel Fearon, by which those two officers must consequently be the last to leave the vessel on whose decks the consuming fire was making such rapid strides. Also noticed is the loss of the *Commerce* on Lake Erie in May, 1850, having on board a detachment of the 23rd Fusiliers under Captain Phillott, when deeds of heroism were performed.

Returning to the *Birkenhead*, the writer asks what must have been the mental ascendency of Captain Wright over the many soldiers on board, not of his own regiment alone, but over men of different corps, to whom he could have been scarcely known, and they almost recruits?

Mark the spell his words—so nobly echoed by young Girardot, of the 43rd—had in instantly restraining the men who could swim from obeying the order of the Master of the *Birkenhead*, in jumping overboard, an act which Captain Wright saw must inevitably be the means of swamping the boat in which the women and children had been rescued. Had not "self" at this moment been immolated at the shrine of exalted heroism, Wright and Girardot would have been the first to have availed themselves of the Master's (Salmond's) order, for the former was perhaps the best swimmer on board, and young Girardot had been taught the art in a Military school in Germany.

Unconsciously, and with an incomplete record before him, the writer errs in excluding Colonel Seton from the position his name should occupy in any reference of this kind. In reading the passage quoted it should be remembered also that in one place at least it has been denied, by Mr. Renwick, the engineer, to Mr. David Seton, brother of the Colonel, that the order to swim to the boats was given by Captain Salmond. These matters do not, however, affect the writer's argument, which quite justifies what follows.

Surely such self-possession in the moment of imminent peril—such extraordinary power as that displayed by Captain Wright over the men of detachments of various regiments at a moment when individual self-preservation, one would have thought, would have been the sole consideration—shows that this officer possesses, together with the intelligence which he displayed when on the personal staff of the late General Hare, those qualities which pre-eminently fit him for the command of a regiment, an appointment which would not only be a just reward of merit, but confer a vast benefit on the Service.

The same qualities were, of course, exhibited by Colonel Seton. The merit of Captain Wright was rewarded, and the promotion which he received conferred a real benefit on the Service he adorned.

It was on May 12th that W. M. Thackeray, with rare prescience and mental sagacity, stimulated by the imaginative daring he possessed, made the bold and, as it proved, true prophecy which is recorded on the title-page of this book. It was not a bow drawn haphazard at a venture, but a prediction based upon solid conviction. It was uttered in a speech* which the great author made at the anniversary meeting of the Royal Literary Fund Society, when he

---

* Reported in *The Morning Herald* of May 13th, 1852.

remarked that so long as there was kindness, folly, fidelity, love, heroism, and humbug in the world, so long would his successors have plenty to write about. He had, he said (speaking more with regard to history than the novel, which he thought would have a longer popularity), sometimes fancied what future times might see in that age to write about, and he added the stirring words:

I can fancy a future author taking for his story the glorious action off Cape Danger, when, striking only to the powers above, the *Birkenhead* went down; and when, with heroic courage and endurance, the men kept to their duty on deck.

A noble and inspiring theme, worthy the pen even of the master mind which dictated these glowing words!

"THE LOSS OF THE *BIRKENHEAD*"

The striking and imposing representation of the loss of the *Birkenhead* seen on the page opposite gives in clear detail the picture done from recollection by Captain Bond-Shelton, of the Royal Lancers, an officer who survived the wreck. The picture was shown in 1890 and 1891 at the Military and Naval Exhibitions in London, from both of which Captain Bond-Shelton received diplomas. The doomed ship is here depicted as she appeared shortly before her final plunge beneath the waves. By the falling of the funnel upon the deck at that moment, many of those on board were crushed and killed. Blue lights were being burned as distress signals at the stern, and their ghostly and fitful glare illumined the dreadful scene, throwing into relief the outlines of the sinking vessel and enabling surrounding objects to be discerned upon the bosom of the water. It was this picture which inspired the celebrated painting by Mr. Thomas M. Hemy, which forms the frontispiece of this book, and it may also have suggested the beautiful work by Mr. Charles Dixon, R.I., reproduced in Chapter II.

The Loss of the "Birkenhead"
(From the picture by Captain Bond-Shelton)

CHAPTER VI

A HERO'S WORK FOR HEROES

Take away the sword;
. . . bring the pen!—LORD LYTTON.

WE have seen reflected in the prints of the day the deep impression and sympathetic outburst which the wreck of the *Birkenhead* produced throughout the United Kingdom, and the public admiration universally expressed for the heroism displayed on board the sinking troopship. More tardy was the recognition which conduct so exceptional, and so flattering to the national name and character, received at the hands of the Home Government and of the Military authorities. At this time the Russell Administration had fallen,* and had given place to Lord Derby's Government. Lord Malmesbury became Foreign Secretary, Sir J. S. Parkington was Colonial Secretary in succession to Lord Grey, the Duke of Northumberland (a Rear-Admiral of the Blue) was First Lord of the Admiralty, Major William Beresford was Secretary for War, and Mr. Augustus Stafford was Secretary to the Admiralty. Early in the year Sir Harry Smith, the Governor and Commander-in-Chief of the Cape, a valiant soldier whose deeds in India had won him lasting fame, was recalled by Lord Grey. In the House of Commons on February 9th Lord John Russell said " the despatch recalling Sir H. Smith had been submitted to and received the sanction of the whole Cabinet." The step caused a great outcry. Sir Harry Smith was a popular and much esteemed General, and his recall was regarded as harsh and unjust. The Duke of Wellington, as Commander-in-Chief, defended the General from his place in the House of Lords. The question of the fitness or unfitness of Sir Harry Smith for

---
* February 20th, 1852.

command in such irregular and savage warfare had long been made the subject of angry dispute; but the Duke of Wellington, who knew the conditions and the country, pronounced in favour of the tactics he employed. Sir Harry Smith was superseded by Major-General the Hon. George Cathcart, and certainly, whatever the injustice of the recall, no better choice of a successor could have been made. The new Governor, whose selection for the Cape command was generally approved, embarked at Plymouth on February 10th on board H.M. steamer *Hydra*, Master-Commander Belgrave. He reached the Cape on March 31st, and at once proceeded in the *Styx* for the seat of war, arriving at King William's Town on Good Friday. Sir Harry Smith left for home on the following day, returning in the steam frigate *Gladiator*, and on landing in England he was accorded a hearty reception. The operations conducted subsequently by General Cathcart are familiar to students of the time and of our Empire's history. Under his command men who had survived from the *Birkenhead* fought through the war. Some of them were killed or wounded. Already comrades of theirs had fallen to the spear and bullet of the Kaffir foe, among them three officers of the 74th, including the gallant commander whom Lieut.-Colonel Seton was going out to replace.

This hasty glance at the condition of affairs at home and at the Cape will help the reader the better to appreciate what follows, and to fill in the complete picture of this story. At home the *Birkenhead* had a doughty champion in General Sir William Napier, the Military historian, a soldier of Peninsular fame and one of a family of heroes renowned for their bravery and chivalry, who took up the subject with all the warmth and impetuosity of his ardent and generous nature, and exerted himself energetically on behalf of the survivors. The following letter from his eloquent pen appears in *The Times* of April 9th:

SIR,—Were the late Ministry still in power we should doubtless have an official letter from Lord John Russell prating of "discretion," and from Lord Grey a "despatch"* censuring Captain Wright for not

---

* Alluding to a recent despatch from Lord Grey to the Governor of the Cape, Sir Harry Smith.

sinking with his men; but under the present Ministers it may be hoped that the matchless chivalry of Captain Wright and Lieutenant Girardot, and the responding generous devotion of their men, who went down without a murmur rather than risk the safety of the women and children in the boats, will meet with some public honour and reward—honour for the dead as well as for the survivors. For surely the occasion was great, was noble, was good—the heroism never surpassed? And it was not calculated—there was no time for that. It was the strong fount of Military honour gushing up from the heart.
—Yours respectfully, W. NAPIER, Lieutenant-General.

From this and other evidence which will be adduced it is abundantly clear that General Napier was one of the greatest admirers of the *Birkenhead* who ever lived, and it will be allowed that he was a competent judge of the merits of the case as a whole. When the above letter was written he unfortunately had the impression that the troops on board were commanded by the senior surviving officer. The existence of Colonel Seton, and the share of that officer in the glory of the occasion, seems to have escaped his notice altogether. As we shall see, however, on learning the truth later Sir William at once very fully and effectually corrected this oversight. Meanwhile he did much, under some discouragement, in the direction of securing due recognition of a subject on which he and others felt so strongly. His stirring letter to *The Times* was an appeal which found a response in the hearts of his countrymen, if it did not dispel the official torpor of the day; and he followed it up with letters to every member of Parliament with whom he was acquainted in both Houses; among others to Lords Hardinge and Ellenborough in the Lords, and to Lord Palmerston and Mr. Henry Drummond in the Commons, who all lent their influence to forward his object.

The subject was brought before the House of Commons by Mr. Drummond on April 26th. After observing that Her Majesty had already, he believed, the power of granting compensation in such cases as that to which the question he was about to put referred up to the amount of £80, and also of rewarding deserving officers by promotion, Mr. Drummond asked the Secretary-at-War whether there was any ground for hoping that the Queen's Ministers would recommend

Her Majesty to grant any compensation, by promotion or otherwise, to the officers who survived of the *Birkenhead* for their heroic conduct and the total loss of their property in "that miserable shipwreck"? He mentioned only a single case. One of the officers,* he said, was the son of a poor clergyman. He had lost everything he possessed, to the amount of £300, and it was utterly impossible for him or his friends ever to make that sum good.

Major William Beresford replied that he was glad to have the opportunity of expressing his sense of the heroic conduct of those who lost their lives on board the *Birkenhead*, more especially as the troops were not old soldiers, but recent raw levies going out to join the regiments at the Cape, and it showed that discipline, which made them so efficient in the field and so ready to die for their country, did not depend on a long course of service. The question divided itself into two branches — compensation and promotion. The War Office would be happy to receive any application for compensation on the most liberal principle that, according to the regulations of Her Majesty's warrant on the subject, could be allowed; and although the statement as to Her Majesty having the power of granting compensation to £80 was correct, yet it was in the power of the Secretary-at-War, having received from the board of officers appointed to inquire a special report of special service under special circumstances, when a greater loss had been incurred to increase that amount. Beyond Her Majesty's warrant no one could expect the Secretary-at-War to go, but nothing could be more agreeable to him than, out of the funds in his hands, to make a distribution in favour of such persons as those to whom the report referred. The subject of promotion was in the hands of the Commander-in-Chief, whose past conduct showed that he was as desirous of rewarding Military men as he was capable of appreciating their services. Unfortunately, however, the *Birkenhead* was not the only case of shipwreck in the last few years where the Military had been sufferers and officers had distinguished themselves. There were four instances in which shipwrecks had occurred, and the officers

* Lieutenant Girardot, 43rd Regiment.

who had distinguished themselves in saving life had received promotion or staff appointments. He was glad to see many persons, headed by the most illustrious Lady in the land, had subscribed for the relief of the sufferers in the present case.

His praise of the men of the *Birkenhead* must have been gratifying to Major Beresford, who had himself served with one of the regiments on board. In 1826 he joined the 12th Lancers as captain, and the same year accompanied that regiment to Portugal in the expedition sent out by Mr. Canning. He remained with the 12th Lancers until January, 1831, when he received his promotion as a major unattached. His elder brother fell at Ciudad Rodrigo, and was specially mentioned for gallantry in the Duke of Wellington's despatch. Without in the least desiring to detract from the meritorious conduct of brave men who had distinguished themselves at previous wrecks, as stated by Major Beresford, it may in fairness be said that those were not cases parallel with the *Birkenhead*, the circumstances of which were altogether exceptional. His own well-intentioned efforts did not avail much in favour of the *Birkenhead* survivors.

About this time Sir William Napier was publishing the abridgment of his *Battles and Sieges in the Peninsula*, in the Introduction to which volume he compares the soldiers of his day with those who won the victories in the Peninsula War. He says:

> For the soldiers, it is no measure of their fortitude and endurance; it records only their active courage. But what *they* were, their successors now are—witness the wreck of the *Birkenhead*, where four hundred men, at the call of their heroic officers, Captain Wright and Lieutenant Girardot, calmly and without a murmur accepted death in a horrible form rather than endanger the women and children already saved in the boats. The records of the world furnish no parallel to this self-devotion!

The attention of Mr. David Seton, brother of Lieut.-Colonel Seton, was subsequently drawn to this prefatory notice by friends who pointed out that Captain Wright and Lieutenant Girardot, who really had no more to do with the incident than other officers then on the deck of the sinking ship,* were

---

* Except to issue an appeal which had already been made by Colonel Seton.

made to assume here a position which might well suggest to the mind of the reader the inquiry, Where was the senior officer? and might even leave an impression unfavourable to him on the minds of those who were unacquainted with the particulars. It was no question as to the soldiers. Their heroism was the same in either case. Mr. Seton called Sir William Napier's attention to the omission, and some correspondence followed; and the result was that in all later editions or issues of the book the words given below were added at the foot of the notice in question:

> After the above notice was published, the author was informed that *Lieut.-Colonel Alexander Seton* was the officer in command of the troops on board the *Birkenhead*, that he called to the men not to swim to the boats, and continued in the active discharge of his duty until the vessel sank. He then perished; but the following extract of a letter from the Secretary-at-War to his brother, Mr. D. Seton, dated War Office, May 24th, 1852, bears testimony to the conduct of Lieut.-Colonel Seton.

Then is quoted the first paragraph of the letter in question, which is given in full on another page of this book in the chapter dealing with Colonel Seton, where will be found ample evidence, were any wanting, that "the call of their heroic officers," to which General Napier refers, originated, as it ought to have done, with the commanding officer.

Reference to this phase of the story is made by the Right Hon. H. A. Bruce, M.P. (afterwards the Home Secretary) in his *Life of General Sir William Napier, K.C.B.*, published in 1864.

> The officers and men may almost be said to have gone down with the ship in their ranks [Mr. Bruce says]. Their noble commanding officer —one of the most gifted and accomplished men in the British Army (it is within the knowledge of the writer that he was so)—was drowned. Sir William wrote the following letter on this subject. When it was written, he was not aware of the fact that Major Seton was the officer commanding, and that all the measures taken were taken under his orders.

Then follows the letter printed in *The Times* of April 9th. It will be observed that Mr. Bruce in his explanation of the letter falls into the error of calling the commanding officer "Major Seton." But this is merely a slip. He passes on to make an important statement.

FACSIMILE OF "BIRKENHEAD" LETTER WRITTEN TO MAJOR WRIGHT BY GENERAL SIR WM. NAPIER, IN WHICH THE MILITARY HISTORIAN SPEAKS OF HIS EFFORTS TO RAISE A MONUMENT, AND OF A PROMISE OF PUBLIC NOTICE OF LIEUTENANT GIRARDOT GIVEN BY THE DUKE OF WELLINGTON.

A HERO'S WORK FOR HEROES

Although admired and praised, the survivors did not seem destined to reap any substantial reward for their heroic conduct, for this sort of heroism was beyond the ken of the official mind. The Duke of Wellington was Commander-in-Chief at the time, and he was very chary of recommending officers for promotion as a reward for any special service not before the enemy.

Mr. Bruce mentions the steps taken by Sir William Napier and the bringing of the matter before the House of Commons by Mr. Henry Drummond, and says the result was that after some delay—

the two officers above-named [Captain Wright and Lieutenant Girardot] received promotion, and all the survivors pecuniary compensation for their losses.

Sir William's reference to the *Birkenhead* in his Preface to *Battles and Sieges in the Peninsula* is also given. Concerning the statement that "this sort of heroism was beyond the ken of the official mind," Mr. David Seton, in the interesting privately printed little work on the *Wreck of the Birkenhead* referred to in another chapter, has some strongly worded comments to make.

No doubt he is right [he says of Mr. Bruce's opinion]; but to me there has always appeared something more in this official apathy—namely, an idea that the wreck of the *Birkenhead*, which was undoubtedly caused by remissness and carelessness, could give rise to many teasing questions, which might easily be asked in Parliament, and perhaps not so easily answered. Be that as it may, the Government made no movement towards testifying in any substantial way their approbation of the conduct of the troops on that occasion; and it is even said that the Duke of Wellington (who was then Commander-in-Chief, and almost in his dotage—he died the same year) was decidedly opposed to anything of the sort. But the country was not in a humour to allow the thing to pass "as a nine days' wonder" to please official apathy and red-tapeism. Private individuals took up the matter, and by dint of importunity, through members of Parliament in both Houses, the Government was at length brought to see the necessity of giving promotion to the few surviving officers, with compensation for their losses, and to erect a tablet to the memory of the drowned.

Mr. Seton also declares that, while all the newspapers were filled with applause at the heroism of the troops,

the Government and the officers at the head of the Army manifested all the calmness of indifference. The general orders issued did not do justice to the case, and Her Majesty's Ministers seemed to think it would be a relief if the whole thing could be forgotten.

Mr. Seton apparently formed his opinion of the decaying mental and bodily powers of the Duke from a not very kindly letter, describing a public banquet, written by Sir Henry Havelock and contained in the Memoirs of that General.

> In looking at the Duke of Wellington [the writer of this letter says], and listening to his speech, nearly all that we have read of the ruined powers of Marlborough, after his first paralytic seizure, seemed to be realised. I never witnessed so affecting a spectacle of mouldering greatness. He is so deaf that he seemed to me to utter prolonged inarticulate sounds without being aware of it. He begins, but rarely concludes a sentence, and where he breaks off in a period the spectator doubts from his manner whether he will commence another or fall down apoplectic in the next effort to begin one.

If the occasion referred to was the Royal Academy banquet of May 1st, 1852—and presumably that is meant—the language of the letter is surprising, and in the light of the account of that banquet, given later in these pages, the picture strikes one as being much overdrawn. On this interesting occasion, as will appear, the Duke, in words happily chosen and feelingly expressed, paid a high tribute to the discipline and humanity displayed at the wreck, in which he graciously included the officers of both services. It is recorded, on evidence that cannot be doubted, that in alluding to the saving of the women and children he spoke "with an emphasis and feeling that affected the whole company." It is not astonishing that on his 83rd birthday the Duke should exhibit somewhat the signs of "mouldering greatness," but that his case was as bad as represented it is impossible to believe. That the subject of the *Birkenhead* had the Duke's earnest sympathy cannot for a moment be questioned, and that the Secretary-at-War shared that feeling thoroughly and sincerely is equally beyond doubt. But they did not constitute the Ministry or the Military authorities, to whose charge the neglect complained of may with more reason and justice be laid.

At this point may fortunately be introduced a highly interesting letter of Sir William Napier's which has not

A HERO'S WORK FOR HEROES

hitherto been printed anywhere. It was written by General Napier to Colonel Wright, who preserved it among the valuable papers to which it was the authors' privilege to have access for the purposes of this work. The letter throws light upon three things. It proves that it was Sir William Napier who suggested the *Birkenhead* Monument, and in fact laid the foundation of that national memorial. It shows that, through his heroic brother (who died in 1852), Sir William obtained a promise from the Duke of Wellington of "some public notice" for Lieutenant Girardot. It reveals also the discouragements which beset the praiseworthy efforts of General Napier *after the death of the Duke,* and breathes his disgust. But here is the letter, which will speak for itself.

SCINDE HOUSE, CLAPHAM PARK,
November 5th, 1855.

DEAR SIR,—
Your note is very agreeable to me, and would have been more so if you could have followed it up by a visit, though I am so feeble as to be scarcely able to see company. What I wrote in *The Times* about the *Birkenhead* was the sincere feelings of my heart. I thought, and still think, it was perhaps the finest instance of heroism ever exhibited in the world.

I endeavoured to obtain a Monument of it, with the names of all who perished as well as those who survived engraved, to be placed in some conspicuous place, but I failed. The action was too great for the feeling of the age—the vulgar, newspaper-ridden age! For Girardot I sought also to obtain some advantage, and at my suggestion my late brother, Sir Charles Napier, spoke to Dr. Babbage on the subject, who thus stimulated actually obtained a promise of some public notice from the Duke of Wellington; but nothing came of it: why I know not.

Believe me to be, with the greatest esteem,
Your faithful servant,
W. NAPIER.

MAJOR WRIGHT, 91st Regiment.

A facsimile of this historic letter appears on another page. It is not difficult to guess why the promise spoken of was not kept. The Duke was looking into the matter, but he moved slowly, his time was short, and he died before his word could be redeemed. We are here led to the consideration of this question of recognition of the *Birkenhead* heroes. Mr. Bruce, in his *Life of Sir William Napier,* says that

Captain Wright and Lieutenant Girardot "received promotion, and all the survivors pecuniary compensation for their losses," and this is echoed by Mr. David Seton in what has been quoted. We only know that Captain Wright of the Military officers was directly rewarded. He received a Distinguished Service pension, was promoted, and eventually was made a C.B. His splendid conduct at the wreck was mentioned specially in general and battalion orders. But who, reading the record of his services, will not say that all the rewards he ever received were more than earned? We have Lieut.-Colonel Girardot's word for it that none of the subalterns who survived the wreck received promotion, and speaking for himself he ridicules the idea of any compensation ever having been given them.* To the members of the ship's company some pecuniary recompense was awarded by the Admiralty for their losses. Staff-Surgeon Bowen became a surgeon-general, and on the Naval side as well as the Military it will be found that here and there an officer rose in rank subsequently; but that came in the ordinary course of their career. How much their connection with the *Birkenhead* ever counted in their favour, if it influenced their lives at all, cannot now be known. All that can be said, safely and regretfully, is that the heroism so warmly eulogised by Sir William Napier and applauded by their countrymen was never recognised or rewarded as it ought to have been.

The movement alluded to in Parliament by Major Beresford, that for the relief of the relatives of those lost in the *Birkenhead*, was widespread and well supported, and afforded the country an opportunity which it readily seized of backing up its praises in a substantial manner. A meeting of officers of the Navy and Army and heads of establishments at Portsmouth was held at the Royal Naval College in that dockyard on April 10th, the Commander-in-Chief, Admiral Sir T. Briggs, in the chair, for the purpose of organising measures to collect subscriptions. A committee composed of "highly influential and many distinguished officers of both services" was formed, bankers appointed, and a handsome subscription list at once opened. Queen

* See notice of Colonel Girardot, further on.

A HERO'S WORK FOR HEROES 91

Victoria and Prince Albert authorised their names to be put at the head of the list. The members of the Cabinet subscribed, and among others Mr. Stafford, M.P., the Secretary to the Admiralty, contributed £10. The officers at Portsmouth, and the officers and men of all the ships in commission at Plymouth, Sheerness and Woolwich, gave one day's pay to this United Service Fund. Public feeling at the time concerning the *Birkenhead* was well voiced by Dr. Rolph* at a large meeting of Portsmouth inhabitants, which resolved to raise a relief fund also.

> The afflicting catastrophe which has brought us together [said this gentleman, and his words were frequently cheered] in its sad and stern reality appeals far more forcibly to our feelings and sympathies than any language that could be uttered or any argument that could be employed. The noble steamship which quitted this harbour but a few months since, gigantic in its dimensions, symmetrical in its proportions, durable in its materials, perfect in its machinery, apparently impregnable, and built as though it was destined to defy the wind and waves; steaming from our shores amidst the acclamations of hundreds, gazing with admiration and with joy that she was appointed to convey succour to our suffering fellow-subjects in another portion of our wide dominions; that this noble vessel should have proved the coffin for more than 450 human beings is a fact too impressive, too startling, too solemn, and too terrible for description.

But the picture has two sides. The speaker turns to the conduct of these troops in a calamity so appalling, and highly and proudly extols it.

> In the simple and affecting narrative of Captain Wright there is, however, a testimony to the worth and virtue of our matchless troops too valuable and too important to remain unnoticed. It is true that on every page of British history there stands recorded some act most honourable to the British Army: but whether as at the masterly retreat on Torres Vedras; at the brilliant victory of Corunna, after enduring unheard-of hardships and in a state of the greatest physical prostration; at their unsurpassed and chivalrous valour on the heights of Minden, their steady fortitude on the scorching sands of Egypt, or the unbroken front which they maintained on the field of Waterloo, exciting alike the admiration, astonishment, and terror of their foe—never did their incomparable bravery, unflinching fortitude, or unequalled discipline shine with more lustre than in the fearless, heroic, noble, unmurmuring manner they met their sad and melancholy fate on board the *Birkenhead*.

* Whose speech is preserved among Colonel Wright's papers.

Poor fellows! It is quite certain that the heroism and submission, the calm and unruffled mien, with which they met their death, proved how well they were prepared to die. Peace to their manes! Be ours the pleasing duty and the grateful task to assuage their widows' and their orphans' grief by every effort in our power.

Such was the spirit in which the appeal was made and responded to. Dr. Rolph continued his eloquent speech with an argument in favour of the employment of wooden instead of iron ships for the transport of troops, contending that wooden vessels had in the past been singularly fortunate in their freedom from serious loss of life. He gave the interesting instance of a brigantine which, in 1839, while conveying the headquarters of the 14th Regiment with women and children on board on her passage from Antigua to St. Lucia, was wrecked on the reef of rocks five miles from the island of Guadaloupe before daylight on Christmas Day. Boats were sent from the shore, and owing to the steady discipline and good behaviour of the troops not a soul perished. Had the vessel been iron instead of wood, it was maintained, not one could have been saved. Again, when Lord Aylmer quitted his government in British North America, he left Quebec in the *Pique*. Passing through the Straits of Belleisle she was wrecked on the coast of Labrador, was got off the rocks with the utmost difficulty, crossed the Atlantic Ocean without a rudder, and dropped anchor in the English Channel without loss of life. Then the ship *Malabar* in 1846 ran on a reef of rocks off Prince Edward's Island and remained there all day, knocking with great violence and receiving much damage before she was released. She proceeded afterwards to Halifax, Bermuda, and England without loss of life.

In a later chapter it will be noted that this question of wooden *versus* iron troopships, raised by the sinking of the *Birkenhead*, was a subject of controversy, and that opinion was divided upon it. Dr. Rolph's speech attracted attention and brought the question prominently into notice. But to return to the *Birkenhead* dependents.

Up to May 1st nearly £1,000 had been subscribed to the borough and United Service funds at Portsmouth, and relief

The Clipper Ship "James Baines" with Troops for India
(Inspected before leaving Portsmouth by Queen Victoria and the Royal children, when Colonel Wrigh explained to them the *Birkenhead* disaster)

was afforded to numerous widows, orphans and relatives of persons, Military and Naval, who perished at the wreck; while to the widows and relatives of officers sums of money were awarded in proportion to their necessities. Subscriptions continued to flow in, and the funds were dispensed until the following spring. Nor was the timely aid afforded confined to charity at home. The Legislative Council at the Cape early voted £500 towards the relief of the sufferers, and about £1,000 was subscribed out there to the end of March. The committee of the United Service Fund nominated Miss F. S. Salmond, eldest child of the unfortunate Commander of the *Birkenhead*, as a candidate for admission to the Royal Naval Female School, and there was a presentation from Captain Stephenson for a girl to the Orphan School at Cheltenham.

Before his death in 1860 Sir William Napier would have the great satisfaction, as it must have been to him, of knowing that the desire of his heart, to which he gave expression in his letter to Colonel Wright, was at last accomplished as regarded the dead. For in the previous year (1859), seven years after the wreck, a Memorial to them was completed and erected by command of Queen Victoria in the colonnade of Chelsea Hospital. There is no doubt that the Queen concerned herself personally in this commemorative work. We have direct evidence in the Memoir of Colonel Wright that Her Majesty was deeply interested in the subject; for did not the senior surviving officer in the August of 1857 escort the Queen and Royal children, who were then in residence at Osborne, over certain troopships, when, as Colonel Wright tells us, Her Majesty "desired me to tell the children how a ship was lost and some of those on board saved." It was a beautiful incident, and nothing in the whole range of the subject is more pathetic than the touching record of it. The story does honour to the womanly feeling and sympathies of Queen Victoria, and reveals not only her real and lively interest in the *Birkenhead*, but the fact that in the end it was owing to her gracious intervention that the measure advocated by Sir William Napier was carried into effect.

94   A DEATHLESS STORY

The Memorial placed in the piazza at Chelsea Hospital bears the inscription which appears below.

>   THIS MONUMENT
>   is erected by command of
>   HER MAJESTY QUEEN VICTORIA,
>   to record the heroic constancy and unbroken discipline shown by Lieutenant-Colonel Seton, 74th Highlanders, and the troops embarked under his command on board the *Birkenhead*, when that vessel was wrecked off the Cape of Good Hope on the 26th Feby. 1852, and to preserve the memory of the Officers, Non-Commissioned Officers and Men who perished on that occasion.
>
>   Their names were as follows.
>   LIEUT.-COL. A. SETON, 74th HIGHLANDERS, COMMANDING THE TROOPS.
>   Cornet Rolt, Sergt. Straw, and 3 Privates, 12th Lancers.
>   Ensign Boylan, Corpl. McManus, 34 Privates, 2nd Queen's Regt.
>   Ensign Metford and 47 Privates, 6th Royals.
>   55 Privates, 12th Regiment.
>   Sergt. Hicks, Corpls. Harrison and Cousins, and 26 Privates, 43rd Light Infantry.
>   3 Privates, 45th Regiment.
>   Corporal Curtis and 29 Privates, 60th Rifles.
>   Lieutenants Robinson and Booth and 54 Privates, 73rd Regiment.
>   Ensign Russell, Corpls. Mathison and William Laird, and 46 Privates, 74th Highlanders.
>   Sergt. Butler, Corpls. Webber and Smith, and 41 Privates, 91st Regt.
>   Staff-Surgeon Laing, Staff Assistant-Surgeon Robertson.
>
>   In all three hundred and fifty-seven officers and men. The names of the privates will be found inscribed on the brass plates adjoining.

Then follow in columns all the names of the private soldiers. They are recorded in this book in the list already given of those who died at the wreck. In the piazza of the Hospital is also a tablet erected by order of Queen Victoria in memory of Lieut.-Colonel Willoughby Moore, Veterinary-Surgeon Kelly, and several non-commissioned officers and soldiers of the Inniskilling Dragoons, who perished on board the *Europa* transport when that vessel was burnt at sea on May 31st, 1854, " affording a noble example of courage and discipline in the discharge of duty." The *Europa* was totally destroyed by fire about 200 miles from Plymouth while on her voyage to the East with the headquarters of the 6th

A HERO'S WORK FOR HEROES

Dragoons and a detachment of the regiment, when the commanding officer of the troops and others refused to quit the post of duty, and nobly perished.

This chapter would be incomplete did it not include some notice of the Royal visit paid during August, 1857, to the troopships *Lady Jocelyn* and *James Baines* at Portsmouth. In company with her children[*] and Colonel Wright, Queen Victoria inspected the soldiers on board the *Lady Jocelyn*; but in the case of the *James Baines* Her Majesty, under the guidance of Colonel Wright, made a thorough survey of the vessel itself, and it was then no doubt that the senior surviving officer repeated the story of the *Birkenhead*, and for the information of the Royal visitors explained "how a ship was lost and some of those on board saved." The Black Ball Line clipper-ship *James Baines*, and her sister ships *Lightning* and *Champion of the Seas*, were owned by Messrs. Baines of Liverpool. The *James Baines* was commanded by Captain Macdonnell. She was a very fine vessel of 2,093 tons register and 3,000 tons burden, her length being 243 feet and her beam 44 feet. Queen Victoria during her inspection highly eulogised the clipper and its appointments, and is said to have declared that she was not aware that so splendid a ship existed within her dominions. The *James Baines* had been chartered as a transport for the Indian Mutiny, and at the time of the Royal visit had on board the 97th Regiment. She sailed on August 8th, and on August 17th, when met by the mail steamship *Oneida* on her voyage to Calcutta, she presented a magnificent appearance, having, in addition to her ordinary canvas, studding-sails, skysails, and moonsail set and drawing—in all thirty-four sails, a perfect billowing cloud of white. The *Champion of the Seas* was not far astern, and both vessels were making great way.

The picture of the *James Baines* given on another page is from a sketch made by a passenger on the *Oneida* and reproduced in *The Illustrated London News*. The clipper was indeed a stately and beautiful spectacle. The troops on board, of the 97th, later the Queen's Own Royal West Kent

[*] The Prince of Wales, afterwards King Edward VII., was then fifteen years of age, and in later years doubtless well remembered the visit.

Regiment, formed part of the reinforcements ordered out to India. The regiment was commanded by Lieut.-Colonel Ingram, and consisted of 33 officers (including paymaster and doctor), eight staff-sergeants, 45 sergeants, 23 drummers, and 739 rank and file. The voyage terminated on November 22nd, and after remaining at Calcutta until January 4th following the troops left for Lucknow, forming part of the Jounpore Field Force under the command of Brigadier-General Franks, C.B. The regiment afterwards took part in the actions of Nusrutpore and Sultanpore, and joined the main army before Lucknow under Sir Colin Campbell, sharing in the assault and capture of that place and winning "Lucknow" for the regimental colours.

FIELD-MARSHAL THE DUKE OF WELLINGTON, K.G., COMMANDER-IN-CHIEF
1827-28, 1842-52

(Photo by Lombardi of painting from a daguerreotype by Claudet. Specially presented by his Grace Arthur Wellesley, 4th Duke of Wellington, in honour of the *Birkenhead*)

CHAPTER VII

THE IRON DUKE AND THE BIRKENHEAD

Foremost captain of his time.—TENNYSON.

THE great Duke of Wellington, the Commander-in-Chief, completed his 83rd year on May 1st, 1852. We know that in the eventide of his life, the falling shadows of which were fast gathering around him, the thoughts of the veteran warrior and statesman, mighty in battle and a force in the Senate which he ornamented almost to the last, dwelt proudly upon the heroes of the *Birkenhead*. It is true he did little to reward them; but that must not be taken as the measure of his estimate of them. The evidence tends to show that he would have done them justice had he lived. Unfortunately he died on September 14th of the same year. In the House of Lords less than three months before, on June 22nd, on the motion of the Duke—

returns were ordered of several regimental reports, *showing the state of discipline among the Military* * on board the steam troopship *Birkenhead* at the time that vessel was lost.

Copy of an order with respect to the transmission of reinforcements to the Cape was also asked for. This was the Duke of Wellington's final public act within the walls of the House of Lords, if we except his formal attendance at the ceremony of the prorogation of Parliament on July 2nd. It is conceivable that his Grace wished to have the evidence officially and properly before him, and that, having it, he would have acted upon it. This seems the more likely when we read of the Duke that a characteristic of his mind was—

patient examination into details, and a careful study of the whole in order to arrive at a right conclusion. He made allowance for contin-

* Italics ours.

gencies, passions, interests, estimated things at their real value, and was rarely wrong. His great principle of action seems to have been a sense of duty, rather than the stimulus of glory or ambition.

In spite of the stern severity in repressing pillage and all excess which earned for him the name of the Iron Duke, no one could have taken more care of his soldiers, and he was habitually considerate and kind-hearted.

Before his final action in the House of Lords, the Duke had on a notable occasion marked publicly his appreciation of the men of the *Birkenhead*, and had given the weight of his personal testimony to the extraordinary steadiness and discipline displayed at the wreck, the circumstances of which were then present in all men's minds. The tribute was paid, with warmth and sincerity, at the annual banquet of the Royal Academy at the rooms in Trafalgar Square on May 1st, 1852, the Duke's last birthday. The gathering was a distinguished one, including as it did many British and foreign Ministers. The Secretary-at-War was there, and so was the First Lord of the Admiralty. The President of the Academy proposed the toast of "The Army and Navy," coupled with the name of the illustrious guest whose birthday he reminded the company it was. The Duke of Wellington, in his reply to the toast, used these words:

Gentlemen, the Services will be rejoiced upon learning that it is considered they continue to deserve the approbation of their country. Both Services, but particularly the Army, have been involved in great difficulties; but I do not doubt, gentlemen, that it will turn out that the approbation of this company is founded upon a just estimate of the manner in which they have performed their duty. It has been highly satisfactory to me, as it must have been to all of you, to have observed that in the great difficulties and misfortunes which all services are liable to, the officers and soldiers of the Army have conducted themselves as they ought to do. They have shown under the most difficult circumstances the utmost subordination, order, and discipline, and the officers of the Navy were in these trials the first to provide for the relief of the helpless. The women and the children [continued his Grace, "with an emphasis and feeling that affected the whole company," the *Times* report said] were all saved—and account was given and rendered of every child and woman. This, gentlemen, is a proud fact for the Services of this country—it must have been satisfactory to you all, and it shows that under any circumstances you can rely upon their subordination and discipline.

The Duke, whose heartfelt utterances were cheered to the echo, withdrew shortly after concluding this memorable speech.

Then there is a significant thing to remember. Almost the last official act of the veteran Commander-in-Chief was his signing the document which conferred a Distinguished Service pension on the senior surviving *Birkenhead* officer, afterwards Colonel Wright. That was done less than three weeks before he died; and from the letter written by Sir William Napier to the same officer, which is printed in another chapter, we now know that the Duke of Wellington gave a promise of "some public notice" for Lieutenant Girardot also. Who can doubt that he meant to redeem that promise? The Duke was a man of his word, and had he lived he would have kept it.

Then there was a powerful personal reason which would impel him to recognise such conduct as made the *Birkenhead* famous. Discipline was the first cardinal law in the Duke of Wellington's Military code. It was his strongest bulwark—the rock upon which his glorious victories were built. At Waterloo our men chafed impatiently in the squares, upon which the French hurled themselves impetuously in their unavailing attempts to break through them. Wellington knew that his strength lay in those squares—that they meant victory, if it was to be had. So he maintained the squares, and the French were broken. But what was it that enabled him to do so? Discipline. Would, then, one who was himself so rigid a disciplinarian—the Iron Duke, who so thoroughly appreciated the value of order and discipline—be likely to neglect such a noble example of what discipline could accomplish as that furnished by the *Birkenhead*? He would not.

It has been charged against the Duke that he was of a cold and haughty temperament, and indifferent to the merits of his younger contemporaries. This was not so. It is well known that he never missed an opportunity of doing honour to an old comrade-in-arms. His noble defence of Sir Harry Smith, when that General was assailed for his conduct of the Kaffir War, is evidence that the Duke was not the cold and impassible man he is sometimes represented to have been, and that, when occasion required, he could spring to the aid and the honour of the brave. There is a personal link associating the Duke of Wellington with the memory of the *Birkenhead*. He began his illustrious career in a *Birkenhead* regiment. The Duke was appointed Ensign, March 7th, 1787, to the 73rd Regiment, then the Royal Highlanders; and in the Army List for 1788 his name stands among the ensigns of that corps as the "Hon. Arthur Wesley."* He afterwards transferred into the 33rd Regiment, in which he long served.

The interesting portrait here given of the Duke is a photo by Lombardi of a painting from a daguerreotype taken by M. Claudet on May 1st, 1848, his Grace's 79th birthday. It represents the Duke sitting in ordinary dress, with a white waistcoat; three-quarter face, stooping a little, and with a bland expression. There is no question about the likeness. So far as can be ascertained, this was the only photograph ever taken of the Duke of Wellington. There are, of course, numerous paintings and portraits of the Duke, many of them great historical works of art. The interest of the portrait here reproduced is enhanced by the autograph attached of the illustrious soldier-statesman, consisting of a portion of a letter written by the Duke at the time and bearing his signature.

* In the Duke's early letters the family name is spelt Wesley; the change to Wellesley was made about 1790.

Extreme Peril of the "Castor's" Launch, sent to survey the "Birkenhead" Rock

CHAPTER VIII

MORE PERILOUS ADVENTURES

> Ye gentlemen of England
> That live at home at ease,
> Ah! little do you think upon
> The dangers of the seas.—MARTYN PARKER.

HISTORY at Danger Point, that spot of awful memory, came perilously near repeating itself just one short month after the troopship disaster. The first attempt to lay down with accuracy the position of the rock on which the *Birkenhead* was wrecked was attended with an adventure of a dangerous character, and one which, but for a providential escape, would have added other memories of affliction to those already associated with it. Towards the end of March, 1852, directions were given to Lieutenant O'Reilly and ten men of H.M.S. *Gladiator* to hold themselves in readiness for this duty. Mr. Mann, assistant astronomer at the Cape Observatory, son of the late General Mann, Royal Engineers, was directed to accompany the party in order to execute the desired work, as well as to make a map or chart of Danger Point.

The *Gladiator's* boat not being considered "A1," the launch of the *Castor* was selected. At midnight on March 25th, there being scarcely any wind, orders came to embark, and the party left. Little progress was made; but after knocking about for two days, they arrived off Danger Point at midnight. Failing to find any place to anchor, the boat lay to, her crew hoping to discover one on the morrow. Before morning, however, a strong south-east wind sprang up, and it increased to such a violent degree that there was nothing left but to "run for it." So they stood away to the westward, running all day, until the launch was quite 140 miles from shore.

When day dawned they were out of sight of land, a long way west of Cape Point. The gale still continued, and the boat was with difficulty kept afloat. Once a heavy sea struck her and the waves closed over the heads of the whole party. But by good fortune and the noble efforts of Lieutenant O'Reilly and his companions, who behaved in a spirit of calmness and order similar to that of their brethren of the *Birkenhead*, the boat was saved; and after various escapes, during eighteen hours' exposure to the fury of the storm, they made Green Point on the morning of the 29th, being unable to enter Table Bay on account of the continuing gales. There were defects in the equipment of the boat, a not uncommon occurrence at that period; but the dangers and difficulties encountered were, with the spirit characteristic of our seamen, met in a worthy and undaunted manner and successfully overcome. The party, on reaching land, were congratulated on their happy escape, and complimented on the seamanship as well as the courage, they had displayed. The accompanying sketch of the small launch, beset by angry seas which threatened every moment to engulf her, was afterwards made by one of their number and sent home.

The same month yet another providential escape was experienced. Considerable interest attached to the return to England at the end of April, 1852, of H.M. corvette *Amazon*, 26 guns, Captain Barker, with fifty-eight survivors of the *Birkenhead* on board. The *Amazon* arrived at Spithead from the China station and the Cape of Good Hope. She was ninety-five days out from Trincomalee, and had run over a distance of 54,076 miles during her commission. She sailed for Trincomalee January 24th, arrived at the Cape on the evening of March 2nd, and sailed on the afternoon of the 7th. The *Castor* and *Rhadamanthus* were at anchor in Simon's Bay, and the *Styx* in Table Bay. While in Simon's Bay the *Amazon* received on board fifty-eight officers, seamen, marines and boys, survivors of the *Birkenhead*, whom she brought to England. The corvette arrived at St. Helena on the morning of April 16th, and sailed on the afternoon of the same day. She reached Ascension on Sunday the 21st, and was detained there until

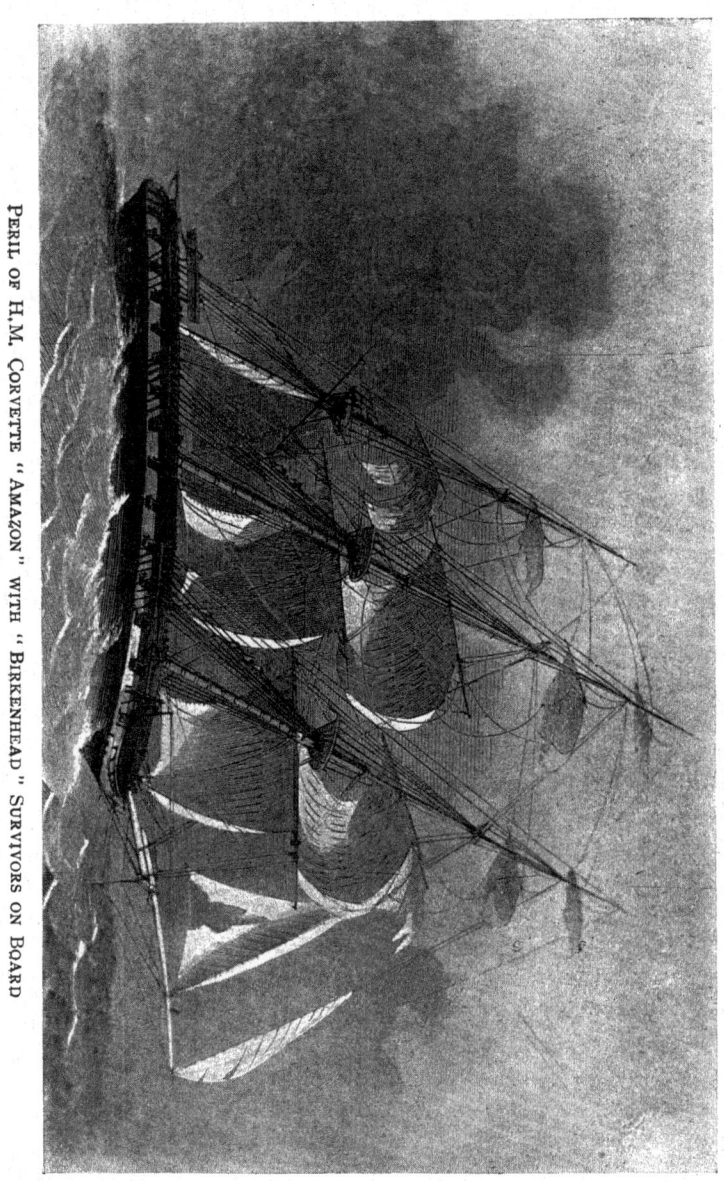

Peril of H.M. Corvette "Amazon" with "Birkenhead" Survivors on Board

Monday afternoon to bring home eight invalids, five of whom were engaged and wounded in the expedition against Lagos. About eight o'clock on the evening of March 30th, when in latitude 2 deg. N., longitude 21 deg. 40 min. W., the *Amazon*, while nearly becalmed, was struck by a sudden squall which made her heel over nearly 23 degrees. She had at the time thirteen sails set, of which ten were split by the fierceness of the blast—namely, fore royal, fore topgallant-sail, fore topmast studding-sail, jib and flying jib, main royal, main topgallant and main-sails, mizen top-sail and topgallant-sail.

The sketch on another page, showing the vessel caught by the squall, was made by an officer who was on board. Like that of the *Castor's* launch, it is a beautifully descriptive picture. Both are reproduced from the originals as published at the time in *The Illustrated London News*.

CHAPTER IX

NAVAL SURVIVORS COURT-MARTIALLED

Most heartily I do beseech the court
To give the judgment.—SHAKESPEARE.

AGAIN the scene is changed. The Naval survivors of the *Birkenhead* were not at the end of their troubles yet. After escaping from the deadly peril of one shipwreck, and being almost involved in another as sudden and fraught with possibilities equally tragic and fatal, the chief among them were selected to undergo the disquieting experience of trial by Court-Martial. That was when at last they reached home. The step was in accordance with an invariable rule of the Naval service. It was *primâ facie* evident that there was no person on whom any responsibility for the loss of the ship could rest, all the senior Naval officers on board having unhappily perished at the post of duty; so that the Court assembled to investigate the conduct of these survivors at the wreck was really a matter of form. Still, there were one or two things which required clearing up in the interests of the survivors themselves, some of whom must have welcomed this opportunity of rebutting certain statements which had been circulated to their injury. The evidence also threw fresh light upon the circumstances of the disaster. The Court was held on board the flagship *Victory* at Portsmouth, and the proceedings aroused great interest. The first to be subjected to the ordeal were Mr. R. B. Richards, master's assistant, the only executive officer saved, and four of the crew—namely, John Bowen, A.B., Thomas Dunn, A.B., Abel Stone, ordinary seaman, and John Ashbolt, stoker. The Court was composed of Rear-Admiral H. Prescott, C.B., President; Captain Chads, C.B., of the *Excellent*; Captain G. B. Martin, C.B., of the *Victory*; Captain Scott, of the

Neptune; Captain Henderson, C.B., of the *Blenheim*; Captain S. T. Innes, of the *Sampson*; Captain Robinson, of the *Arrogant*; Captain Loch, C.B., of the *Winchester*; Captain Warden, of the *Retribution*; Captain Symonds, of the *Arethusa*; Captain Harris, of the *Prince Regent*; Captain Matson, of the *Highflyer*; and Sir G. L. Greetham, Deputy-Judge-Advocate of the Fleet.

The first sitting of the Court was on May 5th, 1852, when the witnesses included Thomas Coffin, who had the first middle watch on the night of the wreck; Thomas Daley, who had the first watch and was look-out man on the forecastle; Colour-Sergeant Drake, Royal Marines, who was on the poop when the ship struck; John T. Archbold, the gunner, who was in bed when the accident happened; and Mr. William Culhane, assistant-surgeon, who was in his cabin at the time. All these witnesses underwent lengthened examination, and deposed to a number of facts connected with the disaster; but their evidence did not disturb materially the main features of the story as already known. One of them stated that, had the boats remained near the wreck and not pursued the schooner, more lives might have been saved; but all seemed to agree that, both on board the ill-fated ship and after she had sunk, every effort was made to save life that under the circumstances was practicable. The occupants of the boats declared that they could not, without danger, take in more than they had; that they heard no cries, and saw no cases of distress which they did not seek to relieve; that the heaviness of the surf, in their judgment, rendered landing impossible; and, in short, that they acted for the best in the trying emergency. As to the course which the ship was steering, it was proved that she was some three miles from the shore, which, however, was not visible in the darkness; that soundings were taken; that the rate of speed at the time was $7\frac{1}{2}$ knots; that a light had been discerned shortly before the catastrophe took place; and that the sound of the surf was not distinguishable. It was also stated that the boats were in good order for launching had time permitted; that the Captain was perfectly collected, and that the orders which he issued were obeyed; that the engines were backed for two minutes after the ship struck, and that she yielded to them; that in ten minutes the fires were completely extinguished, and that the vessel went down in less than half-an-hour. Questions were put to the witnesses not only by the Court, but by the prisoners, and the Court adjourned.

The inquiry was resumed on May 6th, when additional evidence was given by Edward Wilson, the boatswain's mate, who was washed off the paddle-box and, with fourteen others, got ashore on the sponson; by George Till (coxswain of the cutter containing the women and children, commanded by Mr. Richards), who said the other cutter was a ten-oared boat (his was only an eight-oared boat), and he had as many in his boat as she would hold—eighteen women and children, and fourteen men; by John Lewis, coxswain of the first cutter, who stated that his boat was also full, having thirty-eight souls in her; and by Mr. C. K. Renwick, the second engineer, who described the effects of the ship running upon the rocks. Mr. Renwick explained exactly what happened in the engine-room.

> I was on board the *Birkenhead* on the day she struck [he said], and was at the time sleeping in my cot. The engines were stopped. Mr. Whyham, the chief engineer, and his assistants, Mr. Kitchingham and Mr. Barber, were in the engine-room. Orders were given to reverse the engines, which was done, and was continued till the water rose and put out the fires. The fires were extinguished in consequence of the rapidity with which the water rose in the engine-room. We took the injection from the bilge, but it had no effect in lessening the water. Mr. Whyham reported to the Captain that the fires were out, and the Captain sent for me and asked if nothing more could be done. I answered that the water was making 3 or 4 feet a minute. I then proceeded on to the poop and witnessed the efforts made to get the port paddle-box boat out. The safety-valves, about a minute after I entered the engine-room, were eased to take the shock off.

He was questioned by the President of the Court.

> I am of opinion [he answered] that the "back turn" hastened the crisis of the wreck by rending the bilge of the vessel and admitting an immense flow of water. After the "back turn" I heard the rending of the iron plates. If the "back turn" of the ship had not been given I believe the framework of the vessel would have remained intact for some time—at least sufficient to have enabled the paddle-box boats to

FIELD-MARSHAL H.R.H. THE DUKE OF CAMBRIDGE, K.G.,
COMMANDER-IN-CHIEF 1856-95

(Photo by W. S. Stuart, Richmond. Specially presented in honour of the *Birkenhead*)

NAVAL SURVIVORS COURT-MARTIALLED 107

have been got clear. The flow of water was not very great in the engine-room before the "back turn" was given, but it was in the fore part of the vessel. She struck very severely a second time after the "back turn." I do not believe the "back turn" made a second hole, but extended the previous rent. The ship was divided below by bulkheads into compartments: the fore-and-aft ones were sub-divided, and were watertight. I conceived that the whole of the fore divisions were made one by the bilge being "buckled" up the whole extent of the forward part.

Captain Chads was not quite satisfied, and questioned the witness further.

I consider [answered Mr. Renwick] that the hole was made in the fore part of the bilge of the vessel. The main and other compartments, had they remained intact, ought to have resisted the flow of water. The amidship main division was filled in five or six minutes after the ship striking, which was caused by the extension of the fracture forward. I believe the action of the swell, with the motion given by the engines, to have shifted the vessel in such a way as to give her a fulcrum; she thus rested on the rock and broke her back. I do not know of any misconduct on the part of the prisoners.

Mr. Richards also asked a question. It was an important one, and the reply of the assistant-engineer vindicated his action when in charge of the boats.

I do not consider you could have landed without staving the boats [declared the witness]. I did not see any appearance of a landing-place. I consider that the second cutter had as many people in her as she could carry with safety.

Mr. William Robert Madge, master of the *Victory*, deposed that the *Birkenhead* was swung under his direction on February 15th, 1851, when she got a new standard compass. She was also swung before that on October 22nd, 1850. In reply to the President, the witness said the Commander of the vessel was supplied with the result, and he added, "She was also swung here by Mr. Thompson, the late Master. I think she had been swung at Greenhithe by Captain Johnson." Mr. Madge was requested to look at the chart, and to state whether he would steer such a course as that marked down.

It depends on the deviation [he replied]. If it had been easterly it would not have cleared the point, but if westerly it would have cleared the inner point by two miles. It would depend very greatly on circumstances; had there been any swell or a current, I might not have taken that course; if it had been smooth, I might have taken that course.

This concluded the trial. The Court was cleared for deliberation, and after remaining closed for two hours was re-opened, when the Judge-Advocate read the finding. The Court had to observe in the first place that—

from the unfortunate circumstance of the Master commanding, and the principal officers of the ship, having perished, they feel that it is in the highest degree difficult and that it might be unjust to pass censure upon the deceased, whose motives for keeping so near the shore cannot be explained; but they must record their opinion that this fatal loss was owing to the course having been calculated to keep the land in too close proximity. If such be the case, they still are not precluded from speaking with praise of the departed for the coolness which they displayed in the moment of extreme peril, and for the laudable anxiety shown for the safety of the women and children to the exclusion of all selfish considerations.

With respect to the prisoners "tried under the authority of this order," meaning the Admiralty warrant, the finding went on—

the Court, having maturely and deliberately weighed and considered the whole of the evidence, are of opinion that no blame is imputable to them, and doth judge the said Mr. Rowland Bevan Richards, and John Bowen, Thomas Dunn, John Ashbolt, and Abel Stone to be fully acquitted, and they are hereby fully acquitted accordingly.

This was a triumph for the master's assistant more especially, and an answer to the critics who blamed his handling of the boats.

The Court re-assembled on May 7th, to try Mr. John T. Archbold, the gunner, and the other survivors not tried in the first party. This trial had reference, it was understood, more particularly to the conduct of Mr. Culhane, the assistant-surgeon, " whose character," *The Times* remarked,

seems to have been hastily aspersed by people at the Cape without making themselves fully acquainted with all the facts and bearings of the case as applied to him.

Colour-Sergeant Drake deposed that he saw Mr. Culhane in his cabin one minute before the ship went down. Mr. Richards spoke to hearing Mr. Culhane hail the boats; he was in the water and about fifty yards distant, and he swam to the gig. Henry Bewhill deposed that he heard Mr. Culhane hail the boats after he was in the water, and he took him into the gig, and two more persons besides. After chasing the schooner, said witness, they thought the other boats were following them, and not they following the boats. On Mr. Culhane wishing to ask the witness if the officers with "swimming belts" on in the water were not Military officers, the President said he could not see the object of putting that question, as there was nothing before the Court imputing more blame to Mr. Culhane than to the other prisoners. No defence was offered by any of the prisoners, and after the Court had been closed for deliberation and re-opened the Judge-Advocate delivered the finding, which was:

> That no blame is imputable to Mr. John T. Archbold, or the other surviving officers and crew of the said ship, tried under the authority of the above-mentioned order, for the loss of the said ship or for their conduct subsequently thereto, but on the contrary [ran the judgment], the Court see reason to admire and applaud the steadiness shown by all in the most trying circumstances, and the conduct of those who were first in the boats, and who, to the best of their judgment, made every exertion for the rescue of the portion of the crew and passengers who remained upon the wreck. In this expression of praise they desire to include those who have been acquitted on the previous and present Court-Martial, and the Court doth fully acquit the said Mr. Archbold and the other surviving officers and crew of the said ship *Birkenhead*, tried under the authority of the above-mentioned order, and they are hereby fully acquitted accordingly.

Could any decision of any court have been more completely satisfactory? Well might survivors who stood their trial ask for a judgment which could by any good fortune clear them as effectually as this one did. The proceedings of the Courts-Martial were printed by order of the House of Commons dated June 3rd, 1852 (Sessional Paper No. 426). The Paper was by no means a model of care and accuracy. Complaint was made of its slovenly appearance, its misspelling and distorting of names and phrases, and the general tendency of the report as issued to perplex and confuse the unfortunate reader of it. In the succinct account and review of the evidence here presented, with the inclusion of all the salient points arising, no such difficulty will be encountered.

CHAPTER X

FROM THE CRADLE TO THE GRAVE

Our royal, good and gallant ship.—SHAKESPEARE.

As fine a ship as any afloat in her day, the *Birkenhead* had a chequered career, as well, alas! as a short one. The life of the noble vessel was barely six years. She was built by Messrs. Laird of Birkenhead, under the immediate inspection of Mr. G. D. Banes of Chatham Dockyard, and was launched towards the end of December, 1845, when the ceremony of naming her was performed by the Marchioness of Westminster.* The *Birkenhead* was designed to be one of the largest iron steamers belonging to the Government, her breadth within the paddle-wheels with which she was propelled being $37\frac{1}{2}$ feet; breadth outside the paddle-wheels, $60\frac{1}{2}$ feet; depth of hold, 23 feet; tonnage (carpenter's measurement), 1,400 tons. Her engines were fitted by Messrs. George Forrester & Co. The model, approved by the Admiralty, was by Mr. Laird himself. The vessel was considered to be all that could be desired by the most critical judges in Naval architecture, the character given of the ship being that she was very sharp at both extremities, yet with that fulness and rotundity of bottom and bearings which would enable her to do her work well, "blow high or blow low." She had a round but handsome stern, with few but chaste decorations, and her bow terminated in a large figure of Vulcan, holding a hammer in one hand, and in the other some of "the bolts of Jove" which he had just forged. Vulcan, the reader will scarcely need to be reminded, was the mythological god who presided over fire, and was the patron of those who worked in iron. The Cyclopes were his attendants, and with them he forged the

* Lady Elizabeth Leveson-Gower, second daughter of the first Duke of Sutherland, who married the second Marquess of Westminster in 1819. Her husband died in 1869, but the Marchioness lived to a much later date.

thunderbolts of Jupiter, or Jove. The striking figure-head thus evolved for the new iron warship was designed and executed by Mr. Robertson, of Liverpool. The vessel was clencher-built below water, and carvel-built below her top sides. It was intended that the armament of the *Birkenhead* should be two 96-pound pivot guns, one forward and the other aft, and four 68-pounder broadside guns. The round stern of the ship was recognised as being "peculiarly adapted for the working of the huge Long Tom abaft"; and when, it was declared,

to the artillery stated we add the men and musketry she will carry, and the power of her steam to place her in any position, offensive or defensive, there can be no doubt but she will prove to be a most formidable opponent to any adversary.

The vessel had, however, another destiny. Although originally designed as a frigate, she never sailed as such, but was converted into a troopship. How the *Birkenhead* originated, and the change in her character as a ship came about, was told afterwards by Mr. Laird, of the great Mersey firm which built her. On the successful trial of the *Guadaloupe*, he was called upon by the Admiralty to supply plans and a tender for the construction of a frigate of the first class, and to guide him in designing her he applied for, and was furnished with, a statement of the weights she would have to carry.

The designs I submitted [wrote Mr. Laird], and which were finally approved, were of a vessel 210 feet long (being about 20 feet longer than any vessel of her class had been built), and 37˙6 beam, with a displacement of 1,918 tons on the load water-line of 15˙9. The only change made by the authorities at the Admiralty in these designs was in the position of the paddle shaft, which was ordered to be moved several feet more forward. The change was unfortunate, as it makes the vessel, unless due care is taken in stowing the hold, trim by the head. With this exception I am answerable for the model, specification, displacement, and general arrangement of the hull of the vessel. The *Birkenhead* was launched in 1845. Her hull was at that time complete, with the exception of some cabin fittings estimated at 15 tons. Her launching draught was 9 ft. 9 in., showing the weight of the hull to be 903 tons; leaving for the machinery, stores, &c., given me at 1,007 tons 14 cwts., 1,000 tons. If these weights had not been exceeded, the vessel would have gone to sea within one inch of her calculated draught, say 15 ft. 9 in. The *Birkenhead* was never tried as a frigate. Before she was commissioned, it was taken for granted that iron frigates would not answer, and her destiny was altered to a troopship, a poop added to her, and she is loaded with coals and stores generally to 2 ft. beyond her intended load water-line. With all these additions, I am informed by those who have sailed in her that she is a fast and remarkably easy vessel, and I have no hesitation in saying that if loaded only with the weights for which I was directed to construct her, she will not be excelled in speed and seagoing qualities by any steamer, private or public, of her size and power.

The *Birkenhead* left Liverpool in 1846, and on her passage round to Plymouth was reported by the officer in charge to have made twelve or thirteen knots an hour. She was at that time in "fair trim," not being fitted with the heavy poop and forecastle afterwards added to increase her accommodation as a troopship. For some time she was laid up, but eventually she was commissioned by Captain Ingram, and employed in various ways on the coasts of England, Ireland, and Scotland. She also towed the *Great Britain* from Dundrum Bay to Liverpool. Her next employment was carrying troops to the Channel Islands, Lisbon, and other places. This service she was considered to have performed very satisfactorily, making some remarkably quick runs. Early in 1851 she was commissioned by Commander Salmond and sailed to Halifax, the Cape of Good Hope, and other ports. The run she made from Halifax to Woolwich, with a large number of troops on board, was completed in $13\frac{1}{2}$ days.

By a judicious arrangement [it was afterwards stated], and only working one boiler and the engines expansively, Captain Salmond was enabled to steam long distances with a very small expenditure of fuel.

Her speed may be best tested by contrasting the passage she made to the Cape with troops (the 2nd Queen's Regiment), in 1851, with the voyages of other vessels in the Navy sent on similar service: *Birkenhead*, 45 days; *Vulcan*, 56 days; *Retribution*, 65 days; *Sidon*, 64 days; *Cyclops*, 59 days. Her return home in October of that year was made in 37 days, including stoppages. The last voyage of the *Birkenhead*, commenced in January, 1852, in very bad weather, occupied 47 days between Cork and the Cape.

The evidence as to the good sea-going qualities of the *Birkenhead* was supported by a correspondent whose state-

THE "BIRKENHEAD" TROOPSHIP

(The only known picture of the ship as she actually existed. Owned by the late Mr. Barber, Chief Engineer, R.N., a survivor, and the work of a brother officer)

FROM THE CRADLE TO THE GRAVE

ment on the subject was printed by *The Times* on April 20th, 1852.

On the whole, her performances [says this writer] prove her to have been the fastest, most carrying and comfortable vessel in Her Majesty's service as a troopship, and one that could be fully relied on both in hull and machinery. The Admiralty appear to have taken every precaution to keep her in efficient condition, as she was docked on her return from the Cape in October, 1851, and her hull examined and reported in perfect order; her machinery was improved with the view of economising fuel; and on her trial at Spithead after this refit she made, with 40 tons of coal, 60 tons of water, and four months' stores on board, fully 10 knots per hour.

The writer goes on to discuss the vexed question, alluded to in a previous chapter, of the relative safety of wooden and iron ships, and to support the value of watertight compartments.

All accounts from the survivors of the *Birkenhead's* melancholy loss [he observes] agree in one respect, that the cause of the accident was striking upon a sharp-pointed rock while going at a speed through the water of $8\frac{1}{2}$ knots; and when we consider that her weight, or displacement, at her load-draught as a troopship was upwards of 2,000 tons, the effect of such a blow may be readily imagined. The *Birkenhead* was divided into eight watertight compartments by athwartship bulkheads, and the engine-room was sub-divided by two longitudinal bulkheads into four additional compartments, forming the coal bunkers—making in all twelve watertight sections. The first blow (from the description of Captain Wright and other survivors) evidently ripped open the compartment between the engine-room and fore peak, and to such an extent that the water instantaneously filled it, as stated by the engineer, Mr. Renwick; and the next blow stove in the bilge of the vessel in the engine-room, thus filling the two largest compartments in the vessel in four or five minutes after she struck. Had she been a wooden vessel, or not built in compartments, she must have gone down like Her Majesty's frigate *Avenger*, in five minutes after she first struck. As it was, the buoyancy of the after compartment alone was the means of giving time to get the boats out and saving most of those who were rescued from death. Evidently the long swell, and at least 1,000 tons weight of machinery, coals, &c., amidships, acting against the buoyancy of the after division, caused her to break off as described, and sink in deep water. The case appears to be parallel with the *Orion's*, the sides and bilge having in both instances been ripped open in the forward and engine-room compartments.

And the writer adds that many other accidents have happened "proving the vast superiority of iron vessels in cases of grounding." The correspondent appears to be familiar with the construction of the *Birkenhead*, but his statement as to her watertight compartments does not agree with that made in the House of Commons by the Secretary to the Admiralty the day following the publication of his views, when, in answer to a question by Captain Scobell, Mr. Stafford replied "that the *Birkenhead* was in compartments, and that they were five in number." Opinions contrary to those of the writer above quoted were expressed in *The Times* by "A Captain in the Royal Navy," whose dislike of iron ships was similar to that which, in a former chapter, is shown to have been possessed by Dr. Rolph at Portsmouth. "Navigator" had asked if the *Birkenhead* was fitted with watertight compartments.

I can answer that she was [the Naval Captain replied], and that, having been originally intended to carry a heavy armament (as a ship of war), her talented and well-known builders, Messrs. Laird, spared no trouble and expense in constructing her as strongly as iron could make her. When she struck on the rock off Point Danger, it appears that as soon as the foremost compartment filled all that part of the vessel broke from the midship compartment; that on this filling it broke from the after one; and in 20 minutes, in a fine night and the sea so smooth as not to endanger her two overloaded cutters, did this large ship break into three pieces as if she had been built of card-paper, sending 438 human beings to a horrible and sudden death. It appears, from the loss of this ship and that of the *Pasha* in the China Sea, that the socalled watertight compartments are useless; that the destruction of these iron ships was so rapid as not to afford time for getting out their boats or resorting to many of the usual means of saving life; and that sheet iron is unable to bear the weight of the sea when one compartment is full of water, immediately tearing away, as in the case of the *Birkenhead*, and the ship sinking in three separate pieces.

The questions here involved have, of course, long since been decided now; but it is noteworthy that those who at the time condemned the material and the construction of the *Birkenhead*, seem to have overlooked the important fact that the direct cause of so much loss of life was not the character of the ship at all, but the inability to launch the majority of her boats. Could the boats, with which she was particularly well equipped, have been got out promptly, a very different tale would have been told.

FROM THE CRADLE TO THE GRAVE 115

The question of compasses also claimed attention. One of the officers of the Cape Screw Steam Navigation Company's vessel *Propontis*, which returned to England in April,* made a statement in reference to the compasses on board his ship which it was thought at the time might—

go far to account for the accident to the *Birkenhead*, as the extraordinary circumstance referred to happened upon the same day the latter unfortunate steamer was lost.

The report was that:

Some days before making the Cape land, on board the *Propontis*, in February, we found there was nearly six points difference between our standard and binnacle compasses, the standard having nearly three points west variation, and the binnacle nearly three points easterly variation. On approaching the land, the night of the 25th February, we found the binnacle compass so unsteady, and oscillating so much, at times taking nearly a round turn, that we could not steer by it, but coursed the ship by the standard, which remained steady.

The statement is rather remarkable and suggestive; but there is nothing on record to support its application to the *Birkenhead*, the disaster to which is too clearly attributable to other causes. The matter was looked into by the Rev. Dr. Scoresby, in his *Magnetic Investigations*, published about this time. Dr. Scoresby concluded that there may have been, and probably was, an error in the *Birkenhead's* compasses to the extent of about half a point. Such an error, even if it existed, was not sufficient to account for the wreck. The ship was altogether too near the land for safety. Questions put at the Naval Courts-Martial in May show that no direct evidence could be obtained as to the state of the compasses at the time of the wreck, and it must remain a matter of conjecture whether some slight error existed or not. It seems, at any rate, to be admitted that, according to all the experience of navigation, steps should have been taken at Simon's Bay to ascertain the local deviation. But at Simon's Bay, as his own last letter home too clearly proves, Captain Salmond had no time for such investigations.

Before the *Birkenhead* sailed on her fatal voyage to South

* On board this mail-packet was Mr. Freshfield, clerk to the ill-fated Captain Salmond.

Africa, a large quantity of wines was shipped on board of her. These wines were duly insured as far as the Cape of Good Hope; but as only a portion was landed at Simon's Bay, the remainder being lost in the vessel, the underwriters at Lloyd's are reported to have refused to pay the amount, stating as their reason for not doing so that the voyage was completed on the arrival of the vessel either at Table Bay or Simon's Bay, and that there was no clause in the policy by which the *Birkenhead* was allowed to proceed (with the wines) on a fresh trip, and an additional risk be incurred. What was perhaps more to the purpose was the consignment of firearms of a new pattern which the ship carried. It consisted of 350 double-barrelled rifle carbines for the use of the 12th Lancers. The balls which they fired were of the then new conical type "found so effectual at long ranges, doing great execution at 600 or 800, and in many instances at 1,000 yards." These identical carbines were fated not to do any execution, as they went down with the ship, and the weapon was soon superseded because it was found to be too heavy, and otherwise defective. Its disuse will not be wondered at when it is learnt that it "ignited at the sides of the barrels by a superfluously long communication with the charge, and with the left cock so far away as to suit only a very large hand." This curious firearm was replaced by one three pounds lighter and "ignited by putting the seat of the nipple on the centre instead of at the side of each barrel," a decidedly more sensible arrangement.

Speaking of some of the things which the vessel carried suggests the interesting question, Was anything ever recovered from the wreck? This inquiry can be answered in the affirmative. From the deep water and dangerous position in which the *Birkenhead* sank, Commodore Wyvill did not entertain hopes of saving anything of value, and there was a good deal on board well worth the effort, could it have been made. As he reported to the Admiralty, however, the Commodore sent Commander Bunce to the vicinity to recover what property he could and dispose of it as he thought best. The articles so secured were flotsam cast up from the wreck and washed ashore, and many a poor fellow drowned, or what remained of him, came to land in this manner. Early in May it was announced that—

forty-nine bodies have been washed up from the wreck of the unfortunate *Birkenhead*. One of them was recognised as that of Dr. Laing, staff-surgeon, by a gold watch and £18 in money which he had about his person. A number of packages of clothing, &c., have also been washed up.

Captain Wright had already reported that one of the five horses which reached the shore belonged to Staff-Surgeon Laing. The wreck itself, with all that it contained, was sold by public auction by the agents of the Admiralty at the Cape, acting in conjunction with the officers of the Customs there or other Colonial authorities, and early in 1854 it was announced that a Mr. H. Adams and a band of divers were engaged on the wreck at Danger Point, "and so much property is recovered that Mr. Adams will be amply rewarded." Some papers belonging to Colonel Seton, and a few silver articles engraved with his crest and motto, were in this way brought ashore, and, as stated in another chapter, were ultimately restored to his family; but a good deal of property was no doubt recovered and dispersed of which nothing is further known. These salvage operations were resumed by permission many years afterwards, even so late, if we mistake not, as 1894, when some diving was done at the scene of the wreck. There is a romantic fascination about this delving in the grave of a noble vessel, seeking for treasure and relics, like those of King Richard's dreams,

All scattered in the bottom of the sea.

But beyond the excitement of the pursuit, little could result from it in the case of a ship sunk in the situation of the *Birkenhead* after any lapse of time.

Our belief in the diving operations of 1894 was strengthened on later investigation. They received official sanction, which carried with it reservations of a somewhat curious and instructive character. Perhaps the circumstances of this enterprise will be best explained by a communication made to us on the subject by Major A. D. Seton.

At the end of 1893 [writes the nephew of Colonel Seton], a certain Mr. Bandmann at the Cape got leave from the Government to dive at the wreck of the *Birkenhead* in search of some supposed treasure on board, said to amount to about £240,000 in gold, for payment of the troops, &c., at the seat of war. My late uncle, David Seton, hearing of this, was apprehensive lest, if any of his brother's effects not affected by sea water, such as silver spoons, dirk, shoe buckles, &c., were recovered, they might be sold or exhibited as relics of the wreck. He therefore got a memo. sent to Lord Loch, the then Governor at the Cape, by which he was to instruct Mr. Bandmann that in the event of any articles belonging to officers or men on board the *Birkenhead* being recovered and identified, they were to be handed over to their relatives. The minute went on to say that, as regards any treasure that might be recovered, one-third was to be handed over to the authorities at the Cape, and Bandmann could keep the remaining two-thirds. It also went on to say "that in making this arrangement, Mr. Bandmann must clearly understand that it is not now (1893) known whether there was any treasure on board the ship or not." *

At any rate the search, if undertaken, was a fruitless one. These secrets of the *Birkenhead* lie buried for ever with the ship.

* Personally, I believe not. Archbold said he had never heard of its being on board. He would, I think, certainly have known. Fancy the Treasury not knowing fifty years after !—A. D. S.

H.M.S. "Castor," flying the Commodore's Pennant as Flagship at the Cape
(The only existing picture of this noted frigate in full rig)

CHAPTER XI

SISTER SHIPS AT THE CAPE

> Like a stately ship . . . .
> With all her bravery on, and tackle trim.—MILTON.

TWO ships of the Royal Navy of the period have an interesting connection with the subject of the *Birkenhead*. These are the *Castor* frigate and the steam vessel *Rhadamanthus*. The former was the flagship of Commodore Wyvill at the Cape, and her Commander Mr. B. H. Bunce was, as the reader has learnt, sent in the steamer to the scene of the wreck to render the survivors assistance.

The *Castor* was built to the design of Sir Robert Seppings, and was launched at Chatham in 1832. She was a 36-gun frigate of 1,293 tons, and carried a complement of 350 officers and men. A sister ship, the *Amphion*, was built at Woolwich at the same date. The *Castor* of 1832 was successor to the *Castor* of Lord Howe's day, which had an eventful record, being captured by the French and afterwards retaken. These circumstances, which occurred at the time when France was making a bold bid for Naval supremacy, are worthy of recall. The French fleet was at that period divided into two squadrons, one of which was commanded by M. Villaret, and the other by M. Neilly.

On May 19th, 1794, M. Villaret was joined by the *Patriote*, from M. Neilly's squadron, with the news that she had captured the British 32-gun frigate *Castor*, Captain Thomas Troubridge; also the chief part of the convoy from Newfoundland which the frigate had in charge. Captain Troubridge and most of his crew were afterwards transferred to the French ship *Sans Pareil*, in which they remained as prisoners until June 1st, when the *Sans Pareil* was captured by the *Majestic*, being one of the seven ships taken by Lord

Howe at his famous victory. Captain Troubridge and his crew, who had been sent below during the action, afterwards came on deck and assisted in navigating this noble two-decker into port, 380 of the *Sans Pareil's* crew having been either killed or wounded.

The *Castor* was valiantly recovered. On May 29th, in Lat. 46° 38′ N., Long. 9° 40′ W., the British 28-gun frigate *Carysfort*, Captain Francis Laforey, fell in with the French (late British) 32-gun frigate *Castor*, Captain L'Huillier, having in tow a Dutch merchant brig, in chase of which, five days before, she had parted from M. Neilly's squadron. The brig was cast off and an action commenced, which lasted without intermission for an hour and a quarter, at the end of which time the *Castor* hauled down her flag. The *Carysfort* was only slightly affected, her loss out of a crew of 180 men and boys being one seaman killed and three seamen and one marine wounded. The *Castor*, on the other hand, had suffered considerably, having had her maintopgallantmast shot away, her mainmast damaged, and her hull struck in several places. Her loss out of a crew of 200 was 16 officers, seamen and marines killed, and nine wounded. This successful engagement reflected much credit on Captain Laforey, whose ship was the smaller of the two; it also effected the release of one officer and 18 seamen, part of the *Castor's* original crew. It is only fair to the French to state that their knowledge of the working of the ship was limited, owing to the short time she had been in their possession.

The *Castor* of our illustration was rather a larger ship than her predecessor, and although not possessing such an eventful record, she completed many years of foreign service, which included the undermentioned commissions.

    1833–36 Lisbon and on particular service.
    1838–40 Mediterranean.
    1843–47 East Indies Station.
    1850–52 Cape of Good Hope.
    1855–58 Cape of Good Hope, East and West Coasts of Africa.

On August 27th, 1834, an unfortunate collision occurred off Dover between the *Castor* and the *Cameleon* cutter, which resulted in the loss of the cutter and thirteen lives.

SISTER SHIPS AT THE CAPE

In 1840 the *Castor* took part in the operations on the Syrian coast with the allied fleets of England and Austria, the Powers having decided to support the Porte, in order to destroy the influence of the rebellious Pacha Mehemet-Ali. During these operations the *Castor* and *Pique* captured Caiffa and Tyre. The *Castor* also shared in the bombardment of St. Jean d'Acre on November 3rd, 1840, when the forts were stormed by the allies under the command of Sir Robert Stopford, and taken after a bombardment of a few hours. The Egyptians lost 2,000 killed and wounded in the engagement, while the British had but 12 killed and 42 wounded. In 1858 the *Castor* was engaged with other vessels in the suppression of the slave traffic on the West Coast of Africa, where a number of slave-ships were captured and many slaves liberated as the result. In 1860 she was dismantled and sent to North Shields as a drill ship for the Royal Naval Reserve. There she remained until 1895. She was subsequently taken to Sheerness, and was sold in 1902 to Messrs. Henry Castle & Sons, Limited, shipbreakers, Woolwich.

The *Castor's* figurehead represents Castor (Castor and Pollux) in heathen mythology, one of the twin sons of Jupiter, said to preside over the destinies of sailors. Castor was numbered among the fifty heroes (the Argonauts) who sailed to Colchis in the ship *Argo* under Jason in quest of the Golden Fleece. In the New Testament (Acts xxviii. 11), we read that Paul sailed from Malta (A.D. 62) in a ship of Alexandria whose sign was Castor and Pollux. When the *Castor* was broken up at Woolwich * the interesting figurehead of the frigate was put aside, and with many other relics of similar ships was religiously preserved by Messrs. Castle. Our illustration is from a specially prepared drawing showing the *Castor* as she appeared at the period when the *Birkenhead* was wrecked. It is believed to be the only existing picture of this venerable and beautiful ship in full rig. The reproduction of the *Castor's* figurehead given

* Before she passed into the hands of the breakers, Mr. D. Addison went over the stout old ship in which he spent a portion of his youth. He found her below-decks little changed from the *Castor* of the Fifties, and the inspection awoke a crowd of happy memories. He was accompanied on the visit by a son (Sergt.-Major J. L. Addison, Royal Engineers) and a grandson.

separately is from a photograph. The figurehead of the former *Castor* was no doubt the same; this has, in fact, been a design favoured by sailors from the early ages, as proved by the passage in the New Testament.

Commodore CHRISTOPHER WYVILL, of H.M.S. *Castor*, joined the Navy as lieutenant on July 10th, 1813, and as such served successively in the *Towey*, 24 guns, Captain Hew Steuart; *Tagus*, 36 guns, Mediterranean, Captain J. W. D. Dundas; *Cydnus*, 38 guns, Portsmouth, Captain the Hon. F. W. Aylmer; *Pactolus*, 38 guns, Bermuda, Captain William Hugh Dobbie; and the *Arab* sloop of 18 guns at Cork, Captain Charles Simeon. He was promoted to first lieutenant on the *Dover*, 28 guns, at Leith, Captain Samuel Chambers, date of commission November 14th, 1821. His appointment as commander came on July 29th, 1824. He was given the command of the sloop *Cameleon* in the Mediterranean in 1827, and in the following year joined the *Asia*, of 84 guns, in the Mediterranean, Captain W. J. H. Johnstone, under whom he also served in the *Britannia*, 120 guns, on the same station. He was promoted captain on February 22nd, 1832, and served two commissions in the *Cleopatra*, 26 guns, one on the North American and West Indian Station, and the other at the Cape of Good Hope. Then came his appointment to the *Castor* at the Cape as commodore, to date May 7th, 1849. In 1854 (dating June 14th) he went as captain to the *Wellesley*, 72 guns, at Chatham. Subsequently he was promoted to the rank of admiral, and he was for several years superintendent of Chatham Dockyard. He died at the Grange, near Bedale, Yorkshire, on January 29th, 1863, his successors to the family estate being Mr. Marmaduke Wyvill, of Denton Park, Yorkshire, his nephew, and the son of that gentleman, Mr. Marmaduke D'Arcy Wyvill, M.P., of Denton Ben Ryhdding, Yorkshire, and Constable Burton, Finghall, to whom letters of administration were granted as recently as May 4th, 1900. The portrait of the Admiral given on another page was kindly lent for reproduction here by Mrs. Wyvill of Bournemouth, his niece by marriage.

Commander BENJAMIN HOLLAND BUNCE, of the *Castor* frigate, who was despatched by Commodore Wyvill to the

ADMIRAL WYVILL.
(From a photo).

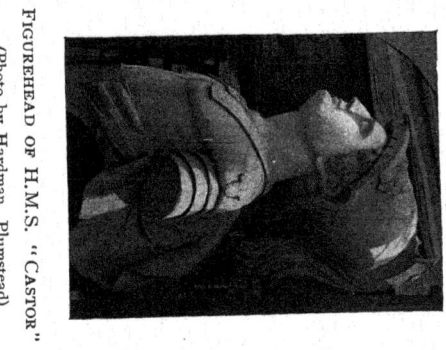

FIGUREHEAD OF H.M.S. "CASTOR".
(Photo by Hardman, Plumstead)

SISTER SHIPS AT THE CAPE 123

scene of the wreck, and after towing in the schooner *Lioness* with her 116 passengers returned to Danger Point and took off 68 other survivors, joined the Navy as lieutenant on June 28th, 1838, his first ship being the *Rover*, 18-gun sloop, on which he served under Commander T. W. C. Symonds on the North American and West Indies Station. In 1843 he joined the *Tyne*, of 26 guns, Captain W. N. Glascock, for service in the Mediterranean, and in 1847 he was appointed to the *Superb*, of 80 guns, Captain Armor L. Corry, serving on the coast of Portugal and in the Mediterranean. He was promoted to the *Castor*, 36 guns, Cape of Good Hope, Commodore Christopher Wyvill, in 1849,* his commission as commander dating from May 9th. In 1853 he transferred to the *Prince Regent*, of 90 guns, flagship of the Western Squadron, Captain Frederick Hutton, and later he returned to an old commander, now Rear-Admiral Armor L. Corry, on board the *Neptune*, 120 guns, flagship in the Baltic, the date of his final commission being March 7th, 1854. This was Commander Bunce's last ship. He died the latter part of this year, after returning to England, having taken part in the earlier stages of the Russian War.

The paddle-sloop *Rhadamanthus*, of 813 tons, was launched at Woolwich in 1831, and was one of the first steam vessels built for use in the British Navy. Her engines were 220 h.p., and her armament consisted of four guns. She carried a crew of fifty men. In 1834 the *Rhadamanthus* was attached to the North American and West Indies Squadron, and from 1838–40 she completed a commission in the Mediterranean. She was afterwards chiefly engaged in particular and transport service, and it was in this capacity that the vessel happened to be at the Cape when the *Birkenhead* was wrecked. She was commanded at the time by Master-Commander John Belam. The *Rhadamanthus* was employed on similar service until 1864, when she was disposed of. The figurehead of

---

* The will of Commander Bunce, appointing his wife, Susan Henrietta Bunce, and William and Thomas Stilwell, of Arundel Street, Strand, London, his executors, bears date June 10th, 1849, and was witnessed by Robert Jenkins, lieutenant of the *Castor*, and G. J. Hodges, master.

this vessel represents Rhadamanthus, a son of Jupiter and Europa, one of the three mythological judges before whom the spirits of the departed appeared to hear their doom. The principal judge was Minos; Æacus judged the Europeans, and Rhadamanthus the Asiatics. Says Dryden of the latter:

> These are the realms of unrelenting fate,
> And awful Rhadamanthus rules the state;
> He hears and judges each committed crime,
> Inquires into the manner, place and time.
> The conscious wretch must all his acts reveal,
> Loth to confess, unable to conceal;
> From the first moment of his vital breath,
> To the last hour of unrepenting death.

Our illustrations of the *Rhadamanthus* represent a model of the vessel made in 1850 by Mr. T. Roberts, Naval architect, to illustrate the advent of steam into the Navy, and presented to the Royal United Service Institution by Miss Roberts. The model is a beautifully finished specimen of its kind. It was specially photographed for this work, by permission of the Council of the Institution, by Mr. J. West, of Anerley, London, who obtained pictures from two positions so as to include all details. The illustrations are unique.

It remains only to add that the *Lioness* schooner, which picked up the boats and was towed into Simon's Bay by the *Rhadamanthus* with *Birkenhead* survivors on board, was afterwards sold and went to Australia. She sailed later on for England, and was finally broken up at the St. Katherine Docks, London. A grandson of Captain Thomas Ramsden, of the *Lioness*, Mr. J. D. Woolward, was at the 50th anniversary of the wreck of the *Birkenhead* a mail officer in the G.P.O. at Capetown. His identity was established by Mr. Richard Jeffery Herd, son of the late Robert Herd, who with eighteen others formed part of the starboard watch and were the only survivors of H.M.S. *Captain*, which foundered off Cape Finisterre on September 7th, 1870, when Captain Hugh Burgoyne, V.C., and 500 men perished.

It is interesting to note here also that the screw steamer *Megæra*, which as we have seen left Dover on January 2nd and put into Plymouth disabled, arrived at the Cape on

MODELS OF H.M. PADDLE SLOOP "RHADAMANTHUS," SHOWING
(1) DECK DETAILS AND ARTISTIC FIGUREHEAD; (2) BROAD-
SIDE OF VESSEL

(By permission of the Council of the Royal United Service Institution, Whitehall)

SISTER SHIPS AT THE CAPE

March 24th after a passage of 81 days, the duration of which had caused the greatest anxiety. She experienced an eventful voyage. Three times she took fire. After leaving Sierra Leone on February 7th her fuel ran short, and the men on board were placed on half-rations. She carried 650 rank and file of the 1st Battalion Rifle Brigade, 18 women, and 29 children. Colonel Buller, C.B., was in Military command, and his officers included Lord Alexander Russell (a brother of the Premier) and Captain Somerset, M.P. The *Hydra*, which was also employed in this troop-carrying service, but sailed later, reached the Cape at the end of March. The *Megæra* seems to have been an unfortunate vessel. She was wrecked some years afterwards, when a disaster was narrowly averted. In February, 1871, she sailed for Australia with about 400 souls on board. On June 8th she sprang a leak, when it was discovered that her bottom was nearly worn away with corrosion. She was beached on St. Paul's Isle, in the Indian Ocean, on June 16th, when the stores were landed and huts erected, and the crew settled down ashore. On July 16th Lieutenant Jones was taken on board a Dutch vessel, and on August 26th the *Oberon* came to the relief of the castaways with a supply of provisions. They were taken off the island by the *Malacca* on September 3rd, during a storm, when it was necessary to leave the stores behind—a cheap price, the crew would doubtless consider it, to pay for their liberation.

CHAPTER XII

GALLANT AND GIFTED COLONEL SETON *

The shining quality of an epic hero.—DRYDEN.

LIEUT.-COLONEL ALEXANDER SETON, the heroic officer who commanded the troops on the *Birkenhead*, was the second but eldest surviving son of Mr. Alexander Seton of Mounie, a Deputy-Lieutenant and Justice of the Peace for Aberdeenshire, who was descended from the second son of Sir Alexander Seton of Pitmedden, Bart., a senator of the College of Justice as Lord Pitmedden.† Colonel Seton was born on October 4th, 1814.

His early youth [says *The Biographical Dictionary of Eminent Scotsmen*, a work originally edited by Robert Chambers, and afterwards revised and corrected by the Rev. Thomas Thomson] was marked by great talents, which were carefully cultivated by private education; but his prevailing bias was towards the Military profession, which he studied as a science, and to which all his acquirements were made subservient. When not quite fifteen years old he accompanied his parents to Italy, where he remained behind them to study mathematics and chemistry under Professor Ferdinando Foggi, of Pisa; and there also he became a perfect Italian scholar, being previously well acquainted with the Latin, Greek, and French languages.

On November 23rd, 1832, young Seton was gazetted as second lieutenant by purchase in the 21st Royal North British Fusiliers, and soon afterwards sailed with a detachment of his regiment to the Australian colonies, where he was

---

* This interesting and instructive chapter was prepared from materials kindly furnished to the authors by Major A. D. Seton, nephew of Lieut.-Colonel A. Seton.

† The 1st baronet, Sir Alexander Seton, was an eminent lawyer, M.P. for Aberdeenshire, a senator of the College of Justice, and a Lord of Justiciary, with the title of Lord Pitmedden. The 2nd baronet was M.P. for Aberdeenshire, and one of the Commissioners appointed to treat about the union between England and Scotland.

EARLY PORTRAIT OF COLONEL SETON IN UNIFORM OF THE
ROYAL NORTH BRITISH FUSILIERS

(From a miniature in the possession of the family)

stationed chiefly at Van Diemen's Land. In the course of a few years he returned to England on leave of absence, and was promoted by purchase to a first lieutenancy on March 2nd, 1838. He made a short tour in Germany in order to perfect himself in the German language, which he had previously studied, and then rejoined his regiment in India as adjutant, the duties of which position he discharged so ably during a long and trying march from Dinapore to Kamptee, near Nagpore, as to win the approbation of his commanding officer. While in India this gifted and studious young officer mastered the difficulties of Hindustani, and made himself familiar with other Oriental languages, including the Sanscrit and Persian. Having been promoted to a company without purchase on January 14th, 1842, he returned to Europe, and exchanged from the 21st into the 74th Highlanders, then expected home from foreign service; and on their arrival he joined, in 1844, the depôt of that regiment at Chatham.

In January, 1846, he obtained permission to become a student in the senior department of the Royal Military College at Sandhurst, and after a two years' attendance there brilliantly passed his final examination in November, 1847. His signal success on that occasion is recounted in the report of the examination in Colburn's *United Service Magazine and Naval and Military Journal* for January, 1848.

Captain Seton, who was particularly distinguished for the talent displayed in the highest departments of mathematical science, and for the great extent of his acquirements, was presented with a certificate of the first class, on which was expressed the sense entertained by the board of his superior merit.

After the examination Captain Seton was personally commended by the Duke of Cambridge, Sir George Brown, Deputy-Adjutant-General, and others. His scientific knowledge was so varied and profound that it embraced not only natural philosophy, mechanics and mathematics, and subjects more closely associated with his profession, such as fortress construction and Military surveying, but also botany and geology, and to all this he added a thorough knowledge of music and drawing; while his wonderful linguistic powers had enabled him to acquire no fewer than fifteen languages! He was an Admirable Crichton indeed, whose surprising talents as here outlined cannot be at all doubted on the evidence upon which this sketch is based.

At the close of 1847 Captain Seton rejoined his regiment, the 74th Highlanders, then stationed at Dublin, and in 1849 he was appointed Assistant-Deputy-Quartermaster-General to the Forces in Ireland. This appointment he held until his promotion by purchase to a majority in the 74th in May, 1850, when, on his resigning the post mentioned, he was assured by Sir Willoughby Gordon, the Quartermaster-General, that "on any future opening occurring on the staff consistent with the work of a field officer, he would not be forgotten at the Horse Guards." In March, 1851, the 74th Highlanders, with their commander, Lieut.-Colonel Fordyce, were ordered for foreign service at the Cape of Good Hope, and embarked for that colony; while Major Seton was left at home in command of the four-company depôt, according to the usual custom of the service. A change, however, speedily took place, for Colonel Fordyce having been killed in an encounter with the Kaffirs,* Major Seton was promoted to the rank of lieutenant-colonel of the 74th, and sent to the Cape to succeed him in January, 1852. The rest is known to the reader—how this gallant and promising officer sailed in the *Birkenhead* from the Cove of Cork on January 7th in charge of drafts from ten different regiments to reinforce the troops in South Africa; and how the voyage had a premature and tragic but a glorious ending. Colonel Seton, one almost believes, had some sort of foreboding of what was to happen.

Among his many endearing qualities [says the Memoir in the *Biographical Dictionary* already quoted], Colonel Seton was distinguished by the virtues of domestic life that constituted a principal charm in his parental home; and the letters which he wrote to his widowed mother during every brief halt of this voyage formed a mournful solace to her subsequent regrets. In one of them he says, "I will, if possible, write

* In an attack on the fastnesses heading the Waterkloof Pass, the stronghold of Macomo's Kaffirs and of the Hottentot banditti who had joined him, when not only Lieut.-Colonel Fordyce, but Lieutenants Carey and Gordon, of the 74th, were killed.

to you again the last thing. I never felt leaving you so much before."
In this way, at every stage of the voyage, and finally from the Cape
only a day before his disastrous end, he endeavoured to alleviate her
anxiety for his safety, while he sought to amuse her with an account
of whatever he had seen at Madeira, Sierra Leone, St. Helena, and
Simon's Bay.*

Speaking of Colonel Seton's character as an officer, the Memoir says that—

In Britain, India, Australia, and Ireland he had always maintained the character of a strict disciplinarian, so that no breach of duty could escape his notice or reprehension. But he was as strict with himself as with others, and whatever might be their labour or fatigue, he was ready to bear his part in it. This combination of two opposite qualities, so rare in Military officers, attracted the admiration of his soldiers, and their usual remark was, " If he does not spare others, he does not spare himself." It was a union of qualities only belonging to those who are born to be the veritable leaders of men, and through which they convert their men into heroes. By the controlling might of such an example, wielded by a superior intellect, a captain may become a conqueror or a king ; and all that such aptitudes require for the purpose is a proper field of action, which is not always to be found. These professional qualities of Colonel Seton during this voyage were called into full exercise. The men under his command, instead of composing a single regiment and possessing the usual regimental *esprit de corps*, were drafted from ten regiments, and therefore had no such bond of union ; they were also a motley assemblage of Irish, English, and Scotch, who had never been under fire, and most of their officers were young and inexperienced. How then, in the hour of such fearful peril, did they exhibit a courage, a firmness, a devotedness to which few veterans would have been found equal? It can only be attributed to the admirable discipline which their commander had established among them, and by which he acquired such marvellous power over them in the valley of the shadow of death. From what danger in the field would an army shrink when conducted by such a leader?

This fine passage is well worth quoting, because it gives us a good insight into the Military character of Colonel Seton, reveals something of his lofty qualities and magnetic personality, and helps us to account for his remarkable

* His last letter, dated February 22nd, 1852, was written when nearing the Cape, and finished "in haste" at Simon's Bay three days afterwards. It concludes: "We sail to-night. . . . I, with some draughts, disembark at Algoa Bay. . . . I have got two horses, which I think will suit me very well. . . . I am in perfect health, and all is going on well." This letter passed into the possession of Major A. D. Seton.

ascendency over the troops, who first he trained to soldierly obedience, and then inspired by his example to such noble conduct as they displayed at the wreck. In the light of it we are the better able to appreciate the concluding eulogy of the heroes of the *Birkenhead*.

When the news came home of the loss of the *Birkenhead,* and the circumstances attending it, not only Britain, but all Europe, was astonished at the narrative. The heroism of the 300 at Thermopylæ, or the 600 at Balaclava, is intelligible, where these daring handfuls went to death in the light of day, and with an admiring world looking on. But how much more heroic still to exhibit at least equal courage and self-devotedness where there was neither the hot excitement of the fight nor the knell of fame for the fallen. All wondered at the steadiness and promptness of raw recruits under such a terrible ordeal, their implicit obedience to orders when death was inevitable, and the resignation with which they submitted to their fate. And what a commander he must have been who could thus control them, and whom they were so ready under such circumstances to obey! The story of the *Birkenhead* will be imperishable, and it will enshrine to all time the name of Colonel Alexander Seton.

Truly a Deathless Story!

In one direction the Memoir above quoted has been considered not to do full justice to Colonel Seton, and that is as regards his modesty of character. With all his brilliant parts, and the soldierly qualities he possessed, he was really one of the most simple and unpretentious of men. This prominent trait is noted by a lady, who wrote of him after his death:

Few are like him, so talented, so highly cultivated, so attractive, and correct in their conduct, and with all his acquirements so simple, unaffected, and unpretending.

Mrs. Strong, wife of the Rev. Linwood Strong, rector of Sedgefield, in a letter to the family said that—

Few could sustain such a loss—for it is rarely given to man to unite attainments so solid and varied, accomplishments so brilliant, with such a noble character.

And the writer added:

The loss of the *Birkenhead* is one of the most tragic events that history can record. A more noble example of discipline and fortitude and unselfishness will never have been given "when the sea shall give up its dead."

Miss Agnes Strickland, author of *The Queens of England* and other historical works, in a letter of sympathy which she addressed to the family, expressed herself in admirable terms with regard to the deceased officer.

It is a proud thing [she said] to have been the mother of so glorious a man. I am sure you must feel like the great Duke of Ormond when he stood by the lifeless remains of the Earl of Ossory, and exclaimed, "I would not exchange my dead son for all the monarchs in Christendom." The reflection of his self-sacrifice must be your comfort, and I hope you will take comfort from the reflection that it was one of the noblest deaths ever recorded, winning more true glory than the brightest laurels that ever graced a conqueror from the battlefield.

No less beautiful were the words of Miss Catharine Sinclair, author of *Hill and Valley* and numerous other works.

I have always thought [she wrote to a friend] the most distinguished instance of deliberate heroism on record was the death of that noble officer, Colonel Seton; and the more I read or think of him the more I think what his country lost, and what a grief beyond all expression it must have been to his family that, in the very prime of his days, with such talents and such marvellous energy to render them available, he should in so fearful a manner have been called on to testify his fortitude and his submission to the will of God.

A former Convener of a county in Scotland, who had good opportunities of forming a correct estimate of Colonel Seton's character, declared that—

Besides being a first-rate officer, his learning, knowledge, and accomplishments exceeded in depth and variety anything I almost ever heard of since the days of the Admirable Crichton, and were accompanied by a modesty hardly less unusual. He was also most truly amiable, and the best and most devoted of sons.

This fragmentary but genuine testimony of those who knew him well emphasises not a little the sterling worth of the late officer, whose character and whose conduct at the wreck we shall have further opportunity of studying in what is to follow.

There is some interesting correspondence relative to the wreck of the *Birkenhead*, with special reference to Colonel Seton's share in the Military proceedings on board the sinking ship. This correspondence was the outcome of action taken by Mr. David Seton,* brother of the deceased officer, who, being anxious to ascertain the facts at first-hand, lost no time in communicating with survivors and asking them for particulars of the last moments of his brother. The result must have been as gratifying to Mr. Seton as it will be satisfactory to the readers of these pages, because it helps to do justice to a gallant soldier's memory, and at the same time it renders a public and historical service by more truly apportioning the deserved credit of the officers present at the wreck. The correspondence establishes beyond all dispute the fact that the heroism and chivalry displayed on board originated, as it ought to have done, and as one would have expected it to do, with Colonel Seton, who, after superintending the removal of the women and children, returned to his place near the mizzen rigging, where he remained giving orders with the greatest coolness and self-possession till the vessel finally broke up and sank; and not only so, but in the meantime he more than once issued that noble appeal to the men around him not to jeopardise the safety of the boats. Mr. David Seton, as he has expressed it, thought it but just that the name of a commanding officer who died so gallantly in the service of his country and in the discharge of his duty as a man and a soldier should at least be associated with the memory of the event. The name of Colonel Seton is more than merely associated with the memory of that event: it stands out prominently and gloriously in connection with it.

Before proceeding to the testimony of survivors, it should first be noted that an important letter on the subject was addressed to Mr. Seton by Major William Beresford, the Secretary-at-War. In this communication, which is dated War Office, May 24th, 1852, Major Beresford says:

The first official report, as well as all the accounts which have been given in all private letters, bear a concurring testimony to the noble

* Formerly of the 93rd Highlanders, afterwards of the 49th Regiment, who succeeded his unmarried brother, Lieut.-Colonel Alexander Seton, in the family estates. Mr. David Seton died in 1894, and being also unmarried, was succeeded by his nephew, Alexander David Seton, Captain and Hon. Major Forfar and Kincardine Artillery Militia, only surviving son of Major George Seton, Sutherland Highlanders.

FIELD-MARSHAL H.R.H. THE DUKE OF CONNAUGHT, K.G.,
INSPECTOR-GENERAL OF THE FORCES

(As Colonel-in-Chief of the Highland Light Infantry, of which the 74th
Regt. is now the 2nd Battalion. Photo by W. & D. Downey, Ebury
Street, S.W. Specially presented in honour of the *Birkenhead*)

GALLANT AND GIFTED COLONEL SETON

and self-devoted conduct of Lieut.-Colonel Seton, who, being the commanding officer on board the *Birkenhead*, must be considered by all Military men to have originated by the authority which he had acquired, and to have stimulated by the example which he set, that display of discipline and of self-devotion which the troops, without exception, exhibited on that melancholy occasion.

Major Beresford refers to the discussion on the subject in Parliament on April 26th.

I did venture in the House of Commons to draw their attention to the fact that the troops on board the *Birkenhead* were composed of raw levies, sent out in different detachments to join their respective regiments; consequently their conduct, amidst dangers and horrors which are not the natural incidents of their professional career, reflects indisputable credit upon the commanding officer, who in a short period of time united so many detached portions of different corps in one unanimous competition to do their duty to the last moment like soldiers and like men.

Major Beresford does not overlook the other officers.

It would be great omission, however, if I did not extend to all the officers on board their share of just praise. They all vied with the senior officer in attending to the fulfilment of their duty, not to the safety of their own lives, and from the lieutenant-colonel to the ensign have shown that it does not require the excitement of a battle, nor the hopes of victory, to empower a British officer to face death with the readiness of a hero and the calmness of a Christian.

There is also a letter received by Mr. Seton, dated July 7th, 1852, from Lieut.-Colonel Patton, commanding 74th Highlanders. It was addressed from the Camp, Botha's Hill, on the frontier, where the regiment was at this time engaged with the enemy at a great distance from the scene of the wreck.

I have spoken to Captain Wright on the subject some time since [says Colonel Patton], but I did not learn any additional particulars from him than what I had previously heard—viz. that your brother behaved in a most noble manner. He called every officer on the poop of the vessel, and gave his orders with extraordinary coolness and presence of mind, entirely forgetful of self. Your brother's death [the Colonel affirms] is an irreparable loss to the regiment, and is deeply regretted by us all, knowing him to have been a good and truly upright honest man.

Dr. Robert Bowen, the senior staff-surgeon of the *Birkenhead*, then in the Rifle Brigade, one of the survivors interrogated by Mr. David Seton, replied that he perfectly recollected seeing Colonel Seton on the poop of the *Birkenhead* after she struck—

and to the best of my belief he remained near the port mizzen rigging. I spoke to him several times while standing there, and at the poop ladder, a conspicuous part of the ship. He was on deck when I went there, and he remained to the last. I heard him issuing orders to the officers and men under his command, and giving effect to the suggestions of the Master of the ship, with the greatest coolness and self-possession. The last time I saw him he was standing with the Master of the ship near the mizzen rigging. At this time the vessel was in two parts—the forward half had nearly disappeared, and the poop was fast settling down; this could not have been more than two or three minutes before the wreck was finally submerged.

Sergeant David Andrews, 60th Rifles, another of the survivors, was at this time Staff-Sergt.-Major Andrews, King William's Town, C.G.H., and he wrote to Mr. Seton as "late Acting Sergt.-Major" on board the *Birkenhead*.* He says that Colonel Seton was looked up to by all as the friend of the soldiers and their wives.

During the short time that elapsed from the striking to the sinking of the vessel [proceeds Sergt.-Major Andrews] Colonel Seton was most calm and firm in all his orders, his first care being directed towards putting in the boats the women, children, and sick; and then, on account of the heavy lurching of the vessel, which caused the horses to lunge and plunge, thereby endangering the lives of those on board, he ordered the horses to be thrown overboard. [This would probably be at Captain Salmond's suggestion.] Colonel Seton was most kind, although at the same time he was most calm and firm in all his orders, and even at the most critical moments his instructions were carried out without a murmur from either side, for he was so much esteemed by all present. His last words to me were, "Sergeant-Major, keep the men steady and quiet, and I shall be the last man that shall leave this ship." During the time the vessel was on the rock it was pitch dark,† and the commander of the ship was trying to capsize the paddle-box boats; but with all the confusion on board, all listened most attentively to Colonel Seton's orders, and so great was the silence that a pin might be heard to drop.

The duties of Sergt.-Major Andrews after the wreck would appear from the concluding sentences of this letter to have

* This distinction is also claimed by Colour-Sergeant Kilkeary, late 73rd. Perhaps the duties were shared by these non-commissioned officers.

† They had a lantern or two on the poop—Surgeon Bowen and Cornet Bond afterwards said so: the binnacle light, at all events.—Mr. D. Seton.

been similar to those of Sergeant B. Kilkeary, as he then was, for the writer says:

The mail steamer was detained two days, whilst I was employed in collecting the names of those drowned to send home to England,* and I am sorry and very much regretted to find that Colonel Seton's name was not amongst the living. The Colonel [he adds] was esteemed the whole way out as an officer and a gentleman, on account of his great urbanity of manner, and his great firmness and deliberate calmness in all his commands.

Colour-Sergeant John Drake, Royal Marines, wrote giving Mr. Seton the result of—

the observations I made during the awful moments immediately preceding the breaking up of the ship and Colonel Seton being lost. I was on the forecastle at the time the ship struck, and immediately after I saw your late brother make his appearance on the quarterdeck, dressed in his pantaloons, a morning-gown, and a Glengarry cap.

This latter, Mr. Seton thought, was probably the Colonel's regimental Highland forage cap.

I heard him distinctly [says Colour-Sergeant Drake] give orders to the various officers that soon surrounded him to order the troops to fall in, which they immediately did on both sides of the quarterdeck. Colonel Seton was very firm and composed in his manner. I distinctly heard him say to the troops, "Silence, men, steady!" I then saw him take up a position on the port gangway, where he continued to superintend the embarkation of the women and children in the boats, preventing the men getting into them (several of whom attempted to do so).

The writer concludes by declaring that—

During the whole of this time no officer could have behaved in a more collected, soldierlike manner than Colonel Seton did, and I am happy in being able to bear my humble testimony to that effect, and I am sure no one had a better opportunity of observing him than I had, having been on the quarter-deck the whole of the time.

There is a letter from Captain Wright, 91st Regiment.

My acquaintance with those on board during the voyage was but short [wrote this correspondent of Mr. D. Seton's], but it was long enough to cause me a deep feeling of sorrow at the loss of so many, amongst whom none was more regretted than your poor brother, for we were a good deal thrown together, being the only two old officers amongst a number of young ones; and he had no easy task with so

* This was the man on whom all the trouble of preparing the lists, &c., really fell after the wreck; but not being a commissioned officer, his name does not appear.—Mr. Seton.

many of different regiments. The men, too, composing the different drafts were all young recruits almost. How well he succeeded up to the last moment the result showed. I did not see him again after the commencement of the wreck. I do not think he succeeded in reaching any floating piece of wood, as I could not hear from any of the survivors that he had been seen, although I made repeated inquiries.

Captain Wright adds that all the heavy baggage was on board the ship at the time she sank. He had Colonel Seton's horse, which had got ashore, sold by auction at Capetown for £11 19s. 6d., which he paid to the paymaster of the 74th Highlanders to be remitted to the Secretary-at-War.

How unfortunate the 74th has been in its double loss! [says Captain Wright]. I need not say how well your poor brother would have filled the gap caused by poor Colonel Fordyce's death, had he not been cut off thus early.

There are two interesting letters from Captain G. A. Lucas, 73rd Regiment. The first is dated "Camp, Keis Kama Hoek," July 15th, 1852, and in this Captain Lucas says:

I believe I was the last person who spoke to your brother while on the deck of the ship; and from all I can learn from those who were saved, no person appears to have seen him in the water.

As a matter of fact, Colonel Seton was seen in the water by Mr. C. K. Renwick, as will appear a little later on. Mr. Renwick was picked up by the boats and conveyed to Simon's Bay. Ensign Lucas swam ashore, was injured, and had to be left up-country at Captain Smales' farm, so that it is unlikely they ever met again. But, says Captain Lucas,

I saw Colonel Seton several times during the time we were going to pieces, and received orders from him. When the order was given for every person to save themselves if they could, I went on the poop-deck, where I met Colonel Seton. We spoke together for some minutes, and when the water was only a few feet from the deck I shook hands with him, and hoped we should meet ashore. Your brother was as cool and collected at this time as if he had been on parade. We were grasping the same piece of rope, and not half a foot from one another.

In a subsequent letter, written from Pietermaritzburg, Natal, Captain Lucas makes important statements.

With regard to your inquiries as to Colonel Seton superintending the embarkation of the women and children on board the *Birkenhead* into the ship's boats, I am happy to say that I can probably give you as much information on the subject as any of the survivors of the wreck, for on my coming on deck from the pumps for a few minutes I met your brother at the head of the companion-ladder, when he told me that he had stationed a sergeant of my regiment at the gangway to see that the boats were not overcrowded, and to prevent the men getting into the boats with the women, at the same time desiring me to see that he did his duty, as his (Colonel Seton's) presence was required elsewhere.* And afterwards, when the boats had been shoved off from the ship and were lying at some distance, I distinctly remember your brother desiring the men not to swim to the boats, lest they should thereby endanger the women and children. I heard Major Wright of the 91st reiterate the order a short time after.

He denies an amusing report which had somewhere been set abroad.

I have, since my last communication with you, heard it stated that Colonel Seton, at the time the ship went down, had a leather bag fastened round his body containing £50 in half-crowns. Now, as I before stated to you, Colonel Seton and myself were grasping the same rope, and spoke together for some minutes before I went overboard. Consequently, I have always considered this as a totally unfounded assertion.

Which no doubt it was. The idea of a man who expected soon to be in the water, and knew he could not swim, as Colonel Seton told Ensign Lucas he could not, weighting himself in the manner suggested, is too preposterous to be entertained for one moment. Besides, the Colonel was not the man to let considerations of this kind influence him at such a time; if he had attempted to save anything at all it would have been his valuable papers and MSS., which we know were lost with the ship.

Let me again assure you [adds Captain Lucas] that, as far as my testimony can be of any service in establishing your brother's character as a man and an officer, who did his utmost to save the lives of all on board and set an example of self-possession, courage, and cheerfulness to those under his command, for which I, for one, am extremely grateful, you are truly welcome to it.

We pass on to the testimony of Mr. C. K. Renwick, the assistant-engineer, who was rescued by the boats. In

---

* The statement of the sergeant of the 60th reported by the Hon. Wm. Hope, also those of Sergeant Drake and others, show that Colonel Seton's absence from the gangway could have been only for a few minutes, and that he had returned there.—Mr. D. Seton.

October, 1852, Mr. Renwick made a verbal statement to Mr. D. Seton, which he afterwards attested. In this he says that he remained on the poop deck, standing close beside Colonel Seton, till they were all thrown off by the final lurch of the ship. He observed Colonel Seton in the water near him, and it appeared that he was seized hold of and dragged down by some of the men who were clinging to one another, and struggling around in such numbers that it was difficult to escape their grasp; but for this he thinks the Colonel might have been saved. Colonel Seton was perfectly cool and collected during the whole time of the wreck. The Colonel himself superintended the embarkation of the women and children into the boats, standing by and directing as they were passed down. At a later period, when the men were advised to swim to the boats, then lying at a short distance from the wreck, Colonel Seton called to them not to do so, as it would only swamp the boats and drown the women and children. While bearing this strong testimony, which confirms that of Captain Lucas, as to the appeal being made by the Colonel, Mr. Renwick denies that it was Captain Salmond who told the men to swim to the boats. This memorandum, signed by Mr. Renwick, concludes by stating that—

Shortly before the poop went down, Mr. Renwick, Colonel Seton, and all the other officers still standing there, shook hands and took leave of one another.

Mr. Renwick supplements the foregoing by a letter to Mr. Seton, in which he says:

I very readily certify to the accuracy with which you have rendered the substance of our conversation. I remember most distinctly, a few moments before the ship's final disappearance, while standing by the side of Colonel Seton, hearing that officer, simultaneously with Captain Salmond, call on us not to endanger the safety of the boats in which were the women and children. I confess to you it has always appeared to me inexplicable that, while the truly heroic bearing of the troops (the majority of them so young and inexperienced) on that occasion has been fully done justice to, the scantiest credit, if any, has been meted to the memories of the noble spirits whose intrepid example, I firmly believe, went very far to produce that cheerful indifference to face death which most undoubtedly was exhibited in a degree scarcely to be conceived. No survivor can ever forget the pre-eminently cool and placid demeanour of Colonel Seton and Cornet Rolt during those trying moments; and I

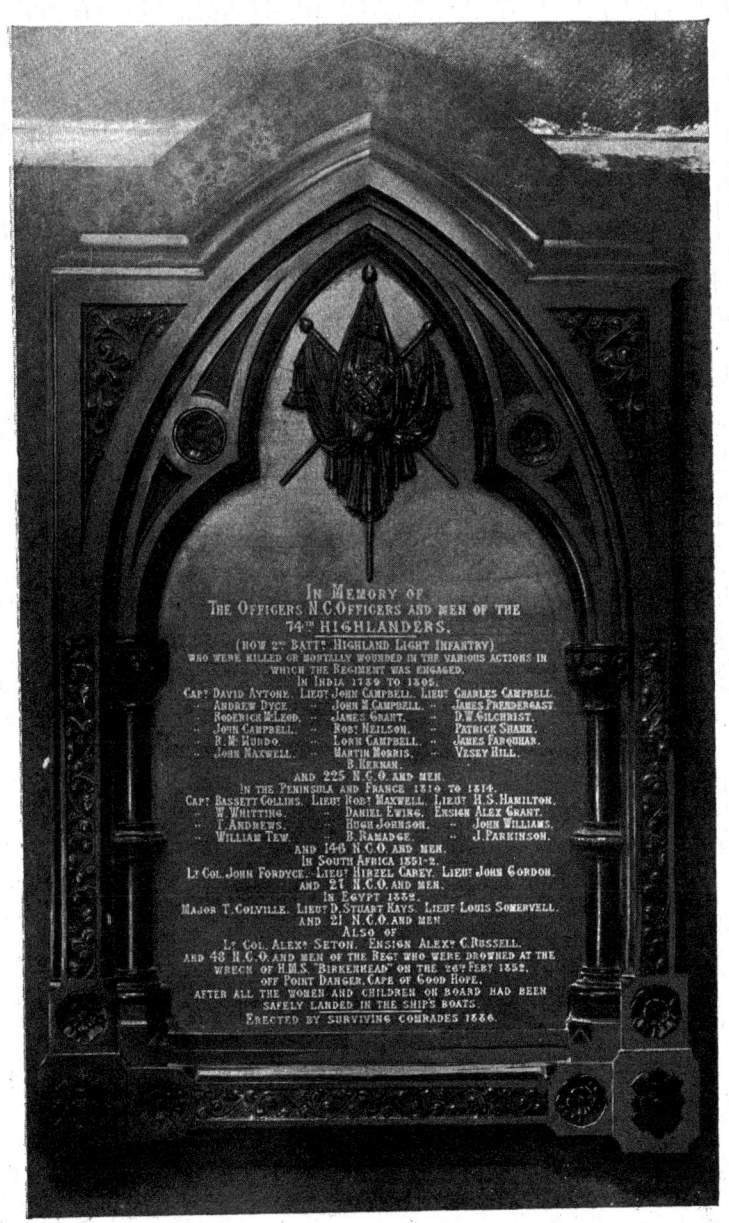

MONUMENT TO THE 74TH HIGHLANDERS IN ST. GILES' CATHEDRAL, EDINBURGH

(Commemorating Colonel Seton and *Birkenhead* heroes. Special photo by Alex. A. Inglis, Edinburgh)

cannot believe it possible that any would hesitate in expressing a sincere and fervent desire to have justice done to their memories.

With this letter Mr. Renwick enclosed the signed memorandum of verbal statement he had already made to Mr. Seton. This evidence, by a Naval officer who would not be unduly biassed towards the Military, should finally remove any existing doubt as to the origination of the appeal with respect to the boats.* The heroism of the troops was never doubted. His manly letter does Mr. Renwick great credit.

There is a memorandum in Mr. Seton's handwriting of a conversation he had with Lieutenant Bond, 12th Lancers, at Canterbury in 1856. It sheds welcome light on a matter which otherwise must have remained in doubt.

This officer said that he remembered Colonel Seton standing by the gangway when the women and children were being put into the boat; that Colonel Seton asked him (Mr. Bond) to fetch a table-knife from the cabin, which he did; that Colonel Seton did not assign a reason for this, but that his object was clearly that he might be able to cut the rope which held the boat, and so let it go, if any rush should be made for it before it was shoved off. No necessity arose, however, for using the knife.

So that the story about the table-knife is strictly true. It is an interesting incident, and it shows how determined Colonel Seton was to secure the safety of the women and children. Lieutenant Bond also bore his testimony to the Colonel being "perfectly cool and self-possessed."

The last of this correspondence to be noticed is a communication from the Hon. Wm. Hope, Auditor-General, C.G.H., received in reply to an inquiring letter by Mr. John Cook, writer to the Signet at Edinburgh. Mr. Hope says he feels certain the body of Colonel Seton was not discovered and identified, because—

the Custom House officer who remained for three weeks on the beach near the wreck told me the body was never found—and he made particular inquiries from the Field Cornet, who held inquests on forty-eight

* The evidence both of Mr. Renwick and Captain Lucas is strengthened quite independently by the following extract from a letter of Major A. D. Seton: "Most certainly the order to the men not to go to the boats originated with my uncle. Archbold told me he was standing alongside my uncle when he gave the order which Wright and the others took up." Major Seton met Mr. Archbold and other survivors personally.

bodies washed on the shore, and which he buried—and he could not find anything to indicate that any of these were the remains of poor Colonel Seton. In fact, the bodies were so mutilated by the sharks that none could have been recognised. A sergeant of the 60th, who was saved, says that Colonel Seton was at the gangway with a drawn sword in his hand, keeping the way clear for the women to get into the boats, and preserving order; and when he had done this, he gave the sergeant the sword and went on the poop to give some orders, when the vessel broke in two pieces, and Colonel Seton went down with all on the poop. All authentic accounts speak in the highest terms of his conduct and behaviour during most trying and awful scenes.

Through the kindly exertions of Mr. Hope, acting as a friend and not in any official capacity, two bundles of articles belonging to Colonel Seton which had been washed up from the wreck were sent home to the family. Both of them were things of a nature that could be easily identified, the one being papers, but unfortunately only some old letters and accounts of no further use, and the other containing a few silver articles of trifling value but each engraved with Colonel Seton's crest and motto. What other property of his, if any, may have been recovered and fallen into the hands of strangers could never be ascertained by Colonel Seton's family. In recording this result of persistent efforts which he made after the wreck to secure any personal belongings of his brother, Mr. David Seton says:

I knew that my brother could not have had anything with him of any pecuniary value; but at the same time, I knew that he had many writings and other things which would have been of interest to myself and to his family generally. I very soon heard that one box, at least, which had belonged to him had been broken open, by authority, on the beach, and the contents dispersed. Conceiving that I had a right to be informed as to what became of any property of that sort, and believing, as I still do believe, that the Admiralty was the only department responsible in the matter, I wrote to the Secretary for information. A correspondence of some length ensued. The answers which I received, being vague and indefinite, although always civil, convinced me at length that the Admiralty had really no definite information on the subject, and it was ultimately allowed to drop.

The result was unfortunate. Mr. Seton states it in an interesting little book on the *Wreck of the "Birkenhead"* which he had printed in Edinburgh in 1861, and again in 1873 and 1890, for private use and not for publication and sale. The book treats more especially of matters concerning Colonel Seton, and its modest and faithful character may be judged by what follows.

With regard to the memory of my brother [writes Mr. Seton], none, it is true, could ever have had opportunities of knowing his great and excellent qualities of heart and head as I have known them, and none, I am certain, could ever have appreciated those qualities more thoroughly than I have done. But I considered that anything that I could say would, to those who knew my brother, seem superfluous, and by others would be set down as the result of fraternal feeling or partiality. It is, therefore, some satisfaction to me that I am able to include in this little collection a short account of his life and talents, written by a gentleman* who, being no relation or kindred, must be regarded as a perfectly disinterested admirer of my brother's character. It is to be regretted that the material at his command was scanty, because, unfortunately, Colonel Seton, as was his custom, had taken with him all his MSS., drawings, and writings of every description, and all of these perished in the wreck.

As Mr. Seton says, none could know the excellent qualities of his brother as he had known them. They were, nevertheless, known and appreciated by others who speak with authority. Of this we have seen something already. The Right Hon. H. A. Bruce, in his *Life of Sir William Napier*, says of him from personal knowledge that he was "one of the most gifted and accomplished men in the British Army." Again, the author of *Medals of the British Army, and How they were Won* (Thomas Carter, of the Adjutant-General's Office, author also of *Curiosities of War and Military Studies*), after observing that Colonel Seton at the wreck of the *Birkenhead* "exhibited an example of the highest coolness and self-possession, and died at his post with the courage and resolution of a British soldier," and declaring that —

such conduct merits every encomium, for true valour never appears in a brighter light than on these awful occasions, when the prospect of glory and the excitement of the battlefield are wanting,

says :

In the death of Lieut.-Colonel Seton the country lost the services of a talented officer, possessing high scientific and professional attainments.

* The Rev. Thomas Thomson, in *The Biographical Dictionary of Eminent Scotsmen.*

This sketch of the gallant and gifted senior officer may be fittingly closed with a reference made to the *Birkenhead* in *The Comprehensive History of England* of Messrs. Blackie & Son, the publishers of the work containing the Memoir of Colonel Seton before alluded to. The wreck is held up as "a unique specimen of heroism, in which the coolest courage and intrepid daring were combined with the purest humanity and disinterestedness," and as such, the history goes on to say,

it roused the emulation of our soldiers and was the parent of similar achievements in the subsequent campaigns of the Crimea and India. As long as the British Army nurses such a spirit as that which was shown upon the deck of the *Birkenhead*, and possesses such officers as Colonel Seton, our country, let the enemy be who they may, has nothing to fear.

Who that reads the Deathless Story can ever doubt this!

COLONEL E. W. C. WRIGHT, C.B.
(From a photo)

CHAPTER XIII

*THE CAREER OF COLONEL WRIGHT, C.B.**

Act well your part, there all the honour lies.—POPE.

COLONEL EDWARD WILLIAM CARLILE WRIGHT, C.B., had, when he passed away many years after the great occasion with which his name is so gloriously associated, a record of Military service of which his country has reason to be proud. His Army career began in 1832, when he obtained a commission without purchase from the Royal Military College. He passed to lieutenant and captain by purchase, was promoted to battalion-major and battalion-lieutenant-colonel for service in the field,† and became colonel by length of service. He was in all the operations during the Kaffir Wars of 1846-7 and 1852-3. In 1852 and part of 1853 he commanded a field force of cavalry, artillery and infantry, and was twice mentioned in general orders for successful operations against the enemy. He commanded the Fort Beaufort district and 91st Regiment on the frontier for two years, and was mentioned in general orders and despatches by Major-General Hare, commanding the forces in the field in 1846-7, and by Sir Peregrine Maitland, Sir Harry Smith, Sir George Cathcart, and Sir James Jackson, Governors and Commanders-in-Chief at the Cape, between 1847 and 1855. Colonel Wright possessed the medal for service in the field during the two Kaffir Wars. He was mentioned in general orders

---

* Written and illustrated from original documents and memoranda, and a photograph, left by Colonel Wright and kindly placed at the authors' disposal by his executor, Mr. Octavius Leigh-Clare, M.P. for the Eccles Division of Lancashire, afterwards Vice-Chancellor of the Duchy of Lancaster.

† "Promotion to major for service in the field was antedated 18 months in order that I might have the benefit of that rank for services I had performed whilst in command of a field force as a captain."—Note in the handwriting of Colonel Wright

by command of the Queen and Duke of Wellington, as Commander-in-Chief, for his conduct as senior surviving officer at the wreck of the *Birkenhead*, and received a pension for distinguished service. Again we find him mentioned in general orders by Sir George Cathcart for having constructed a road across the Eilands Mountain for the passage of the force under Sir George's command on the Berea Expedition; and he was specially thanked by the Secretary of State for the Colonies in 1853, on the conclusion of his duties as Commissioner for Frontier Affairs.

As commandant of Eiland's Post, Captain Wright, as he then was, and the forces under him, experienced stirring times in those eventful days of frontier warfare in South Africa. The natives were active and fearless, and gave them little rest. A general order issued from headquarters, Fort Beaufort, in July, 1852, for instance, recounts how, while several columns directed to march on the Waterkloof were concentrating, the rebel bands of Uithaalder's Hottentots made a bold demonstration to attack Eiland's Post, "which," says Sir George Cathcart, "was ably defeated by the judicious and soldierlike dispositions made by Captain Wright."

At last, after a long stay in South Africa, "the Reserve Battalion 91st Argyleshire Regiment" was ordered to return home, "with every prospect of being speedily employed in the Crimea." Apart from its excellent work on the eastern frontier, the regiment had won the respect and high regard of the civil inhabitants of the Colony. The Commander of the Forces, Sir James Jackson, in a general order, expressed his reluctance at losing a corps which had served with so much credit and gallantry, and had rendered such essential benefit to the frontier districts. In parting with it with regret, he wished Major Wright ("whom he has found a valuable officer") and his officers and veteran soldiers all happiness and success. Seventy-eight of the men took their discharge, preferring to remain in the Colony. The rest of the regiment embarked at Algoa Bay for England on board the steam frigate *Penelope*.* Before they left they were the

* This was one of the ships in which Captain Salmond served, on the West Coast of Africa, before joining the *Birkenhead*.

THE CAREER OF COLONEL WRIGHT, C.B. 145

recipients of a warmly-worded address signed by nearly all the inhabitants of Fort Beaufort.

The harassing and extremely arduous duties imposed upon you during the last two most obstinate and determined wars which have devastated this country [said the signatories], and the intrepid and inflexible manner in which those duties have invariably been performed by your brave regiment, have been such as will ever lead us to refer to them with feelings of extreme gratitude.

They also expressed thankfulness to the regiment for providing for the safety of their wives and families by allowing the regimental quarters to be used as a place of refuge for them "at a period when this town was threatened with a combined attack of our traitorous enemies." Major Wright replied to the address in the name of the officers, non-commissioned officers and men of the regiment.

It is now fifteen years [he said] since the 91st Regiment made its appearance in Fort Beaufort, and from that period to the present time all the officers and men in the regiment have exerted themselves to the utmost to do their duty to their country, not the least part of which duty was the protection of the lives and property of the inhabitants of the district of Fort Beaufort, and other parts of the frontier.

An address was also received from the inhabitants of the city of Grahamstown and its vicinity, speaking appreciatively of the services of the regiment on the frontier. This address is noteworthy for an interesting allusion it contained to Major Wright and the *Birkenhead*.

During the eventful period referred to, it has fallen to your lot, sir, to take a prominent part in one of the most awful occurrences within the memory of man. We allude to the melancholy loss of H.M.S. *Birkenhead* off Danger Point, on this coast. The heroic fortitude exhibited by you on that occasion, and the high Military discipline which your character and influence enabled you to maintain, was then, and still is, the admiration of all to whom the fearful events of that night became known. To the heroism and discipline then displayed by you and by those under your command must be attributed (under Providence) the fact that ALL on board that ill-fated ship did not share the fate of those who perished on that memorable night.

The signatories declared they should feel a lively interest in the future of the regiment—

knowing, as we do from experience, that it is officered by gentlemen possessed of the highest Military qualifications, and that the men whom they command are conspicuous for their orderly and soldierlike conduct.

In his reply to this address Major Wright refers to the fact that he has the honour to command the regiment in the absence of Lieut.-Colonel Yarborough "owing to wounds received whilst leading the 91st against your enemies." He replies modestly to the reference to the *Birkenhead*.

I can but make slight allusion to that part of your address relating to the melancholy event of the loss of H.M.S. *Birkenhead*. I thank you for your commendations of myself, which I cannot apply; but I acknowledge the interposition of that Power which was on that occasion, and ever is, watchful over us.

The address from the citizens of Grahamstown was presented while the regiment was actually on its way to the coast. The corps, or what was left of it, all told 294 strong, had bivouacked at Botha's Hill, eight miles east of Grahamstown. On the morning of departure it entered the town at Dundas Bridge, and headed by the drums and fifes of the 12th Regiment, also a *Birkenhead* corps, was played to the Drostdy Ground. Here the whole of the troops in garrison were drawn up, and on the arrival of the 91st it was inspected by General Jackson, after which it resumed its march, accompanied by Sir James and his staff, the 12th Regiment, and a detachment of the Cape Mounted Rifles. At the eastern entrance of Howison's Poort the escort formed in line and presented arms, and the 91st moved off amid cheers and the playing of "Auld Lang Syne" by the Cape Corps' band. The whole march was a veritable triumphal procession, so popular were the men of the 91st. The inhabitants had not done with them yet, for they waited on them in the middle of the pass, where a halt was called for tiffin, and the address was here presented by Messrs. G. Wood and R. Godlonton, members of the Legislative Council. It is recorded of the ceremony that Major Wright, standing in the centre of the circle formed, made his reply "in an unassuming, soldierlike tone of voice." There was much cheering, and the final leave-taking was of a quite unusually affecting kind. One can well imagine the emotion of the men and their gallant leader on quitting for ever

City July 14. 52. Paris

My dear Girardot

In the event of my wishing
to make use of your evidence
on the subject touching our
any objection I elicit where I
was at the time the supposed
club of the "Birkenhead" has
disappearing below the surface
of the Sea.

Edwd Wright
Capt H M 91st

Edwd Girardot
43rd Reg Lt.
R. Matoun.

COPY IN CAPTAIN WRIGHT'S HANDWRITING OF QUESTION CONCERNING THE WRECK WHICH HE ADDRESSED
TO LIEUTENANT GIRARDOT; AND LIEUTENANT GIRARDOT'S REPLY, MARKED BY CAPTAIN WRIGHT

THE CAREER OF COLONEL WRIGHT, C.B. 147

scenes which, in spite of countless perils and hardships, had from the associations of years and friendships formed become dear to them. But for a desire to face the Russians in the Crimea, we are assured that many more of them would have remained behind as settlers in the Colony.

Before Major Wright bids adieu to South Africa we must note some interesting correspondence concerning him with which his stay in the Colony is identified. First there is a letter he received out there from Colonel Parkenham (afterwards Lord Longford), who was acting at the time as Military secretary to the general commanding at Malta. It is dated April 24th, 1852, and expresses the pride felt by all soldiers at the conduct displayed on the *Birkenhead*.

> I believe [writes Colonel Parkenham] that all the Army have heard the sad account of the loss of the *Birkenhead* with the same feeling of admiration of the coolness and courage shown by those on board, and by none more than by you. I can answer for the garrison of Malta. General and Mrs. Ellise beg me to tell you how glad they are to hear that you have escaped, and with honour, from a scene where so many good men perished. You will not require me to assure you that I cordially concur with them. We all hope that you may obtain the promotion which Sir W. Napier so justly claims for you.

The next correspondence relates to an unfounded statement which appears to have been made in some quarter to the effect that Captain Wright deserted the ship! Such a misconception would have been impossible at any time in the case of anyone at all acquainted with the circumstances; but Captain Wright, with characteristic thoroughness, determined to kill the lie at once, and he accordingly, on July 14th, 1852, wrote from Eiland's Post to Lieutenant Girardot, of the 43rd Light Infantry, who stood with him to the last on the poop of the *Birkenhead*, asking:

> In the event of my wishing to make use of your testimony on the subject, would you have any objection to state where I was at the time the poop deck of the *Birkenhead* was disappearing below the surface of the ocean?

Lieutenant Girardot replied promptly and with a soldierly straightness from Keis Kama Hoek, where he was stationed:

> I am quite surprised to see by your letter that anyone has had the

face to say* that you deserted the ship, and you may call on me at any time you please to prove that you remained till the poop, the last part of the ship that remained above water, went down.

The canard must have died almost at its birth, for happily we hear nothing further of it anywhere.

Of real importance was the communication which Captain Wright received towards the close of the same year from the Military authorities at home. This announced to him the well-earned grant of a Distinguished Service pension, and the original document, bearing the signature of the Commander-in-Chief, which is copied below, is interesting as supplying the only evidence of direct and tangible recognition bestowed on any surviving officer of the wreck. †

HORSE GUARDS, *25th August*, 1852.

SIR,—I have the satisfaction to acquaint you that Her Majesty has been pleased to approve of your receiving from the Grant for Distinguished Service an allowance of £100 per annum from the 20th inst.

In order that this reward may lose none of the value which was considered to attach to the publication in the Army List of the names of the officers holding garrison appointments, it is intended to insert in the Army List, under the head of Garrisons, the names of officers who have received rewards for distinguished service, so that your name may be kept as constantly before the public as if a garrison appointment had been conferred upon you.

You will receive a communication from the Secretary-at-War as to mode in which this allowance is to be paid to you.

I have the honour to be, Sir, your most obedient, humble servant,

WELLINGTON.

CAPTAIN E. W. C. WRIGHT, 91st Foot.

It was with much satisfaction to himself, he announced, that Major D. Forbes, commanding the 91st Regiment at Fort Fordyce, inserted in battalion orders of December 5th following a copy of a letter he had received " conveying to Captain Edward W. C. Wright, of the Battalion, a high

---

* In the accompanying facsimile reproduction it will be seen that the words " has had the face to say" have been crossed out, and the sentence made to read " has said."

† Colonel Wright was created a Companion of the Bath eighteen years later; but, as will be shown, the services he rendered in the meantime well entitled him to that distinction.

Apsley House,
25th August 1852.

Sir,

I have the satisfaction of announcing to you the honor of the Queen having been pleased to approve of your having received a Pension of the Distinguished Service, to that from the Public as a Contribution to enable one to keep up Constantly before the Public eye a Lasting Acknowledgment that this Corps of the Army has received a Commendation from the Sovereign at the Head of the Country. It is to this that alone is to be referred the anxiety of the Army to attain to the List of Candidates to attain to the same position in the Army List of the Officers holding such appointment. It is intended to enter in the Army List under the Head

I have the honor
Your most obedient
humble Servant
Wellington

Captain S.V.C. Wright
91st Foot.

mark of Her Majesty's approbation for his distinguished service."

Next year Captain Wright heard from a *Birkenhead* survivor, James Jeffery, the purser's steward, whose lot he did much to alleviate at the time of the wreck. Jeffery was then serving as boatswain on H.M. steam frigate *Tiger*, and the letter, which is dated Malta Harbour, May 9th, 1853, acknowledges a remittance sent to him by Captain Wright and other acts of kindness.

With much pleasure and thankfulness for your kind consideration for me [says the writer], I take the liberty of addressing to you an answer which I hope you will condescend to receive from one who received so many little comforts from your hands at a time when so much in need—that glass of wine you had so much trouble to preserve for me, a covering for my naked feet while travelling round the rocks, and a number of little things you no doubt think it nonsense of me to mention; but at such a time [and] place, and [in] our deplorable situation, even now too horrible to think of, come feelings of the greatest love and respect.

This is the wording of a letter which speaks the promptings of a grateful heart.

You of course heard some time since [it goes on] of our arrival, court-martial and result, &c., in England. The officers are distributed to [their] respective ships, Dr. Culhane on board [the] *Vulcan*, steam troopship. Mr. Freshfield was appointed to her, but he went sick and to the hospital—did not like another iron ship, I suppose. The Gunner has his promotion, as well as the Engineer, and the Sergeant of Marines has a commission, as I have heard since I left England, and poor me received £2 13s. for my chest of clothes, [worth] close upon £40, as well as £60 value of private things for a few men at the Cape who I was asked to oblige when first we went there (2nd Queen's).

Jeffery's information as to promotion and a commission was of course wrong, but there is much to be said for the hardships of "poor me," especially in the light of what follows.

I have saved myself, thank God, so I must put up with it. My wife heard I was drowned by a letter from the *Castor* flagship. Rather a disagreeable note. She was surprised when she received a letter from me, but it was a very agreeable one.

The writer passes on to other things.

I am most happy to hear your name mentioned in the papers for £100 per annum for your noble conduct at the wreck. I hope it is true, and glad I am to think that the Admiralty are acquainted with those that merit their rewards. There is one did not deserve what he had or has got—that is, one of the engineers. I was very ill while on the passage to England—33 days under the surgeon's hands, and they had no bed or blanket for me or any one else belonging to the *Birkenhead*.

Jeffery here makes an interesting statement respecting Captain Salmond's watch.

I was often at the Captain's widow's, and I gave her the watch, which was the only thing saved from her [the *Birkenhead*] belonging to Captain Salmond.* I hope Dr. Bowen received his plate correct, as they took it from me, which I believe I informed you of, as well as those pieces of linen we had so much labour to bring with us.

The writer, in conclusion, wishes Captain Wright "every success on the battlefield, and good health, with a quick return from the Cape." He adds by way of postscript, "I am very nervous even now in rough weather at sea. I should like a situation on shore, if possible, and under Government." Poor Jeffery's experience of the sea was altogether unfortunate. According to a statement by Sergeant Kilkeary, made on another page, he had previously been wrecked in the *Thunderbolt*, and after the *Birkenhead* disaster he was again shipwrecked in the Black Sea. He died at an infirm old age in London.

Finally in this South African correspondence we have a letter sent home by Sir George Grey, Governor of the Cape of Good Hope.

GOVERNMENT HOUSE, CAPE TOWN, *August 3rd*, 1855.

MY DEAR TULLOCH,—At the moment I am going overland to Natal, Major Wright, of the 91st, has called to wish me good-bye. He sails for England on Sunday. I know not yet (my despatches being missing) whether or not they will send me the pensioners I have applied for, but suppose they will. If you send them out, I should wish to say that you could get no better man in the world, that I know, than Major Wright, either to direct in chief the whole plan, or to carry out any part of it. No appointment, I am sure, would be more advantageous to the service than his. He knows the country well, is a first-rate officer with a good service pension, surveys, is devoted to his profession, and has an excellent manner both with men and officers. If you send the pensioners

* Mr. Freshfield, the ship's clerk, in the letter he wrote home to Mrs. Salmond informing her of the wreck, mentions that Captain Salmond handed his watch to the purser's steward, who was saved.

FACSIMILE OF BATTALION ORDER CONVEYING TO CAPTAIN WRIGHT THE QUEEN'S APPROBATION OF HIS SERVICE AT THE WRECK

you end the Kaffir War—that is, in a few years. All is quiet here at present, and matters are going on well.—Truly yours, G. GREY.

The pensioners spoken of were required for mounted police purposes at the Cape, and this arm of the service was reorganised on the lines suggested with excellent results.

Major Wright returned to England with a record of meritorious service which, working zealously at the profession he was so much attached to, he quickly enhanced. Promoted to be lieutenant-colonel, he was appointed Assistant-Quartermaster-General to Major-General Breton, commanding the South-Western District, and in that capacity superintended the transit of troops and stores between this country and the Crimea during the war with Russia. The duties were as arduous as they were important, and that they were thoroughly well performed is abundantly testified. The work included the embarkation and disembarkation of 185,000 men, 7,000 horses, and war stores, and all this, as expressed in general orders, was completed without a single accident or mistake, or any one thing having gone wrong.

On the disembarkation of the Army of the East, consisting of 6,400 men and 4,500 horses, besides guns, stores, and other things, Lieut.-Colonel Wright was specially thanked in the highest quarters.

Of my Assistant-Quartermaster-General [said Major-General Breton in reporting the result to the Quartermaster-General] I can speak in the highest terms. Upon him fell, through the illness of Lieut.-Colonel Dalgety, the general arrangements from the date of the arrival of the very first ship. Eminently qualified for the office from his excellent temper, clear judgment, patience under difficulties, and an application to details occupying his attention from sunrise till late at night—often, also, nearly the whole day through (whatever the weather might be), at the Dockyard Railway Station or in his boat visiting the ships—he never once gave in, sorely tried as he often was. I have dwelt the more strongly upon Lieut.-Colonel Wright's good qualities, as, I candidly admit, without him my difficulties would have been very great, and in all probability the transit of the troops would have experienced many untoward checks, whereas, through his able arrangements, not a man has been mis-sent, though from one ship alone men of no less than 45 corps were landed, and in a single day men from 60 different corps disposed of, nor has any one thing gone wrong.

Bravo! one is tempted to exclaim. How one sees in all this the brave and energetic senior surviving officer of the *Birkenhead*—working and encouraging, cheerful under difficulties, knowing no fatigue, with one object only steadily in view—his duty! No wonder he made headway in the profession he adorned. He took it seriously.

Major-General Breton's report was made on August 28th, 1856. The Quartermaster-General replied that he had laid it before the Duke of Cambridge, the Commander-in-Chief, to whom it had given great pleasure, and the Major-General was requested to express to Lieut.-Colonel Wright "how much His Royal Highness appreciates the services rendered on this duty." Admiral Sir George Seymour, Commander-in-Chief at Portsmouth, wrote to General Breton—

on the conclusion of a service which is so creditable to all concerned in its execution. The manner in which Lieut.-Colonel Wright carried out the details with which he was charged had attracted my observation as well as your own, and I have no doubt will be recognised by those at the head of the department to which he belongs.

In district orders which he issued on August 30th, Major-General Breton expressed—

his high sense of the unremitting zeal and attention with which all the necessary arrangements have been carried out by the staff, particularly by Lieut.-Colonel Wright, A.Q.M.-General, upon whom the most material arrangements fell.

Since the middle of the previous May, more than 64,000 men had passed through Portsmouth without accident or delay. In a single day more than 7,000 men were disposed of, and during a period of heavy work and many difficulties the duties of the district had been admirably performed. But General Breton was not content with even this testimony. He wrote the subject of it a personal letter, the sincerity of which must impress all who read it.

My dear Wright,—

Although your character as a working officer is pretty well known so far as my opinion of it may weigh at the Horse Guards, you may like to have a line under my hand expressive of my entire satisfaction with all you have done for me during the last two years of my serious responsibility in the details of a command in which a very slight mistake might have been productive of an unpleasant result.

To a certain extent a general officer must necessarily be dependent upon his staff. But although responsible for their acts, it is next to impossible he could carry on his various duties if obliged to interfere in the minutiæ of the several departments. Under the most favourable circumstances, also, there must be an occasional difference of opinion in which he will naturally like to have his own way. What a weight, then, is removed from the mind of one so fortunate as I have been in yourself and Nelson—working on as we have done, and through a trying period, without a word of argument or mistake of any kind. Feeling safe in trusting you both, I have experienced no anxiety in the complications connected with that most difficult of all duties, the transit of troops. I need only add that all who have had anything to do with you have spoken in praise of your temper and patience, sorely tried as both must often have been. My best wishes for your rise in the department will always attend you, and glad should I be to have it in my power to promote your interest in any way.—Yours very sincerely,

HENRY W. BRETON.

LONDON, *August 16th, '57.*

This kind and sensible letter reflects credit equally upon the writer and the receiver of it. Promotion to the rank of colonel came in due course. A district order by Sir J. Yorke Scarlett, K.C.B.,* then commanding the South-Western District, dated August 23rd, 1858, "whilst congratulating Colonel Wright on the promotion his services have so well earned," stated that the Major-General—

cannot but be sensible that he is deprived in his district of an officer whom it will be very difficult to replace. The duties of the district during Colonel Wright's tenure of office on the staff have not only included the usual routine business of a very considerable body of troops belonging to the district, but also the embarkation and disembarkation of upwards of 180,000 men and 7,000 horses, and the arrangements necessary for despatching them from Portsmouth and receiving them from other stations by rail. Not a single accident has occurred, nor a man nor horse been mis-sent, or any sort of unnecessary delay taken place, owing to the admirable arrangements of Colonel Wright, combined with his instructions from headquarters. Vessels at Spithead have been visited in all weathers and at all hours when necessary, and no pains spared by Colonel Wright to ensure by due inspection the orders of Government for the comfort of the troops on board being carried out and every

---

* The General who led the famous charge of the "Three Hundred" at Balaclava.

Abstract from record of service. Col. E. W. Wright obtained a Commission without purchase from R. M[ilitary] College in 1832.
Lieut. by purchase
Captⁿ. do
Bᵗ. Major For Service in the Field
Bᵗ. Lᵗ. Colonel. — do — do.
Colonel. Length of service.
Campaign. In all the operations during the Kafir Wars 1846.47. 1852 & 53.
Commanded a Field Force of Cavalry Artillery and Infantry during the Year 1852 and part of 53. Twice mentioned in General orders for successful operations against the Enemy.
Commanded the Fort Beaufort District and 91ˢᵗ. Regᵗ. for 2 Years on Frontier. C. G. Hope.
Mentioned in General orders and despatches by.
Majr. Genl. Hare. Comdᵍ. Forces in the Fields 1846.47.
Sir Peregrine Maitlands. Govr. & Comdᵍ. in Chief 47.
Sir Harry Smith ———— do do 52.53.
Sir George Cathcart—. do do 52.53—
Sir James Jackson ———— do 54.55.
Medal for Service in the Field 1846.47. 52 & 53.
Pension for "distinguished Service".
Mentioned in General orders by Command of the Queen & Duke of Wellington Comdᵍ. in Chief. as senior officer on the occasion of the wreck of H.M.S. "Birkenhead" off Danger Point, C. G. Hope.
Mentioned in General orders by Sir George Cathcart Govr. & Comdᵍ. in Chief C. G. Hope for having constructed a road across the Islands mountain for the passage of the Force under his Command on the Berea Expedition. Specially thanked by Sectᵨ. of State for the Colonies in 1853. on conclusion of duties as Commissioner for Frontier affairs.
Thanked by. H.R.H. the F.M. Comdᵍ. in Chief 28 Aug. 1856 also by Majr. Genl. Breton & Sir J. Yorke Scarlett Comdᵍ. S.W. Dist. and by Admiral Sir George Seymour Naval Comdᵍ. in Chief on the

> Completion of the Embarkation and disembarkation of 185,000 men, 7,000 horses & War Stores during the War in the Crimea as expressed in General orders "Without a single accident or mistake, or any one thing having gone wrong."
> Assn. Dr. Mr. Gnl. S.W. District for 3 Years.
> Commanded a Depôt Bat. 5 — -
> Passed an Examination at the Senior Dept. R. M. Staff College, and obtained a certificate of the highest Class.
> Dept Inspector Field Ac.d Inspector General Reserve Force 5 Years.
> Full pay service 38 Years — Half pay, None
>
> E. H. C. Wright.
> Col.
>
> Promotion to Major for "Service in the Field" were antedated 18 months in order that I might have the benefit of that rank for services I had performed whilst in command of a Field Force as a Captain.

FACSIMILE OF COLONEL WRIGHT'S RECORD OF SERVICE IN HIS OWN
HANDWRITING

convenience secured to them. In the zealous and uncompromising performance of these duties Colonel Wright has, by his temper and discretion, gained the confidence of all with whom he has had intercourse, and of none more than the general officers under whom he has served.

More could not be said. Colonel Wright's removal was genuinely regretted. "I am sorry to hear we are likely to lose you from Portsmouth," wrote Sir G. Seymour from Admiralty House on July 1st. "You will take with you our best wishes for every success attending you."

A letter possessing great interest received by Colonel Wright before this time, that of Sir William Napier on the subject of the *Birkenhead*, is included in an earlier chapter. While at Portsmouth Colonel Wright was honoured with an invitation to meet Her Majesty Queen Victoria at a time when the Emperor and Empress of the French were on a visit to Osborne. The invitation is dated August 6th, 1857, and it will be seen from the memorandum he made upon it that this was not the first occasion upon which Colonel Wright came in contact with Royalty.

> Received this the day after I had shown the Queen and Royal children over the *Lady Jocelyn* and *James Baines* troopships, when Her Majesty desired me to tell the children how a ship was lost and some of those on board saved.

To tell them "how a ship was lost and some of those on board saved." What a story! What a teller! What an audience! One conjures up the scene, a picture needing but the artist's brush to make it live again; listens almost to the words, and turns instinctively to those imperishable sentences* which, with the vision of it all so fresh and clear, were penned for the world for ever. Colonel Wright was Assistant-Quartermaster-General in the South-Western District for three years, and commander of a depôt battalion for five years. He passed an examination at the Royal Military Staff College and obtained a certificate of the highest class. He was Deputy-Inspector-General and Acting-Inspector-General of Reserve Forces for seven years. His full-pay service was thirty-eight years; half-pay, none. Truly a proud record. He died at 25, Walpole Street, Chelsea, in the autumn of 1871, if not bowed with years, possessed of honours, not the least of which was conferred upon him a year previously, when on September 2nd, 1870, *The London Gazette* announced that the Queen had been graciously pleased to give orders for the appointment of Colonel Wright "to be an Ordinary Member of the Military Division of the Third Class, or Companions of the Most Hon. Order of the Bath."

In the colonnade of Chelsea Hospital is a memorial brass

---

* Of the official Military Report on the loss of the *Birkenhead*. The visit of the Queen and Royal children, accompanied by Colonel Wright, to the *Lady Jocelyn* and *James Baines* troopships is described in Chapter VI.

FACSIMILE OF INVITATION TO OSBORNE, INSCRIBED WITH THE RECORD OF AN INTERESTING EVENT IN CAPTAIN WRIGHT'S HANDWRITING

THE CAREER OF COLONEL WRIGHT, C.B.

to Colonel Wright, erected in 1873 by his brother officers. It adjoins the *Birkenhead* Monument, and tells of the service, reward, and promotion of this gallant officer.

> To the Memory of
> COLONEL EDWARD W. C. WRIGHT, C.B.,
> late 91st Highlanders
> and Deputy-Inspector of Reserve Forces,
> who died 26th August, 1871, aged 57.
> Captain Wright was the senior
> surviving Officer of the Troops
> embarked in Her Majesty's
> Ship *Birkenhead* wrecked off
> the Cape of Good Hope on
> the 26th of Feby., 1852. For his
> distinguished service on this
> occasion he was promoted to
> the rank of Major and awarded
> a good service pension. He was also
> engaged in the Kaffir Wars of 1846-47
> and 1852-53, for which he
> was granted the medal and promoted
> for service in the Field to the rank of Lt.-Colonel.
> This Tablet is erected by his brother Officers.
> MDCCCLXXIII.

All honour to his name! It is good to remember that such a man won just appreciation in our Army.

CHAPTER XIV

CAPTAIN SALMOND'S PATHETIC END

<small>A brave man struggling in the storms of Fate.—POPE.</small>

ON the eve of departure from Simon's Bay, February 25th, the Commander of the *Birkenhead* wrote home to his family at Gosport, Hants, a letter which, in the light of subsequent events, is of tragic interest. That letter the reader is here privileged to have before him. Below are given the first three pages of it—the fourth is of too private and sacred a nature to be published; and these pages, with the signature brought over from the last page, are also reproduced in *facsimile*.

SIMON'S BAY, CAPE OF GOOD HOPE,
Wednesday, 25th February, 1852.

. . . We arrived here on Monday at noon, just one day longer than my last passage, viz. 46 days. The Commodore expressed himself well pleased. I am as busy now as Old Nick, coaling, watering, provisioning, and getting all ready to be off to-night with my troops, and about 30 horses in addition, for Buffalo mouth. I hope to [be] back on or about the 10th of March, when I am to proceed to England, so that if all goes well, please God, I may be with you about the end of April; but I shall leave Freshfield to give you all the news. I leave him behind to recruit at the Commodore's—poor fellow, he has been very ill—so that he will be able to give you [more] information than I can about our movements. The packet will leave this about the 12th of March, but she has not arrived yet. You must write the old Admiral, for I have not time, and give him all the news. Young Rolt goes to Buffalo with me, with some others. He has bought three horses, which I take for him. Others, again, I land at Algoa Bay on my way up. The Commodore tells me I shall be full of passengers going home. . . .

R. SALMOND.

"I shall leave Freshfield to give you all the news." There was something fatally prophetic in those words. "All the

CAPTAIN ROBERT SALMOND, R.N.

(From a portrait painted some years before the wreck)

CAPTAIN SALMOND'S PATHETIC END

news" was indeed sent home by John Freshfield, the Commander's devoted clerk, but it was not of the kind in contemplation on February 25th. To Mr. Freshfield fell the sad task of informing Mrs. Salmond of the disaster to the troopship and of her husband's death. The letter was despatched from Admiralty House, Simon's Bay, on March 2nd. It is a pathetic document, as the reader will see.

> However painful may be the task, still I think it a duty imperative on me to inform you of the total loss of the *Birkenhead*, involving a fearful sacrifice of human life. Most providentially, when we arrived here, I was not well, and the Commodore invited me to stay with him whilst the *Birkenhead* went to the Buffalo. The *Birkenhead* sailed from this bay at 6 p.m. on the 25th February, and eight hours after she ran on a shoal off Danger Point, and in twenty minutes broke up and went down. Upwards of 400 souls were drowned; amongst them, I am deeply grieved to say, poor Mr. Salmond was one. Mr. Brodie, Mr. Speer, Mr. Davis, and Mr. Whyham all perished. The Commander remained to the last, and was taken down when the poop sank. He had given his watch to the purser's steward, who was saved.* The total number saved is 192. A poor lady who has only been married nine weeks lost her husband,† and, I am much afraid, is left quite unprovided for. It certainly is the most melancholy thing I ever knew, and please God, I hope never to have such a task again as the present. I had promised poor Captain Salmond I would write to you, but I little thought at the time what fearful news it would contain. I trust, my dear Mrs. Salmond, you will give me credit for feeling most deeply both with and for you under this dreadful bereavement. Poor Mr. Salmond had been always most kind to me, and had it not been for his kindness in asking the Commodore to allow me to remain behind, I should most probably have shared the same fate. The survivors have been brought in here, and are on board the *Castor*. The Commodore has ordered me to England in the mail packet *Propontis*; the others are to go home in the *Amazon*. On my arrival I shall proceed immediately to London, and I have no doubt but I shall be ordered on board the *Victory* to make out pay-books for the remainder. I will call on you directly, and when in London will call on the agent, and I trust you will make use of me in any way that I can be of any service.

Captain ROBERT SALMOND, the brave but unfortunate Commander of the *Birkenhead*, became a master in the Royal

---

* James Jeffery, who duly delivered the watch to Mrs. Salmond. See letter in Colonel Wright's notice.

† Ensign Metford, 6th Royals.

Navy on August 17th, 1838, his first ship being the *Hydra* steamer, in which he served under Commander Anthony W. Milward in the Mediterranean, and afterwards on the North American and West Indies Station. In 1843 Mr. Salmond was in the *Penelope* steam frigate, Commodore W. Jones, on the West Coast of Africa; in 1845 he joined the *Retribution* steam frigate, Captain Stephen Lushington, attached to the Channel Squadron; and he then went with the *Vengeance*, of 84 guns (date of commission October 15th, 1846), to the Mediterranean, still with Captain Lushington, who was succeeded in the command by the Right Hon. the Earl of Hardwicke,* under whom Mr. Salmond continued to serve. His commission to the *Birkenhead* as Master-Commander is dated February 8th, 1851. Shortly before the *Birkenhead* sank, on that fatal February night a year later, he spoke to Dr. Bowen on the poop, and he was at the wheel with Mr. Speer, the second master, when the poop went down. When last seen alive he was swimming from the sternpost of the ship to a portion of the forecastle deck which was floating about twenty yards from the main body of the wreck; something struck him on the back of the head, and he never rose again.

Captain Salmond came of a distinguished Naval stock, whose deeds upon the sea, dating back to Elizabethan days, won them renown in more modern times. His father was mortally wounded in the American War of Independence in 1776. His four brothers all died while on active Naval service. One of them, William Salmond, was killed in the action between the *Java* and *Constitution* in 1812. Another, John Salmond, was wounded while serving under Nelson at Copenhagen. A third, Peter Salmond, died while in command of H.M.S. *Asia*, after the battle of Navarino in 1827. Captain Robert Salmond had two sons. The eldest was killed on duty at sea before he was fifteen years of age. Truly the death-toll of this family of heroes was a heavy one! The second son died in the 50th anniversary year of the loss of the *Birkenhead*, and is

---

* Author of *Our Naval Position and Policy*, containing a reference to the discipline on board the *Birkenhead*, which, with comments thereon, appears on another page.

FACSIMILE OF LETTER WRITTEN BY CAPTAIN SALMOND ON THE EVE OF THE WRECK

CAPTAIN SALMOND'S PATHETIC END

spoken of on a later page. The accompanying portrait of Captain Salmond is from an oil painting done by a messmate some years before the wreck, and preserved by the Gofton-Salmond family.

OTHER "BIRKENHEAD" OFFICERS

In the account we are able to give of other *Birkenhead* officers, it will be noted as a singular and interesting circumstance that Dr. Culhane and Mr. C. K. Renwick subsequently sailed together as surgeon and chief engineer in the *Chesapeake* screw steam frigate, of 51 guns, in which they saw service on the East Indies and China Station. The *Chesapeake* was successor to the ship of the same name which was captured on June 1st, 1813, by the *Shannon*, Captain Broke. She was wooden built and launched in 1852, length 212 feet, breadth 50 feet, tonnage 2,358; the heaviest of her 51 guns was a 68-pounder, and she carried 530 men. It will thus be seen that she was a larger vessel than her famous predecessor, the American frigate, which had 48 guns, the heaviest a 32-pounder, was of 1,622 tons, length 160 feet and breadth 48 feet 8 inches, and carried 315 men. Models of these ships were shown at the Royal Naval Exhibition of 1891.

Mr. WILLIAM BRODIE, the Master of the *Birkenhead*, joined the Navy on December 19th, 1843. He was appointed Second Master of the *St. Vincent*, 120 guns, flagship at Plymouth, Captain Richard F. Rowley, his commission dating from January 6th, 1844. His next ship was the *Media*, steam sloop, serving in the East Indies under Commander Thos. H. Mason, the appointment dating from January 2nd, 1847. Afterwards he was attached to the *Fisgard*, of 42 guns, Commander Henry Eden, for special service at Woolwich, the date of the commission being December 3rd, 1850. Finally he was appointed Master of the *Birkenhead* on June 6th, 1851. Mr. Brodie was stated by one survivor of the wreck to have been killed while trying to clear the starboard paddle-box boat. According to Mr. Archbold, however, he was afterwards seen clinging to a truss of hay floating in the water.

Mr. ROWLAND B. RICHARDS, the young master's assistant,

who at the wreck got the women and children away in the second cutter and was in charge of the boats, was appointed Second Master on October 8th, 1852, and on December 11th following was commissioned to the *Resistance* troopship, 10 guns, Master-Commander Mauser Bradshaw, for particular service. His next ship was the *Oberon*, a 3-gun iron paddle-wheel steam vessel, Lieut.-Commander John O. Freeland, in the Mediterranean. Mr. Richards left the Navy at his own request in the latter part of 1856. He still held the rank of second master.

Mr. WILLIAM CULHANE, assistant-surgeon on the *Birkenhead*, who landed with the gig and carried the news of the wreck to Capetown, entered the Navy in 1847, his appointment being dated May 12th, and in the October following he was commissioned to the *Bellerophon*, Captain Robert L. Baynes, for particular service, which he continued in the *Birkenhead* from February 8th, 1851. After the wreck his next ship was the *Vulcan*, 6-gun screw steam troopship, Commander Edward P. B. Van Donop, to which he was commissioned on June 16th, 1852. In 1854 he joined the *Scourge*, a 6-gun paddle-wheel steamship, and sailed for the West Coast of Africa under Commodore John Adams; and in 1855 he was on the same coast in the *Minx*, an iron screw steam gun-vessel, Lieut.-Commander Richard H. Roe. Promotion to surgeon came in 1856, and on June 3rd, 1858, Dr. Culhane was commissioned to the *Chesapeake*, 51-gun screw steam frigate, as additional surgeon, on the East Indies and China Station, under Commodore Edgell and Rear-Admiral Hope, C.B. It was on the *Chesapeake* that Dr. Culhane again became a messmate of Mr. Renwick, who was serving on the frigate as chief engineer. Dr. Culhane died in England in the spring of 1860. The accompanying portrait of Dr. Culhane, the only one extant, was kindly lent for this work by Dr. O'Mahoney, of Sutton, Co. Dublin, a near relative of the Naval surgeon. In a letter written in 1904 the Rev. Stephen Culhane, C.C., of Ballingarry, Co. Limerick, a more distant kinsman of Dr. Culhane, after reading the earlier edition of this book, notes a circumstance which generally has been lost sight of—

SURGEON WM. CULHANE, R.N.

(From a photo)

namely, the absence of any clergyman on board the *Birkenhead*. He also speaks very moderately of Dr. Culhane and Colonel Girardot.

> I note with sorrow [he says] that a large number of the troops were Irish. Poor, poor boys! At that time the famine drove them from their homes in thousands. "*Quæ regio in terris nostri non plena laboris?*"* It is painful also to note that they had to go into eternity without ministration or encouragement from a clergyman of any religious persuasion. As far as Dr. Culhane's action is concerned, I think, under the circumstances, you deal fairly enough with him in leaving your readers to draw their own conclusions, and I for one would feel inclined to attach not too much importance to what an old man of 73 years remembered 50 years after.

At this time Miss Kate Culhane, a first cousin of Dr. Culhane, was living at Limerick; Mrs. Dillon, another first cousin, was residing with her nephew, Dr. J. F. Barrett, at Highgate; and Dr. F. W. S. Culhane, M.R.C.S., was at Glin House, Hastings. The family came from Glin, Co. Limerick. The father of Dr. F. W. S. Culhane was at one time in partnership at Croydon with his first cousin, Dr. Morgan Culhane, uncle of Dr. William Culhane, of the *Birkenhead*.

Mr. C. K. RENWICK, first-class assistant-engineer on the *Birkenhead*, as already seen, sank with the ship, was picked up by the gig, and afterwards was transferred to the first cutter, of which he took charge. He was appointed third-class engineer on June 8th, 1852, so that his promotion followed soon after the wreck; and it was speedily continued, for in the following year we find him commissioned as chief engineer of the *Phœnix*, 8-gun screw steam sloop, Commander Edward A. Inglefield, for service in the Arctic Seas, the warrant bearing date April 4th, 1853. In 1856 Mr. Renwick was appointed chief engineer to the *Chesapeake*, 51 guns, screw steam frigate, at Chatham, which, in July, 1857, was commissioned for service on the East Indies and China Station, first under command of Commodore Harry E. Edgell, and afterwards under that of Rear-Admiral James Hope,

* "What region of the earth is not full of our works?" Said by Æneas of the Trojans. Great Britain might justly, as the writer indicates, assume this as her motto.

C.B. He transferred in 1859 (commission dated August 30th) to the *Fury*, 6-gun paddle-wheel steam sloop, Commander W. A. J. Heath, on the same station; and he served subsequently as chief engineer on the *Majestic*, of 80 guns, coastguard ship at Liverpool, under his old commander, now Captain E. A. Inglefield, his commission here dating March 27th, 1861. Mr. Renwick died in the early part of 1864.

Mr. BENJAMIN BARBER, assistant-engineer third class on board the *Birkenhead*, was in the engine-room when the ship struck, and stayed there with the other engineers till the water rose and put out the fires. He reached the shore on a piece of wreckage * after twelve hours' immersion in the sea. Mr. Barber continued in the Naval Service for twenty-five years after the loss of the *Birkenhead*. He had an eventful career. Born on April 29th, 1829, he entered the Navy as an engineer apprentice at Woolwich in December, 1842. His first ship was the *Gorgon*, Captain Sir Charles Hotham, and after completing his apprenticeship he was made third-class assistant-engineer in November, 1847. He was on board during the recovery of the ship from the beach at Monte Video, and was present at the destruction of the batteries at Obligade and all the operations in the Parana and Uruguay. He joined the *Birkenhead* under Captain Salmond in 1851, and after the wreck was promoted to second-class assistant-engineer in June, 1852. His ship was then the *Brisk*, Captain F. B. P. Seymour, from which he was invalided as the result of fever. His next service was with Captains A. Kynaston and F. Shortt in the *Spiteful*, which on October 17th, 1854, engaged the sea forts at Sevastopol and towed the *Rodney* off the ground under a heavy fire.

Mr. Barber was now promoted to first-class assistant-engineer, in which capacity he served in the *Royal Albert*, Captain R. W. Mends, 1855-6, and in the three following years he was engineer in charge of the *Ariel* under Captains A. F. Maxse and C. Bromby. On March 21st, 1861, he was appointed chief engineer of the *Tribune* frigate, of 31 guns, at Portsmouth, and subsequently he held the same

* See statement of Mr. Archbold, the gunner.

MR. BENJAMIN BARBER, CHIEF ENGINEER, R.N.
(From a photo)

CAPTAIN SALMOND'S PATHETIC END 165

post, dating from June 5th, 1863, on the *Salamander*, a sloop of 6 guns commanded by the Hon. John Carnegie on the Australian Station; the *Terrible*, a frigate of 19 guns, Captain W. H. W. Bennett, from May 22nd, 1869; and the *Doris*, a frigate of 24 guns, Captain W. H. Edye, from October 4th, 1872. In his discharge from the *Doris*, dated July 20th, 1874, Captain Edye wrote: "Mr. Barber has always shown great attention and zeal, and I regret that ill-health renders it necessary for him to leave the ship." Mr. Barber was placed on the retired list from June 1st, 1877. He was then residing at De Vaux Cottage, The Close, Salisbury; but he afterwards removed to Liverpool, where he died at 5, Pelham Grove, Sefton Park, on April 29th, 1882, the 53rd anniversary of his birthday, and was interred on May 3rd at St. James's Cemetery, below St. James's Mount, the site of the new cathedral. This work is indebted to Mrs. Barber for her husband's portrait in Naval uniform, and also for the valuable picture of the *Birkenhead* done by a brother officer of Mr. Barber's, showing the troopship as she actually appeared.

CHIEF OFFICER OF COASTGUARDS W. H. MATTHEWS

Among those saved from the wreck of the *Birkenhead* was William Henry Matthews, a second-class boy on board, whose escape from the doomed vessel was truly marvellous. He had, almost at the last moment, been sent below by a ship's officer to fetch an overcoat, and on returning found, to his horror, the hatchway battened down against him. He shouted loudly for help, and luckily his voice was heard and recognised above the tumult by a shipmate, who released him. It was only just in time, for immediately afterwards the ship sank. His subsequent rescue from a watery grave was almost equally wonderful. Being a good swimmer, he struck out in the direction of the boats, which were standing off at some distance. Fortunately he came up with the second cutter, containing the women and children, the crew of which ceased rowing and picked him up in response to the pleadings of the women, who wished him to be taken in on account of his youth. And so the boy's life was saved. Young Matthews and several of the soldiers were afterwards ordered to bale out water from the overladen boat, which was leaking badly—the soldiers, who still possessed their caps, using them for this purpose. These exertions helped to repel the cold during the thirteen hours they had to remain in their wet condition.

After serving afloat for some years, Wm. Matthews joined the Coastguard Service, in which he rose to the rank of chief officer.

The long and interesting career of this *Birkenhead* survivor commenced in 1849, when he joined H.M.S. *Illustrious* at Portsmouth. He came of a family of sailors, his four brothers and himself all entering the Navy, in which their father also served; and after leaving the Isle of Wight, where he was born at Fishbourne on May 4th, 1836, he spent his early boyhood days in Dorset. His father,* a Coastguard stationed last at Langton, Dorset, had some interesting tales to tell of engagements with smugglers in which he had taken part. These recitals no doubt fed William's youthful enthusiasm for a seafaring life. His elder brother Richard, after serving in the Russian War of 1854-5, died of fever on board the frigate *Impérieuse* in the Straits of Malacca in 1859, during a voyage to China. A younger brother, Joseph, lost his life when H.M. revenue cutter *Curlew* was run down by the London and Antwerp steamer *Baron Osy*, near the Mouse Light at the Nore, on April 23rd, 1857, upon which sad occasion Mr. William Shepherd, the commanding officer of the cutter, and six men were drowned. †

The adventures of William Matthews himself began early. While serving in the *Illustrious* he had a narrow escape. He was racing with another boy to the masthead, when he fell sixty feet from the rigging into the water, just clear of the ship's side, against which he would have been dashed to pieces had he struck it. His body was much discoloured by the fall, and he was unconscious when picked up by an officer,

---

* He was one of the old Preventive men, and afterwards joined the Coastguard Service.

† At the inquest held the jury found that the officers of the *Baron Osy* were not to blame, and that the occurrence was due to failure on the part of the cutter to exhibit a light.

CHIEF OFFICER OF COASTGUARDS W. H. MATTHEWS
(Photo by J. W. Thomas, Hastings)

CAPTAIN SALMOND'S PATHETIC END

Mr. Grant, who jumped overboard and held him until a boat came to the rescue. As the result of this accident he was in hospital six weeks.

In 1851 he was transferred to the *Britannia*, and from thence drafted to the ill-fated *Birkenhead* on March 20th of the same year. He made two voyages in the *Birkenhead* previous to the one when she was wrecked. In April, 1851, she took drafts of Royal Artillery from Woolwich to Halifax and Quebec, and brought other drafts back. She next sailed to the Cape with the 2nd Queen's Regiment, calling at Ascension, and returned home empty. Then, early in 1852, came her last memorable voyage. The account which Mr. Matthews left of his experiences at the troopship disaster makes mention of two facts which we do not find recorded elsewhere—viz. the number of boats on board, eleven, eight of which proved useless or were lost, and the blindfolding of the horses before they were cast overboard.

> We left England for the Cape of Good Hope [he says] with 638 souls on board, the majority being soldiers whom we were conveying to Cape Colony. On February 26th, at 2 a.m., our ship struck on a reef three miles from land, the night being very dark. I was sleeping in the forecastle at the time of the collision, and was thrown from my hammock. We sent up lots of signals of distress, which met with no response, owing to the land being uninhabited, and there being few ships sailing the waters. Almost immediately after the vessel struck she became a total wreck, the rock penetrating her bottom just aft the mainmast. The rush of water was so great that most of the men who were on the lower deck were drowned sleeping in their hammocks. I was sleeping on the deck above, and I was thrown out of my hammock by the shock. I immediately ran aft, when I heard Major Seton, who was in command of the soldiers, order sixty of them down to the pumps. They went and were battened down, remaining till they were drowned in the execution of their duty.* Mr. Harris, one of the ship's officers,† sent me down below to fetch his coat, it being very cold, and on my return I found the hatchway—the only way of escape—battened down against me. I shouted, and, marvellous to say, my voice was heard amid the awful tumult. The hatch was opened, and I was let out by my chum, Tom Drackford. Had I been a moment later I should have been drowned,

---

* Fifty men were drowned at the pumps, together with Lieutenant Booth, of the 73rd, the officer in charge at the time.

† Mr. T. Harris, the boatswain, who was drowned. Young Matthews was boatswain's boy

as the ship went down immediately.* Previous to this Captain Salmond, the commander of the ship, ordered the horses to be blindfolded and thrown overboard, and the women and children to be put in the boats, which was done with splendid discipline, not a man attempting to save himself. These orders had just been obeyed, and the boats pulled away, when the entire bow broke off from the mainmast, and the funnel fell over the side, crushing many to death. There were eleven boats on board, eight of which went down with the ship. About five minutes later the vessel broke in two, and the Captain then ordered all those who could swim to jump overboard and try to save themselves—this being his last order, as he went down with the ship and perished with the rest. I, with many others, jumped overboard and made for the boats, by means of which I was picked up. Many were eaten by sharks, which were very numerous. After pulling seaward for thirteen hours we were picked up by a passing vessel—the *Lioness*, of Capetown —which at once proceeded to the wreck and found thirty more poor fellows clinging to the maintopsail-yard of the submerged vessel. Those who reached the shore had to cross the mountains, which were covered with bush. Only 192 were saved, the remaining 446 of the troops and crew being drowned.

After the loss of the *Birkenhead* Mr. Matthews returned to England in H.M. corvette *Amazon*, a sketch of which is given in Chapter VIII. showing her as she appeared when struck by a sudden fierce squall on the voyage home. He left England again in 1852 in H.M.S. *Vestal*, which proceeded to Port Royal, Jamaica, where on May 6th, 1852, he was drafted to H.M. schooner *Bermuda*, in which vessel Mr. Matthews had another experience of shipwreck almost similar to that of the *Birkenhead*. On the night of April 13th, 1855, the ship was driven about 8.30 on a reef at Long Green Key Island, in the East Caicos, West Indies. It was very dark at the time, and there was a moderate gale with thick rain. The vessel struck with such force that the rocks penetrated her bottom and she soon filled with water; the sea broke clean over her, and the officers and crew took to the rigging. It was well for them that the tide was ebbing instead of flowing, or they would have perished. As it was, they succeeded in getting the boats over the reef, and by that means all (fifty-two in number, including Lieutenant William Cashman in command) reached land in safety, two miles

* The hatchway referred to was in the fore part of the ship, and the first to be submerged.

distant. Shortly afterwards the vessel became a total wreck.

On their reaching *terra firma* the island was found to be uninhabited, and they suffered much from numerous large sand-flies, the faces of some of the men being so badly stung that they were unable to open their eyes, and had to be led about. To prevent further injury from these pests, they smoked the bush and turf and lived in the smoke, which kept the flies away. These flies were such a terror that it would have been impossible for cattle to live on the island, as the torment they inflicted would have caused the animals to run themselves to death. Mr. Matthews said that when the men were stung they could see the bodies of the flies swell out like bladders with the blood. It was with great difficulty they were able to make a fire, most of the matches in their possession having been destroyed by sea-water. When the fire at last was kindled, it was necessary for their preservation that it should be kept constantly burning, and in order to accomplish this relief parties were organised, whose duty it was also to maintain a sharp look-out for passing vessels.

Deliverance came on the seventeenth day, when the castaways were taken off the island by two small merchant schooners, whose attention had been attracted by the fire and also by a piece of serge attached to a spar, erected as a signal of distress. During their stay on the island, the men's food consisted chiefly of roots and berries, the ship's provisions and ammunition having, of course, been lost. They were conveyed to Turk's Island, where they remained twelve days, the inhabitants, mostly black men, providing them with a temporary shelter. The schooners having reported the disaster at their next port of call, H.M.S. *Wolverene* was despatched to the relief of the shipwrecked crew, and took them to Bermuda, whence H.M.S. *Calypso* brought them to England.

Young Matthews was destined to renew his personal acquaintance with the frigate *Castor*, on board which, in Simon's Bay, he with other survivors was conveyed after the wreck of the *Birkenhead.* On returning from Bermuda in the *Calypso*, he joined the *Castor* on July 13th, 1855, when she was ordered to the South African Station on a three years' commission. She was commanded by Commodore Trotter, and subsequently by Captain Henry Lyster, and had a complement of 350 officers and men. The *Castor's* duties also embraced a survey of the east and west coasts. She was one of the ships to welcome Dr. Livingstone's return from the interior after his perilous exploration of the Zambesi in 1856. Instructions had been received from the Admiralty to give the doctor any assistance he needed, in order to facilitate his return to England. To carry this into effect H.M. brigantine *Dart*, which was acting as a tender to the *Castor*, was ordered to proceed to the mouth of the Zambesi, sixty officers and men, who had formed part of the *Castor's* crew, having been transferred to the vessel for this purpose. Soon after arriving at their destination, a boat's crew, in charge of the commander of the *Dart*, together with a lieutenant of Marines, left the ship in order to proceed to Quilimane, where the doctor was expected. An unfortunate disaster, however, occurred. In trying to cross a dangerous bar near the river's mouth the boat capsized, the two officers, three men, and a black boy who was accompanying them, being drowned. The remainder of the crew, consisting of three men, were afterwards rescued in an exhausted condition. The *Dart*, having lost her officer in charge, returned to the *Castor*, and the doctor was subsequently conveyed to the Cape in H.M. brig *Frolic*. He was there visited by Commodore Trotter, of the *Castor*, when a quantity of correspondence was handed to him, which included a number of letters from his friends at home.

Mr. Matthews told how on one occasion the *Castor* was ordered to look for a missing boat's crew, consisting of five men and an officer in charge, who, it was feared, had been massacred by cannibals while the boat was hidden in the bush. When near Zanzibar, the captain and five others, including Mr. Matthews, left the ship about three miles in the offing and proceeded to the shore. As soon as they had landed and were about fifty yards from the sea, two cannibal chiefs came slowly down the beach, evidently with the object

CAPTAIN SALMOND'S PATHETIC END 171

of drawing them as far from the boat as possible. The two men left in charge of the boat had orders to keep it afloat. When the cannibals thought the sailors were far enough from the boat for them to cut off the means of escape, hundreds of black men sprang to their feet from the thick bush, sounding their war-cry. The captain turned pale, and exclaimed, "For God's sake, men, run for your lives, or we are lost!" They rushed back and fell almost breathless into the boat, and had just got off from the shore when numbers of the cannibals dashed into the sea, and tried to keep the boat from going out, throwing spears and other missiles after it. No one, however, was injured.

The *Castor* afterwards paid a visit to the West Coast, where our ships were engaged in the suppression of the slave traffic. Mr. Matthews was thus able to share in these experiences. A large slave-ship having been sighted in the Bight of Benin, the frigate started in pursuit. After a prolonged chase the slave-ship, finding she was getting the worst of it, ran ashore and hoisted the American flag. Captain Lyster disputed the right of the slaver to claim protection in this way, and decided to capture the ship. The *Castor*, which carried 36 guns, found she was unable to approach the vessel owing to the shallow water. H.M.S. *Sappho*, a 12-gun sloop which happened to be in the vicinity, was therefore sent in to demand her surrender. This the slaver refused. A boat's crew were then ordered to board the ship, when they were fired upon, and the coxswain killed before they had accomplished their object. The slave-ship was found to contain men, women and children, who were closely packed in the hull of the vessel, several having died of suffocation. The slaves were liberated, after which the slave-ship was destroyed. The crew of the *Sappho*, who had taken part in many similar exploits, never reached home to relate their experiences. Shortly after this incident the sloop sailed from Simon's Bay for Cape Horn, and was not afterwards heard of. Having served three years in African waters, the *Castor* returned to England and was paid off at Chatham on August 2nd, 1858.

Mr. Matthews was attached to the *Victory* till September

11th, and was appointed to the Coastguards on September 12th, 1858. His first station was Atherfield, Isle of Wight, where he remained six months. He was then transferred to Brixton, Isle of Wight, where an important event was his marriage. After completing seven years' service at Brixton, he was promoted to commissioned boatman at his former station, Atherfield, an isolated spot between the Needles and Blackgang Chine, Isle of Wight. During his stay of two years on that dangerous part of the coast he assisted in saving many lives of shipwrecked mariners. Among the vessels wrecked was the ship *Marabeta*, from Malta, laden with corn, the crew numbering thirty-three. Of these thirteen were drowned, and the remainder saved. Those who lost their lives included the captain and mate, who were brothers. After they had been buried for several months their poor distressed father came from Malta to "fetch their bodies." The vessel, when she struck, became a total wreck before the lifeboat could reach her, the storm raging so furiously. Those who escaped were washed to shore on pieces of wood. It so happened that on the same night the local lifeboat had already been called to the wreck of a small schooner, all of whose crew were saved, and she was thereby prevented from going sooner to the help of the *Marabeta*.

Another wreck which was the cause of some exciting scenes in the neighbourhood was that of the *Cedarine*, from Bermuda. She had on board 134 convicts, who were about to be liberated after having served their sentences of transportation. These, together with the ship's crew, were rescued by the lifeboat and rocket apparatus. The convicts, wearing garments picturesquely marked with the "broad arrow," soon took charge of two public-houses in the quiet village of Brixton. They conveyed all the casks of beer and spirits into a field adjoining, and sat down to a regular orgie, the villagers being afraid to come out of their houses. A messenger was despatched to Parkhurst Barracks for a company of soldiers, who escorted the carousing convicts to Parkhurst Prison. The smell of the cedar-wood composing the wreckage remained about the shore for years. By a strange coincidence Mr. Matthews and the captain of the convict ship were old

CAPTAIN SALMOND'S PATHETIC END 173

acquaintances, they having met while serving in the West Indies some years before.

Many other interesting experiences in connection with wrecks befell Mr. Matthews while serving at Atherfield. We need only mention one. A large steamer with a general cargo, the *Fortuna*, from Malta, carrying a crew of twenty-seven men and several others who had been picked up from a wreck at sea, came to grief during a dense fog, in spite of which a rescue of all those on board was effected by means of the rocket apparatus fired from the top of a high cliff. The fog was so thick that the Coastguards were unable to see the ship, and their aim in firing had to be guided by the sound of the cries for help which came from the poor fellows on board. Every rocket fired had failed to touch the ship till they came to the last, the result of which was awaited with keen anxiety. To their great joy the last shot proved a successful one, and the cheers of the shipwrecked men were described as being most touching. The rescue of the whole of the ship's company was then soon accomplished.

Shortly after this Mr. Matthews volunteered for removal, and he was sent to St. Leonards Station, Hastings Division, remaining there about eight years. In 1873 a visit was paid to the Coastguard Station by the Prince of Wales, then the Duke of York, and his brother, the late Duke of Clarence, who were staying at St. Leonards. To recognise this honour the Coastguards had been summoned, and arrangements made to enable their Royal Highnesses to witness the rocket drill. The supposed ship in distress was No. 39 Martello Tower, from which a number of men were rescued, the Royal visitors appearing very interested, and somewhat amused by the proceedings.

On April 1st, 1876, Mr. Matthews got his second step in the Coastguard Service, being made chief boatman at Langley Station, between Pevensey and Eastbourne, in the Hastings Division. His stay there, however, was very brief, for he had two sick children, and on their behalf he made an early application to be allowed to leave this bleak and open part of the coast. He removed to Government House, Marine Parade, Hastings, where he stayed two years and attained his chief-officership. He was then placed at Pevensey Sluice, when he had under him a chief boatman and eight men, with a detachment at 57 Tower consisting of a chief boatman and four men. For nearly five years he had charge at Pevensey Sluice, after which he was transferred a second time to Government House, Hastings. Having been eight years at Government House, Mr. Matthews' term of service expired, and he retired on a pension in June, 1890. He had standing to his credit the long term of thirty-seven years' man's service, and possessed two medals, that for the Kaffir War (during which he assisted to escort native prisoners to the coast), and that awarded for long service and good conduct. Mr. Matthews did not live many years to enjoy his well-earned retirement. He died of pneumonia on November 11th, 1898, after an illness of nine months, at the age of sixty-two, a victim finally to hardships in his early days which undermined a robust constitution. He was buried in the Hastings Cemetery, where his tombstone records the fact that he was a *Birkenhead* survivor. Eight Coastguards who had served with him, at Hastings and elsewhere, bore his body to the grave.

Mr. Matthews was a member of the Wesleyan Church at Hastings, and in conjunction with his wife had maintained an active interest in religious work for many years. A prominent result of their efforts was the erection of a mission-hall at Pevensey Sluice in 1885. He left a widow and five children, four sons and a daughter. His anxiety was that they should have a good start in life, and it was a source of comfort to him in his later years to know they had made the most of their opportunities. His eldest son, W. H. Matthews, joint author of this book, had in 1905 held a position in Lloyds Bank at Hastings (late Beechings & Co.) for nineteen years; the second son was Postmaster of Chislehurst; the third was Borough Engineer of Bridlington-on-Sea; and the fourth was in the Surveyor's Department of H.M. Office of Works at Westminster. It is needless to say that their father's was a sacred memory, and that they honoured and cherished its association with the name of the *Birkenhead*.

THOMAS DRACKFORD
(From a photo)

THOMAS DRACKFORD

This was the seaman to whose promptness and presence of mind William Henry Matthews owed his life at the wreck. Thomas Drackford afterwards formed one of the crew of nine of the boat which picked young Matthews up. Mr. Richards directed them, and the boat also contained four soldiers, besides the seven women and thirteen children, or about thirty-five souls in all. A Londoner by birth, Drackford was born in Tothill Street, Westminster, in 1828, in a house demolished subsequently to make way for the Royal Aquarium. Drackford made an early choice in favour of the sea. Joining the frigate *Warspite* in 1842, he served on that ship for some time, when he was allowed the option—a privilege then extended to boys—either of remaining in the Navy or being transferred to the mercantile marine. He decided on adopting the latter course. He was then apprenticed for five years on board a collier sailing between the North of England and southern ports. His last voyage was to Valparaiso, where his vessel dragged her anchors in the harbour during a gale of wind and became a total wreck. It was during his stay at Valparaiso that Drackford renewed his connection with the Navy. A British gunboat which was at anchor in the harbour was short of men, and her commander having made inquiries for English sailors, Drackford, whose five years' apprenticeship had now expired, offered his services, which were accepted. He then returned to England as a seaman in the gunboat. These circumstances led up to his joining the *Birkenhead*, to which he was transferred in the early part of 1851 as a seaman. He made two successful voyages in the ship, one from Woolwich to Halifax with Artillery, and another to the Cape with the 2nd Queen's Regiment. Drackford then left England with her on the voyage which was destined to end so fatally.

After the *Birkenhead* struck the rock, he with others was ordered to batten down the fore hatchways, the crew who occupied this portion of the ship having been summoned on deck. It was during the execution of these orders that the incident occurred which nearly cost his shipmate, William Matthews, his life. Mr. Matthews refers to the mishap in his narrative on a previous page. When this work had been completed Drackford assisted the women and children, who were being transferred to the second cutter, when he was told to accompany them as one of the crew of the boat. Pulling away a short distance from the wreck, they remained until the *Birkenhead* had gone down, when, together with the two other boats containing survivors, they decided to row towards the shore, where it was hoped they would be able to effect a landing; but owing to the thick weed on this part of the coast, and the surf which was breaking on the shore, their efforts were unsuccessful. Mr. Richards, the officer in command, then resolved to pull seaward, thinking that they might possibly fall in with a passing vessel. In doing so the three boats soon parted company. After pulling for twelve hours under circumstances of great difficulty, the second cutter was picked up by the schooner *Lioness*, of Capetown, whose master, Captain Ramsden, as we have seen, treated the castaways with the utmost kindness. The first cutter had been picked up by the same vessel about two hours earlier. The schooner proceeded to the scene of the wreck, where the two cutters rescued forty-five men from the topsail-yard of the ill-fated ship. Captain Ramsden then sailed for Simon's Bay with 116 survivors, who were transferred to the *Castor*.

After the wreck Thomas Drackford returned to England with other survivors in the *Amazon*. He was attached to the Home Fleet until 1854, and was then transferred to H.M.S. *Porcupine*, a paddle-wheel steam vessel carrying three guns (Lieut.-Commander G. M. Jackson), which proceeded to the Baltic to engage in the Russian War. As one of the smaller vessels, the *Porcupine* was able to take a prominent part in the operations which followed, the coast in many places being inaccessible to the larger ships. Her commander was one of the killed. On returning again to England, Drackford was awarded the Baltic medal for his services. He was then transferred to the frigate *Monarch*, in the Home Fleet, as leading seaman. There he served for two years, when he met with a serious accident, which neces-

Surgeon-General Robert Bowen, F.R.C.S.
(From a photo)

CAPTAIN SALMOND'S PATHETIC END 177

sitated his retirement from the Navy. A block which was being hoisted aloft broke away, and falling to the deck narrowly missed his head, but smashed two of his fingers. He was at work on the deck at the time, and was in a kneeling position. Drackford had now completed fifteen years' service, for which he received a small pension.

Although incapacitated from further employment in the Navy, Drackford's seafaring career was not yet at an end. He next joined a West Indiaman, in which he made a number of voyages to the West Indies. He was also mate of a schooner, the *Ann and Sarah*, trading between Portsmouth and the North of England. In this capacity he spent several of his later years. After retiring from the sea Drackford went to live at Landport, where he died on December 24th, 1890. He was buried in the Mile End Cemetery at Portsmouth. For most of the information contained in this sketch of his life history the book is indebted to his brother, Mr. Joseph Drackford, of Erasmus Street, Westminster, also an old sailor for many years in the Orient line of steamships.

Surgeon-General Bowen

An interesting figure in the group of *Birkenhead* notabilities will always be Staff-Surgeon Robert Bowen. Dr. Bowen, as he is familiarly designated in connection with the wreck, entered the service on May 18th, 1841, as an assistant-surgeon, and retired with the rank of surgeon-general on June 26th, 1877. He served abroad in Gibraltar, Jamaica, South Africa and Canada; also in the Crimean campaign. He went through the Kaffir War, 1852-3 (medal), and acted as principal medical officer to the expedition against the Kaffir chief Kreli in August, 1852; served in the Eastern Campaign of 1854-5, including the battles of Alma and Inkerman and siege of Sevastopol (medal with three clasps and Turkish medal); and was acting principal medical officer of the 4th Division during the march from Old Fort to Cathcart's Hill, and for a short time afterwards.

Dr. Bowen was highly esteemed in his profession, and was elected a Fellow of the Royal College of Surgeons. He died at Eastfield, Weston-super-Mare, on June 7th, 1895, aged seventy-seven. A year or two before his death a photograph of Surgeon-General Bowen was taken for the British Museum of Portraits, and a copy of it is kept in the Art Library of the Victoria and Albert Museum at South Kensington. "Not nearly such a good one as mine, I am sorry to say," wrote Mrs. Bowen in reference to this portrait, when she kindly sent for reproduction in this book the excellent photograph of the Surgeon-General which appears on another page. The portrait preserved at South Kensington has pasted on the back a signed record of service, which mentions the fact that Dr. Bowen was shipwrecked in the *Birkenhead*.

There was for long in existence a legend to the effect that Dr. Bowen escaped from the wreck on a white charger which swam with him to shore. The story gained credence in the Rifle Brigade, where it passed into a tradition, and it was accepted in other places also. As late as 1905 Mr. W. J. Milne, of Capetown (son of Captain David Milne, Hornsey, N.), put forward, as something he had from boyhood been familiar with, this remarkable version of the doctor's deliverance.

At the time of my birth (1860) in the 1st Battalion Rifle Brigade, of which my father was then Sergeant-Major [wrote Mr. Milne], the regimental surgeon was the late Dr. Bowen, who rode a white charger (mare) of which he was very fond, and which he cherished till it died of old age. I recall being told that he owed his life to this mare, as he was on board the *Birkenhead*, and when, at the last moment, the order came *sauve qui peut*, he leapt with her into the sea and she carried him safe to shore.

A delightful little fiction! Dr. Bowen, as he has told us in an earlier chapter, lowered himself from the poop of the sinking ship and was picked up by the first cutter, whose occupants were rescued by the schooner *Lioness*.

CHAPTER XV

GRAPHIC NARRATIVE OF AN OFFICER

'Tis a fearful night,
There's danger on the deep.—THOS. HAYNES BAYLY.

ENSIGN LUCAS of the 73rd Regiment, who was saved after a terrible struggle to get ashore, where he was injured on the rocks, sent home three weeks after the wreck an account of his experience which is of great interest. It remained for many years a treasured possession of the family, and eventually returned to the hands of him who penned it. Written while the circumstances were fresh in the mind of the young officer (he was only nineteen), the narrative presents a vivid picture of the scene on that fearful night in February, 1852, and brings before the reader very realistically the surroundings of the life-and-death struggle in which so many gallant men engaged. It is here given to the world for the first time, with footnotes made by Captain Lucas, who was one of the surviving officers at the 50th anniversary, to accompany it in this work.

H.M.S. *Birkenhead* sailed from Cork Harbour about the end of December, 1851. On board were, in addition to the crew of 90 men, drafts of regiments going out to join their corps in South Africa, in all 490 men and officers. We had rough weather for some 14 days after our departure, notwithstanding which we made a very good passage to Simon's Bay, arriving about February 22nd, 1852. On the evening of the 25th we sailed from Simon's Bay to Algoa Bay and Buffalo mouth, where several drafts were to be landed.

It being my watch from four to eight the next morning, I turned in early. I was roused by a severe shock, and when well awake found myself sitting bolt upright in my berth. Two severe shocks followed immediately. I then got out of my bed and ran on deck, where I found all in confusion, the men crowding up from the troop-deck, mostly without any clothes but their shirts. On asking the ship's carpenter, Roberts, what had happened, his answer was, "We have struck a rock and are going down fast." Asking him not to tell the men the extent of our danger, fearing a panic, I returned to my cabin, where I dressed, and again went on deck, where everything had been restored to order, every soul being on deck, the men at "quarters."

Mr. Girardot, 43rd Regiment, and myself then undertook to go down in turn and work the pumps, which were on the lower deck. Mr. Girardot superintended getting the horses overboard—they were plunging so violently that nothing could be done till they were gone; besides, it was only right to give them a chance of their lives. Eight out of nine got ashore. The boats were then lowered and got ready for sea—that is, those that hung on the ship's quarters. By this time it became my duty to relieve Mr. Girardot at the pumps with a fresh spell of 50 men, as no set of men could work longer than a few minutes at a time. *Nothing could exceed the order that prevailed. Every word of command could be heard as plainly as on parade.** I remained at the pumps as long as the men could, when Mr. Girardot again relieved. On reaching the deck I was ordered by poor Major Seton, 74th, to superintend the getting of the women and children into the ship's boats.

The ship was now rolling her yardarms in the sea, and it was no light matter to keep one's legs. It is not easy to imagine a more painful task than that of getting the wretched women into the boats. This was in several cases done by main force. Tearing them from their husbands, they were carried to the bulwarks and dropped over the ship's side into the arms of the boat's crew. The whole of the women and children, thirty in all, were safely stowed in the boats, when they shoved off and pulled away. It is hard to describe the sensation of oppression removed from one's mind on knowing the utterly helpless part of the ship's living cargo had been deposited in comparative safety. Thank God, it can seldom be said that Englishmen have left women and children to perish and saved their own lives!

I again returned to the pumps, and when tired went on deck. I found poor Booth, of the 73rd, who relieved, Mr. Girardot being out of the way. Poor fellow, he had hardly reached the pumps when the water rushed in and swamped himself and men (50).

About this time the fore part of the ship broke off and went down immediately, covered with men. I was next sent to help to get one of the paddle-box boats over into the sea. We did not succeed, the ropes breaking. A similar fate happened to the other paddle-box boat—thus losing the means of saving three hundred men. Just at this moment the funnel fell with a fearful crash on deck, killing and maiming several of my party who had been endeavouring to get the boat over the ship's side.† We now ran for our lives to the poop deck, the water being

---

* Italics ours.

† A man of the 6th Regiment had one eye knocked out. He was saved, but the agony he suffered must have been terrible, by salt water and sun next day.

CAPTAIN G. A. LUCAS
(Photo by Hy. Kisch, Durban, Natal)

GRAPHIC NARRATIVE OF AN OFFICER 181

knee-deep on the quarter-deck. All hands were ordered aft, as the ship appeared to be going down by the head, in hopes that their weight would bring her stern again into the water. For some minutes she remained with the heel of her rudder completely out of the water,* during which time the order was given for everybody to swim to those boats that were afloat, or save themselves as best they could. Those boats still hooked to the falls were instantly swamped, the men crowding into them. Three boats only got clear of the ship, including that containing the women.

During this time I stood looking over the stern of the ship, Major Seton with me. I had made up my mind to swim if possible to the shore, as being my only chance. I, however, dared not jump into the water, as it was literally alive with men. A dreadful sight it was! Some in their last dying efforts, others striking out manfully and suddenly going down with a yell of agony—their shrieks seem still to ring in my ears; some pulling others down in their efforts to keep above water. The rigging was crowded from the deck to the trucks.

The ship broke off just aft of the mainmast with a tremendous crash. There was a general rush into the water. Major Seton and myself still remained in the same place. The ship's stern, now being relieved of all weight forward, settled steadily down. It was quite evident that there was nothing for it but to get away from her as soon as possible. Up to this moment I had had some hopes of her remaining above water till daylight. I shook hands with Major Seton, and hoped we should meet ashore. "I do not think we shall, Lucas, as I cannot swim a stroke," he answered. Just then my name was called, and on looking back I saw my servant, as faithful a fellow as ever lived.† He asked whether he was to follow me. Poor fellow, he could not swim! I could give him little advice, except to get as high as possible into the rigging. I never saw him again.

I then jumped into the sea, the poop deck being little more than a foot out of water. I struck out with a will, fearing the suction caused by the ship's foundering. How far I swam I know not, when I heard a fearful shriek, and on turning I could see nothing. The ship had struck at 2 a.m., and little more than half-an-hour had elapsed. Several large fires were now burning on the hills along the shore, the grass being on fire. I struck out again in the direction of the fires, resting every now and then on pieces of the wreck. I had swum some distance when I came up with some large object. At first I could not make out what it was. It turned out to be a large boat turned keel uppermost. I crawled upon it. I could distinguish several forms on the other end, but did not speak, fearing they might shove me off again. Right glad was I to find myself crouched, up to my middle in water, on the boat! The boat

---

* Dr. Bowen, who was saved, told me that he swam under the heel of the rudder.

† He had brought my purse out of my cabin to me.

drifted towards the shore for some distance, when a current took her close alongside the remains of the ship. Nothing could be seen but the mainyard above water. Through the gloom I could see that the rigging was crowded with men. To my great horror we drifted past the ship, or, rather, where she had been. It was a black look-out, for had we gone to sea the chances were greatly against our being saved.

Our fate seemed inevitable, when the boat again drifted towards the shore. The sea was beautifully calm. The stars shone out, but no moon was visible. The cold was intense. As the fires on the land burned up, we could see the light reflected by the breakers. By this time I had made my presence known to the other men on the boat, five soldiers and one sailor—Maxwell, one of the ship's quartermasters, as fine a fellow as ever lived. We drifted through large quantities of wreck, to which were many unhappy wretches clinging, and, as we passed, begging for help.

When day broke we found ourselves about a mile from the beach, on which the sea broke with fearful violence.* Three of our party were naked. Maxwell had three shirts and two pair of trousers, the surplus of which he gave to them. Our great danger now was that, should the wind set off shore, we were sure to be drifted out to sea, as we had no means of helping the boat along. An oar floated past us, which I, being the best swimmer, went after. I had some distance to go. When I turned towards the boat it appeared so far off that I almost despaired of reaching it, which the men I suppose seeing by my face, cheered me. I struck out, and gained the boat pretty nigh exhausted. The oar was of the greatest service in keeping our side to the seas. One man acted as a "rolluck," and three at a time rowed it, first one side and then the other. While we drifted slowly, many pieces of timber drifted by us with men on them. Some, getting done, let go their hold and went down. The most painful sight was two men swimming alongside of each other. For a long time they struck out well together. After a time one got evidently tired—the other helped him along—it was no use, and at last he swam some distance towards shore, but returned again to help his comrade. It was of no avail, and he at last left for the shore. Poor fellow, he had expended his little remaining strength in helping his companion, and went down soon afterwards.

Our boat drifted within a few hundred yards of the shore when we struck on a rock, over which the sea broke with great violence. After several unsuccessful endeavours to get her loose, we gave up and determined to remain as long as possible. We were several times knocked off our boat into the sea. Presently another boat passed us with six men on her bottom. She was upset within arm's length of the rocks, and only one man came up out of the six. We were losing our strength fast, so I proposed making a start for the nearest rocks. The sea was covered for several hundred yards with a weed called "sea

* The bay was full of "blackfins" (sharks).

bamboo," a most difficult thing to swim through. We, however, left our boat. I went down once among it, and for the first time my heart really failed me. By good luck I came up to the top, and swam on by mere instinct more than anything else, as I was nearly exhausted.* Several large waves, following one after the other, lifted me upon the rocks, where I managed to hold on till they receded. The reef runs a long distance into the sea. I was on the very extreme point of it. I laid down for some time, and then crawled towards the beach, for walk I could not. Judge of my horror when I found the reef broken by a piece of water about a hundred yards wide. It looked shallow. I tried to wade it, but went over my head. I had just sufficient strength to swim to rocks on the opposite side, and clutched them and dragged myself out with some difficulty. One of the men of my own company came and helped me up to the sandy beach, where I laid down and fell asleep. I was awoke by the same man, who had collected what people he could find along the beach. We then started to look for water or some habitation. As we could see neither house nor any indication of one, we walked along the shore for a short distance, when I gave in and refused to go any further. A halt was called. A pipe was hunted for among us; nothing turned up but a piece of "baccy," well wet by the sea—several of us took a bite. I still would go no further, so the men carried me whether I would or no, saying, "I had got so far, and they would never leave an officer behind to die." I was so stiff and sore from the cuts I had received on the rocks that I cared little what my fate was. The sun had burned my legs until I had little or no skin left on them.

We had walked along the beach for about five miles, and were nearly done up, when to our great delight a waggon was descried on the beach. I had become ashamed of my want of courage, and had walked sooner than let men little better off than myself carry me. The waggon belonged to a Dutchman who had come to fetch a load of fish for the Caledon market. Nothing could exceed this man's kindness. He gave us all the fish he had caught, and showed those who could walk the way to Stanford Cove, a fishing station about seven miles further up the coast. I remained with those men who were unable to move at the waggon. The next morning he lent me a horse, upon which I got to the fishing station. On my offering my ring as payment, he refused, saying that "if I could pay hereafter, well and good; if not, it did not matter." At the fishing station I found about sixty men who had made their way there the previous day. I then heard that two officers had also been saved—Lieutenant Girardot and Cornet Bond. Every man who could move came up to welcome me. Could anything be greater than their kindness to me? In the afternoon a waggon came down to

* I remember trying to get into the boat, in-shore of me, but fell back into the water and made for rocks. Maxwell got into the boat, remaining there until following morning, when rescued.

bring us to the nearest farmhouse, about fifteen miles inland, where we arrived in the evening. I was carried to bed, where I remained some days. The men were fed and clothed by our host, Captain Smales, late 7th Dragoon Guards. In a few days a steamer was sent to the fishing station to convey the men and officers round to the Cape. Being unable to move, I remained for some time with Captain Smales, until perfectly recovered. I can never say enough of the kindness of Captain and Mrs. Smales. Had I been their own son, better care could not have been taken of me.

The writer of this moving narrative mentions in conclusion that the *Lioness* schooner took forty people off the mast several hours after the wreck, and that one boat was beached near the Bot River, some miles up the coast. It will have been noted that Ensign Lucas refers to the senior officer on board the *Birkenhead* as "Major" Seton. He was generally known by that title, but really, as already explained, held the rank of lieutenant-colonel.

CHAPTER XVI

FIFTY YEARS AFTER

>   Deposited upon the silent shore
>   Of memory, images and precious thoughts
>   That shall not die, and cannot be destroyed.—WORDSWORTH.

DOWN through the years the deathless story of the *Birkenhead* has been a memory, ever fresh and green. The 50th anniversary of the wreck fell on February 26th, 1902, when evidence was forthcoming that the tale of heroism and devotion had still as strong a hold as ever upon the minds and affections of the British people. At Boston, in Lincolnshire, was organised a public testimonial to a survivor then living there, Sergeant John O'Neil, who was with the 91st Regiment on board the troopship. Field-Marshal Lord Wolseley promptly came forward with an eloquent letter, holding up the *Birkenhead* and its heroes as an object-lesson of the value of Military discipline, which made a deep impression. Not less timely was the kindly interest displayed in the movement by Field-Marshal Lord Roberts, then Commander-in-Chief, and also by the Prince of Wales; and the testimonial had a supporter in Mr. Robert Gofton-Salmond, of the New Hermitage, Central Hill, Norwood, S.E., the only surviving son of the Commander of the *Birkenhead*.

It was thought at the outset that Sergeant O'Neil was probably the only survivor of the *Birkenhead* living. A year previously the announcement was made that "the last survivor" of the wreck had died at Floore, in Northamptonshire, and the fact that another survivor remained in the person of O'Neil was then notified in the Press. Nothing further was heard, and the inference drawn was that Boston possessed the sole survivor. This many people believed. The publicity given to the O'Neil testimonial, however, quickly and very happily established the fact that other survivors were left. Lieut.-Colonel Girardot subscribed to the fund on seeing a letter in *The Standard*, and by degrees the others were heard of. The heroes of the *Birkenhead* were not men to proclaim themselves from the housetops, and they took a good deal of looking for. It required a Diogenes' lantern, almost, to find them all out.

The search extended far and wide. Two were discovered in Ireland—Captain Bond-Shelton, late 12th Lancers, and Colour-Sergeant Kilkeary, 73rd Regiment. Then John Smith, of the 2nd Queen's, was heard of, living at St. Ives, Hunts, and Thomas Coffin, late Quartermaster, Royal Navy ("The Man at the Wheel"), was announced from Bristol. Colour-Sergeant Drake, a Royal Marine who had "won his spurs" for gallantry before the *Birkenhead* episode, was found to be living in Lambeth. Mr. Archbold and Benjamin Turner, Naval gunner and boy respectively on board the troopship, were at the same time discovered in the neighbourhood of Portsmouth—Mr. Archbold at Buckland and Turner at Landport. It is rather remarkable that Turner should have served Mr. Archbold as his personal attendant when in the *Birkenhead*. Next an agreeable surprise came about. Captain Lucas, formerly of the 73rd Regiment, was found to still survive and to be residing at Penkridge, in Staffordshire. Nor was the list yet completed, for William Tuck, late Royal Marines, "fell in" at Brockhurst, Gosport. These survivors numbered altogether eleven—six Military, including three officers, and five Naval, including one officer of the *Birkenhead* and two Royal Marines. A "Roll Call" had in the meantime been prepared, consisting of a parchment with a heading artistically designed in gold and colours. This was in turn signed by the survivors known up to that time and despatched to the King, together with a letter of explanation. His Majesty was pleased to accept the historic document.

It was shortly after this that Captain Lucas was heard of and communicated with, and the fact that he also survived, although his name did not appear upon the "Roll Call," was at once notified, when the Hon. Sidney Greville replied

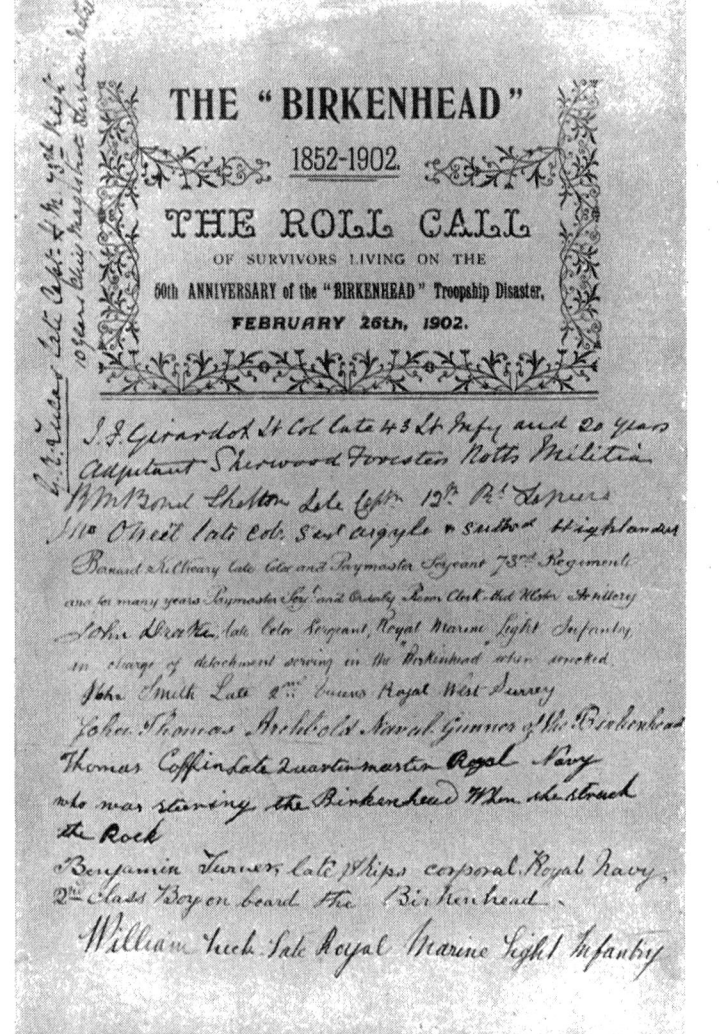

THE "BIRKENHEAD"

1852-1902

THE ROLL CALL

OF SURVIVORS LIVING ON THE
50th ANNIVERSARY of the "BIRKENHEAD" Troopship Disaster,
FEBRUARY 26th, 1902.

[Handwritten signatures of survivors, including:]

J. E. Girardot, Lt. Col. late 43 Lt. Infy. and 20 years Adjutant Sherwood Foresters Notts Militia

W. M. Bond Shelton, late Capt. 12th Rl. Lancers

J. McO'Neil late Colr. Sert. Argyle & Sutherd. Highlanders

Barnard McCleary late Colr. and Paymaster Sergeant 73rd Regiment and for many years Paymaster Sgt. and Orderly Room Clerk Ulster Artillery

John Drake late Colr. Sergeant, Royal Marine Light Infantry, in charge of detachment serving in the Birkenhead when wrecked

John Smith Late 2nd Queens Royal West Surrey

John Thomas Archbold Naval Gunner of the Birkenhead

Thomas Coffindale Quartermaster Royal Navy who was steering the Birkenhead When she struck the Rock

Benjamin Turner, late Ships corporal, Royal Navy, 2nd Class Boy on board the Birkenhead

William Tuck late Royal Marine Light Infantry

DUPLICATE OF DOCUMENT PRESENTED TO THE KING

that he would "take an early opportunity of informing the King of the omission of Captain Lucas's name." A duplicate of the document had been signed by the survivors as well as the parchment presented to His Majesty. To this the signature of Captain Lucas was duly added, and also that of William Tuck; and the "Roll Call," bearing these names of men left "fifty years after" of those saved from the wreck, is reproduced in this work. It further received the record of William Smith, formerly a corporal of the 12th Foot, whose story of the shipwreck is given in these pages, together with an account of his interesting adventures in South Africa. He was living at Middleton Cheney, near Banbury, at the 50th anniversary, but was not heard of till later; when it also became known that Francis Ginn, a late sergeant of the 43rd Light Infantry who was present at the wreck, had died at Sudbury, his native place, in Suffolk. The reader will find, as he proceeds, that two *Birkenhead* survivors perished under remarkable circumstances in South Africa within a few months of each other during 1903. One was on board the troopship as a Cape Mounted Rifleman, and the other as a passenger. The end of both these poor fellows, unheard of, probably, in England up to this moment, but here properly authenticated, was exceedingly sad. The statements of two more South African survivors, Colonel Nesbitt, C.B., a boy saved from the wreck, and William Butler, who belonged to the 12th Lancers' draft, are also given.

From what has been said it will be seen that the total number of men survivors "fifty years after" was seventeen, of whom six had died before the end of 1904—those who had passed away being Colonel Girardot, Gunner Archbold, Sergeant O'Neil, Sergeant Ginn, and Sergeant McCluskey and Mr. Charles Daly who died, one fatally injured and the other murdered, in South Africa. Colonel Nesbitt expired suddenly towards the close of 1905. The death also occurred at Beckingham, near Gainsborough, of Mrs. Parkinson, a "daughter of the regiment" who, as Marian Darkin, a child under four, was saved with her mother at the wreck; and the record of survivors is complete if we include Thomas Kelly, of Leeds, son of Timothy Kelly, 73rd Regiment, who, as a boy of three, escaped with his mother and a brother from the scene in which his father perished.

The wife of one of the men who went down with the *Birkenhead*, Thomas Cave, of the 43rd Light Infantry, died in the infirmary of Portsmouth Workhouse on March 13th, 1905. She was not on board the troopship, but was landed with her children, four or five in number, when the vessel called at Simon's Bay. Some years after the wreck Mrs. Cave married again, the name of her second husband being Murphy. He in turn died, and Bridget Murphy, formerly Cave, was admitted to the Portsmouth Workhouse in 1897. At the time of her death she was eighty-four years of age, and some of her children were living in Portsmouth.

The melancholy fact has to be recorded that Mr. Robert Gofton-Salmond, the surviving son of Captain Salmond, died on August 31st of the 50th anniversary year at Worthing, where he had gone to recoup his health. He was buried in Elmer's End Cemetery. Mr. Gofton-Salmond engaged extensively for many years in philanthropic work. He was best known as the secretary of the British Home for Incurables, the foundation-stone of whose building in Streatham was laid by the then Princess of Wales, afterwards Queen Alexandra. He was hon. secretary of the Trained Nurses' Annuity Fund, and an original member of the Committee of the Hospitals' Association, and his good works extended in many other directions. Mr. Gofton-Salmond was not twelve months old when his heroic father, Commander Salmond, was lost with the *Birkenhead*, and his own education was obtained at the Royal Naval School at New Cross, afterwards known as Eltham College. His mother came of an old Northumberland family, the Goftons, of Eland Hall, whose name he took in later years. In 1879 he married Lucy, the daughter of Mr. John Wotherspoon, of Denmark Hill, who survived him.

James Jeffery, the purser's steward of the *Birkenhead*, died in London shortly before the 50th anniversary. Jeffery was the man to whom Captain Salmond handed his watch as the ship was sinking, and who, on his return home, as we have seen from the letter he afterwards wrote to Captain

FIELD-MARSHAL VISCOUNT WOLSELEY, K.P., COMMANDER-IN-CHIEF
1895–1900

(Photo by Werner & Son, Dublin. Specially dated and presented in honour of the *Birkenhead*)

FIFTY YEARS AFTER 189

Wright, gave the watch to his commander's widow. Poor Jeffery! He was very old and infirm when the end came. When we heard of him later, through John Drake, his daughter, Mrs. Winter, was still living in London.

Below is given the finely-worded letter of Field-Marshal Lord Wolseley which has been referred to.

FARM HOUSE, GLYNDE, NR. LEWES,
February 17th, 1902.

DEAR SIR,—It must be a very great source of satisfaction to Sergeant O'Neil to feel that he was present when the *Birkenhead* sank 50 years ago. The news reached England at the time when I obtained my first commission in the Army, and I can remember the pride all soldiers felt at the heroic conduct on the part of the soldiers upon that occasion.

In all Military annals, it is one of the very finest instances of heroism, and the attention of young soldiers of to-day cannot be too frequently called to it. It teaches all ranks in the Army the inestimable value of Military discipline; and without discipline, firmly administered and thoroughly appreciated by all ranks, no Army is worth its salt.

Please tell Sergeant O'Neil that I wish him long life and prosperity. He has already won the admiration of all who admire heroic deeds.

I remain, faithfully yours,
(Signed) WOLSELEY.

On the date of the 50th anniversary Lord Wolseley wrote a short letter on the subject of a reminiscent character which is also interesting.

FARM HOUSE, GLYNDE, NR. LEWES,
February 26th, 1902.

DEAR SIR,—I enclose with great pleasure a copy of the last photograph I have had taken of myself. In my many wanderings I have been at the place where the *Birkenhead* disaster occurred, and I knew the two surviving officers Colonel Wright and Captain Bond, of the 12th Lancers, very well. From both of them I have heard many times particulars of that disaster: if anything so glorious in the annals of an Army can be classed under such a head.

Believe me to be, faithfully yours,
(Signed) WOLSELEY.

The subjoined letter from Lord Roberts, the Commander-in-Chief, breathes sincere admiration of the heroes of the *Birkenhead*. The gratifying testimony of the Field-Marshal will be valued for all time, and will do much to impress the lesson which he so forcibly recommends.

WAR OFFICE, LONDON, S.W.
May 26th, 1902.

DEAR SIR,—I am directed by Field-Marshal Lord Roberts to acknowledge with thanks the receipt of your letter of the 20th instant, which he has read with interest, and I am now to say that he wishes you all possible success in the publication of your Story regarding the loss of the *Birkenhead*.

The heroism displayed upon that occasion represents vividly the sterling characteristics of the British race, and the Field-Marshal trusts that all the Military readers of your work will take to heart the splendid lesson of discipline which is conveyed by the action of the troops when overcome by a catastrophe in which so many of them perished.

I am, dear Sir, yours faithfully,
GEORGE J. GOSCHEN, Major.
Per Lieut.-Colonel, Private Secretary.

A splendid lesson indeed. Well might General Maurice exclaim, in " An Anniversary Study " in *The Cornhill Magazine* of February, 1897 * :

This is a day to be much observed in all British households for ever. The record of the doings of Britons at the time of that wreck has stirred blood other than British. We have learnt of late years to look upon Prussia as the nucleus of the proudest Military monarchy in Europe, and on the discipline of Prussian soldiers as the rock on which the grandeur and unity of Germany have been built. Yet, in 1852, the lesson in discipline which had been taught the world by Britons on February 26th seemed to the King of Prussia so precious that he ordered the record of it to be read out at the head of every regiment in his service. It may be doubted if in the history of the world the like compliment has been ever paid by the monarch of one proud race to the martial qualities and training of another. One thinks that every schoolmaster in Britain who can be detected in having one scholar in his school who does not know the true story of that day, ought to be handed over for some such sentence as Judge Jeffreys might have passed for a far more venial offence on an unhappy woman shrinking before him. Alas! the executions would be too numerous. British history in its heroism and its example is scarcely a subject of British education. So far as my experience goes, most men have heard of the *Birkenhead*; but they would tell you, if pressed, that they believed the men went down standing in their ranks singing " Rule Britannia " or " God Save the Queen." I appeal to the mothers of England to remedy these crimes, and to teach their children the plain, unvarnished tale.

* Quoted by courtesy of Major-General Sir J. F. Maurice, K.C.B., and the editor of *The Cornhill*.

FIELD-MARSHAL EARL ROBERTS, V.C., K.G., COMMANDER-IN-CHIEF AT DATE OF FIFTIETH ANNIVERSARY

(Photo by J. Robinson & Sons, Dublin. Specially presented in honour of the *Birkenhead*)

For on that February morning, as the writer recalls, the sons of Britain did nothing theatrical.

The dignity of the whole scene lies in this, that it consisted in nothing but the calm, ordinary performance of duty at a time when every man had before him the immediate prospect of a watery grave on a rock-bound coast densely covered with fatal sea-weed, in a sea known to be full of sharks; and that, whilst out of a total number of 630, only 193 men were saved, not one woman or child was drowned, because the men, after all further work was impossible, in obedience to the appeal of their officers, remained on the poop of the sinking ship rather than leap into the water, lest they should swamp by their numbers the boat that was carrying off the women and children. The whole story is, however, pregnant with suggestions of the course that should be taken in such an emergency, and for that cause, even if not for the far higher one of a lofty example, it ought to be studied in all its details.

General Maurice points with the pen of an expert to the nature of the discipline on board, and of the test which it withstood.

If every regiment which contributed a detachment ought not, as I think it ought, to bear on its banners the name *Birkenhead*, at least the bead roll of honour ought to omit no regiment that was there represented. For what, perhaps, comes home more to a soldier than he can ever bring home to the minds of those who have not themselves realised the full significance of that wonderful thing—the vital unity of a well-trained regiment—is this, that here was no highly organised and complete unit, but broken fragments, specimens only of that discipline which had been taught in each complete unit at home, put now to the severest of trials—a great emergency, faced not under their own commanding officer, but under a stranger.

He speaks further of the vitality remaining to the Army—

in the splendid regimental discipline, in the relations of officers and men, in the power of such men as Seton, Wright, and Girardot, to arouse such a feeling as kept those men standing on the poop of the *Birkenhead*,

and says:

If only that grand story would put a little of such enthusiasm into the mothers, the schoolmasters, and the painters of England as it roused at Cambridge when my father read it to a few graduates and undergraduates, I would venture to ask them not to forget the 26th of this month.

The writer's allusion is to a touching scene in class at the reading of Sir Francis Doyle's Poem, as to which he gives the testimony of eye-witnesses.

The date, February 26th, is never likely to be neglected. While its incidents may have been confused, or in part forgotten, the memory of the event associated with the day has not in its main features faded away. On through the intervening years the glorious episode of 1852 has not been lost sight of. From time to time it has been conjured up by public speakers and writers, and used by them "to point a moral, and adorn a tale"; while in some of the public schools of England the "Wreck of the *Birkenhead*" has been selected as the subject of the Prize Poem, as at Rugby in 1858, and at Bedford. Eight stanzas on the *Birkenhead*, by Henry G. Hewlett, appeared in *The Academy* of March, 1882.

At the period of the 50th anniversary a hearty welcome was accorded everywhere to *The Story of the "Birkenhead,"* and the Press renewed its praises of the subject. Nor have the sentiments expressed with regard to it all been confined to this country. The *Birkenhead* has had and still possesses many sincere admirers among our Continental neighbours. Count Montalembert, the French Academician, for instance, in his *Political Future of England*,* gives generous prominence to the story as embodying, or representing, the sterling constituents of the English character—a tribute as deserved by the soldiers on board as it is flattering to their fellow-countrymen.

But as regards the indomitable energy shown in great dangers, contempt for death, and the upholding of discipline, it (the British Army) is second to none. Who can forget the example of high-mindedness, and of Christian self-denial, which the whole of an English regiment showed some years ago, whilst doomed to death by shipwreck? This regiment had embarked on a frigate named the *Birkenhead*, in order to proceed to garrison duty at the Cape of Good Hope. The ship struck on a reef a short distance from its destination. The means which were to hand to enable those on board to be saved only permitted deliverance to the women, children, and a few sick passengers. Officers and soldiers stood to arms, and ranged themselves in rank and file on the deck whilst the means of safety were carried out, and as the vessel was slowly engulfed by the waves. Not one of these men, although young, strong, and armed, attempted to take the place of the weaker ones who were within reach

* "De l'Avenir Politique de l'Angleterre, par le Comte de Montalembert, l'un des quarante de l'Académie Française," 3rd edition. Paris, 1856. Extract preserved among Colonel Wright's papers.

of safety, and the whole regiment perished, martyrs to obedience and charity. To my mind, the name of the *Birkenhead* and the date of this shipwreck would figure on the colours of the regiment by as good a title as the most brilliant victories.*

The Count's errors of description are obvious, but he has caught the true spirit of the situation, and his testimony is enhanced by the fact that it applies, not to one solid regiment, but a collection of Military fragments.

The tale of years is spanned, and in the *National Zeitung* of Berlin of January 16th, 1902, we find a contribution signed by a German which reveals something of another country's real estimate of the English. It was a time when abuse of the British Army, which gave place to better feeling, was rife on some parts of the Continent. The writer appealed to the sense of justice of his countrymen, and against the prevalent falsehood ranged the deeds of British arms on hard-fought fields, including Waterloo, the glory of which, he reminded them, was shared by Prussian troops.

Have the people of Germany [he asked, crowning the recital] quite forgotten the sad and dreadful shipwreck of the English troopship *Birkenhead*? There were on board 638 souls—*i.e.* 464 soldiers, and 174 sailors, women, and children. In the awful excitement following the two shocks as the ship ran upon the water-hidden rocks, the doleful wailings of the women were all in keeping with the doings (behaviour) of the men. The latter quietly and resolutely discharged the duties assigned them at the pumps and lifeboats, and so loyally did they work that every woman and child was saved; but of the men very few only reached the near shore. The maintenance of order was rendered more difficult as the inestimable and worthy feeling of good fellowship forsook the soldiers, as they were only drafts, a motley crowd of men thrown together out of ten different regiments and not commanded by their own officers. Fancy, again, that the water, here tangled with wreck and seaweed, was swarming with sharks, and death in its grimmest aspects stared the men in the face. So heartrending was the occurrence that the King of Prussia issued orders that the official account of it should be read out to each of his Regiments as an example of true Teutonic Military discipline and virtue. But now the question comes, whether it beseems folks of the same Teutonic stock to slander and brandmark men of such stamp?

An example of "true Teutonic Military discipline and

* Quoted in Hayward's *Selected Essays*, ii. 298. See also Kingsley's *Life and Letters*, ii. 267.

virtue." Such in fact it was ; as such it was honoured at the time, and is proudly remembered still ; and as such it will be handed on in the years to come—a Deathless Story. Note well what a Naval authority has to say about this discipline.

It is *discipline* [foretells the author of *Our Naval Position and Policy*, a Naval peer *], not seamanship, that will decide future battles by sea as well as land, and this is a matter well worth considering. Nearly all Englishmen are individually brave and pugnacious, but a *body* of Englishmen, or men of any other country, will be brave according to the degree of their mutual confidence. It is the essence of discipline to give this confidence, by so organising a body that they become, as it were, one man, and no individual can leave his post without betraying himself to his own companions-in-arms, as well as to his superiors. In a well-organised body, so strong are the bands of discipline that inevitable death cannot break them, as some very beautiful instances have shown.

And the author adds in a note :

The very striking one of the soldiers who perished in the *Birkenhead*, to the very last obeying their officers and sacrificing their own lives to discipline, may be remembered.

This splendid conduct is contrasted with the loss of discipline at the storming of the Redan in the Crimea, when different regiments became mixed ; and as this " might lead to the inference that the case of the *Birkenhead* was that of a single regiment," another author, Andrew Bisset, M.A., in his book *On the Strength of Nations*, takes the question up and points out—

that the troops on the *Birkenhead* consisted of draughts from no less than *ten* different regiments, and that the admirable discipline maintained on that sad and memorable occasion—a discipline which death, coming in an unusual and horrible form, could not destroy—was due to the authority and example of the commanding officer on board, Lieut.-Colonel Alexander Seton, who perished. Undoubtedly the other officers [continues this writer] commanding the various detachments did their duty admirably also. But the fact that the orders of the senior, and therefore commanding, officer on board were obeyed with the same alacrity by all the men of the various other regiments as by the men of his own regiment, the 74th Highlanders, proves that with firmness and intelligence in the officer commanding, several bodies of men taken from

---

* Admiral the Earl of Hardwicke. He was the last Naval officer under whom Captain Robt. Salmond served. Lord Hardwicke commanded the *Vengeance*, 84 guns, of which Mr. Salmond was Master, in the Mediterranean, before Mr. Salmond took command of the *Birkenhead*, his next ship.

different regiments may possess all the qualities of a single well-organised body. What renders the case of the *Birkenhead* still more striking is that the troops on board were mostly composed of young soldiers and raw recruits. Yet such was the force of discipline on that occasion that the utmost order was preserved to the last.

And the bands of that discipline were so strong that, as Lord Hardwicke finely and truthfully says, the hovering presence of inevitable death, even, could not break them. His words found an echo some years afterwards on an occasion when the display of the same spirit which prompted them again excited grateful admiration.

Speaking of the loss of one of Her Majesty's ships in the China Seas, *The Times* of January 5th, 1865, adverted to the powerful influence at crises of habits of duty as inculcated among our soldiers and sailors.

There is nothing sublimer on record than the discipline of the troops on board the *Birkenhead*, and the finest specimens of self-sacrifice in modern times have been displayed by common sailors in shipwrecks. It is consolatory to know that this heroic spirit was not wanting among those who clung to the wreck of the *Racehorse*, and that, if we have lost a fine ship and gallant crew, we have gained at least a new assurance that habits of duty are superior to the fear of death.

Could more than this be said?

Here may be noted the changes in designation of the *Birkenhead* regiments brought about by the introduction of the territorial system. At the 50th anniversary the regiments were named as stated below :

2nd QUEEN'S.—Royal West Surrey Regiment (The Queen's).
6th.—Royal Warwickshire Regiment.
12th LANCERS.—The 12th (Prince of Wales') Royal Lancers.
12th FOOT.—The Suffolk Regiment.
43rd.—1st Battalion Oxfordshire Light Infantry.
45th.—1st Battalion Derbyshire Regiment (The Sherwood Foresters).
60th RIFLES.—The King's Royal Rifle Corps.
73rd.—2nd Battalion Royal Highlanders (The Black Watch).
74th.—2nd Battalion Highland Light Infantry.
91st.—1st Battalion Argyll and Sutherland Highlanders (Princess Louise's).

CHAPTER XVII

"ALL THAT WAS LEFT OF THEM"

When to the sessions of sweet silent thought
I summon up remembrance of things past.—SHAKESPEARE.

THE senior surviving officer at the 50th anniversary of the wreck was Colonel J. F. GIRARDOT, who as Lieutenant Girardot commanded the detachment of the 43rd Light Infantry on board the troopship. After the sinking of the vessel, with which he went down, he was cast ashore with others on some driftwood, which under Providence was the means of their preservation. It is justly claimed for Colonel Girardot that he was one of the great heroes of the *Birkenhead*. A son of the Rev. John Chaucourt Girardot, and Sophia his wife (*née* Chaplin), he was born at Averham, Newark, Notts, in 1829. He entered the Army in 1847, and went through the Kaffir War of 1852-3, including the expedition over the Orange River under General Cathcart and the battle of Berea. At the close of the Kaffir War he proceeded with the 43rd to Madras and Bangalore. He became Adjutant of the Sherwood Foresters Militia in 1856, retaining that position until 1875, and he retired in 1880 with the honorary rank of lieutenant-colonel. In 1894 Colonel Girardot married Mary, daughter of the late Mr. James Evans, of Trevanghan, County Carmarthen. He was for many years a Justice of the Peace for the county of Notts. Lieutenant Girardot wrote home the following letter shortly after the wreck.

SIMON'S BAY, *March* 1st.

MY DEAR FATHER,—I wrote one letter to say I was safe, but for fear that should not reach you I will send this to say I am quite well. I remained on the wreck until she went down; the suction took me down some way, and a man got hold of my leg, but I managed to kick him off and came up and struck out for some pieces of wood that were

LIEUT.-COLONEL J. F. GIRARDOT
(Photo by Debenham & Smith, Southampton)

"ALL THAT WAS LEFT OF THEM"

on the water, and started for land, about two miles off. I was in the water about five hours, as the shore was so rocky and the surf ran so high that a great many were lost trying to land. Nearly all those that took to the water without their clothes on were taken by sharks. Hundreds of them were all round us, and I saw men taken by them close to me; but as I was dressed (having on a flannel shirt and trousers) they preferred the others. I was not in the least hurt, and, am happy to say, kept my head clear; most of the officers lost their lives from losing their presence of mind and trying to take money with them, and from not throwing off their coats. There was no time to get the paddle-box boats down, and a great many more might have been saved but the boats that were got down deserted us and went off. From the time she struck to when she went down was 20 minutes. When I landed I found an officer of the 12th Lancers,* who had swum off with a life preserver, and 14 men who had got on with bits of wood like myself. We walked up the country 11 miles to a farm belonging to Captain Smales, formerly of the 7th Dragoon Guards, who was very kind to us, and all the men that were got on shore came up to him. I hope the Government will make up our loss to us, as I have saved nothing. Metford, of the 6th, the ensign I spoke of as having his wife on board with him, went down.† She, poor thing, was left here when the ship sailed for Buffalo mouth; I have just been to see her, and she looks more dead than alive, left all alone at this distance from her home, but we shall do all we can to be of service to her. There is a report that many have been killed in the Amatola Mountains, and our poor doctor was killed some little time back. God grant that we may all be spared to meet again.—Ever your affectionate son,

FRANK GIRARDOT.

Writing with reference to the testimonial to a survivor from "L'Agulhas," his residence in Northlands Road, Southampton, at the 50th anniversary of the sea tragedy in which he played so conspicuous a part, Colonel Girardot thanked his correspondent—

for your kind note *re* Sergeant O'Neil, with enclosed cuttings from papers, which are very incorrect, as are all I have seen, except that by General F. Maurice in *The Cornhill Magazine*, February, 1897, which is about as correct as any that could be given, even by those that were present, when each officer was attending to his own duties. The men [says Colonel Girardot] were never fallen into ranks, and the boats never

---

* Cornet Bond.

† Ensign Metford, whose melancholy fate is here referred to, was married the previous Christmas, a few days only before embarking on the *Birkenhead* at Cork, to Maria, daughter of Dr. Falkiner, of Nenagh, and niece of the late Dr. Sadleir, Provost of Trinity College.

passed between the ship and the land, but remained near the ship. No one knew where the land was, as it was pitch dark. The only boat that did not stay by the ship was that Dr. Culhane was in, which went away, and had it remained until it was light might have saved many lives, as there was no one in it but the doctor and the crew.

Anyone who had the privilege of his acquaintance at all would know Colonel Girardot to be incapable of doing the slightest intentional injustice to any man. His disposition was all the other way. It is nevertheless plain that the veteran soldier retained to the last something of the prejudice which in early days he shared against Dr. Culhane. In his letter to Captain Wright dated Keis Kama Hoek, July, 1852, the first page of which is facsimiled in this book, Lieutenant Girardot wrote:

I have not the slightest doubt that Dr. Culhane set up the report [that Captain Wright deserted the ship]. I only wish you or I had been in England at the time of his Court-Martial, and he would have had something else to think about than writing lies in the papers.

As he said in 1902, immediately after the wreck the young Lieutenant went on to the frontier for two years' war, and never saw any of the newspapers—so that he would not know about the statements made there; and presumably he was unaware of the finding of the Naval Court-Martial which acquitted Dr. Culhane. This short explanation is necessary as much in the interest of Colonel Girardot as that of the unfortunate but absolved doctor himself. To resume.

I was in charge of the party at the chain-pumps below [continues Colonel Girardot in his letter written at the 50th anniversary] until about five minutes before the *Birkenhead* parted and went down, when I was on the poop with Colonel Wright and a number of men. I shall be very glad if you will forward me an account of the presentation to Sergeant O'Neil. I am pleased to hear that one who took part in that grand display of discipline by drafts of several regiments, not even under their own officers, has lived to be so well appreciated.

In a subsequent letter the senior surviving officer said:

I was glad to see Lord Roberts had taken Sergeant O'Neil's case up. I thought, perhaps, the case being mentioned in so many of the London papers, you might have heard of others still living of those saved from the wreck; but considering the small number who escaped, and fifty years having passed, perhaps it is not so much to be wondered at, although most of both officers and men were very young. You may have observed,

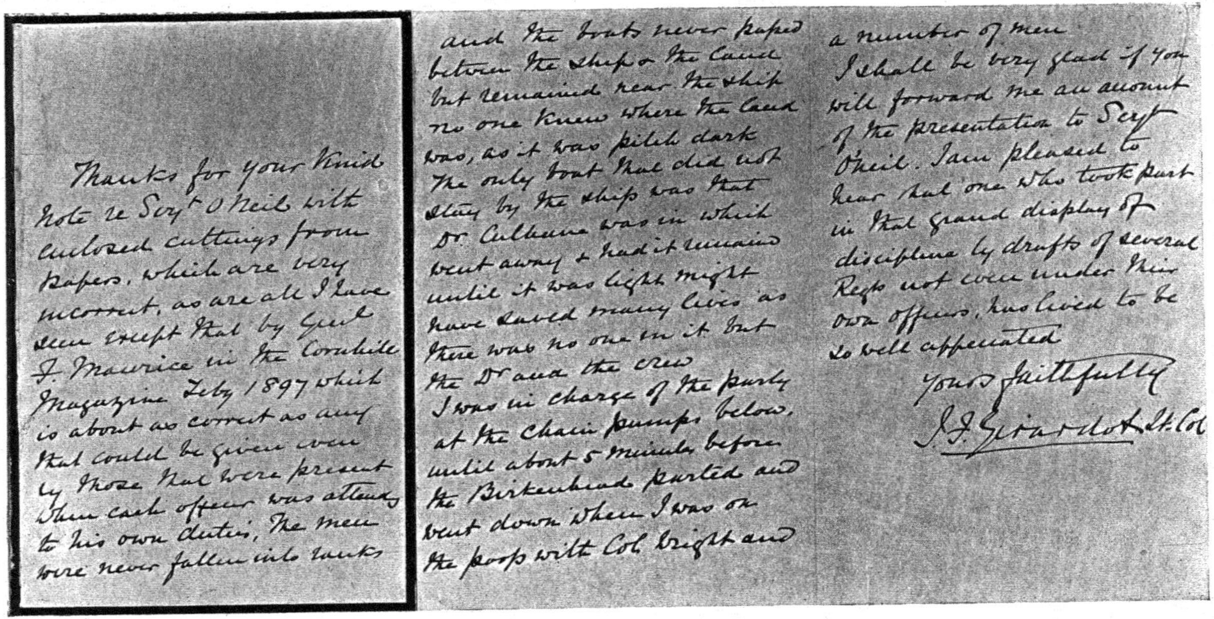

Thanks for your kind
note re Sergt O'Neil with
enclosed cuttings from
papers, which are very
incorrect, as are all I have
seen except that by Genl
F. Maurice in the Cornhill
Magazine Feby 1897 which
is about as correct as any
that could be given even
by those that were present
when each officer was attending
to his own duties, The men
were never fallen into ranks

and the boats never passed
between the ship & the land
but remained near the ship
no one knew where the land
was, as it was pitch dark
The only boat that did not
stay by the ship was that
Dr. Culhane was in which
went away & had it remained
until it was light might
have saved many lives as
there was no one in it but
the Dr and the crew
I was in charge of the party
at the chain pumps below,
until about 5 minutes before
the Birkenhead parted and
went down when I was on
the poop with Col. Wright and

a number of men
I shall be very glad if you
will forward me an account
of the presentation to Sergt
O'Neil. I am pleased to
hear that one who took part
in that grand display of
discipline by drafts of several
Regts not even under their
own officers, has lived to be
so well appreciated

Yours faithfully
J. F. Girardot Lt. Col

Facsimile of Letter written by Colonel Girardot at Date of Fiftieth Anniversary

"ALL THAT WAS LEFT OF THEM" 199

by *The Cornhill Magazine*, that the behaviour of the troops on board was thought much more of in Prussia than it was in England, where no order was given to read the record at the head of every regiment, as in Prussia; but the Duke of Wellington, then Commander-in-Chief, was not much in the habit of rewarding those under him. I fear you will find the making of a book giving a clear account of the wreck a very difficult affair. Even the papers of that date give most inaccurate accounts. They, of course, had to depend on what they heard from those who escaped, whose ideas of what took place differ most widely. Sergt.-Major Kilkeary says he "went off in the boat with the women," that "the sea was rough," and that he "saw the ship go down." I went down with her standing on the poop, and could not see more than a few feet from the ship *—the sea perfectly calm except a long swell, ever present on that coast. Other accounts say, "The troops stood on the deck with arms presented." The *Cornhill* is the best account I have seen. It is very good of you to take so much interest in an event that took place so long ago. Going on to the frontier immediately after for two years' war, and never seeing any of the newspapers, I do not know whether much interest was taken in it by the country at large, but certainly nothing like what is taken in African affairs now. Only the senior officer saved was promoted. The remainder being subalterns, no notice whatever was taken of them at the War Office, except that I had a letter from the Paymaster-General asking where the money was that I had for the payment of the forty men under my command!

This should settle the question, if it be anywhere in doubt, as to whether the junior Military officers who survived were promoted, or any officer was compensated. It is some satisfaction to know now that the Duke of Wellington gave a promise that Lieutenant Girardot's conduct at the wreck should receive public recognition. How gratifying it would have been to be able to tell him this, had it been possible while he lived! But he was not unhonoured. On the memorable date February 26th, half-a-century after he helped to make it so, Colonel Girardot received a message which must have given him pleasure.

On the 50th anniversary of the wreck of the *Birkenhead*, the officers of The Queen's, whose regiment was represented on board, send hearty

---

* But they had a lantern or two on the poop. Sergeant Kilkeary wrote in explanation of the above: "I saw the *Birkenhead* list over and sink quite distinctly. Had we tried to land in due course after leaving the place where she struck, we should, in my judgment, have been capsized. I knew the nature of the task assigned to those steering the boat on a rock-bound, shark-infested coast, and I made up my mind to run no risk of that kind."

greetings to one who did so much on this memorable occasion to uphold the glorious traditions of the British Army.

To this kindly remembrance he returned the reply:

Lieut.-Colonel Girardot begs sincerely to thank the officers of The Queen's for their hearty greeting on the 50th anniversary of the wreck of the *Birkenhead*. He well remembers poor Ensign Boylan, who commanded the detachment of The Queen's.

Poor Colonel Girardot. He died on September 11th of the 50th anniversary year. The world is the poorer for his loss, but it is the richer for the page he helped to write on the tablets of our national history. He possessed in a marked degree the modest reserve of brave men. Of his thought for others and forgetfulness of self, a striking instance may be cited here. It relates to something which occurred at the wreck of the *Birkenhead*, and the fact that he always kept the story back is *prima facie* evidence that it redounded to his credit. We only heard of it after his death. It seems that when the raft upon which young Girardot and others were drifting was within 300 yards of the shore, it got among rocks and seaweed. He told the men they would have to swim to land. All started to do so except Lieutenant Girardot and one man, a soldier, who said he could not swim. The officer thereupon said he would take him on his back, if he would promise not to pull him down. The promise was given, and officer and private reached the beach together. Who the man was Colonel Girardot never knew; he did not ask—it was sufficient for him that he had saved him. But that soldier owed his life to an act which, for gallantry and generosity, equals anything in the whole story of the *Birkenhead*. Such a man was Colonel Girardot. All honour to his name!

One who was near and dear to him wrote of his illness and death:

The end at last was painfully sudden at 7 a.m. He had suffered from heart disease for six years, but he had been much better till the last six months.

He fell peacefully into the long, calm sleep which had been gradually stealing over him, and a noble spirit went to its rest and to its reward. Colonel Girardot left a widow, and a young son for whom nothing better could be hoped than that he might follow worthily in his father's footsteps. The Colonel was buried in Rownhams Churchyard, Southampton, close by the grave of Field-Marshal Sir Neville Bowles Chamberlain. It is a satisfaction to recall that during his last days he read with interest manuscripts prepared for the first edition of this book, and to remember that a work of which he was capable of judging met with his approval.

The death of Colonel Girardot was a blow to the other surviving officers.

I saw in the papers the notice of poor Colonel Girardot's death [wrote Captain Bond-Shelton], which has made me very sad. I did not know he had been ill. Captain Lucas and myself are now the only officers surviving of the *Birkenhead.*

I feared the worst [said Captain Lucas], as I had not heard from Colonel Girardot. I am sad at the loss. Although we had not met for years, I always had an affectionate memory of my old chum. The "Roll Call" is fast becoming less and less. Well, we have all got to go when the time comes. Girardot always did his duty as a man should.

Within a year of his death the officers of the Oxfordshire Light Infantry (formerly the 43rd) had placed in the colonnade of Chelsea Hospital a memorial bearing the inscription printed below.

LT.-COL. JOHN FRANCIS GIRARDOT,
Late 43rd Light Infantry and Adjutant Sherwood Foresters Militia,
Who died 11th September, 1902,
Aged 73 years.
Erected by brother officers of the 43rd Light Infantry.

He was one of the last surviving officers of the *Birkenhead*, on board which vessel, as a lieutenant, he commanded a detachment of the 43rd Light Infantry, and by his personal valour saved many lives. He subsequently served in the Kaffir War, 1852-3, and received the medal and clasp.

This tablet is erected by his brother officers of the 43rd Light Infantry as a token of their appreciation of his gallant service.

Captain Bond-Shelton

The name of Cornet Bond, 12th Royal Lancers, the next surviving officer, stands forth prominently in connection with the *Birkenhead.* This is the officer referred to by Field-

Marshal Lord Wolseley in his second letter on the subject. Cornet Bond and his Lancers worked hard after the ship struck, rendering much useful help where needed and performing humane deeds. The plunging and terrified horses were got up on deck by them, and into the sea, and at the last moment Cornet Bond jeopardised his own safety by staying to secure and carry up from the saloon cabin two young children who, in the confusion following the striking of the vessel and the rush upon deck, had been forgotten and left behind to what, but for Cornet Bond's timely intervention, must have been inevitable death. This act of self-forgetfulness in the face of danger, and consideration for others first, is but an isolated example of the conduct generally of officers and men on board the doomed troopship. Scarcely had it been performed, and the children passed to the boats, than their heroic preserver went down with the ship. As will have been gathered from his description of the wreck, he managed to get ashore with the help of a life-saving appliance he had secured, which he filled while swimming in the water. When he got there he found that his charger had already reached land, and was standing on the beach to welcome him! The home of this gallant gentleman, Captain R. M. Bond-Shelton, at the period of the *Birkenhead* anniversary in 1902, was "The Argory," Moy, Co. Tyrone. Writing from there on April 14th the Captain enclosed a copy of the sketch he made of the wreck from recollection.

> The original [he said], which is large, I exhibited at both the Military and Naval Exhibitions held in London a few years ago. I was given diplomas from both. An artist saw the picture there, and made a very large picture from his own idea, which was submitted for the Queen's inspection at Osborne and has been exhibited all over the world.

This large picture was the work of Mr. Hemy, the painter of dramatic sea subjects. It is reproduced in these pages, together with Captain Bond-Shelton's realistic sketch and other pictures.

> I have the pleasing recollection [proceeded the Captain's letter] of carrying up two little girls that I found on the floor of the saloon cabin

CAPTAIN R. M. BOND-SHELTON
Photo by Bassano, Old Bond Street, W.)

quite alone, and handing them to some one on deck, who put them into a boat with the women.* I had been sent below by Colonel Seton to get something out of his cabin. I do not think I can add anything to the few words printed on the back of enclosed photo of explanation, except that *every one behaved equally well* in that most trying time of the wreck.

Captain Bond-Shelton was the son of a large landed proprietor in Co. Armagh and in Wiltshire. He was born at Cheltenham, and joined the Army in 1851, his war service including the Cape (Kaffir War, 1852-3), Crimea, and Indian Mutiny. He retired in 1858; but his adventures were not yet finished.

After I left the service [he wrote on May 20th, 1902] I was with the Italian Army in 1859, when they and the French were fighting with the Austrians. In 1864 I took a bag of despatches for the Princess of Wales to the King of Denmark. I was going to join the Danish Army, who were fighting the Prussians, at Dybol. I was with the headquarters at Sonderburg. I knew the King of Denmark and the Crown Prince very well. I dined with the King twice after delivering the despatches. Any papers I had about the *Birkenhead* were burned about four years ago, when I had the great misfortune to have my house nearly completely burned down.

This was indeed a heavy blow, in suffering which the Captain would have the sympathy of everybody. The elder and only surviving brother of Captain Bond-Shelton, Mr. Joshua Walter MacGeough Bond, D.L., of Drumsill, Armagh, died in Paris on August 29th, 1905, in his 74th year. Mr. MacGeough Bond sat in the Palmerstonian interest for the city of Armagh in the Parliament of 1859-65. He was formerly in the Army. A younger brother of Captain Bond-Shelton's was a Captain in the Grenadier Guards; he was a child when the *Birkenhead* was lost.

* One of these children was believed to have been Marian Darkin, whose mother was going out to join her husband, Drum-Major John Robert Darkin, of The Queen's. Marian Darkin was surviving in 1902 as Mrs. Parkinson, at Beckingham; she died in November, 1904. Her letter to Lieut.-Colonel Mackie, printed elsewhere, shows, however, that she was carried on deck by her mother and lowered into the boat, so that she could not have been one of the children rescued by Cornet Bond. The other little girl, Captain Bond-Shelton says, he believed was a bandmaster's daughter. If so, she was the daughter of Mr. Zwyker, of The Queen's, the only bandmaster on board,

Captain G. A. Lucas

Captain Gould Arthur Lucas, late 73rd Regiment, the third surviving officer, was at the 50th anniversary of the wreck residing at Mitton Manor, Penkridge, Staffordshire.* His father was the Right Hon. Edward Lucas, of Castle Shane, Co. Monaghan, Ireland. It was this gallant officer, then Ensign Lucas, who superintended the placing of the women and children in the boat. Captain Lucas, after serving with the Army through the troublous times following the *Birkenhead* disaster, retired from his regiment in 1859, having got his company, and for many years subsequently he was a magistrate, and filled other appointments in Natal, S.A., during the latter portion of the period occupying the important post of Chief Magistrate at Durban. He returned to England in 1897. This officer and Lieutenant Girardot, of the 43rd, were on watch together the night the *Birkenhead* was wrecked. Captain Lucas heard the night orders given to the Naval officer of the watch. He was always under the impression that a small grass fire, high on the shore at Danger Point, misled that officer, who probably mistook it for Cape Agulhas lighthouse.

The graphic story of the wreck sent home by Ensign Lucas at the time will have been read earlier in these pages, to which the writer of it kindly contributed the narrative, with a few footnotes, fifty years after it was penned. His interesting correspondence with Mr. David Seton, brother of Colonel Seton, will also have been perused. Captain Lucas was in command of a squadron of the Cape Mounted Rifles for eighteen months, and he commanded the Natal Frontier Guard at Ladysmith for some years.

Writing to Lieut.-Colonel Mackie, of The Queen's Regiment, after the 50th anniversary, Captain Lucas said:

> I remember Boylan quite well. I only saw him once that night. The Queen's and the 73rd were in Eyre's Brigade in the Frontier War of 1852. I have never had the luck to meet your regiment since. I often think that too much credit was given to us for our conduct at the wreck. We were disciplined officers and men, did our duty, and did all we could for helpless women and children, as, thank God, Englishmen have the

---

* He afterwards removed to Rockdale, Abersoch, nr. Pwllheli, North Wales.

CAPTAIN LUCAS IN HIS ROBES AS CHIEF MAGISTRATE OF DURBAN
(Photo by Hy. Kisch, Durban, Natal)

habit of doing. John Smith, of The Queen's, was one of the men who, with language more forcible than polite, declared "it should never be said that they left an officer to die," and carried me along.

Having observed that his contribution to this work was "written a few days after the wreck—I was just 19 then," Captain Lucas concludes :

> Dear old Girardot! I did not know he was so ill until too late to go and see him. We were a bit tired when the order was given for each to do the best he could. Girardot and I got a stiff b.-and-s. out of the messman's storeroom, then went on to the poop.

A year later Captain Lucas was asked about another survivor who had turned up :

> The only man I knew in South Africa a survivor of the *Birkenhead* [he r eplied] was Dobson, who had been in the carpenter's crew. He was not badly off, and did me a good turn by putting me on my guard against being "stuck up" by a gang when in charge of a heavy sum belonging to the Government.

Later on Captain Lucas was surprised to receive a letter from Corporal William Smith, who was with the draft of the 12th Regiment at the wreck, and afterwards, as a Cape Mounted Rifleman, was under Captain Lucas's orders at the execution of Hans de Lango at Ladysmith, when the rope broke. It was at that time that Captain Lucas commanded a squadron of the Cape Mounted Rifles in Natal, and he was not aware of the fact that one of his troopers was a *Birkenhead* survivor. His surprise on receiving William Smith's letter, in December, 1904, was therefore pleasant as well as real, and the reminiscent character of the letter would both interest and amuse him.

The Master Gunner

No more striking figure presents itself in the survey of *Birkenhead* heroes surviving after the lapse of fifty years than Mr. John Thomas Archbold, the Naval gunner on board the ship. Mr. Archbold, the *doyen* of the survivors, was in the *Birkenhead* days, judging from the photograph taken of him later and here reproduced, a seaman of the true "hearts of oak" type which is so gloriously associated with our national history. He was washed ashore after the wreck on the driftwood to which Lieutenant Girardot and others also clung. For some time he was on the same raft as Captain Wright, who says of him that—

> while there he was, as usual, active to a degree, and encouraged the other 15 men who were also on it; but this was no more than his daily custom when on board the ship, for there he was perpetually at work, and to some purpose too.

Mr. Archbold was one of the surviving officers whose statements concerning the wreck were sent home to the Board of Admiralty by Commodore Wyvill. The Master Gunner's account of what occurred is short, but interesting.

> On the morning of February 26th I was aroused from my bed by a severe shock. I instantly ran on deck, and found the ship had struck on a rock and was rapidly sinking. I was ordered by the Captain to fire the rockets and burn the blue lights, which I did. After so doing, I went on the port sponson to clear away the port paddle-box boat. We had canted the boat when the fore part of the ship went down. At the same time I and Mr. Brodie (master) were washed overboard. When rising to the surface of the water I held on to part of the wreck. Leaving the piece of wreck I swam towards a truss of hay, where I found Mr. Brodie. Finding it impossible to hold on to the hay any longer, I made for part of the wreck, where I found Captain Wright, 91st Regiment, and nine or ten men. They assisted me on the raft floating towards the shore. We picked up Mr. Barber, assistant-engineer, and a boatswain's mate (James Lacey). We arrived on shore about one or two o'clock. Previous to landing on shore I observed a sail in the offing, distant about eight miles. After landing, I saw the schooner making for the wreck. We then proceeded on to Stanford Bay, at which place Captain Wright left us and procured some refreshment. Next morning proceeded to Captain Smales', where we were clothed and fed until sent on board Her Majesty's steamer *Rhadamanthus*.

Gunner Archbold adds a memorandum concerning the boats.

> In respect to the boats, I saw none but the port paddle-box boat, bottom up, with some seven or eight hands on her, drifting towards the shore. I heard several voices calling loudly, and in that strain of voice that I fancied some boat or boats very near at hand; and if there had been any boat or boats present to have taken the men from the floating pieces of wreck, they might with good management have been safely landed in the same cove where Captain Wright and myself were landed, and could have made several trips to and fro to the shore and saved a large number of men, as they were some time kept upon the surface of

*Yours faithfully,
John T. Archbold

P.S. I believe I am the
only Naval Officer that
is now Living that was
saved from the Wreck
of the Birkenhead   J.A.*

MR. J. T. ARCHBOLD, THE GUNNER OF THE "BIRKENHEAD"

the water by floating pieces of wreck.* My opinion is that the boat that had the women and children in saved time and lives by getting the assistance of the schooner, there being a great number on and about the wreck.

Writing from his home at Buckland, Portsmouth, in April, 1902, Mr. Archbold supplemented with a few observations the report he made to his superior officer fifty years before.

I was some eight or ten hours in the water before I reached the shore, being most of the time on a piece of the wreck. It was not our good swimming that took us ashore—it was the current setting in-shore that enabled those that were saved to reach it. Best part of us were in a state of nakedness when we landed. We were all taken to a farmhouse, where a good man was able to furnish us with a bit of clothes to put on, as he kept several Hottentots on his farm. We remained there till a ship was sent for us and brought us back to Simon's Bay. As near as we could judge, about 440 were drowned, but the women and children were put into the boats and were all saved, being picked up by a little coasting-vessel and taken to the Cape. I should be pleased to give you any information that lays in my power, but I am now nearly eighty-four years of age, and my recollection is not very good at times. Captain Wright, of the 91st Regiment, got ashore the same time as myself. I see he has passed away—a great friend of mine. I believe I am the only Naval officer that is now living that was saved from the wreck of the *Birkenhead*.

Mr. Archbold did not long survive the 50th anniversary of the wreck. He died in April, 1903, just a year after the letter above-quoted was written.

Colour-Sergeant Drake

The file of Royal Marines on board the *Birkenhead* was in charge of Colour-Sergeant John Drake, a young non-commissioned officer who had a few years previously been specially promoted for gallantry. John Drake was standing on the forecastle when the troopship struck the rock, and was thrown down by the force of the shock. In the terrible moments which followed he bravely attempted to save the life of Cornet Rolt, of the 12th Lancers, and almost succeeded in doing so. When the ship sank he was one of those who,

---

* The boats were afraid to venture in for fear of being swamped by the breakers, which they probably would have been had they made the attempt.

on regaining the surface, clung to the maintopmast, from the yard of which he was taken, with another Royal Marine (John Cooper), on the following afternoon by the schooner *Lioness*. Sergeant Drake always spoke warmly of the courageous conduct of Captain Salmond, who gave him orders which he carried hither and thither on the sinking ship.

This veteran survivor of many perils of the sea was Dorsetshire born and bred. His father was a gamekeeper to the Lord Portman of his day, and young Drake was trained to be a woodman; but he was destined for other things, and in September, 1843, he joined the Royal Marines. The circumstances of his subsequent special promotion are noteworthy. H.M.S. *Waterwitch* captured the Brazilian slave-vessel *Romeo Primero*, which the prisoners on board made a desperate attempt to retake, and John Drake, who was one of the party in charge of the prize, continued to fight gallantly after receiving two wounds. The facts were reported by Commander Mansfield, R.N., to the Lords Commissioners of the Admiralty, who in January, 1848, were—

> pleased to mark their approbation of this Private's excellent conduct by directing that he be immediately and specially promoted to the rank of Corporal, and that this order be read at the head of each of the Divisions of Royal Marines. This highly creditable circumstance is to be recorded at the Portsmouth Division in favour of the Corporal.

In the July following, by further direction of the Lords of the Admiralty, Corporal Drake, then serving on the *Frolic*, was disembarked at headquarters and there promoted to the rank of sergeant.

In 1850 John Drake, then a colour-sergeant, was drafted to the *Birkenhead*, lying at Portsmouth. In those days the vessel was considered an excellent trooper, and Sergeant Drake esteemed himself lucky in being appointed to her. Being a Marine, he was under the immediate orders of the commander of the ship, not of the officer commanding the troops.

After the *Birkenhead* episode Colour-Sergeant Drake did much good service for his Queen and country, as the official record of his decorations testifies.

COLOUR-SERGEANT JOHN DRAKE, R.M.L.I.
(Photo by Alfred Hughes, Strand, W.C.)

Served in the Baltic and Black Sea in 1854 and 1855, and has the Baltic and Crimean medals, with clasps for Sebastopol and Azov, also the Turkish medal. Served in China in 1860, and has the medal for that service with clasp for Taku Forts. Has long-service and good-conduct medal.

The gallant Marine took his discharge on September 22nd, 1864,* after serving "honestly and faithfully"—as the certificate sets forth—" for the space of 21 years and 11 days," of which long term he was colour-sergeant 13 years and 237 days. Yet a sixth medal, awarded specially by the Admiralty for meritorious service, and carrying with it an additional pension of £10 per annum, was bestowed upon this veteran in the autumn of 1901. He was then residing in South Lambeth.

For twenty-eight years John Drake was an attendant at Westminster Abbey, a post which he vacated in 1905, when he went to live with his married daughters at Limetrees Farm, West End, near Hayes, Middlesex. This peaceful retirement, to which he had long looked forward, was unfortunately of short duration. It terminated with painful suddenness as the result of a fatal apoplectic seizure. The veteran died on Easter Monday, April 24th, in his 85th year, and was buried in Greenford Park Cemetery, the mourners including a grandson, H. Goodliff, serving on H.M.S. *Montagu*, attached to the Channel Fleet.

COLOUR-SERGEANT O'NEIL

Colour-Sergeant John O'Neil, of the 91st Regiment (Argyll and Sutherland Highlanders), was living in quiet retirement at Boston, Lincolnshire, in 1902. He was then in his 75th year. O'Neil went to Boston in 1863 as drill instructor to the Rifle Volunteers; he became also drill master at the Grammar School. Shortly before the *Birkenhead* jubilee he retired from his post at the Grammar School, after thirty-eight years' service; he had ceased to be drill instructor of the

---

* An interesting account of the veteran soldier-seaman and his exploits was published about this time in *The British Army and Navy Review*, under the title "Remarkable Passages in the Life of John Drake, Marine." This we are able to give further on by permission of the successors to the property in the *Review*, which had only a short existence.

Volunteers a few years previously, when he received a presentation watch and other gifts from the Rifle Corps. The son of a farrier-major of the 7th Dragoons, O'Neil was born a soldier on shipboard at Malta. As a boy he sailed to South Africa with the 91st Regiment in 1842, and was shipwrecked in Table Bay. He fought in the Kaffir War under Sir Harry Smith, and also in operations conducted in those early days against the Boers. In 1852 O'Neil, a corporal then, was sent on escort duty to Robben Island with prisoners. He afterwards, with the two privates who accompanied him, went on board the ill-fated troopship *Birkenhead* at Simon's Bay to return to the headquarters of his regiment. At the 50th anniversary of the disaster which followed, he made a statement of his experience at the wreck.

The drafts on board [he said] included 100 of the Argyll and Sutherlands, and an officer of ours, Major Wright, was in command of the troops.* I and my escort had only been on board half-an-hour when the vessel struck on a rock between Simon's Bay and Port Elizabeth, somewhere near Danger Point.† She struck a mile and a quarter from shore. It is fair to suppose the disaster was caused by reckless navigation, because outside the breakers the sea was as smooth almost as this floor; there was scarcely a ripple on the surface of the water. It was a strange scene when she struck. The Captain of the ship, ah! I recollect well the last words he uttered. He rushed down below and told the sailors to man the boats. "Lower your boats, men," said he, "we are all lost!" I never saw him again.‡ Major Wright gave the order, "All hands fall in on deck," and we fell in, every man. He told off so many soldiers and so many sailors to each boat, to get them out and save the women and children. I forget how many boats there were, but every boat available was got over the side. No man was allowed to leave the ranks till the boats were pushed off. Major Wright threatened to shoot any man who stepped towards the boats, but no one thought of doing it. Any rush

* Colonel Seton was in command of the troops. Captain Wright was second in command, and his own detachment numbered sixty men.

† The escort must have been on board eight hours, the time which elapsed between the ship leaving Simon's Bay and her striking.

‡ As to this, Captain Lucas, on reading the statement subsequently, wrote: "The wreck happened so many years ago that Sergeant O'Neil's memory may have failed. No blame is to be attached to him in consequence. I am sure that his memory has failed him as regards the Captain of the ship, who was as cool as any of us—in fact, he was the Naval officer who desired me to take my 'pump spell' and try to get the paddle-box boat into the water, sending another Naval officer to direct me." Similar testimony is borne by others.

COLOUR-SERGEANT JOHN O'NEIL, 91ST REGT.
(Photo by G. E. Hackford, Boston)

would have swamped the boats for certain. Discipline was maintained till the last. The ship went down twenty minutes after striking. It was a terrible time, but we stood on. We all expected to die, but the women and children were got safely off. Not one of them were drowned, thank God! They and their escort comprised the greater part of the 179 who were saved. The water rose as the ship was sinking. Before we left her we were up to our necks in water on the top deck. Just before the end came Major Wright addressed us. "You men who cannot swim," said he, "stick to some wreckage—whatever you can lay hands on. As for you who can swim, I can give you no advice. As you see, there are sharks about, and I cannot advise you how to avoid them," which of course he could not. There was many a quiet hand-shake and silent good-bye. Few of us hoped to live through it. The breakers between us and the shore were awful. At last the ship sank. There was a lurch and a plunge, and all was over. I found myself in the water and struck out for shore. I had next to nothing on in the way of clothing. It was a fight for life. We were not above a mile and a quarter from land, as far as my eye served me; but that is plenty far enough when there are breakers and sharks! The breakers were so big. Luckily I knew how to swim breakers, or I should not be here now. Any one not knowing how to would have been drowned, as sure as fate! They would smother him. With proper management a breaker will sometimes sweep you in for hundreds of yards. The backwash was the worst. I stuck to it and got ashore at last, escaping the sharks. I saw nothing of the rest, or of the ship's boats. All the trouble was not over when I got ashore. I had to walk sixteen miles stark naked under a blazing sun before I met any one or obtained any assistance. I shall never forget Major Wright. If it had not been for him all hands would have been lost, women and children and all. You may know that he was afterwards granted an annuity of £100, and he deserved it. I believe there was a lot of treasure on board the *Birkenhead* when she foundered. The military chest was on board for the troops—so we were led to understand. I think it is true, because for some time afterwards we were paid with Mexican dollars. They never recovered anything from the wreck.

This survivor of a tragedy of the sea the record of which is imperishable afterwards fought the Kaffirs a second time, was wounded, and served a couple of years in India. He possessed the Kaffir and long-service medals. The public testimonial raised in his honour was presented to O'Neil on May 22nd, when he was the recipient of an address signed on behalf of the subscribers by Mr. Wm. White, M.A., Headmaster of Boston School; Lieut.-Colonel R. W. Staniland and Major W. H. Gane, Volunteer officers; and A. C. Addison, hon. secretary.

The kindly interest of Field-Marshals Lord Roberts and Lord Wolseley in yourself and in the fund [read the document] will have been very gratifying to you, and the notices in the local Press have expressed the admiration which we, in common with all Englishmen, feel for that historic and stirring example of the performance of duty heroically displayed at the loss of the *Birkenhead*, in which you, sir, took part half-a-century ago. We who have known you personally for years, as one of the survivors, wish to mark our sense of the privilege by offering you on your retirement, after long years of service, from the post of Drill Instructor of our Grammar School, a small earnest of our heartiest good wishes that you may enjoy many remaining years of health and happiness.

Sergeant O'Neil in his reply, alluding to the cheerful obedience of orders at all times by the boys of the school, made a touching reference.

Now small matters like this [the old soldier said] are the seeds of discipline, which is a plant of slow growth but bears fruit in due season; and as I am on the subject of discipline I might be allowed to say a word or two about that memorable disaster, the wreck of the *Birkenhead*. My share in that is soon told: simple obedience of orders, standing on deck slowly but surely sinking, whilst the women and children got safely away in the boats; then by God's providence, and a long and perilous swim 'midst sharks, breakers, and seaweeds, I managed to scramble ashore.

The wishes expressed that the Sergeant's life might still be spared for many years were not, unhappily, realised. He died on Christmas Day, 1904, and an imposing Military funeral further testified to the respect felt for him, and for the association of his name with the heroic episode of '52. Among the mourners was his son, Frederick George O'Neil, of the Royal Marines. A holly wreath, sent in memory of the *Birkenhead* and on behalf of the survivors, bore a verse from Sir Francis Doyle's famous poem:

> There rose no murmur from the ranks, no thought,
>   By shameful strength, unhonoured life to seek.
> Our post to quit we were not trained, nor taught
>   To trample down the weak.

The wreath was also inscribed "Danger Point, S.A., Feb. 26th, 1852," the place and date of the historic shipwreck. On a marble headstone raised to the veteran was carved in a panel the badge of his old regiment, the 91st.

COLOUR-SERGEANT KILKEARY

Colour-Sergeant Bernard Kilkeary, late of the 73rd Regiment, a *Birkenhead* survivor, was residing at Dungannon, Co. Tyrone, at the 50th anniversary. For this work he gave a short account of his personal experience at the wreck, from which he was saved by one of the boats.

There were [he wrote], besides the troops, some half-dozen Marines for the four guns which the frigate carried, and a crew of about 120. When I stepped on board the vessel in January, 1852, I little thought that she would never again sail over British waters. Colonel Seton, 74th Highlanders, who commanded the drafts, amounting to about 500 men, appointed me at Cork sergeant-major for the voyage, and all went well until that memorable morning in February when the ship struck the reef off Cape Agulhas.* Immediately upon impact I went on deck, where, meeting Colonel Seton, I received from him a last command to disembark the women and children into a quarter-boat, and take charge of the occupants.† In this work I was ably seconded by Cornet Bond, of the 12th Lancers (now Captain Bond-Shelton), to whose indefatigable exertions many of the children owed their deliverance from the vessel. He himself was saved by swimming to the shore, two miles or so off. Before leaving I heard Captain Salmond tell Colonel Seton there was no danger, and it was my intention to have landed the women and children on shore and returned on board ship; but we had scarcely pulled away 200 yards when suddenly, and in our full view, the *Birkenhead* listed and sank, carrying down her living freight.‡ A very heavy sea was running at the time, and we decided to stand out to sea, where, after being tossed about for twelve hours, we were picked up by the schooner *Lioness*, of Capetown. On getting aboard the *Lioness* I suggested to her captain that our quarter-boat and one of his boats should proceed to the scene of the wreck. This he gladly assented to, and it resulted in the rescue of some forty or fifty men who were found clinging to the rigging. These were also brought on board the *Lioness*, whose captain treated us all with the greatest kindness. On the next day the *Lioness* spoke the *Rhadamanthus*, and signalled, " Troops on board from the wreck of the

---

* Danger Point.

† A letter written by Captain Lucas to Mr. David Seton, given in the chapter devoted to Colonel Seton, shows that Sergeant Kilkeary did receive the command he speaks of as to disembarking the women and children, a work which Ensign Lucas superintended at the request of Colonel Seton. Mr. Richards, master's assistant, took charge of the boat. Sergeant Kilkeary says, "For disciplinary purposes I had command of the Military section, soldiers, soldiers' wives, and children. The Naval portion steered the boat and looked after themselves. Mr. Richards conferred with me in moments of doubt or difficulty."

‡ See observation of Colonel Girardot, in statement made by that officer.

Birkenhead," whereupon the *Rhadamanthus* took the schooner in tow, and brought us to Simon's Bay. At Simon's Bay we were transferred on board the guardship *Castor*, while the *Rhadamanthus* proceeded down to the vicinity of the wreck and found and brought to Simon's Bay those survivors who had succeeded in getting ashore. At Simon's Bay I compiled the official narrative of the sad occurrence for the Military authorities at the Cape.

In regard to this last statement, Sergeant Kilkeary explained that it refers to a roll which he prepared of officers and men on board. It was drawn up at Simon's Bay—

from which place it was forwarded under the covering letter of the senior surviving officer, Major Wright. I conferred with the survivors of rank of each detachment, and ascertained the strength of each at time of sailing and the then effective strength, and from this data I compiled an alphabetical roll of the drowned.

The wreck itself was officially reported at the Cape some time earlier by Dr. Culhane. Sergeant Kilkeary adds that—

the boat in which I left put off after the ship was backed, which caused a second rent, and Cornet Bond, at great risk, went below, the engine-room fires being extinguished by a water inrush, and rescued the two last children and handed them to me. You mention in your letter Colour-Sergeant John Drake. I knew him very well. He has a romantic record. He told me at Simon's Bay he was saved by holding on to a hay bale, and the purser's steward, James Jeffery, got ashore on a table. Jeffery had been previously wrecked in the *Thunderbolt*, and afterwards he was wrecked in the Black Sea about 1854. On the occasion of the wreck of the *Birkenhead* all ranks, officers and men, acted nobly, each doing his duty to his country and his Queen; the coolest and most heroic, if I must differentiate, being Colonel Seton, commanding the troops, who from the impact was on deck in full regimentals, giving his orders as if on parade, at the last dying like a hero at the post of duty. He set a very inspiring example, conducing to that perfect discipline never surpassed in the annals of our Army.

Born at Parsonstown, King's County, Ireland, in 1827, Bernard Kilkeary joined the Army at an early age. He served 12 years and 201 days with the colours, and afterwards for 20 years in the Auxiliary Forces, his last corps being the Mid-Ulster Artillery, of which he was Paymaster-Sergeant. Of his total service of thirty-two years, thirty years were in non-commissioned rank. His active service comprised the Kaffir War, 1852-3, the expedition across the Orange River to Basutoland (battle of Berea), and the Indian Mutiny.

COLOUR-SERGEANT BERNARD KILKEARY, 73RD REGT.

(Special photo of this veteran survivor as Paymaster-Sergeant of the Mid-Ulster Artillery. Taken at the time he received the Meritorious Service Medal by W. J. Trimble & Sons, Dungannon.

"ALL THAT WAS LEFT OF THEM" 215

The long and honourable career of this Military veteran certainly called for some form of special recognition, and it was a source of satisfaction to all who knew him when, in 1905, he was selected as a recipient of the meritorious service medal, which carries with it an annuity of £10. The medal was presented to Mr. Kilkeary in the King's name at an interesting parade on August 14th of the year mentioned, when the permanent staff of the Mid-Ulster Royal Garrison Artillery formed up in review order in the quadrangle of the quarters at Castle Hill, Dungannon, and Warrant-Officer Phil Donohoe, R.A., having brought the parade to attention, Captain E. W. M. Walker, R.A., the Adjutant, proceeded with the presentation ceremony, which he said had happily fallen to him to perform before leaving Dungannon.

He holds, as you know, a most honourable record [observed the Adjutant of Mr. Kilkeary]; in fact, the medal has never been bestowed in a more deserving case. As you are aware, his military record has extended over thirty-two years, twelve of these being with the colours—the 73rd Regiment—and the remainder here on the permanent staff, as well as upon the staff of the Leinster Regiment. Besides seeing active service in South Africa and in the Indian Mutiny, he was present at the wreck of the *Birkenhead*. Doubtless this distinction would have been granted to him many years ago had he not thought right to wait so long—so patiently—before making application.

Captain Walker hoped in concluding that the owner of the medal would live many years to wear it, a sentiment in which doubtless all heartily joined. Mr. Kilkeary acknowledged the presentation in a well and modestly worded little speech.

I beg to return my grateful and dutiful thanks to his most gracious Majesty the King for the signal honour which he has been pleased, through your medium, to confer upon me. To you, sir, I also respectfully tender my sincere acknowledgments. It is particularly gratifying to me to receive this medal standing in close proximity to Warrant-Officer Donohoe and the members of the permanent staff Mid-Ulster Royal Garrison Artillery—a regiment in which I served many years, and whose officers, non-commissioned officers, and men have at all times upheld the best traditions of the British Army. Believe me, this ceremonial, the recollection of which will never fade from my memory, will be deeply appreciated by the Royal Highlanders, that distinguished regiment in which I commenced my Military career.

The honour thus done him, so well deserved, would not fail to give pleasure to his old Corps, the 73rd, in which he served on the *Birkenhead*.

Sergeant Francis Ginn

One of the body of brave young soldiers who maintained at the wreck the exemplary discipline afterwards extolled by Captain Wright was Private Francis Ginn, of the 43rd Light Infantry, then a recruit just turned eighteen. Obedient to orders he, with others, stood upon the troopship, awaiting patiently what seemed certain death, while the safety of the women and children was secured by means of the boats. When finally the *Birkenhead* went down, Francis Ginn found himself battling for life on the surface of the dark and troubled waters. He was a good swimmer, and divesting himself of his clothing he contrived, by alternately striking out shoreward and clinging for support to passing wreckage, to keep himself afloat during the long weary hours of that dreadful night and the following morning, until at midday he was picked up in a benumbed and exhausted condition by a Dutch fishing-boat. He was landed by the Dutchmen and carried on the back of one of them to what served as a hospital, where he remained three months before he fully recovered. The survivor thus brought ashore and tended back to health and strength always remembered with gratitude the kind treatment of his rescuers. On rejoining his regiment he served with it in the Kaffir War, and afterwards through the Indian Mutiny.

Born at Sudbury, in Suffolk, Francis Ginn was brought up to the peaceful occupation of silk weaving, a calling which he quitted on November 12th, 1851, when he enlisted in the 43rd Light Infantry. He was then a fine young fellow of seventeen years and eleven months, standing well on to 6 feet—his actual height when in the Army was 5 feet $11\frac{1}{4}$ inches. He was a good soldier as well as a tall one, and served his Queen faithfully, for the most part in India, until, at the age of twenty-eight, he bade farewell to his comrades-in-arms at Fort St. George, Madras, on December 14th, 1861.

SERGEANT FRANCIS GINN, 43RD LIGHT INFANTRY
(Photo by J. H. Abbott, Lavenham)

"ALL THAT WAS LEFT OF THEM" 217

He then held the rank of sergeant, and his discharge certificate states that he—

served in the Army for 10 years and 121 days; was corporal five months and sergeant one year; was at the Cape of Good Hope one year and nine months, in the East Indies seven years and ten months; was granted a medal for the Kaffir War of 1851-2-3, and also a medal for the suppression of the Mutiny and Rebellion in India, 1857-8.

For many years subsequently this survivor was employed by the British and Foreign Wharf Co., Ltd., at Lower East Smithfield, E., where he received every consideration. When no longer able to remain there he returned to his native town of Sudbury, where he died, after twelve months' residence with his brother-in-law, Mr. William Wright, on January 13th, 1904, and was buried with every mark of the respect and honour due to the memory of so worthy a Military veteran.

Corporal William Smith

No sterner fight for life was made at the foundering of the troopship than that fought amidst sharks, kelpweed and breakers by William Smith, of the 12th Foot. When the vessel was sinking he assisted in rigging, and for some time worked at, the chain-pumps below, and he afterwards claimed to be the only private soldier who returned from them alive. He sprang up the companion-ladder just before the deck parted amidships, when he was washed into the sea. Handicapped as he was by inability to swim, this young stalwart struggled desperately for the land, or drifted towards it when his efforts slackened, clinging to portions of the wreckage. He got ashore at last, more dead than alive, after being twenty hours in the water. Following the wreck, Smith saw active service with his regiment in the bush of South Africa. He next joined the Cape Mounted Rifles, served as a Volunteer in later South African wars, and, among other occupations, filled for a time that of convict warder. His whole career was exceptionally varied and interesting. Discharged as full corporal possessing four badges, the holder of several war medals, and with a record of twenty-one years' honourable service to his account, he was, at the 50th anniversary of the wreck, living at Middleton Cheney, near Banbury, in Oxfordshire, there luxuriating on the munificent pension of 1*s*. 1½*d*. per day.

A native of Eydon, Northamptonshire, William Smith enlisted at Weedon, Bucks, in 1848, in the 12th Regiment of Foot, then commanded by Lieut.-Colonel J. M. Percival. Let him tell his experience at the shipwreck in his own words.

After four years' service in England I embarked on board the *Birkenhead* at Spithead, on January 1st, 1852. We took in men and stores at Queenstown. We had it very rough in the Bay of Biscay; made Madeira; then sailed on to Sierra Leone; from thence to St. Helena. At Simon's Bay we took in stores and a few Colonial troops. We left Simon's Bay about 6 p.m. on February 25th, *en route* for Port Elizabeth and East London, as our different corps were stationed on the frontier. We surmised that Captain Salmond, R.N., commanding the vessel, was anxious to get ahead of H.M.S. *Styx*, then on the Cape coast. At two o'clock in the morning, on the wheel being relieved, a tremendous shock was felt, and we knew the ship had struck. This was on Danger Point, a short distance from Cape Agulhas. There was a panic for a short time, but admirable discipline was maintained through the efforts of the officers. A few Congreve rockets were thrown up, but were of no avail. A gun could not be fired, as the magazine was almost instantly under water. Good order was eventually restored, but the shock was so sudden. I believe twenty minutes had hardly elapsed before the vessel was in pieces. I was sleeping on the lower deck when the shock came, and crowded up the ladder with others, but found it difficult work. Some never came up at all, but were drowned in their hammocks, the water rushing in so suddenly. Most of the troops were fallen in on deck, with the exception of some sixty men who were told off below to man the chain-pumps; they never came up again, but were all drowned like rats in a hole. After gaining the deck I went and assisted the crew in rigging the chain-pumps; I remained there, and I think it was about the hardest twenty minutes' work I ever did in my life. We all worked like Trojans.

As I have said, there were sixty men told off. I remember nothing about reliefs; I know I remained below the whole time. I know very little about what happened on deck during this time. I think I was the only man that ever came up again from the pumps. Lieutenant Girardot was on the ladder giving orders and encouraging us. I was over my knees in water, and it was gaining fast on us. I happened to be working nearest the companion-ladder when one of the ship's officers told Lieutenant Girardot that it was no use attempting to keep the water down, and we had better try to get the boats out, or anything in the shape

Yours faithfully,
William Smith

CORPORAL WM. SMITH, 12TH FOOT
(Photo by Beales & Co., Banbury)

of a raft. With that I sprang up the ladder on deck, and not a moment too soon, as immediately the main deck was under water, which poured down the hatchway, so that it would be impossible for any to escape. In about two minutes the main crash came, and I was washed into the sea. I saw Captain Salmond on the poop deck with a lantern in his hand surrounded by a crowd. I heard him say, "I will save you all and the ship too." Some short time after this the poop deck gave a lurch and went under. I don't remember his telling the men to swim out to the boats; I might have been too far off, together with the noise of falling timbers. The women and children were placed in the second cutter, and the horses thrown over the gangway, most of them swimming ashore. A master's assistant, Mr. Richards (who, I think, afterwards became admiral)* took charge of the boat, which cleared from the sinking ship at once; had they remained the boat would have been drawn in the vortex. This and one other small boat † were all that could be got afloat. Had there been time to get the long-boat and the two paddle-box boats afloat, many more would have been saved. The boat with the women and children was fortunately sighted and picked up at sea the next day by a coasting schooner, the *Lioness*, and taken into Simon's Bay. A small portion of the wreck was jointed into the sunken rocks with a part of the mainmast standing, to which a few men clung for some hours, till, becoming exhausted, they fell off one by one into the sea and were drowned.‡

I managed, fortunately, to meet one of the ship's spars when in the water, to which I clung, and getting on top I stuck tight to it, as I could not swim. I was about twenty hours in the water. Some others managed to get ashore in much the same way.§ I should think it would be about two and a half miles. I believe most of the swimmers were drowned in miscalculating the distance, as the mountains looked much nearer across the water in the darkness. Many lost their lives by the falling and smashing of timbers, others by the sharks which infested this part of the sea, as the waters were tinged with blood in many places. The *Birkenhead* was an iron vessel; had she been a wooden ship she might not have broken up so quickly, and there would probably have been more time and a better chance to escape. After being a long while without food, we managed to scramble to a sort of farm owned by

* Mr. Richards left the Navy in 1856, with the rank of second master.
† Three boats, the gig and two cutters, got away.
‡ Several of the men were taken off the yard by the schooner *Lioness*.
§ The writer of this narrative supplemented it with the following interesting incident, which is described in his own words: "On a sort of raft were several men, and also Captain Wright of the 91st, who had on a life-preserver. After passing through the difficult seaweed, Captain Wright jumped off and swam the remainder of the distance to shore, at the same time giving us a stave of 'The Bay of Biscay, O!' The men who got ashore about the same place will no doubt remember this incident."

Captain Smales, who had a small store. Here we got a glass of grog each, and procured clothing, food, and shelter. Captain Wright, the senior officer saved, who had served at the Cape before, was the only officer who knew the coast. Information of the wreck was conveyed to the commanding officer at the Cape, who forthwith despatched the *Rhadamanthus* sloop, which took us to Simon's Bay, where we remained a few days to recruit our strength. We then proceeded to the frontier to join our different corps.

Smith continued to serve some three or four years longer with the 12th or East Suffolk Regiment, and was promoted to the rank of corporal. He then transferred to the Cape Mounted Rifles, in which he remained for fourteen years. His discharge from the Rifles is dated August 16th, 1870, when he had to his credit over twenty-one years' service, and received his pension of 1s. $1\frac{1}{2}$d. per diem. This, however, by no means exhausted the service he rendered to his country, for he took part as a volunteer in three subsequent Colonial wars. During the Kaffir War of 1852-3 he was wounded at the Koonap fight in British Kaffraria under Sir Harry Smith. The troops to which he was attached were commanded by Captain Moody, 9th Company R.E., and lost heavily. Smith accompanied the attack on the Basuto chief, Mosheth, under command of Sir George Cathcart.

After one day's sharp fighting [he writes of that affair], the chief, who had been making raids on neighbouring farmers, came into our camp bearing a flag of truce and desiring to make peace, knowing, as he said, it would be no use his contending with the British. Our General fined him a thousand horses and three thousand head of cattle. We lost some men in this little affair. The 12th Lancers lost twenty-eight, left dead on the field, of one squadron. Their draft sent out on the *Birkenhead* was very small; two only escaped from the wreck, Cornet Bond and Private Dodd.* The latter fell in this fight; he was a personal friend of mine. I could say a great deal about the Kaffir War. We had some hard campaigning, many hand-to-hand fights with the natives, and the transport was not what it has since become.

On returning to Cape Colony Smith, with others, joined the Mounted Rifles, the ranks of which required strengthening. In 1857 he made two trips to India with horses during the Mutiny. Mounted police duty, varied by a spell as convict warder, filled up his time in the Colony. Then came the

* A third, William Butler, also got ashore.

volunteering for the Colonial wars. He went through the Transkei War (South Africa) in 1877, across the Bashee River under General Wavell; fought with the Frontier Light Horse in the Zulu War of 1879 under Colonel (afterwards General) Buller, V.C.; and again in the Basuto War of 1880-1 under General Sir Mansfield Clarke.

Smith returned to England in 1888, after an absence of thirty-six years, and when the anniversary in 1902 came round he was seventy-two years of age. Towards the close of 1903 efforts were made by Lieut.-Colonel Mackie, of The Queen's Regiment, to obtain an increase of pension for William Smith, whose case was with this object brought to the notice of the officer commanding the 12th Regimental District. The Commissioners of Chelsea Hospital were, however, unable to recommend him for an increase. They expressed regret that—

being already in receipt of the full amount of pension to which he became entitled under the regulations in force at the time of his discharge, he cannot be awarded any increase, as he was discharged on termination of engagement and was never wounded.

His subsequent services in the Transkei and Zulu Campaigns, the Commissioners wrote, "do not render him eligible for increase of pension from Army funds." This decision, while unavoidable, apparently, under the cast-iron rules laid down, was much regretted. As Colonel Mackie commented in *The Army and Navy Gazette*:

It is a pity that the Regulations are not more elastic, so as to provide for an increase of pension in this and similar cases; but we are not a sentimental nation—other countries appraised the coolness and marvellous discipline shown by the young soldiers on board the *Birkenhead* at a far higher value than we did; witness the order of the then King of Prussia, directing that the official account of the wreck should be read at the head of every regiment in his Army!

Nevertheless, something was done for this deserving veteran. Where the regulations failed, individual sympathy was not wanting, and welcome assistance, received through Colonel Mackie from Colonel Mackenzie, C.B., commanding the 1st Battalion Suffolk Regiment, and others, was handed on to Smith by his friend and neighbour Mr. Chamberlain, of the Schoolhouse, Middleton Cheney. In December, 1905, when seventy-six years of age, he also had the gratification of adding to his war decorations the Cape medal and Basutoland, 1881, clasp, granted by the Colonial Government. Some account in detail of the interesting personal adventures of this *Birkenhead* survivor will be found elsewhere in the book.

Private John Smith

The publicity given in February, 1902, to the movement on behalf of Sergeant O'Neil elicited the statement that at St. Ives, Hunts, there lived another *Birkenhead* survivor in the person of John Smith, who at the time of the wreck was serving in the 2nd Queen's Royals, afterwards the West Surrey Regiment. The identity of Smith was satisfactorily established, and in a letter to us he said: "I was with Sergeant O'Neil on land after we were wrecked, and I am pleased to hear he is alive and well." Smith's age was sixty-nine, so that he was a young fellow of nineteen when on board the *Birkenhead*. He was a native of St. Ives, and on returning there in after years was given the name of "Bushman," we may suppose because of his association with the "bush" in South Africa. Young Smith enlisted in The Queen's at Westminster in 1851, and was stationed in Ireland when the drafts were sent out early in the following year. This is his story of the wreck.

I was asleep below when I was aroused by a tremendous crash. I at once realised that something serious was amiss, and calling to my mate, a Romford man, I told him I thought we must be ashore. We ran up on deck with the rest, and afterwards I stood at the gangway and assisted to hand the women and children into the boat. The men all stood back until they had been got safely away; but there was no "falling in" on the deck. When the vessel went down I was in the long-boat. There were about a hundred of us in it altogether, but when the ship broke in two the falling funnel caught our boat and smashed it, throwing us into the water. I managed to swim about until the ship went to pieces, when I got hold of a bit of the forecastle and clambered on to it, afterwards picking up two other men and helping them on to my raft. It was an awful experience. There were men in the water all around. We could hear them struggling, and occasionally came shouts of "Boat ahoy!" but the shouts became fewer and the struggles feebler, until at last everything was quiet. We were fourteen hours in the water before we drifted to the shore.

When we got in there was a man about 200 yards off floating on a barrel. He couldn't get off without help, and my two mates refused to go back and help him, so I had to go by myself, and I managed to get him ashore. Many were killed close to the shore, and we afterwards buried no less than 45 in the sand. We landed at a place where there was not a soul to be found. We set off to find some one, and part of the time I assisted in carrying Ensign Lucas, of the 73rd Regiment, who had been injured on the rocks. We came upon three blackfellows fishing, but could not make them understand anything, and it was two days before we came to a place belonging to Captain Smales, who had been in the Army, and got something to eat. A schooner (the *Lioness*) came for us when they knew where we were, and we had to go back to the shore to meet it. We were taken back to Simon's Bay, and from there went on to East London and were sent up to the front.

Smith was in the Kaffir War of 1852-3 under Sir Harry Smith and Sir George Cathcart. He returned to England in 1861 in the merchant ship *Belvedere*.

After getting back I went into the service of the Great Eastern Railway Company, and served them for 37 years and six months. I am now superannuated from the railway, and have a small pension from them of five shillings a week, which is my principal source of income.

Smith's case was inquired into by Colonel Nourse, commanding the 2nd Regimental District, and it was ascertained that he was one of the detachment of The Queen's on board the transport. A movement was accordingly set on foot to obtain for Smith a special service pension in his old age, and in June Colonel Nourse and Lieut.-Colonel Mackie received the gratifying intimation that such pension had been granted by the Commissioners of Chelsea Hospital. This augmented the veteran's scanty income by ninepence a day, and the officers of his old regiment sent him a present of a banknote which he thoroughly well deserved also.

"THE MAN AT THE WHEEL"

This was Thomas Coffin, then a seaman of the *Birkenhead*, who after many years of storm and stress in the service of his country was in 1902, at the age of seventy-nine, living in peaceful retirement at Eastville, Bristol, with the rank of quartermaster. Thomas Coffin joined the *Birkenhead* late in

1850 or early in 1851. He was on duty as the man at the wheel when the troopship struck the rock. He was coxswain of the first cutter, which contained Dr. Bowen, the staff surgeon, and a number of men from the wreck. How he came to get ashore in the gig, to which he transferred from the cutter, is told in his story, written for this work.

My first voyage in the *Birkenhead* was to North America with a detachment of Artillery, and we brought back a corresponding number to England. My second was to Ascension Island. My third was to the Cape,* with the 2nd Queen's Regiment. Whilst there, the mail-boat broke down, and the *Birkenhead* was told off to bring home the mails. My fourth and fateful voyage was to the Cape again, with composite troops to fill up gaps in the Kaffir War. We had rounded the Cape and were sixty miles on our journey, just off Point Danger, where there are a number of dangerous, hidden rocks; it was on one of these that the *Birkenhead* struck (on the starboard bow). Never shall I forget that morning! I was at the wheel, and well remember the sentry calling out to the officer of the watch, "Four bells, sir." The officer replied, "Strike them, sentry," which he did not do, for at that very moment she struck the rock and the sentry went rolling on the deck. At the time most of the soldiers were below asleep, but were awoke by the crash (which appeared to me to be enough to wake the dead almost) and came on deck; but on being called to order, fell in and remained so, thus enabling the seamen to get out what boats were left.† My instructions from the Captain were to man my boat and pull off and await orders, which never came. I heard after that he was struck by a falling spar and killed. My boat's crew and myself picked up 32 in all, and we pulled till daylight, when we came across the second cutter and gig, and we sighted a sail in the offing. The ship's doctor, who was one of the saved, called for seamen to man the gig and pull toward her. Eight of us volunteered, and we pulled out, but could not attract her attention, so we decided not to venture any further, but pulled for shore, which we reached about 6 p.m. Fish Bay was our landing place, and fortunately for us the postmaster's daughters of Caledon had just finished bathing and were about to return home. They were very kind and provided us with some coffee and bread, which was very acceptable. After we had tramped to Caledon we were sent to Simon's Town, and then to Algoa Bay, our Naval station. We were brought back to England on the *Amazon*. I was one of the witnesses at the court-martial, and was asked by the Admiral Judge-Advocate if

---

* There was no intermediate voyage to Ascension Island, but the ship called there on her way to the Cape with the 2nd Queen's Regiment.

† Incorrect. Many of the soldiers were set to work, and rendered all the assistance possible under the circumstances.

PRIVATE JOHN SMITH, 2ND QUEEN'S REGT.
(Photo by A. Hendry, St. Ives, Hunts.)

QUARTERMASTER THOS. COFFIN, "THE MAN AT THE WHEEL"
(Photo by Alfred E. Smith, Bristol)

"ALL THAT WAS LEFT OF THEM" 225

the court could do anything for me, to which I replied, "Nothing, thank you, but to allow me to stay in the dockyard at Portsmouth for a time," which was readily granted me. This ended my experiences with all connected with the *Birkenhead*.

Thomas Coffin was very early initiated into the career which he followed for so many eventful years of his life with credit and success. He was born on board H.M.S. *Pitt*, of which his father was at the time shipkeeper. As a little sailor-boy he paraded on Southsea Common at Queen Victoria's Accession. Later, he saw active service on the coast of Syria, was in the Naval Brigade in the Crimea, and fought in the China War of 1860, where he received his only wound, his upper lip being cut through by a Chinaman's boat-hook whilst boarding a pirate junk. Mr. Coffin left the sea service in 1871 as quartermaster, esteemed by all who knew and had sailed with him. The ship's model, seen in the photograph of the veteran here reproduced, is not that of the *Birkenhead*, but of some other vessel in which its maker sailed during his thirty-six years' experience of the sea. He possessed several relics of his adventures, including the shell which he and other seamen used as a drinking-cup on the tramp to Caledon from Fish Bay. During that trying journey they picked up nude, and succoured and cared for, a soldier cast ashore from the wreck who otherwise must have perished in that desert waste.

PRIVATE WILLIAM TUCK

Yet another veteran survivor of the small band of Royal Marines present on board the *Birkenhead* was living at the 50th anniversary of the wreck. This was Private William Tuck, a man who, like his comrade-in-arms Colour-Sergeant Drake, had experienced exciting adventures prior to the disaster of February, 1852. He was wrecked in the *Torch* in 1848. After escaping a second time when the *Birkenhead* sank, he was in the Baltic in 1854 with Sir Charles Napier, and in 1855 served there again under Admiral Dundas and was at the bombardment of Sweaborg. Fifteen years of his service were passed upon the water. Old age found him the possessor of the Baltic medal and a small pension. Writing on May 27th from Brockhurst, Gosport, his place of abode, William Tuck told what befell him that fateful February half-a-century before in these words :

> After the *Birkenhead* struck, the first thing I was called upon to do was to get the women and children into a boat, and dreadful was the scene! We had to push some of the women into the boat. I went forward to help with the paddle-box boat, but I was too late, and the foremast went over the starboard side, and as soon as the masts were gone she broke in two at the foremost part. I was in the water. She broke again on the quarter-deck, and the poop was up on end when I was passing into the water. I was about 15 hours in the water before I could reach the land, and then we did not know where to go. We fell in with several men who got ashore. We wandered about all day, scorched up with the sun, until we reached a house, where we stopped two days and a half and were treated well. We had a glass of grog as soon as we arrived there. An officer of the *Rhadamanthus* came and gave us notice where to get back to, and as soon as I got on board the boatswain's mate of the *Rhadamanthus*, who was wrecked with me in the *Torch* steamer, August 15th, 1848, treated me like a brother. I was 21 years and eight days in the Royal Marines. I only wish I were young enough to serve my country again; I would gladly do it.

A commendable spirit, honouring to the sea veteran who fostered it!

BENJAMIN TURNER

The third Naval survivor living at the 50th anniversary, Benjamin Turner, was a second-class boy on board the *Birkenhead* and servant to Mr. Archbold, the gunner. The son of a shoemaker, he was born at Chichester on July 1st, 1835, and he had sailed in the troopship on her two previous voyages. In a letter written on May 1st, 1902, Mr. Turner gives a clear and interesting account of his own experience at the wreck.

> I was a boy on the *Birkenhead* at the time, and servant to Mr. Archbold, the gunner of the ship. In those days boys were servants to officers in their first experience in sea-going ships. When the ship struck the rock I was in my hammock asleep forward in the eyes of the ship under the topgallant forecastle, and was thrown out on to the deck by the concussion of the ship striking the rock, at the same time the

PRIVATE WILLIAM TUCK, R.M.L.I.
(Photo by W. C. Harvey, Gosport)

boatswain's mate rushing under the forecastle piping "Hands save ship!" I then made my way aft to the quarter-deck, where I saw my master, Mr. Archbold, in the act of sending up rockets and burning blue lights as signals of distress, and I held the staffs for him while he fixed them on. Shortly after this the ship broke in halves in midships, taking all the men down with her that were in the act of getting the paddle-box boats out. I was on the poop at that time with several others, expecting every moment to be our last, and when the poop was only about two feet above water the order was given to try and save ourselves. Seeing there was no other escape, I took off my flannel and trousers and threw them overboard, and jumped into the sea and made for the shore as best I could. It was very dark at the time—you could not see one another in the water. I swam about for some time, resting on pieces of the wreckage, until I came across a part of the ship's bridge, which I lay on the top of, and thank God it enabled me to keep clear of the sharks, which I did not think much about at the time—I thought more about my poor old mother than I did the sharks, wondering if I ever should see her again. I saw many poor fellows during the day, who were hanging with their arms over a spar and their legs in the water, taken down by the sharks. A shark would come up, seize them by the leg, and drag them down. At last I managed to get on shore, along with two others—W. Neal, carpenter's mate of the ship, and a soldier whose name I forget. I must mention that after we landed on the rocks we had a large span of water to go through before we got to the mainland. I had to escort my two companions through it one at a time, as neither of them could swim—in fact, I think I may say that I almost saved their lives, for they were completely exhausted after being about 14 hours in the water. I was so burnt with the sun and salt water that it was quite three weeks before I could lay on my back. We had some distance to travel before we could get any relief, my shipmates carrying me in turns on their backs. At last we came to a farm belonging to Captain Smales, where we were treated very kindly, and on the following Sunday we were taken on board H.M.S. *Rhadamanthus* and conveyed to Simon's Bay, from which we sailed a week later in H.M.S. *Amazon* for dear old England, and boy-like, I was very glad when I arrived home.

After the wreck Turner continued his sea service in the Baltic, on the China Station, and elsewhere in the *Impérieuse, Chesapeake, Euryalus, Bellerophon, Crocodile, Implacable* and *Flora*.

The ship I served in during the Russian War in the Baltic [he says] was the *Impérieuse*, Captain R. B. Watson. Our duties consisted chiefly in cruising about, watching the Russian fleet off Kronstadt. Occasionally we fired a few shells into the back of the forts from a 32-pounder which was slung half-way up the mainmast of the ship. On one occasion we engaged a fort on Hangs Head, driving the Russians out and dismantling the fort. The first ship I served in on the China Station was the *Chesapeake*, flagship of Admiral Sir James Hope. During the attack on the Taku Forts in 1859-60 Flag-Captain George O. Willes was in command, the Admiral directing operations from the gunboat *Plover*. In the course of the bombardment Admiral Hope was wounded. The *Plover* and also the gunboat *Lee* were left high and dry on the mud when the tide receded, and were burnt by the Chinese at night. My next ship on the China Station was the *Euryalus*, flagship of Admiral Kuper. I was present at the attack on the forts of Kagoshima in Japan in 1863. During the bombardment Flag-Captain J. Josling and Commander Wilmot were both killed on the bridge by a round shot from one of the forts. I was also with the landing party at the attack on Simonosaki in 1864, and was present at the capture of the stockade. The English ships taking part in these operations were the *Euryalus, Tartar, Conqueror, Barossa, Perseus, Argus, Coquette* and *Bouncer*. Three of our ship's company were awarded the Victoria Cross for their gallantry on this occasion. The circumstances under which the stockade was captured were as follows : The Japanese had posted two or three of their heavy guns behind a timber stockade among the trees which covered the top of a hill, where the huts or barracks of their soldiery and their principal magazines of ammunition were situated. From this sheltered position they had kept up an annoying fire upon the English and French below, who were engaged during the afternoon in removing the guns from the other batteries, close to the shore, which had been previously captured. Captain Alexander, of the *Euryalus*, with a few hundred men from that ship and the *Conqueror*, proceeded at length to the attack of the masked battery, hastily crossing a paddy-field which was exposed to its full fire, and then ascending a steep, thickly-wooded ravine to the front of the stockade. Several of our men were killed or wounded in this arduous service, and Captain Alexander was severely wounded in the foot, after which the command was taken by Lieutenant Suther, of the Royal Marines, the stockade being eventually captured.

On the return of the *Euryalus* to England in the following year an impressive ceremony took place on Southsea Common, when Admiral Sir M. Seymour, as representative of Her Majesty, decorated Mr. Duncan G. Boyes, midshipman; Mr. Thomas Pride, captain of the afterguard; and William Seeley, ordinary seaman, with the Victoria Cross for conspicuous gallantry during the operations in the Strait of Simonosaki, Japan. A large concourse of people were present, many of whom were unable to witness the proceedings. A royal salute was fired by H.M.S. *Victory* in Portsmouth Harbour at the conclusion of the ceremony. On

BENJAMIN TURNER
(Photo by J. Long, Portsmouth)

August 13th, 1877, Turner retired from the Navy on a well-earned pension. He was holding the rank of ship's corporal, and had nearly twenty-three years' man's service to his credit. He possessed the Baltic medal for the Russian War, and also the China medal for the bombardment of the Taku Forts. In 1905 Mr. Turner was still living at Fratton, near Portsmouth, one of the last of the Naval heroes of the *Birkenhead*.

A Hero's Son

When the *Birkenhead* sank she took down, with many another gallant man, Timothy Kelly, of the 73rd Foot, whose name will be found in the death roll of those who perished. Kelly's wife and two little sons are stated to have been on board and among the last to be placed in the ship's cutter, in which the women and children were saved. As they went over the side, it is affirmed, Private Kelly said to them, with soldierly resignation, " Cheer up! we shall meet in the next world." A few minutes later he was drowned. After the awful experience of that black night, the story goes, Mrs. Kelly remained some time in hospital at Capetown, suffering from the shock of that last sad parting and the effects of exposure in the open boat. Her young sons, James and Thomas Kelly, were taken care of by Kaffirs, and eventually all three were sent home. On Mrs. Kelly was bestowed a Government pension, and from time to time she received gifts of money from Queen Victoria, the Right Hon. W. E. Gladstone, and others. She died in Co. Kildare during 1899. Her sons, James and Thomas, were allowed a small money grant by Government, and were also taught the trade of tailoring in the Army. At the 50th anniversary of the wreck and after Thomas Kelly was hale and well and living in Leeds. His brother James was deceased. Thomas, who was not quite three years old when the troopship was lost (he was born on March 12th, 1849), said he had little recollection of the incidents of the disaster, but he remembered how in after years his mother used to relate with pride and sadness the story of those brave British soldiers who died without murmuring heroes' deaths.

The name of Mrs. Kelly, it will be found, does not appear in the official list of the women and children saved from the wreck, a circumstance which seemed to indicate that she was put ashore with others at Simon's Bay when the ship called there. The case was brought to the notice of the authorities of Chelsea Hospital, who replied regretting to state that—

there is no information in this office to show whether Thomas Kelly, the son of Timothy Kelly, of the 73rd Regiment, was amongst the persons saved from the wreck of the *Birkenhead*, nor [the Secretary was sorry to say] have the Commissioners any means of testing the accuracy of the other statements quoted in your letter.

Thomas Kelly himself was further questioned. He said he could not understand how his mother's name was missing from the official list of women saved, adding :

I have a faint recollection of the wreck. I was the very last of the children to leave it, and was nearly drowned. Myself and my brother were each given £23 from the Government to learn a trade. My mother received ten shillings a week for life so long as she remained single. We stayed two years in Capetown before we came home.

According to this, Thomas Kelly was a survivor of the *Birkenhead* as well as the son of a soldier who perished on board. Other instances have demonstrated that the lists of persons saved compiled at the time are not infallible, and it is possible that Mrs. Kelly may have been overlooked. More cannot be said. Thomas Kelly is responsible for his own statements, which, notwithstanding the lack of confirmation by the official list as to his presence at the wreck, may still be true, and as such we think they may safely be accepted.

THOMAS KELLY
(Photo by M. & F. Smith, Leeds)

CHAPTER XVIII

FATE OF SOUTH AFRICAN SURVIVORS

There is no armour against Fate.—JAMES SHIRLEY.

IT sometimes happens that a man who has passed through the gravest perils in his time comes at last to his end by a trifling misadventure. It is a hard fate to befall such a one. No more melancholy instance of it exists than is furnished by the decease near his veldt home at Mosita, in Bechuanaland, during April, 1903, of that sturdy pioneer settler CHARLES DALY. Mr. Daly's death was caused by the kick of a waggon ox. The veteran was on his way to Vryburg at the time, and the kick, which took effect above the eye, terminated fatally within a few minutes. The unhappy accident aroused far and wide a feeling of keen regret, for Mr. Daly was well known in South Africa and had many friends there and in Australia, England and America, and in Ireland, his native country, who all admired him for his personal qualities and his successful life-work. To readers of this book, Charles Daly and his adventurous career are matters of interest because he was a survivor of the *Birkenhead*. He belonged to no branch of the Government service. He was neither soldier nor sailor, nor a police recruit. How came he, then, it will be asked, to be in the *Birkenhead* when the ship was lost? The reply is that he was there as a passenger on board—under what circumstances shall be explained presently. He was among those saved from the wreck, and he landed on that occasion, for the first and last time in his life, on the shores of South Africa in his shirt only.

Charles Daly died a rich man, but he began the battle of life a poor lad. He was born at Gort, in Co. Galway, on March 17th (St. Patrick's Day), 1832. His father was a bailiff to Lord Clanricarde, and the family, a large one, was reared on the estate. Things were not very prosperous at home, and young Daly decided that he could better his fortunes by going abroad. Accordingly, he left Ireland while still a boy. In 1849 he landed at Durban. Proceeding up country to Bloemfontein, he secured a clerkship in Mr. Palmer's store. He was not without education, and being a sharp youth and energetic, he soon made headway. It was necessary that he should know Dutch, in which language, by hard study, he made himself tolerably proficient, thereby laying the foundation of future successes. He was a friend of the local bank manager, and in after years often recalled the "great talks" they had together. Those discussions were animated and sometimes heated—a fact which is not surprising when it is known that whereas the clerk was fired by Ireland's wrongs, and the prevailing notions of redressing them, the banker, on the other hand, was a "rank Tory," and as such beyond hope of conviction; but the politicians remained good friends.

After spending a year or two in the Free State and saving a little money, young Daly resolved to return home. He set out on the journey, but got no farther than St. Helena, where he was left behind suffering from an attack of fever, on recovering from which he decided to abandon his trip and get back to the Free State. It was now that he joined the *Birkenhead*, and came to participate in the horrors of her last fatal voyage. When the troopship called at St. Helena on her way south, he got a passage on board with the object of accompanying the vessel round to the Buffalo River. It was a project fated not to be realised, for the historic shipwreck intervened. Charles Daly was of the number who were lucky enough to struggle ashore when the *Birkenhead* sank off Danger Point, landing, as already mentioned, in his shirt. Desperate adventures were afterwards his along the Kaffir frontiers, but none of them eclipsed the terrors of that black night, the story of which, as told by this survivor, has thrilled eager listeners by many a camp-fire since. Odd that after all he should be reserved for the death which overtook him! He had completed his 71st year a month earlier, and was still hale and strong when the end came, on April 16th, 1903

MR. CHARLES DALY
(Photo by W. Klisser, Vryburg)

The decrees of Fate were not all unkind to Mr. Daly. We have seen how he was saved from a disaster at sea while so many around him perished, and on land he experienced numerous escapes during his romantic career. Only a year before he died he had the happiness, sweetened by long, long absence, of revisiting his old home in Ireland and sojourning for a space among the well-remembered haunts and still familiar scenes of his boyhood days. True, he was bowed then with the weight of a domestic grief; but that visit must have been a satisfaction and a solace.

After the wreck of the *Birkenhead* friends came forward and helped Charles Daly, and he again found himself in Bloemfontein. Fortune seemed to smile on him, and it was not long before he fell in love with a Miss Roesch, whom he eventually married, and the union was a happy one. On the Basuto War breaking out he was, in common with others, commandeered for active service; but being a shrewd business man, he paid £25 for a substitute, and, taking a couple of waggons loaded principally with brandy, proceeded with the commando. Everything went well until some of the burghers got rather too merry. A court-martial was then held on him and he was put out of camp, to the sorrow of the jovial spirits there assembled.

I then [he said afterwards] travelled around Thaba-Bosigo to another commando, where I was well received; but longing to get back to my old camp, I inspanned one morning early and travelled back, although the Basutos were now fully on the war-path and most of the roads closed. About noon of that day I came upon several hundred Basutos, all armed; to say I was in a great fright is to say the least of it. Upon asking them several questions and eliciting no response, I thought my last hour had come; this continued until late in the afternoon, when several approached the waggon and asked for food. The relief I felt was so great that I gave them all I had, and they became very friendly towards me. The next morning I appeared before camp and some hundreds of Boers came out and escorted me in with great demonstrations of joy. I was completely forgiven, and the next day had to send my waggons back to Bloemfontein for more goods and brandy.

He described a visit he paid to the Chief Masupha, of the Basutos, during an armistice, in company with another gentleman.

We proceeded to go up the mountain to visit the chief. We took two bottles of French brandy and several other articles which we thought the chief might like. Upon reaching the footpath by which we had to ascend, we found it to be very difficult, winding through large rocks. Judge of our surprise when, a little way up, from behind nearly every boulder a Basuto jumped up, fully armed and shouting to us, "Spion! Spion! Go back or we will kill you!" Again I was in a terrible state, but (I expect the old Irish blood asserted itself) eventually thought it best to go forward. Upon reaching the summit we were introduced to Masupha, whom we found seated within a ring of his warriors. I was surprised to see a white man among them who was constantly gibbering and laughing, and as the man had a peculiar fascination for me, I asked who he was, and was informed he was a lunatic! Our visit being ended, bidding adieu to the chief, we got back safely to camp.

We next find Mr. Daly in Bloemhof, a friend of the President, owner of a large store and a palatial dwelling-house—evidences that times had gone well with him, for he was now an affluent man with branch stores in the country. The Stellaland War breaking out, Charles Daly, being the only man near the line allowed a magazine licence, was a great factor in it, supplying arms, food, etc., to the Transvaal forces, an arrangement which proved lucrative to himself and satisfactory to all concerned. An amusing incident occurred during the war. The notorious Scotty Smith broke into Mr. Daly's magazine, and, in company with several boon companions, "cleared it out," leaving their signatures affixed to a postcard on the door as a token that they would pay for whatever had been taken.

Afterwards in 1884, in Warren's Expedition, Charles Daly was at Pudimoe, near Taungs; but soon he was obliged to leave, the British Government considering the ground more suitable for the natives and telling him to seek veldt elsewhere. From here he went to his farm Italie, on the Hartz River, where he put up magnificent dwellings, dams, and a garden; but his restless spirit was not satisfied, and we next find him occupying his Mosita and Molopo farms with great success in cattle ranching. In 1897 the rinderpest came along and swept nearly every living head of cattle away in its path, impoverishing many well-to-do farmers and forcing them to start afresh. The second blow came when Mr. Daly's favourite son, Redmond, died on May 26th, 1898, at the early age of thirty. Redmond was a fine cricketer, whose record had not been broken at St. Andrews, and a good scholar, having matriculated highly. His death was a blow from which neither Mr. Daly nor his wife seemed to recover. In 1899 broke out the Anglo-Boer War, towards the end of which the Daly family were taken to Yana Masibe camp, where Mrs. Daly died on January 2nd, 1902. This appeared to break the veteran down altogether, and he left for Europe with his youngest son, Nimrod—going from Capetown to Durban, thence to Madagascar, where he spent two weeks, then to Marseilles *via* the Suez Canal, from there by train to Paris, and on to London and so to Dublin, whence he went to see his birthplace, finding alive one of his sisters, aged eighty-three. Mr. Daly spent six weeks in Ireland and then returned to his desolate home in South Africa, only, as already shown, to die by the kick of an ox in the April of 1903.

Concluding an anniversary article in *The Bechuanaland News*, from which many of the facts given above are quoted, the writer speaks of Mr. Daly's personal character.

> He was a good father, generous to a fault, a staunch Home-Ruler and a thorough Irishman to the last, a keen sportsman, well educated, an aristocrat to the tips of his fingers, and a man of whom may be said, " He had many friends but no enemies." For the last thirty-five years of his life he was a total abstainer from alcoholic liquor and tobacco.

Charles Daly was a model man and a settler whose name will always be honoured in South Africa. Thanks are due to Mr. C. Zinn, proprietor of *The Bechuanaland News*, for his kindness in placing at the authors' disposal materials for this sketch of so interesting a *Birkenhead* survivor. Indebtedness is also acknowledged to Mr. Zinn for the accompanying photograph.

Sergeant W. H. McCluskey

By a remarkable coincidence—one which can rarely have been equalled in the history of any notable subject—the story of the *Birkenhead* was revived in South Africa a second time under tragic circumstances during 1903. We have already mourned the unhappy fate of poor Charles Daly in April of that year. Six months later almost to the day, on

October 5th, the British settlements in South Africa were thrilled by a tragedy far more intense and pathetic; for on that date a barbarous murder was committed. The victim was William Henry McCluskey, an aged Irishman, who was employed as a guard by De Beers Company at Beaconsfield. And he, too, was a survivor of the *Birkenhead*—the last but two then remaining in South Africa. McCluskey was a veteran of long and honourable service and of many a battlefield. An added touch of melancholy attaches to his end in the fact that he had served in the late Boer War through the siege of Kimberley as a sergeant of the Beaconsfield Town Guard.

The murder of this worthy man was of a particularly atrocious character; and that it was the work of a mad native who should have been under restraint makes it all the more deplorable. McCluskey, who was seventy-three years of age, was engaged in guarding the blue ground on the Bultfontein floors at that portion of the mine nearest the Green Point location. He commenced his usual duties at six o'clock on Monday morning, October 5th, and was seen then and shortly afterwards by other employés of the company in that neighbourhood. About the time that McCluskey began his duties for the day, a native named Michael Mongale left the Green Point location and proceeded in the direction of the Bultfontein floors. The man was missed by a relative, John Malahleve, a native with whom he lived, who knew it was not safe for him to be at large. Malahleve at once went in search of Mongale, whom he espied at some distance in the act of "chopping something on the floor" with an implement, near the guard's hut situate on McCluskey's beat. The weapon used proved to be a spade. Malahleve hurried to the spot, and there found that the object of Mongale's attack was a dead body, that of the unfortunate McCluskey. On being interrogated Mongale admitted that he had killed the man whose remains he was still hacking. Malahleve, who acted in a very creditable manner, seized the miscreant who had so calmly proclaimed himself a murderer, and took him to the location at Green Point, which was but a few hundred yards away.

SERGEANT W. H. McCLUSKEY
(From a photo)

FATE OF SOUTH AFRICAN SURVIVORS 237

There Mongale was handed over to the charge of the headman, who called an escort of some half-dozen natives and marched him off to the gaol. Up to this time there appears to have been no suspicion abroad that McCluskey was dead. The police at Beaconsfield were informed by Mongale's escort that he had "assaulted the guard." In the meantime, however, another employé on the floors had come across McCluskey, and, examining the body, found life to be extinct. The head had been battered in. The dreadful discovery was duly reported, and the police were speedily acquainted with the fact that McCluskey was dead. The first charge against Mongale was thereupon withdrawn, and the capital charge substituted. The unhappy wretch Mongale was about twenty-eight years of age. He had lived in the Beaconsfield district for some time, and was well known in the town itself. He had worked for De Beers at Bultfontein, but was not in the employ of the company at the time of the murder. His appearance immediately after his statement that he had killed McCluskey was described as "not like that of a person under the influence of drink, but rather like that of a native who had been indulging in dagga." He was eventually found to be irresponsible, and incarcerated as a criminal lunatic. The preliminary hearing at Beaconsfield, and trial of the case at the Kimberley Criminal Sessions, aroused an interest almost as intense as the indignation felt when the cruel deed was committed. The proceedings in court are fully set forth in a later chapter of the book. Occurring as it did on a bank holiday, the crime created an extraordinary sensation in the district, and as the local press prophetically commented, "The memory of this particular bank holiday will long remain associated with the sad end of one who had fought a good fight for more than three-score years and ten."

McCluskey, as already observed, was one of the few survivors of the *Birkenhead* disaster—the last but two left in South Africa. By a coincidence remarked on at the time, the preacher at a local place of worship spoke only the previous day (Sunday) upon the subject of the never-to-be-forgotten incidents connected with the loss of the *Birkenhead*, and is said to have alluded to this survivor of the terrible yet grand calamity. In the early 'eighties McCluskey was gaoler at Dutoitspan, and subsequently he was appointed sanitary constable to the Mining Board. He was in the employ of the Mining Board, under Major Maxwell and Mr. Hartog, as a searching officer until about six months from his death, when he commenced duty as a guard. He left a widow and three stepchildren. For many years he had lived near the old United Mine at Bultfontein. It was as one of the Cape Mounted Rifles that McCluskey made that memorable trip on board the *Birkenhead*. His career was a most adventurous one. He fought under Sir Harry Smith in the native war of the early 'fifties, and subsequently joined and served with the Diamond Fields Horse under Sir Charles Warren in 1877-8. Later, in 1887, he again served with the Diamond Fields Horse, ultimately attaining the rank of sergeant in "C" troop. His last service under arms was as a member of the Beaconsfield Town Guard during the siege of Kimberley. He had a share in the Gaika and Gealeka Wars of 1877-8. On the wall of his cabin he had burnt the dates "1848-73" over the letters "C.M.R.," designating his old corps. He was deservedly popular among a large circle of friends and acquaintances.

The funeral of William McCluskey took place on October 6th, the day following his tragic death, from the residence he had lately occupied in the Old Capetown Road. The widespread sympathy evoked by his fate was evidenced by the large number of persons who followed the remains to their final resting-place in the Dutoitspan Cemetery. Among those who paid to his memory a last tribute of respect were Colonel D. Harris, C.M.G., Captain S. Salaman (representing the Kimberley Regiment), Mr. W. Austin Knight, Mr. J. Hopwood Thorp (representing the Mayor and Councillors of Beaconsfield), Mr. Hartog (Secretary, Bultfontein Mining Board), Inspector D. Cowieson and Sub-Inspector Saddler, Cape Police, D. II., and many of the Bultfontein mine and floors employés. The pall-bearers were Captain S. Salaman and Messrs. J. M. Powell, T. Bird, G. Castle, P. Pretorius, and J. Fraser. Service at the house and grave was conducted by the Rev. W. F. P. Marais. Wreaths and floral tributes were many and beautiful, prominent among them being one from the Mayor and Councillors of Beaconsfield, and another from Colonel Harris, Captain Tyson, and Captain Blackbeard (the Mayor), bearing the inscription: " With the respect and esteem of his comrades of the Diamond Fields Horse of 1877-8." There were also wreaths from Mr. Austin Knight (floors manager, Bultfontein), the employés of the Bultfontein floors and compound, the manager and staff of the Bultfontein mine, Mr. and Mrs. C. A. Blackbeard, Mrs. Faulkner and family, Mr. and Mrs. D. Jacobs, Mr. and Mrs. Yates, Misses B. and M. Pretorius.

In a communication received from Captain C. A. Blackbeard, Mayor of Beaconsfield, subsequent to the death of this worthy veteran and *Birkenhead* survivor, the writer said:

McCluskey was a very old friend of mine, I having known him for over twenty years. We were comrades-in-arms in the Griqua War, 1877-8; he was then sergeant in the Diamond Fields Horse, and I was a trooper. In the late Boer War, during the siege of Kimberley, I was captain and he was sergeant in the Beaconsfield Town Guard. As you may imagine, we have often " fought our battles o'er again," but the little service I saw pales before the work of that modest but grand old hero of many battles.

Captain Blackbeard further wrote:

I little thought when my dear old mother used to tell us boys stories of the Kaffir wars, and the wonderful story of the loss of the *Birkenhead*, and the heroism, discipline, and fortitude of its gallant heroes, that I should have the privilege of meeting one of the survivors and have him as a fellow comrade-in-arms in two campaigns, and again hear the story around our camp-fire from the lips of the old warrior.

Captain Blackbeard was invited to contribute to this book any particulars concerning McCluskey and his career vouched for by his own personal knowledge of the veteran and his history. The gallant Captain, himself possessing a meritorious record of service to the Empire in South Africa, readily responded to the invitation with a brightly-written little sketch which is full of interest and value. It is given here in Captain Blackbeard's own words.

William Henry McCluskey was born at Armagh, Ireland, on June 18th, 1830; came out to South Africa with his parents about the year 1843, and lived with them on a farm near Capetown. When nineteen years of age he joined the Cape Mounted Rifles. In the year 1852, he, with other members of the same Corps, was sent on board the ill-fated troopship *Birkenhead*, to proceed to the seat of war in the Eastern Province. When the vessel struck all the troops on board fell into line on deck, by order of Lieut.-Colonel Seton, of the 74th Highlanders, until all the women, children, and the sick were got into the boats. When the ship went down he (McCluskey) was lucky enough to get out of the whirlpool, and being a very strong young man and a powerful swimmer, he made for the shore, and managed after a time to lay hold of a spar, to which another of his comrades was clinging. The waves threw them on to some rocks; they rested here for awhile, then made for the shore, which they reached safely, but all bleeding, torn, and bruised, being buffeted by the waves against the rocks. When he had sufficiently recovered, he with other survivors went to the front and took part in the Kaffir War then raging. In one of the engagements he was wounded in the thigh with an assegai. After serving ten years in the Cape Mounted Rifles he got his discharge, and proceeded to Natal, where he secured a contract for some irrigation work and fencing. When the rush took place to the Transvaal Gold Fields he was amongst the pioneer diggers, but was one of the unlucky ones. In 1871 he came to the Diamond Fields and worked a portion of a claim at the New Rush (now Kimberley Mine), and strange to relate, the neighbouring claimholder was his shipwrecked companion! Not having met for nearly twenty years, they did not recognise each other. Mac (as we always called him) has often told me of this remarkable coincidence, and how puzzled he was to know where he had met his neighbour before, until his curiosity got the better of him; so he said one day: "Old man, what is your name? I fancy we have met before." "I don't know," replied his friend, "but my name is O'Reilly." "Good God!" Mac exclaimed, taking his hand, "don't you know me? Why, I'm McCluskey, who was on the *Birkenhead*. We swam out together on the spar." Needless to say, the delight and surprise of the two men thus thrown so unexpectedly together after a lapse of so many years was great. Mac was not very fortunate as a diamond digger, so about 1875 he again left to try his luck on the gold fields, and went to Lydenburg. In 1876 he was commandeered along with many other diggers by the Boer Government in the Transvaal to go and fight the Kaffirs under Sekukuni. He was wounded in the shoulder with a bullet which was never extracted, and also grazed on the side by a piece of pot leg fired from a gun.

After this war he returned to the diamond fields, and was appointed assistant gaoler at Kimberley, joined the Diamond Fields Horse, and served in that corps under Colonel (now Sir Charles) Warren through the Griqua Rebellion of 1878, being present in many engagements. On his return he was appointed gaoler at Dutoitspan (now Beaconsfield), which post he held for some years, when he resigned to join the Searching Department of Bultfontein Diamond Mine. When this department

FATE OF SOUTH AFRICAN SURVIVORS

was done away with he was taken on as a guard by the De Beers Consolidated Mines, and whilst on duty on the Bultfontein floors, he was brutally murdered by a native lunatic, who must have taken him unawares and stunned with a shovel or a stone, as, notwithstanding his age, seventy-three years, he was remarkable for his strength and activity, being able to lift a bag of mealies, of two hundred pounds' weight, with his teeth, eighteen inches off the ground. He was one of the first to join the Beaconsfield Town Guard during the late Boer War, doing good work the whole of the siege. He held three war medals, Kaffir War, 1852-3, Griqua Rebellion, 1877-8, and the late Boer War. McCluskey was a sincere friend, good-hearted, thoroughly honest and straightforward, a jovial comrade at the camp-fire circle, and most interesting—more especially when you could get him to relate some of his experiences in the various wars, or his ups and downs either as a gold or as a diamond digger. He was one of the many modest and unassuming heroes that our race has just cause to be proud of—men who have always been ready at the call of duty to fight for Queen, King, and country, and who have helped so much to build up our great Empire. Peace be to his ashes!

It only remains to be added that a tombstone was raised to Sergeant McCluskey, than whom no man was ever more highly esteemed by all whose privilege it was to know him.

COLONEL R. A. NESBITT, C.B.

Another South African survivor, a distinguished Colonial soldier, died suddenly near Port Elizabeth in September, 1905. This was Colonel Nesbitt, C.B. When the *Birkenhead* called at Simon's Bay on the eve of the wreck, she took on board, among other passengers, Mrs. Nesbitt, the wife of Quartermaster Nesbitt, who was serving with his regiment, the 12th Suffolk, in the Kaffir War, and her younger boys. An elder son was with his father at the time fighting on the frontier. Mrs. Nesbitt and her sons, R. A. and H. Nesbitt, were saved in the cutter which pulled from the sinking troopship in charge of Mr. Richards. The first boy, Richard Athol, had a narrow escape. He found himself struggling in the sea, but managed to reach the boat and get on board with great difficulty. The subsequent career of this brave youth was one of remarkable interest. He joined the Imperial service three years after the wreck, and six years later became a Sub-Inspector of the Colonial Forces, in which he continued to serve for eighteen years. In 1878 he commanded the troops on the northern border. Wounds and ill-health compelled his retirement in 1879; but he was not idle long, for, recovering his physical strength, he next year raised and placed himself at the head of Nesbitt's Light Horse, which did such good work in Tembuland and Basutoland. This concluded his war service until 1899, when, on the outbreak of hostilities with the Boers, he again emerged from private life, and as Colonel of Nesbitt's Horse, served with distinction through that trying campaign, at the close of which the King rewarded his long and loyal devotion to the Imperial service by conferring upon him the Companionship of the Bath. Honoured and respected far and wide, he now retired to Red House, near Port Elizabeth, where, surrounded by relatives and friends, he resided quietly till his death, which came suddenly on September 5th, 1905, in his 69th year.

The story of his life is told by Colonel Nesbitt himself in a letter which he wrote from Red House on February 10th, seven months before he died. The letter is addressed to Mr. John R. Cocker, the lighthouse-keeper at Danger Point, off which the *Birkenhead* was lost, and the writer first speaks of the wreck fifty-three years before and of his own narrow escape.

Yes, I am one of the *Birkenhead* survivors. I was between fourteen and fifteen years old when it happened, and have a very clear and distinct recollection of all that occurred. I saved myself by making for and fastening on to one of the boats, to which I clung for some time after my fingers were crushed, and was eventually pulled on board. We were afterwards picked up by the schooner *Lioness*, and never shall I forget the great kindness of Captain and Mrs. Ramsden to all the survivors—men, women and children. I got Mr. Addison's book by last mail and have read it carefully through. The different accounts given by some of the survivors are very correct, and very interesting to me. I really cannot add in any way to its contents. Everything was carried out with great regularity and without confusion. I don't think half-an-hour could have elapsed from her striking until she broke up. I believe I am the sole survivor in this Colony. I should indeed be glad to see some memorial of the wreck erected in this country: it was to the assistance of the colonists that the troops were hastening when the ship was wrecked. Captain Nesbitt, of Barkly West, was my elder brother. He got his commission in the 12th or Suffolk Regiment, the same regiment as my father. He retired after getting his company in 1865 and started

FATE OF SOUTH AFRICAN SURVIVORS 243

farming near Barkly East. He has been dead now several years. When the *Birkenhead* was wrecked he was with my father serving in the Kaffir War of 1852.

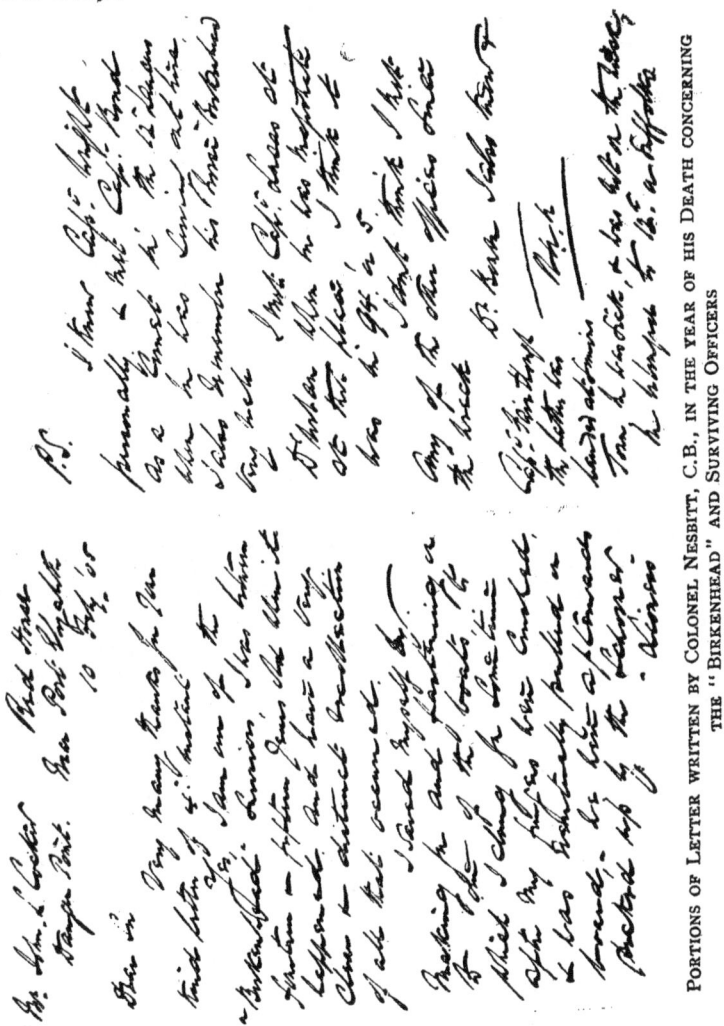

PORTIONS OF LETTER WRITTEN BY COLONEL NESBITT, C.B., IN THE YEAR OF HIS DEATH CONCERNING THE "BIRKENHEAD" AND SURVIVING OFFICERS

Colonel Nesbitt goes on to describe his own adventurous career after the wreck, and the narration is full of interest.

I joined the Imperial Government's service in 1855, and in 1861 came over to the Colonial Forces as a Sub-Inspector in the F.A. and M.P., which was afterwards converted into the C.M.R., from which I retired on pension in 1879, unfit for further service through wounds and ill-health. In 1878 I commanded the troops on the northern border until I was wounded and lost my health. In 1880 I was so far recovered that I, at the request of the Colonial Government, raised and commanded a Colonial corps, Nesbitt's Light Horse, and served with it throughout the Tembu and Basuto rebellions. In 1899, after nearly twenty years' quiet civil life, I was again requested to raise a Colonial regiment for the Boer War. This I did, and the regiment, Nesbitt's Horse, of which I was Colonel, served in most of the principal events of the war, with Lord Roberts' march—Paardeburg, capture of Bloemfontein, Johannesburg, Pretoria, and in clearing the Colony of rebels. His Majesty the King was pleased to decorate me with a C.B. for my war services, and I have now settled down in this pretty river siding, which is about nine miles from Port Elizabeth, where I enjoy, in addition to fair health, boating and fishing and the society of nice neighbours and several married members of my own family.

The writer speaks in conclusion of the pleasure with which he was looking forward to the revised *Birkenhead* book. In a postscript he recalls some of the officers who were at the wreck.

I knew Captain Wright personally, and met Captain Bond as a cornet in the 12th Lancers when he was serving out here. I also remember his horse "Birkenhead" very well. I met Captain Lucas at Durban when he was magistrate at that place, I think it was in 1894 or 1895. I don't think I met any of the other officers after the wreck. Dr. Bowen I also knew, and Captain Fairclough. The latter was landed at Simon's Town. He was sick, and was not on the wreck. He belonged to the 12th, or Suffolks.

The horse "Birkenhead" which Colonel Nesbitt remembered was the charger which swam ashore from the wreck and met its owner, Cornet Bond, on the beach.

The family to which Colonel Nesbitt belonged has been noted for its soldiers. In addition to those who have served in the 12th Regiment, Nesbitt's Horse included Captain N. Nesbitt, Captain C. W. Nesbitt, D.S.O., and Lieutenant W. W. Nesbitt. Then there was gallant Ralph Nesbitt, successively of the Cape Mounted Rifles, the British South Africa Company's Police, and the Mashonaland Mounted Rifles. For his conduct in rescuing the Mazoe refugees in 1896, in the punitive operations against the Rhodesian rebels, this young officer received the Victoria Cross, and three years

COLONEL R. A. NESBITT, C.B.
(Photo by Elliott & Fry, Baker Street, W.)

later he was the first British officer wounded in the Boer War while attempting to run the gauntlet with an armoured train.

Corporal William Butler

A happier fate was that of Corporal William Butler, who after the death of Colonel Nesbitt, claimed to be the only *Birkenhead* survivor living in South Africa. Butler was one of the draft of 12th Royal Lancers at the wreck, and he got ashore with the aid of a piece of wood which had been lying on the long-boat amidships. He was seven hours in the water, and reached the land exhausted and almost dead from exposure and being knocked about in the surf and among the rocks. After engaging in the Kaffir War, he left the service with the rank of corporal. "I am seventy-six years old, and quite hearty and well, thank God," he wrote from his farm in the Whittlesea district of Queenstown when stating these facts in October, 1905. His story was taken down at his dictation by Mr. W. M. Nightingale, a friend of Mr. Herbert Penny, secretary to the Capetown branch of the Navy League, who forwarded the written narrative for inclusion in these pages. Mr. Nightingale described this veteran survivor as "a fine specimen of an Englishman, who has a splendid farm," and said he was "as upright as a dart and as hale and hearty as possible." Mr. Butler's recollections of the wreck are an interesting addition to the personal accounts already recorded.

I was born [he says] at Shortwood Farm, one mile from Hucknall Torkard, Notts, on March 19th, 1830, and in 1848 joined the "Cherry Pickers" (11th Hussars), and went with them to Dublin, where volunteers were requested for the Cape of Good Hope. Five of us volunteered for the 12th Lancers, and were drafted to Cork, where we boarded the *Birkenhead*. As soon as we were out of harbour the sea was mountains high, and we took fourteen days to reach Madeira. From there we went to Sierra Leone, where a stoker swam ashore to desert. He was caught, and the next morning we were all paraded to see him receive fifty lashes. Thence we went to St. Helena, and from there to Simon's Bay, taking 47 days. We remained at Simon's Bay a day or two, taking on board baggage, eighteen horses, hay, etc., so that the main-deck was full, hay being piled nearly to the top of the funnel, leaving

absolutely no room for troops to parade as shown in the noted picture.*
We left Simon's Bay at sunset, and between twelve and one o'clock next
morning, when the sea was very calm, we ran on a reef. It was like
a clap of thunder. Everyone rushed out. The Captain and officers
behaved splendidly; the former sang out, "Soldiers and sailors, keep
quiet, and I will save you all!" There was calm after panic; we
lowered the gangway, and pitched four guns and the horses overboard.
Captain Wright, of the 91st, jumped after his horse and got ashore with
him.† The Captain ordered Mr. Brodie, the 1st Lieutenant,‡ to get
the paddle-box boats loose. In doing so he got his thighs jammed.
When the vessel went down, the boat he had loosened remained in the
water keel up. I saw four men get ashore on her, one man sitting on
the keel with a big coat on, the three others paddling. Three on a
spar also reached the shore, two men and a cabin boy; the boy sat
on the spar, and the men paddled. I saw another get ashore on a truss
of hay.

As to the troops being paraded, it is imagination. She was loaded
to the funnel. It was *sauve qui peut*. The last words I heard the
Captain say were: "Soldiers and sailors, I've done what I can for
you. I can't do more. Those who can swim do so; those who can't,
climb the rigging." Then it was a rush. Two quarter-boats had been
lowered and the women and children put into them, all of whom were
saved. These boats left the wreck at once, and remained on the water
till daybreak; then, seeing a vessel, they went to her, the Captain
bringing her to within two miles of the wreck. She was a schooner.
The *Birkenhead* broke in two at the fore and then at the mainmast, the
hind-part sinking and the officers going down then; the mainmast, with
forty odd on the mainyard, remaining above water. The schooner's
boats saved all the latter; she went into Simon's Bay, where the survivors were put on board the *Castor*, about 75 in all. When the Captain
told us to save ourselves, many of us jumped overboard. I had stripped.
I got hold of a bit of wreckage, on which it took me about seven hours
to reach the shore, where the survivors mustered in lots of six to ten
who knew each other and walked in the direction of Simon's Bay, taking
two days to reach the same. Many, like myself, were naked. I got
two gunny bags, all my covering, my head being bare, and was in the
doctor's hands a month, all my hair and even skin coming off. We
passed several Dutch houses on the road, the inmates of which gave
us food and seemed very much afraid of us! We remained on the
Castor about a month, and then went in the *Rhadamanthus* to East
London. From there I went to King William's Town, and was in the
thick of the war, eventually receiving my discharge as a corporal.

* The troops were assembled on the poop.
† This evidently has reference to the fable of Dr. Bowen and his white mare,
dealt with in a preceding chapter, the names of the officers being confounded.
‡ Mr. Brodie was the Master.

FATE OF SOUTH AFRICAN SURVIVORS

It is not surprising to learn that the weird appearance of some of the castaways alarmed the poor Dutch settlers, who nevertheless behaved very kindly to the sufferers. The whole statement is interesting, and is no doubt conscientiously made; but while he seems to remember well some things which happened at |the wreck, the narrator fails to do any justice to the grand display of discipline which unquestionably took place on board. The boats which put off from the wreck did not leave at once, but stood by the ship for some time. The parading, or rather assembling, of the troops on the poop—not on the maindeck—is not, as he insists, imagination. The order to the men to save themselves, which drew from their officers the chivalrous appeal to them not to endanger the boats, was not issued till the last. One curious fact is revealed by Mr. Butler. This is that the five troopers of the 12th Lancers present at the wreck were volunteers from the 11th Hussars, under two cornets and a sergeant of the Lancers. The original returns, it has been noticed, leave one man of the 12th Lancers unaccounted for. There were, all told, eight of the regiment on board; five (Cornet Rolt, Sergeant Straw, and three troopers) were reported drowned, and two (Cornet Bond and Trooper Dodd) as being saved. This accounted for seven only. Evidently Trooper Butler was the eighth man. The returns were not altogether trustworthy, and it is possible that the William Butler, described as a sergeant of the 91st, included among the drowned may really have been the William Butler who was saved. The lists also show that a John Butler, of the 43rd draft, perished at the wreck.

CHAPTER XIX

A DAUGHTER OF THE REGIMENT

So we made women with their children go ;
Whilst inch by inch the drowning ship sank low,
Still under steadfast men.—SIR FRANCIS DOYLE'S *Poem*.

THERE passed away at Beckingham, in the county of Notts, on November 17th, 1904, a "Daughter of the Regiment" whose personality will always be remembered with interest, especially by The Queen's. The deceased was one of those on whose behalf the 2nd Queen's and other corps showed such marvellous coolness and discipline at the wreck of the *Birkenhead*. Mrs. Parkinson, then Marian Darkin, was going out with her mother to join her father, Drum-Major John Robert Darkin, of The Queen's. Although not quite four years of age at the time, in after life she recollected distinctly some of the incidents of that terrible night in 1852. This will be seen from a letter she wrote at the 50th anniversary of the wreck to Lieut.-Colonel William Mackie, of The Queen's.

I was three years and eight months old at the time of the wreck. There were only my mother and myself of our family on board the *Birkenhead*; my mother was on the way to join my father. I can remember quite well my mother taking me in her arms on deck in our night clothes, and giving me to a cabin boy to hold whilst she went again down below to fetch a cloak, and they lowered me into the boat. When she got back she could not find me, and all the boats had pushed off. Two officers swung mother from the side of the vessel as she was sinking, and she just caught the side of the boat and fell amongst the people. If she had fallen the other way they must have left her, as the boat was being drawn under by the sinking vessel. We were out in the boat till one o'clock next day, and a small vessel picked us up and gave us some biscuits and water, and took us back to Cape Town. We were not long before we started again, and went up country all through the Kaffir War. I was born in The Queen's, and so were my brothers. My father was discharged when I was 12 years old. I was sorry when he left the Army ; I like Military life best.

It will be observed [comments Colonel Mackie] that Mrs. Parkinson

MRS. PARKINSON, NÉE MARIAN DARKIN
(From a photo)

says that two officers caught sight of her mother, just before the ship sank, and lowered her into the boat. In every account of the wreck the same noble, self-denying part played by all the officers shines out brightly. Their marvellous heroism and preservation of discipline were the means by which all the women and children were saved.

Mrs. Parkinson had three soldier brothers and one sister. Her brothers were all born at Fort Hare, Cape of Good Hope: Alfred John Darkin, on March 10th, 1853; Edward Charles, on July 9th, 1855; and Robert Christopher, on October 12th, 1858. Her sister, Catherine Darkin, was born on March 18th, 1861. The brothers all joined the Coldstream Guards, where they represented the fourth generation of the family which had served in that famous corps. Their father was transferred from the Coldstreams to The Queen's as Drum-Major at Winchester in 1846, and his father and grandfather belonged to the Coldstreams before him; so that the Military history of this interesting family was very remarkable. It was equally honourable. The eldest brother of the "Daughter of the Regiment" joined the Coldstreams on June 6th, 1864, and was discharged on July 7th, 1892, with the rank of staff-sergeant, after serving twenty-eight years and one month. Edward Charles Darkin was with the regiment seventeen years, and Robert Christopher Darkin sixteen years. Edward Charles died in London in 1899; the other two brothers were both living at Forest Gate in 1905. Their father, who left the service in 1860, died at Leeds on June 10th, 1883, at the age of sixty-three. He possessed the Kaffir War medal and that for long service and good conduct. Their mother had died at Knaresborough twenty years previously, in July, 1863, at the early age of thirty-six. Marian Darkin herself, on March 11th, 1886, married Mr. George Parkinson, an engineer, and she left a daughter, Rose, born September 11th of the following year. Before her marriage Mrs. Parkinson lived in the service of the Vicar of Beckingham for over twenty years. Her death in 1904 was preceded by a painful illness, which, like a true "Daughter of the Regiment," she bore with great patience and resignation.* Her affliction was unhappily

* "Mrs. Parkinson was a most brave woman in her suffering, which was very great indeed. In fact, as I wrote Colonel Mackie, she was a true soldier's daughter to the very last."—Letter by Miss Sidwell.

caused by the kick of a cow on the breast. She underwent an operation for cancer in Lincoln County Hospital, and at home was tenderly nursed by a step-daughter, and received much kindness also from her friend Miss Sidwell, of Beckingham. In her illness she was much cheered by the sympathy shown her by all ranks of the regiment, conveyed through the commanding officers of the battalions, the depôt, and individual officers, including Major-General Pye Phillipps, who served in The Queen's with Drum-Major Darkin.

At the funeral of Marian Parkinson a wreath was sent tied with the regimental ribbon, and bearing a card with the inscription, " A tribute of affection and respect for a *Birkenhead* survivor, from the officers and all ranks of The Queen's Regiment." In the 2nd Battalion regimental orders of November 19th a compliment was paid to the memory of Mrs. Parkinson by the commanding-officer informing the battalion with regret of her death. Later a memorial tablet was erected by the 1st Battalion of the regiment to one whose long association with it and share in an episode which brought it undying honour was a subject of so much interest and solicitude to the last. The tablet, placed on the west wall of the building, was unveiled in Beckingham Church on June 19th, 1905. It is inscribed :

<blockquote align="center">
SACRED TO THE MEMORY
of
MRS. MARIAN PARKINSON
a survivor of the troopship
BIRKENHEAD
wrecked off the Cape
26th Feby. 1852
under circumstances which
evoked the admiration of
all countries.
She was a daughter of
Drum-Major John R. Darkin
of The Queen's Regt.
and died on 17th November, 1904.
Erected by the Officers and all Ranks
1st Bn. The Queen's Regt.
</blockquote>

Engraved on the brass of the tablet above the inscription is a representation of the sinking troopship from the picture

A DAUGHTER OF THE REGIMENT

of Captain Bond-Shelton. The beautiful little edifice containing the memorial, true type of our English village churches, was filled for the unveiling ceremony, which in the unavoidable absence of Colonel Mackie or any officer of the 2nd Battalion, was, on behalf of the 1st Battalion in India, performed by the author of *The Story of the "Birkenhead."* The company assembled included the Bishop of Southwell (Dr. Hoskyns), the Vicar of Beckingham (Rev. C. R. Round) and several neighbouring clergy, Miss Sidwell of Beckingham (who carried out the arrangements for the memorial), Mr. H. L. Howlden of Sheffield (head of the firm which designed and executed the tablet), and Staff-Sergeant A. J. Darkin, late Coldstream Guards. Although unable to be present in person, Colonel Mackie wrote expressing his well-known admiration of the magnificent behaviour of the *Birkenhead* troops. He alluded to the high tribute paid by Captain Wright concerning that perfect order and discipline of the men which resulted in the saving of the women and children at the sacrifice of their own lives, and recalled that the then King of Prussia commanded Captain Wright's report to be read to every regiment in the Prussian service.

A moving incident inaugurated the unveiling. There in tears before the flag-draped tablet stood a sorrowing young form, Mrs. Parkinson's daughter, her only child, a bowed and sobbing figure clad in black, outlined on the brilliant colours of the nation's flag. It was a sight infinitely pathetic and instantly suggestive. That touch of nature revived as in a flash the whole tragedy of the wreck! It was the picture of a simple village maiden pouring forth her soul in grief. But it depicted something more. It typified Britannia lamenting her gallant sons, as she mourned them more than half-a-century before. The tears shed then, like those wept now for "one of the children" saved in the boats, came from the heart; but they were soon dried, giving place to the applause which rang not through England only, but throughout Europe and the world, and echoes still to-day.

When, following the few spoken words of the ceremony, the fallen Union Jack revealed the memorial, the Lord Bishop offered a special dedicatory prayer.

Grant that as the soldiers on board the *Birkenhead* were faithful and obedient in the hour of trial and danger, so we, Thy soldiers, may have grace to be faithful in the time of temptation.

Then Mr. Howlden, who had been invited to speak by Miss Sidwell, acknowledged the active and disinterested labours of that lady and read from "The Story" the letter given above, written by Mrs. Parkinson to Colonel Mackie, together with the Colonel's comments thereon. Mr. Howlden went on to remark that in these country villages, these "sleepy hollows," were born men often poorly circumstanced, with little influence to back their career, not unused to hardship, but with vigorous, healthy constitutions and a nervous system to be envied. From such material, he said, England's need was supplied. It was grit that was recruited from the country villages and hamlets—grit, a word which seemed to embody the pluck and tenacity of English manhood, and in a measure to typify the sturdy self-reliance and independence forming the backbone of the English character. He remembered as a boy reading of the gallant conduct of the old Queen's Royals; how that upon the sinking *Birkenhead* officers and men stood at attention, silently and heroically facing death, while the women and children were taken off in the boats; and the recollection of such gallantry had been an incentive to him, among, he was sure, many thousands of others, to stand firm for self-discipline, character, and unselfishness, and to strive to play the man against adverse people and circumstances. It had, he declared, been a sincere pleasure to him to come there and to pay, in small measure, his tribute to noble example.

In the course of an eloquent address the Bishop of Southwell referred to what he described as the touching function which had just taken place, and remarked, in eulogising the behaviour of the men on board the *Birkenhead*, that it was only by training, by discipline, by bringing in higher motives and higher ideals of life, that at last we could learn to think of others before self. Dr. Hoskyns mentioned that he had himself sailed very near to the spot where the troopship was lost. In telling words, appropriate to the occasion and the scene of the day's ceremony, he emphasised the lessons of duty,

A DAUGHTER OF THE REGIMENT 253

obedience and unselfishness taught by the *Birkenhead*, and their application to Christian life and church membership.

The part played at the wreck by the 2nd Queen's, or Royal West Surrey Regiment, which had a detachment on board the troopship, is well told by Colonel Mackie, who was personally acquainted with survivors of the draft and heard the story from their own lips.

Fifty years have barely elapsed since this event occurred [wrote Colonel Mackie, from Stoughton Barracks, Guildford, in 1902], and yet it is in danger of being forgotten; whereas the inhabitants of these islands should, as the centuries roll on, be proud to remember that they can claim kinship with those young lads who, going out to maintain the fame of their country on the battlefield, faced death under far different surroundings, thinking only of the honour of their uniform and the safety of the women and little ones. The Queen's Regiment, however, will, it is to be hoped, ever treasure the memory of their comrades of a past generation who took part in this great and moving tragedy. The detachment of The Queen's on board consisted of one sergeant, one bandmaster, and 50 rank and file, Ensign Boylan being in command. Ensign Boylan, Bandmaster Zwyker, and 33 men were never seen again. The few survivors of the detachment had many thrilling narratives of hairbreadth escapes to narrate. Private Robert Page, of The Queen's, with 28 other men, clung to the cabin mess-table, which was floating in the water. He, the sole survivor, was, 24 hours subsequently, rescued by a passing vessel, all his comrades having, through exhaustion, loosened their hold and been drowned, or been seized by sharks. Page was subsequently soldier-servant to the writer of these lines, and related to him his experiences. Private James Boyden, also of The Queen's and of only five months' service, managed to clamber on top of a bale of compressed hay, and was borne towards the shore by the current. A short way in front of him he saw a boy clinging to a spar, and the little fellow, notwithstanding his perilous position, could not resist a joke, calling out, "Come on, Jack Straw." Both were saved, and the nickname clung to Boyden throughout the whole of his regimental service.

Boyden, many years afterwards, was colour-sergeant of the company commanded by Colonel Mackie, and in giving his officer an account of the catastrophe, said:

During the time that Colonel Seton's orders were being carried out one might have heard a pin fall; Colonel Seton walked about the deck giving his orders with as much coolness and presence of mind as if he were on parade, entirely forgetful of self. When the commander of the ship shouted to the men to swim for the boats I saw none attempt to do so—all remained steady. When on the hay I saw the sea literally swarming with sharks, which dashed about among their prey till the air resounded with the cries of their victims. Before reaching the shore I came to a mass of seaweed, so had to leave my bundle of hay and swim ashore. The rigging of the maintopmast remained upright above the water, and about 40 men who were clinging to it were eventually saved.

When he left the regiment, on pension, Colour-Sergeant Boyden was the possessor of the Kaffir War medal of 1852-3, the China War medal of 1860, with clasps for Taku Forts and Pekin, and the medal for long service and good conduct.

Major-General H. P. Phillipps, who was gazetted to The Queen's between two and three years after the wreck, wrote informing Colonel Mackie that—

one survivor of The Queen's was afterwards a colour-sergeant—Law by name. He swam with Ensign Boylan, of the regiment, for some time, and was close to him when Boylan called out, and was drawn under by a shark. Law used to say that Boylan was much the better swimmer of the two, but that they kept together until Boylan was drawn under. Cornet Bond's horse was saved; some of the animals went straight to sea.

The Private Law here referred to, who swam ashore and was later promoted to colour-sergeant, stood as godfather to Drum-Major Darkin's eldest son, Alfred John, born at Fort Hare in March, 1853, and afterwards a staff-sergeant in the Coldstream Guards. Law died at Leeds in 1872. In a letter which he wrote to Colonel Mackie, Captain Bond-Shelton said:

I knew well poor Boylan, commanding the detachment of The Queen's —a very tall, fine young man (and I knew most of the officers at the Cape). I wonder if Mrs. Parkinson was one of the children that I carried up from the cabin. I never heard anything of them afterwards, as I went to the front. I think that the other little girl I carried up must have been a bandmaster's daughter, who, I heard, was married years ago.

The questions here raised by Captain Bond-Shelton are discussed in the pages of this book devoted to that gallant officer himself. The story of Mrs. Kaye, of The Queen's, who went out to the Cape in the *Birkenhead*, and in 1906 was still residing in the Colony, is told at the end of the next chapter,

Danger Point Lighthouse and Keepers' Quarters

CHAPTER XX

DANGER POINT

On a stern and rock-bound coast.—MRS. HEMANS.

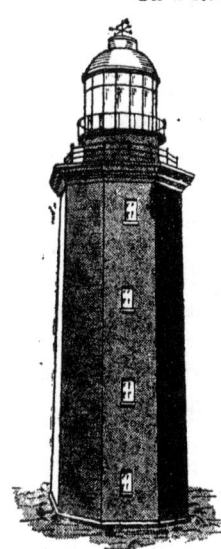

THE accompanying map sections show the chief points and places on the South African coast mentioned in this story, and will help the reader to locate other spots named. Upon Danger Point, where the *Birkenhead* was wrecked, now stands a lighthouse 150 feet in height above sea level. From the octagonal tower, painted with red and white vertical stripes and rising 87 feet from the ground, is shown a triple-flashing white light every forty seconds during the night, which, when at full power, is visible six leagues, or eighteen miles distant. The approximate bearing of the lighthouse is lat. 34° 47′ 45″ S., long. 19° 18′ E. The "Birkenhead Rock" is as nearly as possible opposite the lighthouse, and is distant from the shore slightly under two miles. At very low water, spring tide, the rock can be distinctly seen, although at high water it is covered by twelve feet of water.

DANGER POINT LIGHTHOUSE

There are two old men living a few miles from here [wrote the head light-keeper, Mr. John R. Cocker, to the authors in December, 1904] who clearly remember the wreck and assisted to bury many of the bodies cast up.* I have often spoken to them about it. If you could only see the great rocks and heavy sea that is always here you would marvel that any escaped alive from the wreck. The farm owned by Captain Smales, where assistance was obtained, is now the small Dutch village of Stanford, with a Dutch and English church and a population of about 400.

* One of these men was David Faro, a fisherman, who was still hale and hearty in 1905. Mr. de Villiers, sen., of Caledon, the Field-Cornet under whose orders Faro acted, was also living in 1905.

The other place mentioned, Stanford Cove, better known as Stanford Bay, is a small fishing hamlet with 50 or 60 people living there.

A native of Higher Broughton, Manchester, Mr. Cocker had, at the date of this letter, been out in South Africa twenty-six years, for thirteen years and seven months in the Cape Lighthouse Service, the last seven years and a month of which period he had been head light-keeper at Danger Point, with two assistants. His wife and family of seven children were with him. The Point, being an isolated and out-of-the-way place, attracts very few strangers, and whole months sometimes pass without a single visitor appearing there, except the post-boy bringing the letters and packages once a week from Stanford, and the lighthouse inspector, who makes an official call every two months. Still, judging from Mr. Cocker's cheery letter, there is no feeling of oppression there, and the members of the sequestered little colony would seem to find plenty in their duties and surroundings to occupy and interest them. The accompanying scenes, from photographs supplied for this work by Mr. Cocker, will show the reader what the lighthouse, with the signal station adjoining, is like, and give him an idea of the character of the vicinity ashore and seaward. Point Danger has rocks about it extending off more or less for half-a-mile. "Birkenhead Rock" is situated W.S.W. one mile from the extremity of the Point. Its position is usually indicated by breakers. Owing to the presence of the rock it is necessary for sailing-craft to give the land hereabout a wide berth, especially as it is very steep, the lead dropping from it at once into seven or ten fathoms.

Point Danger is prolonged under water for about three miles in a similar direction to the inclination of the land in the locality, which is W.S.W., by a bank of ten fathoms, deepening to twenty fathoms as that distance from the shore is reached. The bank consists almost entirely of rock and coral. Danger Point affords shelter to vessels during the strong south-easterly gales in summer, and boats may land at Stanford Bay, the small rocky inlet on the north side of the Point five miles from its extremity, during easterly and south-easterly winds, if care be taken to avoid

VIEWS OF DANGER POINT AND VICINITY

the rocky patches off it. Hydra Bay, nearer the end of the Point, is, however, a better place for landing, the swell there not being so strong; but it is necessary to observe equal caution in clearing outlying rocky patches. The bay is only a shallow indentation of the land, and may easily be recognised by a sand patch which marks the face of the hillock over it. As Point Danger is approached from the sea the appearance of the shore is deceptive, being low and backed by high land which in the distance resembles a bluff, but really is quite twelve miles inside the Point.*

Continuing to the south-eastward of this interesting spot, we may here briefly note other familiar names met with round the coast which in some measure are associated with our story. They have not the same attraction for us as Danger Point, but they fill in the whole picture. Cape Agulhas, the most southerly point of Africa and the dividing line between the Atlantic and Indian Oceans, lies about a hundred miles E.S.E. of the Cape of Good Hope, in lat. 34° 49′ S., long. 20° 40″ E. The name, which signifies "Needles," owes its origin to the saw-edged reefs which here run out to the sea, and are very dangerous to navigate landward. The lighthouse on this cape was erected in 1849. The Agulhas Bank, about forty miles broad, extends along the whole southern coast of Africa, from near Natal to Saldanha Bay. Algoa Bay, a broad inlet at the eastern extremity of the south coast of Africa, where part of the *Birkenhead's* troops were to have landed, has a sheltered anchorage, except towards the south-east. On it stands Port Elizabeth. East London, for which point the rest of the troops were destined, is a South African seaport at the mouth of the Buffalo River, thirty-six miles south-east of King William's Town, and seven hundred east of Capetown. It now has a large export and import trade, and is the terminus of the railway to Queenstown.

To return to Point Danger and its useful lighthouse, a

* Should any enterprising reader, combining the spirit of adventure with admiration for the *Birkenhead*, ever attempt to navigate these troubled and treacherous waters for the sake of closer personal acquaintance with the scene and the subject, he will find certain "Sailing Directions" which are obtainable for this coast a safe and reliable guide.

boon to the many mariners who ply their calling off this coast. Why should not the glorious tragedy which suggested the light and led to its creation be permanently commemorated on the spot? This question, we may hope, will before long command a satisfactory answer. Prior to joining the Cape Lighthouse Service, Mr. Cocker, the intelligent head-keeper of the Danger Point light,* was in the Army, where he won two medals with bars for the Zulu War of 1879 and the Basuto War of 1880-1. It is not surprising that the subject of the *Birkenhead*, and his close proximity to the scene of the wreck, should powerfully influence and interest such a man, and that in his letter, already mentioned, he should express gratification that some one was—

endeavouring to keep green the history of such an event as the wreck of the *Birkenhead*, and the names of the brave fellows who died and of those who are still living. I am very much afraid [he continues] we English, as a nation, are very apt to let such events slide, whereas any other nation, the Germans for instance, would have the yearly anniversary of such a signal act of bravery, devotion, and discipline officially kept; and I am of opinion that this could still be done if you could manage to obtain enough influence and pressure to bear in the right direction.

An excellent suggestion, which at any rate is worthy of consideration. Excellent also and more feasible is the proposal which follows.

Seven years ago I spoke to some gentlemen of influence in Capetown on the subject, and tried my best to interest them in the matter. I suggested the erection of a memorial in one of the squares in Capetown, and the placing of a brass tablet on the lighthouse, briefly recording the event, the expense to be defrayed by public subscription; but, other public and political events arising at the time, the matter died out.

Mr. Cocker, however, expressed himself in hopeful terms as willing to try again, and asked for advice and co-operation, which were readily given and promised. Just at this time † Mr. Joseph Chamberlain, the ex-Colonial Secretary, spoke at a public gathering of welcome to the Coldstream Guards at Birmingham, and in the course of an eloquent address declared:

* In January, 1906, Mr. Cocker was transferred as head light-keeper to Robben Island.
† Early in January, 1905.

DAVID FARO

(This remarkable old man, a native fisherman on the coast, assisted in burying the bodies cast ashore from the wreck of the *Birkenhead*. At the close of 1905 he was still living in the neighbourhood of Danger Point, where this photograph of him was taken. He was then reported to be 102 years of age, and in the enjoyment of "fairly good health." Faro is wearing the medal given for the Kaffir War of 1852, in which he served in the Hottentot Brigade under Sir Harry Smith)

I hold it to be a social crime to ignore the nobler side of this great profession [the Military], and not to seize every opportunity to do honour to the men who take the burden and the task upon themselves, and make the sacrifice which is required, and who in their country's cause are loyal even unto death.

The right hon. gentleman was communicated with on the subject. He was reminded that the *Birkenhead* represents the very noblest side of the Military profession, and that the soldiers who stood on the deck of the sinking troopship were indeed "loyal even unto death." He was informed of the proposal emanating from South Africa, and invited to lend his powerful advocacy in furtherance of so laudable a project. Promptly came the answer back from Highbury:

Mr. Chamberlain would be glad to see such a proposal as you suggest carried into effect. HE DOES NOT THINK IT IS WELL FOR A NATION TO FORGET ITS HEROES.

This encouraging message was sent out to Mr. Cocker, with the best wishes for the success of a proposal which does him honour, and the hope that the weighty words of a statesman so prominently identified with South African affairs would lead to its ultimate realisation.

The question was taken up subsequently by the Capetown branch of the Navy League, to whose notice it was brought by Mr. Herbert Penny, the honorary secretary to that influential body. That Mr. Penny personally sympathised strongly with the idea was shown by his letter to *The Cape Times* dealing with it, and speaking also of the book and the correspondence on the subject; and the feeling was shared by the members of the League, who lost no time in taking preliminary steps to give effect to the proposal. The Navy as well as the Army suffered heavily at the tragic shipwreck in officers and men who heroically did their duty; and it was recognised that the memory of those who perished, as well as the conduct of survivors, deserved to be perpetuated near the scene of their deeds in some such manner as that suggested, especially as the troops on the *Birkenhead* were proceeding at the time to the defence of the Colony from a powerful savage foe.

The interesting views of Danger Point and Lighthouse accompanying this chapter were specially taken by Mr. H. R. Beard, B.A., of Capetown. In the small combined pictures, that on the reader's left is a bit of the coast three miles from the Point, and the other shore scene, "All sand," is a mile farther off. Danger Point lighthouse appears in the view above. In the dense bush of the low-lying hill beneath the lighthouse were buried most of the bodies washed up from the wreck of the *Birkenhead*.

Reference is here made to certain aged dwellers in South Africa who assisted in the disposal of the dead and so came to be associated with the wreck. There remained still in Cape Colony in 1906 one who ministered to the living by providing food and shelter for the survivors on their arrival at Simon's Bay. This was the widow of Erick Malcolm Kaye, once of The Queen's. Mrs. Kaye went out in the *Birkenhead* in 1851, when the ship conveyed the 2nd Queen's Regiment to Capetown. Mrs. Darkin and her little daughter Marian were fellow-passengers on the voyage. The regiment marched to the front, and the woman and child stayed at the Cape till the coming of the *Birkenhead* with drafts in the February following. Mrs. Darkin and Marian re-embarked, but Mrs. Kaye was left behind. She thus escaped the wreck herself, and in the period of suffering which ensued, rendered all the help possible to those who were snatched from a watery grave. Her husband quitted the regiment in 1853 on completion of twelve years' service. Mrs. Kaye continued in South Africa after his death, and in 1906 was residing with her son-in-law, Sergeant W. E. Miles, of the Cape Mounted Rifles. "Comrades of the grand old regiment, I am one of you yet, at the age of seventy-seven," she wrote to The Queen's, to whom she discovered herself, a veritable link with the past, on hearing of the memorial erected to the child of former years, Mrs. Parkinson; and the officers of the 1st Battalion, as a mark of their regard, and of the respect and sympathy of the whole corps, presented the worthy recipient with a brooch of the regimental badge, bearing a suitable inscription.

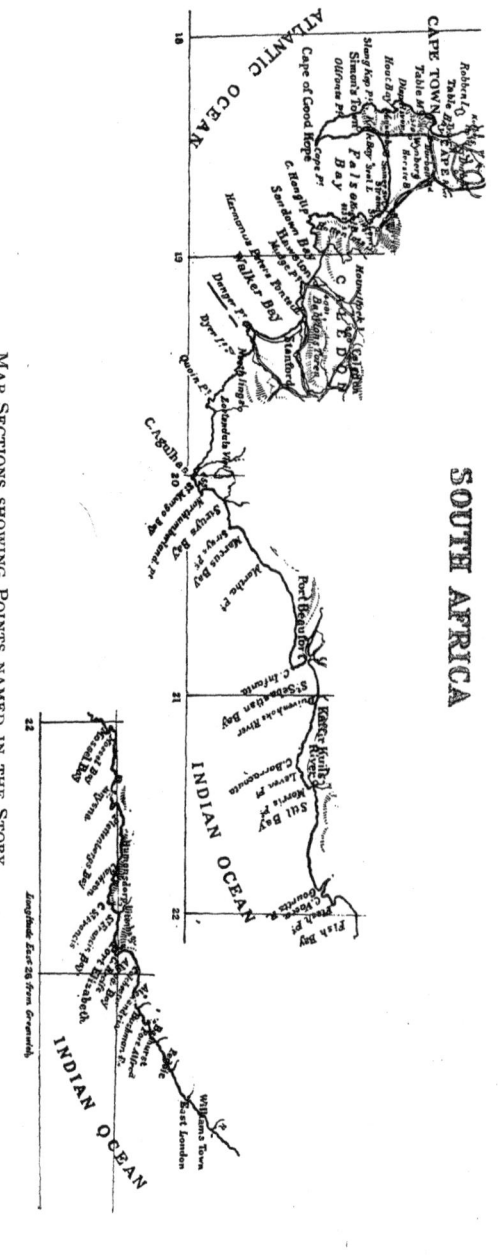

MAP SECTIONS SHOWING POINTS NAMED IN THE STORY

CHAPTER XXI

THE TRAGIC DEATH OF A SURVIVOR*

A deed of dreadful note.—SHAKESPEARE.

IN the notice already contained in these pages of that stalwart old *Birkenhead* survivor, William Henry McCluskey, is stated the fact of his tragic death in South Africa while acting as a guard in the employ of the De Beers Company at Bultfontein on October 5th, 1903. We may here enter more fully into the narration of that terrible story as the circumstances of it were disclosed subsequently. It forms the subject of perhaps the most thrilling and pathetic criminal trial that has ever been heard in South Africa.

The murder of poor McCluskey excited widespread horror throughout the diamond fields, and much curiosity was evinced respecting the native, Michael Mongale, who perpetrated the awful crime. On the morning of October 6th, the day following its commission, the precincts of Beaconsfield Courthouse were thronged with white and coloured people who had gathered together in the expectation of seeing the wretch Mongale brought up. They were not disappointed. The accused, wrapped in a blanket, squatted outside the court among other prisoners who were awaiting trial on various minor charges. He appeared unconcerned and indifferent to the curiosity of the crowd, upon whom he gazed with a stolid demeanour. Inside the court was exhibited a gruesome collection of articles connected with the case, all bearing traces of blood. There was the battered tin can used by Mongale; also a piece of shafting weighing 89 lb. which it was supposed was dropped on the deceased's head after he had been rendered insensible by a blow from a shovel.

---

* The book is indebted to the publishers of *The Diamond Fields Advertiser* for their assistance in the collection of materials for this record.

Mongale's appearance in court was only of brief duration. He was formally charged with the murder and remanded by Mr. E. L. Harries, Acting Ad. R.M., until the 9th of the month. When the day for the hearing came a large crowd collected round the prisoners—among whom was Mongale—before the police proceedings commenced; and after being admitted to the courthouse, the public manifested keen interest in the bloodstained implements associated with the tragedy, which were on view at the solicitors' table. When brought into court Mongale took up a position in a corner of the dock, and he stood there with a piece of paper between his fingers, almost without movement, throughout the proceedings. Only at rare intervals did he display any real interest in the evidence. He was wearing the coat he had on when he left the location on the morning of the murder. Detective-Sergeant Beatty conducted the case on behalf of the police.

The first witness called was John Malahleve, a native living at Green Point Location, who said the accused was his nephew and had been living in the same hut as witness for the last twelve months. Lately, witness had noticed something wrong in Mongale's conduct. On Monday, September 28th, accused started to sing in the middle of the night, and he sang and shouted at intervals for some days. Witness took no steps for a few days, during which this conduct on Mongale's part continued. At night-time he sang and shouted, and during the daytime he walked about the location singing. When witness tried to quieten him he refused to listen, and said, "Don't bother me—I don't interfere with any one." Witness had never seen Mongale smoking dagga. He reported Mongale's conduct to the Rev. Josiah Philip, native minister, who went to the hut and saw him. Mr. Philip said witness had better detain Mongale a few days to see whether he was wrong in his head. On Saturday Mongale got worse, and was violent about six o'clock that morning. As the result of this witness went to Beaconsfield Police Station and reported the matter, as Mongale was looking wild and singing, shouting and dancing. Witness told the police there was a sick boy at the location who was mad. They told him to go back, tie the boy, and bring him to the police station.

THE TRAGIC DEATH OF A SURVIVOR

Then witness was told that as it was late he had better bring the boy to the station on Monday. That was about mid-day. On Sunday Mongale appeared better, and on Sunday night also he was better.

Coming to the morning of Monday, October 5th, witness said he was told by another native that Mongale was running about the floors. Witness had not tied Mongale or fastened him in the hut at all, and he got up about sunrise and went out. When he left the hut Mongale was wearing the jacket he now wore, and a red shirt, with trousers. When informed that Mongale was running across the Bultfontein floors, which were close to the location, witness went and told the Rev. Josiah Philip, as he had promised that if the boy was mad he should be taken to the police station. Then witness set off to catch Mongale, seeing that he was not able to take care of himself, and fearing he would get lost or hurt himself. Witness went along the fence of the floors and saw Mongale come out of the guard's hut. He noticed Mongale stoop down and strike something in front of him when he got out of the hut, and when he drew nearer he saw that this something was a body. Then Mongale went into the hut and brought out a "scoff" tin. Witness called to him, and told him to put the tin down, which he did. Witness then said, "Who killed that man?" and Mongale replied, "I did." The body was inside the fence, and witness was afraid to go to it. At that time Mongale had neither his shirt nor his jacket on—only his trousers. Witness noticed the jacket lying outside the fence, and picked it up; he did not see the shirt produced at all. He took Mongale to the headman of the location.

Questioned by Detective-Sergeant Beatty witness replied that when he went to the police he reported that the boy was "sick—wrong, wrong in his Charlie" (pointing to his head). He was told to bring him to the station; the police told him to "tie the boy and bring him down." When he took Mongale to the station on Monday he said he had killed a man, not that he had assaulted a man. What he said was interpreted by the headman. The object of Sergeant Beatty's questions appeared to be to show that witness was not told by the police to delay bringing the sick boy in till Monday, and that when Mongale was taken to the police station on the Monday the report given to the police was that he had "assaulted a guard."

Josiah Philip, a native Presbyterian minister residing at Green Point Location, who was next examined, said he had known the accused since October 2nd, when the previous witness asked him "to go and see a boy who was sick." Witness saw the accused and asked him if he was sick; he replied, "No." "But I found out he had silliness in his head," added the witness. Asked how he found that out, witness responded, "From his wild eyes." He reported the matter to the headman of the location, who returned with him to Malahleve's hut for the purpose of seeing Mongale, but Mongale had gone out. Witness had not seen the accused since, till he now saw him in the dock. He remembered Malahleve telling him about six o'clock on Monday morning that the "sick boy" was running away across the floors. At that time witness was lying down. Later he heard that a guard had been killed.

The Court then heard the story of Jones Notyoda, headman of Green Point Location and a special constable, who said he had known the accused by sight for some time, but spoke to him for the first time on Monday, when accused was taken to him. Malahleve reported to him that Mongale had assaulted a guard.

<blockquote>The word he used [said the witness] means "assault," but sometimes means "murder"—it can be interpreted to mean either assault or kill. I interpreted his meaning to be "assault," and when we took Mongale to the police station I reported accordingly.</blockquote>

On the way to the station Mongale looked very wild. Witness, thinking it was a case of assault only, did not actually hold Mongale, who jumped about and kicked tins which he came across in the way. When they entered the town Mongale swore at some coolies without any apparent cause. Six men brought Mongale to the police station. On the previous Friday the Rev. Josiah Philip reported to him that he had been informed there was a suspicion that Mongale was mad, and the witness went with Mr. Philip to Malahleve's hut to see Mongale, but he was not there.

THE TRAGIC DEATH OF A SURVIVOR 265

William Robert Spratt, guard in Kimberley Gaol, told the Court that Mongale had been confined there since October 6th, and that he had been under witness's charge. When brought in the accused was a little excited, and at the request of the district surgeon witness kept particular observation on him.

> The first night we had to move him into the padded cell because he kept the other prisoners awake by shouting and singing. There was a tear in one of the pads, and next morning I found he had torn it up. I asked him why, and he said he had dreamt he had to feed the horses and took the straw out.

The hearing was adjourned for the medical report as to Mongale's mental condition, and at a subsequent sitting of the Court the accused was committed to take his trial on the capital charge. The case duly came on at the Criminal Sessions held at Kimberley on November 12th, 1903, before Mr. Justice Hopley, when Mongale, who was described as a "native labourer," was arraigned for the murder of McCluskey, and was defended by Mr. Advocate Wallach "pro Deo." Mr. H. T. Tamplin was the Crown prosecutor. David MacIntosh, traffic manager at Bultfontein Mine, deposed to posting deceased at the bottom of the Bultfontein floors, between Green Point Location and Alexandersfontein Road, at 6 a.m. on October 5th. Prisoner had been in the company's employ for two years, on and off. Witness had never noticed anything peculiar about Mongale, nor could he say that he was addicted to dagga-smoking. Hans Dreyer, a herd, testified that he saw prisoner running along, and heard him shouting and swearing at deceased, who got up and asked what was the matter. Prisoner ran into the guard-house, followed by McCluskey. He came out with a tin, threw it down, and stamped on it. He caught hold of McCluskey and threw him down after a struggle; then, picking up a spade, prisoner struck deceased several blows. Deceased did not get up again.

The next witness sworn was John Malahleve, the uncle of the accused man, who gave such important testimony at the preliminary inquiry. His evidence at the trial contained new matter, and offered some variety as to detail, so that it may be repeated here. Malahleve deposed that he had known Mongale for a year past, during which time he had been well conducted. On the morning of October 5th, in consequence of certain information, he went to look for prisoner, and saw him running along the floors towards the guard-house. Prisoner was behaving like an insane man. On the previous Saturday witness informed the police that his nephew was insane, and was told to bring him to the station. Witness tried to bring the prisoner, who struggled with him, and he thereupon gave it up. It was in consequence of prisoner having been very excited on the Saturday that he reported the matter to the police. Witness understood that prisoner had on one occasion been taken to an asylum in Capetown. [Mr. Justice Hopley interposed with the remark, " Of course, this is very important. The whole case will turn on the prisoner's state of mind." He put some questions to Mongale, who said he was confined in Kimberley in 1896 because of insanity, but could not say whether he was taken to Capetown.] Resuming his evidence, John Malahleve said that when he saw Mongale running away on the morning of October 5th he informed the native minister and then went after the accused, who he saw in the distance hacking at something with an implement. When witness got to the spot he saw McCluskey lying dead, and prisoner walking to and from the guard-room. Witness asked the deceased, pointing to the body, " What is the matter with that man ? " Prisoner replied, " I killed him." Witness told prisoner that he had committed a crime, and that he would have to take him to the police station. Prisoner, who kept on hopping and jumping about, merely said, " All right," and went with witness to the headman, shouting and singing. Replying to questions asked by Court, counsel, or jury, witness said that when the headman came up Mongale seemed to have calmed down. The only time he had noticed anything strange about the prisoner was four or five days previous to October 5th. Mongale was addicted to drink. He did not think the strangeness of prisoner's demeanour was due to drink or smoking dagga. The Monday prior to October 5th Mongale showed strangeness of manner, waking up in the night and singing and shouting. He got over this, but subsequently became worse, jumping and running about and singing. Witness had known Mongale from infancy; he was at Boshof or Pokwani when prisoner was said to have been in an asylum.

Jones Notyoda, the headman of Green Point Location, spoke to the prisoner being handed over to him; and, in answer to Mr. Wallach, said Mongale appeared somewhat strange in his manner, abusing Indian hawkers and kicking tins on his way to the police station. On one occasion, said the witness, accused had to be removed from the church, where he started moaning and groaning. Evidence of the prisoner's arrest was given by P.C. Brooks, who stated that on being charged and cautioned, Mongale said he killed the man because "he spoils the earth."

The Court now came to the medical witness, whose testimony had been awaited with anxious interest. William Walter Stoney, district surgeon, said he saw the body of the deceased on October 5th. He described the injuries in detail, and added that death was due to shock from the wounds inflicted. A shovel might have caused the injuries. Witness had taken considerable trouble in examining the condition of the prisoner, and he had come to the conclusion that he was now perfectly sane. On the afternoon of October 5th prisoner spoke to him voluntarily, and told him the story of the murder. Witness asked him some questions in order to arrive at his mental condition. After that he had the prisoner under observation for a fortnight. On the occasion in question he said that he had killed a Dutchman, as he had been told that he had to do so before the year was out. Prisoner was perfectly sober. The witness was cross-questioned by the counsel for the accused. He said that persons suffering from homicidal mania were sometimes perfectly sane an hour, a day, or a week after they had committed a crime. The evidence of the native witnesses for the Crown who took the prisoner to the police station was not inconsistent with the theory of homicidal mania. Prisoner's explanation of his pulling his bed to pieces in the gaol was that it was infested with lice. In reply to the Court, witness said he considered that the prisoner was suffering from temporary insanity at the time he committed the crime. He had had three natives under observation at the gaol suffering from mental delusions and excitement. Prisoner told witness that he had been smoking dagga, but that might have been a delusion, as there was nothing to prove that he had done; neither his eyes nor his breath bore any trace of the drug. Taking all the prisoner's answers to the various questions put to him, witness certainly considered that he was suffering from temporary insanity at the time he committed the act.

Other witnesses were briefly examined. Daniel Jacobs said he identified the body of deceased in the presence of Dr. Stoney. Fred Num, police interpreter at Beaconsfield, stated that he cautioned the prisoner when brought to the charge office. Mongale said, "I killed the man, because he spoiled the earth." He did not say that he had been assaulted. William Robert Spratt, gaol guard at Kimberley, deposed that prisoner was excited and noisy when first taken there. He subsequently quietened down, and they had no trouble with him after October 7th. Prisoner said he pulled his bed to pieces "because he had to feed the horses."

This closed the evidence, and Mr. Wallach, addressing the jury, pointed out that all they had to consider was the state of mind of prisoner when he committed the crime, and whether he was responsible for his actions. The strongest evidence in favour of the prisoner was that of Dr. Stoney, to whom Mongale gave three different versions of the crime. His relations also deposed that he was excited and jumped about, and seemed to have an aversion to tins, which he kicked whenever he came across them. He confidently asked the jury to say that Mongale was not responsible for his actions at the time of the murder.

In his summing up, Mr. Justice Hopley explained that murder must be the intention to kill with malice prepense, and the jury would have to consider whether the prisoner had that intention, and whether he knew what he was doing at the time. His Lordship lucidly reviewed the evidence at considerable length, quoting cases of mental aberration which had been heard before the Supreme Court

THE TRAGIC DEATH OF A SURVIVOR

and the Chief Justice's remarks thereon. The very manner of the killing of the deceased, continued his Lordship, was hardly that of a sane man, for the prisoner did not leave McCluskey to die after giving him a blow, or two blows, but he went on chopping and chopping until there was no skull left. The evidence of his relatives also tended to show that he had lost his mental balance on previous occasions.

After a long deliberation the jury found as their verdict that the accused killed William McCluskey while suffering from temporary insanity. They added a strong rider to the effect that a man such as Mongale should not be further permitted to be a danger to the public safety. Addressing the prisoner, Mr. Justice Hopley said :

> The jury have found that you killed McCluskey, but that you were not responsible for your actions. Had you been sane I need hardly say that in all probability you would have been hanged. But the law does not punish a man in that way for committing a crime for which he is not mentally responsible. You will not, however, be permitted to go at large. His Excellency the Governor will make some order so that you will no longer be a danger to the public safety. In the meanwhile you will remain in the Kimberley Gaol pending the receipt of His Excellency's decision regarding your case.

His Lordship added that if there had been more vigilance shown by the police at Beaconsfield when it was reported to them that a lunatic was at large, in all probability Mongale would have been saved from life-long imprisonment and McCluskey would have been alive that day. Inquiries would be made into this case, and the public might rely upon every precaution being taken in the future.

So descended the curtain upon a drama the tragedy of which must still awaken a pang throughout our Empire. Poor McCluskey! Fate was cruel to him at the last ; but the bitterness of his end accentuates his personal worth and sturdy, useful life. After all, he fell at the post of duty, and that, at least, was a death becoming such a man. He was a true modest hero, of whose memory we are justly proud.

CHAPTER XXII

THE POETIC PICTURE OF THE BIRKENHEAD
BY SIR FRANCIS H. DOYLE

A poet soaring in the high reason of his fancies.—MILTON.

WHILE the story of iron discipline and perfect duty has engaged the pen of the prose writer, the eloquence of the orator, and the brush of the painter, it has furnished the poet also with a lofty theme. Best known and most popular are the verses of Sir Francis Hastings Doyle, Professor of Poetry at Oxford,* whose lines are put into the mouth of a soldier who survived the wreck, which he is supposed to be describing. The revised and accepted version of this fine poem consists of nine stanzas.

> Right on our flank the crimson sun went down,
>   The deep sea rolled around in dark repose,
> When, like the wild shriek from some captured town,
>   A cry of women rose.
>
> The stout ship *Birkenhead* lay hard and fast
>   Caught without hope upon a hidden rock;
> Her timbers thrilled as nerves, when through them passed
>   The spirit of that shock.
>
> And ever, like base cowards who leave their ranks
>   In danger's hour, before the rush of steel,
> Drifted away disorderly the planks
>   From underneath her keel.
>
> Confusion spread, for though the coast seemed near,
>   Sharks hovered thick along that white sea-brink;
> The boats could hold?—not all—and it was clear
>   She was about to sink.
>
> "Out with those boats and let us haste away,"
>   Cried one, "ere yet yon sea the bark devours";
> The man thus clamouring was, I scarce need say,
>   No officer of ours.

---
* 1867-77. He died June, 1888.

THE POETIC PICTURE OF THE *BIRKENHEAD*

> We knew our duty better than to care
>   For such loose babblers, and made no reply,
> Till our good Colonel gave the word, and there
>   Formed us in line to die.
>
> There rose no murmur from the ranks, no thought,
>   By shameful strength, unhonoured life to seek.
> Our post to quit we were not trained, nor taught
>   To trample down the weak.
>
> So we made women with their children go ;
>   The oars ply back agen, and yet agen,
> Whilst inch by inch the drowning ship sank low
>   Still under steadfast men.
>
> What follows why recall ? The brave who died
>   Died without flinching in the bloody surf ;
> They sleep as well beneath that purple tide
>   As others under turf.

These are beautiful verses, and if only they all spoke truth they would indeed command a high place in the literature of the *Birkenhead*. Unfortunately, however, they present to us an unfaithful picture. The description they give of the scene at the wreck is hopelessly wrong and misleading. The poetry itself is charming and captivating; it has the right ring about it; the spirit of the lines could not be finer, or truer to the scene which the lines misrepresent. Would that the poet had known the facts—that his information had been worthy of his inspiration. Then what a grand production would have been the result! But we have to take the poetry as it stands, with its beauties and its defects, and it is still worth possessing. We would not care to lose it by any means. It speaks of the "timbers" of an iron ship, and of "the planks ... underneath her keel." This may be allowed to be mere poetic licence. Scarcely so the perversion of fact in the implied calculation as to how many the boats would hold ; in the picturesque panic of the brave Commander, who we know was cool and collected to the last ; in the weirdness of the order which "formed us in line to die"; above all, in the imaginary excursions of the boats while the good ship, by slowly diminishing measurement, "sank low." That is all Even these burlesques do not rob the poem of its attraction.

We can only regret them. As General Maurice says, in that striking sketch of his already quoted :

> All that is best in the poetry and thought of the poem is good and true as ever, but the actual scene is falsely painted altogether. The men were not standing, as here represented, drawn up in line waiting quietly whilst the boats, crowded with women, went to and fro to the shore. The suggestion is that of a single regiment under its colonel formed up under his influence to die. There were only detachments, most of them under boy ensigns. Even the "major" who had been in command was dead at the time when the one captain and lieutenant called on the men to make their splendid sacrifice. The suggestion as to the boats and "no officer of ours" is altogether unfair to Salmond, who, though he, as in duty bound, released the soldiers from his Naval authority at a moment when it was no longer applicable, remained himself to the last, calmly giving such orders as were possible, and lost his life by doing so. The ship did not sink inch by inch, but broke up almost at once ; and even the poop itself sank within less than twenty minutes of the striking of the ship. If the three stanzas, "Out with those boats," "We know our duty," "So we made women," had been brought into accord with the truth, they would have been more worthy of some of their grand comrade stanzas, especially the seventh and ninth. Even as it is, however, with all its historical blemishes, it is a poem that ought to be known better than it is.

In this we shall all concur. But even General Maurice himself is not free from error. He commits one oversight which implies another. Colonel Seton was not dead "at the time when the one captain and lieutenant called on the men to make their splendid sacrifice." He was on the poop to the last, and just before the deck sank shook hands with Ensign Lucas. And he had, moreover, already exhorted the men to make the very sacrifice, the call for which Captain Wright and Lieutenant Girardot now so chivalrously repeated. The lapse is, of course, unwitting on the part of General Maurice, who defends the chief Naval officer from unfairness, while unconsciously he allows it to the senior Military officer. It is curious that he should fall into much the same error as Sir William Napier originally did; only General Maurice, while overlooking the fact that Colonel Seton appealed to the troops in the manner described, and counting him as dead prematurely, does acknowledge his active presence at the wreck, and the value of his influence and example.

Only the revised verses of Sir Francis Doyle's poem have

THE POETIC PICTURE OF THE *BIRKENHEAD*

been under discussion. The original poem (given below) is in fourteen stanzas. It would be unfair to say more about the omitted or varied portions than has already been said concerning the accepted lines. The reader will observe that but four of the original verses are contained in the revised poem. Stanzas 2 and 3, 10 and 11 are retained intact. Words in the first verse have been altered, with the apparent object of transforming the scene from sunset to night. Much of the original poem has been changed or eliminated.

> Right on our flank the sun was dropping down;
> The deep sea heaved around in bright repose;
> When, like the wild shriek from some captured town,
>   A cry of women rose.
>
> The stout ship *Birkenhead* lay hard and fast,
> Caught without hope upon a hidden rock;
> Her timbers thrilled as nerves, when through them passed
>   The spirit of that shock.
>
> And ever like base cowards, who leave their ranks
> In danger's hour, before the rush of steel,
> Drifted away, disorderly, the planks
>   From underneath her keel.
>
> So calm the air—so calm and still the flood,
> That low down in its blue translucent glass
> We saw the great fierce fish, that thirst for blood,
>   Pass slowly, then repass.
>
> They tarried, the waves tarried, for their prey!
> The sea turned one clear smile! Like things asleep
> Those dark shapes in the azure silence lay,
>   As quiet as the deep.
>
> Then amidst oath, and prayer, and rush, and wreck,
> Faint screams, faint questions waiting no reply,
> Our Colonel gave the word, and on the deck
>   Formed us in line to die.
>
> To die—'twas hard, while the sleek ocean glowed
> Beneath a sky as fair as summer flowers:
> *All to the boats!* cried one—he was, thank God,
>   No officer of ours.
>
> Our English hearts beat true—we would not stir;
> That base appeal we heard, but heeded not;
> On land, on sea, we had our Colours, sir,
>   To keep without a spot.

> They shall not say in England that we fought
> With shameful strength, unhonoured life to seek;
> Into mean safety, mean deserters, brought
>   By trampling down the weak.
>
> So we made women with their children go,
> The oars ply back again, and yet again;
> Whilst, inch by inch, the drowning ship sank low,
>   Still under steadfast men.
>
> What follows, why recall? The brave who died,
> Died without flinching in the bloody surf,
> They sleep as well beneath that purple tide
>   As others under turf.
>
> They sleep as well! and, roused from their wild grave,
> Wearing their wounds like stars, shall rise again,
> Joint-heirs with Christ, because they bled to save
>   His weak ones, not in vain.
>
> If that day's work no clasp or medal mark;
> If each proud heart no cross of bronze may press,
> Nor cannon thunder loud from tower or park,
>   This feel we none the less:
>
> That those whom God's high grace there saved from ill,
> Those also left His martyrs in the bay,
> Though not by siege, though not in battle, still
>   Full well had earned their pay.

Our only comment shall be the obvious one, that the poem was revised with considerable advantage.

Sir Francis Doyle's contribution is probably responsible in part for the description of the wreck as given in a standard school reading-book which has familiarised the minds of thousands of our young people with the subject. This romantic statement of "The Loss of the *Birkenhead*" contains the historical errors which have long been commonly accepted as gospel truth—the "roll of the drum," calling the soldiers "to arms on the upper deck"; the men themselves standing "as if on parade," and "in their ranks, shoulder to shoulder"; the pulling of the boats between the ship and the shore, "again and again." Officers and men patiently "watching the sharks," that were "waiting for them in the waves," is powerfully imaginative. So is the rigmarole about the boats. The picture is one to seize upon the minds of the young and remain engraven there. And it presents a grand truth when it says that "the waves closed over a band of the truest heroes the world has ever seen." Without its added touches it might lose something of its charm for the juvenile student. Maturer minds will find plenty to admire in the story in the naked truth alone. That needs no embellishment. Unadorned, in fact, it is "adorned the most."

Much the same licence is displayed by an American newspaper as that observable in the English school primer. Speaking of "the loss of the British steamer *Birkenhead* on the coast of Africa," a year or two after the event, *The New York Express* described how the vessel struck on a hidden rock, "stove a plank at the bows," and went to the bottom.

> There was a regiment of troops on board. As soon as the alarm was given, and it became apparent that the ship's fate was sealed, the roll of the drum called the soldiers to arms on the upper deck. That call was promptly obeyed, though every gallant heart there knew that it was his death summons. There they stood as if in battle array—a motionless mass of brave men—men who were men indeed. The ship every moment was going down and down, but there were no traitors, no deserters, no cravens there! The women and children were got into the boats, and were all, or nearly all, saved. There were no boats for the troops; but there was no panic, no blanched, pale, quivering lips among them. Men like these never perish; their bodies may be given to the fishes of the sea, but their memories are, as they ought to be, immortal.

The description is picturesque; but its faults are redeemed, especially as the reference was by way of contrast to the loss of another ship, the *Arctic*, when most of the crew escaped, leaving to their fate the women and children, whose piteous appeals for life, we are told, were unheeded by "the robust cowards who had stolen the boats," and turned their backs on those whom it was their duty to preserve. Well might the *Birkenhead* be pointed to as an example in a case like that, when the manner of the pointing becomes a minor matter altogether.

This American reference to the subject was made in the autumn of 1854. In December of the same year *The Spectator* took up the story, and in an article on War and our Army, spoke of the wonderful transformation effected in the ordinary recruit after a period of discipline, steadily enforced obedience, instruction and good example.

The very men whom we shrank from when we met them flying ribbons in their battered hats, reeling through the streets, were the same who went down in the *Birkenhead*—as which of us can feel sure that he would have had nerve to do?—in their ranks, shoulder to shoulder, standing at ease, watching the sharks that were waiting for them in the waves, at the simple suggestion of their officers that the women and children filled the boats, and must be saved first. No saint ever died more simply; no martyr ever died more voluntarily; no hero ever died more firmly; no victim ever met his fate in a more generous spirit of self-immolation.

All that is here misrepresented is the scene on board the troopship. The rest of the picture is true in fact and in spirit, and does credit to the word-artist who drew it.

Instances of mis-statements as to the facts about the *Birkenhead* might be multiplied. We need only cite another. This is a glaring and less excusable exaggeration, and it shows what fantastic notions concerning the wreck have prevailed in later days in quarters which one would have expected to be better informed. In a little work by Hubert Handley, M.A., *A Christian Knight*, a sermon to young men published by the S.P.C.K. in 1903, the traits of the knightly character are explained, and the writer deals with the high attitude towards women which he holds is confined to no one class.

As bright an instance of it as can be found was in the wreck of the *Birkenhead* off the coast of Africa, on February 27th, 1852. The vessel was steaming along the African coast with 472 men and 166 women and children on board. The men were mostly raw recruits for several regiments at the Cape. At two o'clock in the morning, while all were asleep below, the ship struck violently on a hidden rock. It was at once felt that she must go down. The roll of the drums called the soldiers to arms on the upper deck, and the men mustered as if on parade. The word was passed *to save the women and children*; and the trembling, helpless creatures were brought from below, in night attire, and were handed slowly into the boats. When they had all left the ship's side, the commander of the vessel, meaning well, but thoughtless—called out, "All those that can swim, jump overboard and make for the boats." But Captain Wright, of the 91st Highlanders, said "No! if you do that, *the boats with the women must be swamped*"; and the chivalrous men *stood motionless*. Down went the ship, and down went the heroic band, firing a last salute with a volley in the air as they sank beneath the waves.

Incredible almost, is it not? Really a cruel caricature, though not meant as such. It exceeds the poetic licence, excels the romance of the school-book. One is tempted to forgive even the absurdities rampant in the passage just quoted because of the sincere admiration shown for the spirit exhibited at the wreck, and the evident desire to impress on our young people the grand object-lesson of the *Birkenhead*. But it tries one's charitable feeling. Let us hope that for the future the facts themselves will be better understood and appreciated. The lesson to be derived from them will then be more intensely taught.

By Dr. John A. Goodchild

Whose deeds some nobler poem shall adorn.—Dryden.

There is another poem, "The *Birkenhead*: a Tale for Englishmen," by Dr. John A. Goodchild.* It is not so well known as that of Sir F. H. Doyle, or as it deserves to be. It deals with the broad theme, rather than with incidents, and the subject is nobly treated. These verses sing in praise of heroes, not with the high and silvery note of Sir Francis Doyle, or with his daring, but with a chord deep, and full, and true, that will strike upon all hearts.

> All was silence. All was sleep. Night lay pillowed on the Deep,
>   Neath cold stars that watched unwinking in a cloudless sky,
> And these whispered to the Wave, "Tell us stories of the brave.
>   We would see this night thy pageant, 'How the English die.'"
>
> Then the Ocean called on Death, in his silent watch beneath,
>   "Arm thyself for sudden slaughter. I will be to thee an aid;
> For the stars that rule this night would behold thee ride in might
>   On thy battlesteed of terror o'er the souls of men afraid."

---

* In *Somnia Medici*, 2nd Series. Dr. Goodchild was a physician of eminence in his profession, endowed also with rare literary gifts. The later years of his life were spent at Bordighiera, in Italy, but he was staying at Bath in 1902 when he kindly sanctioned the inclusion of his poem in these pages.

A DEATHLESS STORY

From his stillness Death upstirred at the summons that he heard,
   Echoing back his solemn answer to the mandate of the main,
" I hear and I obey. Who are these thou would'st dismay ? "
   " English men," boomed slow the thunder of the sullen Deep again.

Then Death answered, " Thou hast oft borne my battle flag aloft,
   Till men's voices, shrill with terror, stilled the wailing of the wind ;
But the hearts of English men are as lions in their den.
   Though thou crush them down to silence, neither thou nor I shalt bind ;

"And the stars that look adown shall behold ourselves o'erthrown,
   Bearing witness that our masters are these men of British race.
Though thy billows overflow till their limbs are stilled below ;
   Theirs the glory, theirs the triumph, who shall fight us face to face."

Then the sullen Ocean played round the ambush Death had laid,
   Rocking soft the gallant vessel where she rode its treacherous tide,
Till she touched the hidden rock, and night echoed to the shock
   Of her rending, whilst the waters stormed the breaches in her side.

"A wreck ! A wreck ! A wreck !" Death's that war-cry ; but on deck
   No man cried. The captain's voice alone gave orders to his crew ;
Whilst, like ants, out of the hold streamed young lads and veterans bold,
   Each beholding Death before him as a foeman that he knew.

Every seaman toiled with will, but the boatswain's pipe came shrill,
   " Sixty men to man the pumps." And in a moment forth they stood—
Sixty soldiers stark and strong marched that shattered deck along
   To give battle such as heroes seldom gave on field of blood.

For these sixty, for the crew, there is somewhat set to do,
   And each comrade 'gainst his fellow striveth nobly in the race ;
But four hundred red-coats stand to their ranks on either hand,
   Watching Death draw nearer, nearer, whilst they eye him face to face.

From the long, low line of coast, half a league away at most,
   Life holds out a hand and beckons : " Safe is he that hither flies.
Now your chance is, while she floats. For your lives, men, seize the boats ! "
   But a coward is not found there, and no craven's voice replies.

But those boats, 'tis shame to see, were but five, and are but three,
   Helpless women, little children, are enough to fill them all.
Ah ! the little ones and wives by the stronger stalwart lives
   Are girt round with living breastplates when 'tis need that Britons fall.

THE POETIC PICTURE OF THE *BIRKENHEAD*

So the feebler lives go free o'er the treacherous, smiling sea,
  And the hearts of all are lightened that their toil is not in vain,
Striving till the fierce onrush, when the waters overgush
  All last fragment of denial, and the great ship parts in twain.

Then the one half settles down. Easier so perchance to drown,
  Than to live with these that linger 'neath the hollow eyes of Death.
Cries a leader, " All is o'er ; there is nought we may do more ;
  But 'tis each man's right to strive alone, then strive whilst ye have breath.

" Seize a barrel, seize an oar, so perchance escape to shore."
  " Ay," said one, " but none are cowards, and let no man help his case
Climbing yon o'erloaded boats." Then a cheer bursts from their throats.
  Fear will crouch to men who front him though his leash be slipped for chase.

Then the yearning waters rave, where men living see their grave
  Yawn beneath them, close upon them. Few there are find light again,
Scattered breathless far and wide on the surface of the tide,
  Specks and atoms tossing helpless on the bosom of the main.

Still, the stronger, Britons true, find such deeds as Britons do,
  Yielding each his straw of vantage to the weaker out of twain,
'Mongst them all, scarce one shall stand with the living on the land,
  Till the Spoiler spoil the Ocean, and Death renders up his slain.

War hath champions without end. If one dieth for a friend,
  Highest is his deed of valour, to his great War Captain known :
Strong thin red line, heroes true, ye bear palm o'er Waterloo,
  Or the last man at Isandula who fought and died alone.

The names may yet exist, in some old War-Office list,
  Of five hundred men that perished, heroes all. But tears might trace
With diamonds, not gold, such a tale as here is told,
  How Death met young lads and veterans, and they stared him in the face.

And the stars that shone that night gazed upon a wondrous sight,
  Watching all the deathless story of the good ship *Birkenhead*.
But the pale stars fled away, shamed before the face of day,
  And the sun looks down in glory on the faces of the dead.

It is, perhaps, inseparable from any dealing with the *Birkenhead*, whether in prose or in verse, that the men should be pictured standing drawn up in rank. Dr. Goodchild falls into error in filling the three boats with the women and children. And he overlooks the sixty men put on the tackles of the paddle-box boats. These, in so far as he ventures on the facts, are his only mistakes; and they are far outweighed, and made insignificant, by the strength and breadth and beauty of his lines, which should serve to enshrine in the nation's heart the Deathless Story of the *Birkenhead*.

* * * * *

To take your chance in the thick of a rush, with firing all about,
Is nothing so bad when you've cover to 'and an' leave an' likin' to shout;
But to stand an' be still to the *Birken'ead* drill is a damn tough bullet to chew;
An' they done it, the Jollies—'er Majesty's Jollies—soldier an' sailor, too!

So wrote Rudyard Kipling of the gallant men—soldiers and sailors too—who died doing their duty on the *Victoria* when that ill-starred ship plunged to the depths of the Mediterranean years after the "*Birken'ead* drill" had earned its famous reputation. May the lesson taught upon the deck of the *Birkenhead* never lack apt pupils, and may the observance and the spirit of its drill ever be present when needed, whether afloat or ashore.

CHAPTER XXIII

REMARKABLE PASSAGES IN THE LIFE OF JOHN DRAKE, MARINE *

> Whoe'er amidst the sons
> Of . . . valour . . .
> Displays distinguish'd merit, is a noble
> Of Nature's own creating.—THOMSON.

IT is an old and true saying, that "some men are born to greatness, a few achieve it, and others have greatness thrust upon them." Under which of these three headings should be placed the name of John Drake, late colour-sergeant in the Royal Marine Light Infantry, will, after this story has been told, be no very difficult task to determine. I therefore leave that to the just and impartial reader. Some twenty-three years ago John Drake, then an under-keeper to a nobleman, took it into his head to prefer the life of a Marine to that occupation. Whether he was of a roving disposition, or whether the exploits of his namesake, Sir Francis Drake, attracted him, or whether his life at that time was too hard or too easy, or whether it was the "red coat" that wrought the change, is now of very little consequence. Whatever the cause may have been, the effect was that Lord —— lost his under-keeper, and Dorsetshire a promising young fellow, while Her Majesty gained a smart and gallant soldier. It would likewise be a waste of space to attempt any detailed account of his enlistment, and of his relish for the change in his condition; suffice it to say that he joined the Portmouth Division in 1843. When he had learned his drill, he got appointed to a ship on the first opportunity, and proceeded on active service.

---

* From *The British Army and Navy Review* (Richard Bentley), published 1864-6. By permission of Messrs. Macmillan & Co., in whom is vested the property in the Review.

Although bred inland, he appears to have taken to the sea naturally, as, in the twenty-one years and upwards that he served, four-fifths of this time were passed afloat. It is equally needless to relate any of his first experiences, all of which I will pass over until I come to his undoubtedly greatest exploit, which was also his earliest.

His first ship was the *Waterwitch*, Captain Birch, which went on the African station. It was about the latter part of 1844 that this vessel captured the Brazilian slaver (brigantine) *Romeo Primero*. Those who knew Drake at this time have informed me that, although a powerful lad, he was always remarkably quiet and unobtrusive; and it may probably have been the possession of these qualities which caused him to be selected to make one of the prize crew, a very important duty for so young a soldier to be detailed for. In consequence of sickness the *Waterwitch* was short of men, so Lieutenant Mansfield was only allowed three bluejackets and a Marine, four in all, for his prize crew. In addition to them, however, six of the prisoners belonging to the slaver were left on board to assist in working the ship. As a matter of course, these had no weapons, while the prize crew were armed, a circumstance which left the advantage on the side of the latter. So it was with no uneasy feeling, but rather with a sense of relief, that they saw the *Waterwitch* sail away, and in a short time be hull down, cruising in an opposite direction. It was doubtless pleasant, likewise, for the young lieutenant to find himself his own master for a short time, while his small command were also pleased to be clear of the daily routine and stricter discipline which they had probably been subject to for months. Lieutenant Mansfield divided his ship's company into two watches, larboard and starboard, putting two sailors and half the prisoners in the former, and the remainder of the prisoners with his other two men in the latter. As there were always two of these and usually the commander on deck, and the arms ready to hand, no fear of a surprise was entertained.

The prisoners, however, formed an able plan for re-taking the vessel, and waiting for an opportunity, seized upon it

COLOUR-SERGEANT JOHN DRAKE, 54TH COMPANY R.M.L.I.
(From a photo)

the very first chance. It was about six bells in the middle watch, when one of the Spaniards was steering, that the lieutenant ordered the remainder of the watch aloft to shorten sail. The two Englishmen started away up the rigging, while the two prisoners made a rush at the arms, and being instantly joined by the others from below and the man at the wheel, they made at once a murderous attack upon the officer, at the same time menacing the two sailors who had gone to shorten sail. Surprised, unarmed, and attacked by such odds, still Lieutenant Mansfield met and engaged them gallantly single-handed, never yielding, fighting on until he fell insensible, bleeding from upwards of thirty wounds. Leaving him, the Spaniards then sallied below, feeling confident now that the brigantine was their own again—for was not the commander dead, were not the arms in their possession, two men aloft who were in a manner caged, and easily shot should they attempt to descend, and the other two below sound asleep?—a sleep from which one of them never awoke. Everything was in their favour, so creeping cautiously and stealthily down, they made their attack upon the two defenceless men.

David Wakeham was nearest, and closer and closer they drew towards him. A glittering knife, a sudden quick movement of the arm, a gurgling noise, and there was another Englishman the less. By the time this poor fellow had been murdered two had attacked Drake, who was lying asleep in the next bunk. It is no slight noise that will disturb a sailor. He is accustomed to sleep while the storm rages, amid the hurried rush of feet overhead, or to the tune of creaking wood, the rattle of chains, the squeaking of pullies. Therefore Drake, with death hanging over him and a bleeding corpse alongside, slept on, only to be speedily awakened by a blow from a handspike on the forehead, and at the same time, but by another foe, to be (fortunately) cut across the throat from under the right ear to the collar-blade bone, and then downwards through the chest. *Fortunately* in this wise—that the blood-letting counteracted the effect of the stupefying blow on the temple. Stunned, surprised, and dangerously wounded as he was, Private John Drake did not lose heart as he bounded out on the floor among them. To ward off a second blow from the handspike aimed at his head, to wrest it from the Spaniard's hand, and fell to the ground him and his other enemies with this weapon so providentially placed in his grasp, took but a few seconds. And such good use did he make of the handspike that all were knocked down senseless with blows which two of their number never recovered from. The immense strength and the desperate courage shown by Drake on this occasion, especially when the usage he had just received is taken into account, must have been wonderful.

Streaming with blood from the wound on the head and the cut in the throat, Drake's appearance on deck could not much tend to assure his two comrades in the rigging at first. And the sight of his officer's apparently lifeless body, with no one near it or about the deck, was far from being satisfactory to one who had just had such a narrow escape himself. Consequently his joy was great when the two seamen came down, and showed that he was not the sole survivor, while they could scarcely credit that that bloody figure had saved the ship and their lives. A very few words from Drake told them how the case stood; and first securing the Spaniards, and seeing to Lieutenant Mansfield's wounds, finding him still alive, they then turned their attention to Drake, and looked to his.

His escape had been miraculous; the cut barely missed the jugular vein, and the windpipe afterwards. This was partly owing to his having been lying on his left side, and the knife, being probably used by a right-handed man, had slipped diagonally from under the ear to the collar-bone, and that turning the weapon had caused it to glance downwards. A wide scar in the neck, six inches long, and another three inches farther, at right angles to the first, show *now* what a narrow escape he had. The prize was taken safely into port, and the prisoners were turned over to the civil power, to be tried for the murder of poor Wakeham. Lieutenant Mansfield's wounds, although numerous—thirty-four in all—did not prove fatal; and Drake, having a good thick skull and a strong constitution, also soon recovered. A full report of the whole affair was duly forwarded by the Lieutenant to his superior, who in turn transmitted it to the Admiralty. Lieutenant Mansfield was justly appointed Commander for his gallantry, but no recognition at the same time was made of the service performed by the private Marine. Some three years elapsed, and in the interval Drake had been nearly all over the world, back to England again, and was laid up by sickness in Haslar Hospital. If he had ever dreamt of any favourable notice being taken of him for his conduct in the affair, that had all passed and gone. However, "better late than never," for on January 5th, 1848, the following letter was forwarded to the Commanding Officer of Marines at Portsmouth from the Assistant-Adjutant-General of that force:

ROYAL MARINE OFFICE, *January 5th,* 1848.

SIR,—The Lords Commissioners of the Admiralty having signified their command to the Deputy-Adjutant-General that Private John Drake, of the Division under your command, lately serving on board the *Waterwitch* and now in Haslar Hospital, be promoted to the rank of Corporal in consequence of his having fought gallantly after receiving two wounds, as reported to their Lordships by Commander Mansfield, late in charge of the Brazilian slave vessel *Romeo Primero*, when the prisoners attempted to recapture the vessel; the Deputy-Adjutant-General directs that Private John Drake be so promoted to Corporal accordingly.—I have the honour to be, sir, your most humble servant,

(Signed) S. R. WESLEY, A.A.G.

Two days after a still more satisfactory document came in the shape of a circular.

ROYAL MARINE OFFICE, *January 7th,* 1848.

The Lords Commissioners of the Admiralty having received a report from Commander Mansfield, R.N., late in charge of the Brazilian slave vessel *Romeo Primero*, prize to the *Waterwitch*, of the good conduct of Private John Drake, of the Royal Marines, who, when the prisoners made a desperate attempt to recapture the vessel, "continued to fight gallantly after he had received two wounds"; their Lordships are pleased to mark their approbation of this Private's excellent conduct by directing that he be immediately and specially promoted to the rank of Corporal, and that this order be read at the head of each of the Divisions of Royal Marines.

This highly creditable circumstance is to be recorded at the Portsmouth Division in favour of the Corporal. By command of their Lordships,

(Signed) JNO. OWEN, D.A.G.

This gratifying communication was six months afterwards supplemented by another, giving him a further step in promotion, and which was as follows:

ROYAL MARINE OFFICE, *July* 14*th*, 1848.

SIR,—With reference to the circular letter from this Office of the 7th January last, containing the approbation of the Lords Commissioners of the Admiralty of the excellent conduct of Private John Drake, of the Division under your command, now a Corporal serving on board the *Frolic*, and directing that he may be immediately and specially promoted; I have the honour to request that you will take the earliest opportunity of communicating with the Admiral commanding at Portsmouth for the purpose of the Corporal being disembarked to your Headquarters and there promoted to the rank of Sergeant, provided he be found equal to the duties of that station. I have the honour to be, sir, your most obedient servant,

(Signed) JNO. OWEN, D.A.G.

The Officer Commanding Royal Marines, Portsmouth.

All this was nearly as it should be—a young soldier had distinguished himself and been made sergeant when only five years in the service. Appointed colour-sergeant nine months afterwards, everything appeared in his favour; and should he continue to behave himself well, a commission was in prospect. As my story goes on, it will be seen whether this idea was realised or not. Sergeant Drake was no barrack bird—consequently, he was soon afloat again after his second promotion. In 1850 he was on board of the *Birkenhead*, in which vessel he remained till she was wrecked two years afterwards at the Cape of Good Hope.

As I have already remarked, it is not my intention to give his history in full, but merely to touch upon the salient points in his eventful career. I now come to the wreck of the above-mentioned vessel. His life was here again saved by a miracle; for fifteen hours is a wonderfully long time to remain in water, with only the hold of a spar between you and death. The *Birkenhead* sailed from Cork with detachments for regiments at the Cape on January 7th, 1852 (exactly four years after Drake's promotion), and after a prosperous and short voyage of forty-eight days, reached Simon's Bay on February 24th. Here were landed Mr. Freshfield and eighteen invalids, besides women and children. The ship was commanded by Captain Salmond, and the troops by Major Seton, of the 74th Regiment. I will endeavour to give an account of the wreck in Sergeant Drake's own words.

After landing the invalids we steamed out of Simon's Bay about six p.m. on the 25th. I remained on deck that night, and when we struck on the rock I was standing on the forecastle talking to old Tom Jaffray, the steward. This was about two a.m. on the 26th, and the shock threw me right off my legs on the deck, the crash shaking every timber in the ship. Captain Salmond, Major Seton, [and all the other officers were immediately upon deck, while orders were given calmly, and were as coolly obeyed. Although this circumstance did not strike me at the time, still I have often since wondered how perfectly composed every one seemed after such a catastrophe happening. There was no shouting nor jostling among the men, and very little noise among the women. The Captain gave his orders as if he had been in harbour, and the men by sixties worked at the pumps as if it was only ordinary practice, instead of toiling for life. The commands were obeyed quietly, resolutely, and to the letter. The cutter was lowered, and the women and children placed in safety, with the youngest officer, Mr. Richards (quite a boy), put in charge of them. The Doctor was also sent away in a boat, as his services would in all likelihood be needed. Captain Salmond now turned his attention to the poor dumb animals, and ordered the horses to be loosened and shoved overboard—a merciful thought, too, as they all, I believe, got to land, many of them being found six and even eight miles from where the vessel went down, so that a horse's swimming powers must be great. One, I think an officer, leapt his horse overboard, and got safe to shore. At this time scarcely fifteen minutes had elapsed since we struck on the rock. Immediately after the cutter had left, and while Mr. Brodie was trying to have the port paddle-box [boat] lowered, the fore-part of the ship snapped off by the foremast; then her back broke, and the water poured in. Captain Salmond at this instant shouted for the men to "jump overboard." I leapt out then, I believe, but would not be positive. In fact, the whole affair passed so quickly that many circumstances connected with it appeared to me afterwards like a dream. I had taken my clothes off, and still I did not discover this until I had been some time in the water.

I can remember something of the vessel going down, and seeing the water, as it were, alive with human beings. But the Destroyer had more deadly agents than water at work. As if they had been in waiting for this to happen, scores of sharks made their appearance as soon as the vessel went down. At the sight of these monsters many a poor fellow's heart quailed, and he made but little effort to escape drowning, that being the easier death. Others, trying manfully to gain the shore, were dragged under by these creatures. A cry, a splash, and a tinge of blood on the wave told the survivors what had occurred, and what they might themselves expect at any moment. I had swum to a truss of compressed hay which was floating about, and getting upon that, found myself in a manner partly secure. I think it was Captain Salmond I saw sink, from being struck by a drifting piece of wood, but could not be certain. Cornet Rolt, of the 12th Lancers, who had been very kind and civil on the voyage, asked me to save him. I readily gave him my hand, and pulled him on to my strange and uncertain support. He was very much exhausted, and I had to hold him on; this fatigued me greatly. Twice he slipped off, and twice I rescued him, encouraging him all I could by telling him the cutter would be safe to return for us soon. I managed to keep him up for an hour and a half, until the truss surged against a rock, capsized us, and we both sank; when I got righted and looked round, there was no trace left of Cornet Rolt. The hay, after being so long in the water, became saturated, when I fortunately got on to the topsailyard, where there were already several others. The minutes became hours, and they seemed to drag on with leaden wings, while we could see no hope of assistance, no chance of escape, although the land appeared so near. Many a poor fellow I saw silently drop off from the spar he was on, and sink to rest. They were evidently worn out and tired of hoping; but still I clung on, keeping my spirits up as best I could. Having no clothes on caused me to feel the cold bitterly, and sometimes I wished that it was all over; and then the thoughts of home, and the wife and child*—Harry was but a baby then—made me strive, and almost hope against hope. At last, after we had been fifteen hours in the water, the schooner *Lioness*, which had picked up the cutter with the women and children, bore down, and, taking us on board, conveyed us to Simon's Bay. When there we were transferred to the *Castor* frigate,† where I soon got a rig-out of one sort or another. It was no time to stand to niceties; therefore a pair of duck trousers, a mile too short and yards too wide, a blue long-tailed coat, a frilled shirt, and, last of all, a long-sleeved hat, were very acceptable—not altogether the uniform which would have been approved by the Inspector-General when reviewing the Division; but still, it did for me very well until I got back to old England. We remained in barracks until H.M.S. *Amazon* reached Simon's Bay, when, being homeward bound, she took the seamen and Marines to

* His eldest son.

† At the time Drake was relating this there came in a sergeant of Marines, from the *Tamar*, who shook hands with him. Drake did not remember him until he said, "I can remember you when you had not a shirt to your back." Drake then immediately recollected he was the man who gave him a rig-out of underclothing on board of the *Castor* frigate after he had been wrecked.

England. When I joined again at Portsmouth, I had still the same suit of clothes on that I had got together on board of the *Castor*, and when I reported my arrival to the Commandant, he for a second or two could not make me out. I certainly looked a hybrid sort of animal, not resembling in the least degree the Marine species. However, when I announced my name I was received heartily, and then ordered to the Quartermaster's store, when I was soon fitted out with a Joey's* suit. I forgot to mention that old Jaffray, the steward, was also one of the survivors; we had many a talk together in the *Urgent* about that night's adventure, when we were sipping souchong at Canton, or drinking a stronger liquid in Japan. Tom is still a steward, and if you wish to converse with a proper polar bear unshaved, just go on board H.M. troopship *Tamar*, and inquire for Jaffray, the steward; then mention Jack Drake's name, and a hundred to one but you get a glass of as good stuff as there is to be found in Her Majesty's fleet, for Tom was always a good judge of liquor.

Although Sergeant Drake had again had a narrow escape for his life, his propensity for service afloat had not decreased; wherever there was danger he was near. It is not, therefore, surprising to find that he was on board of H.M.S. *Sphinx*, in the Baltic, at the commencement of the Russian War, was present at the bombardment of, and assisted to capture Bomarsund. His ship being selected to proceed home with the Russian prisoners taken there, he found himself soon back again in England, but remained scarcely long enough to see what o'clock it was.

On the following day the *Sphinx* tripped her anchor, and steered for Balaklava, at which place she duly arrived on October 18th, and Sergeant Drake was immediately detailed for duty on shore. He soon landed and soon engaged, for being stationed on the heights by the hospital above Balaklava harbour, he formed one of that small band of Marines who acted as support to Sir Colin Campbell's "thin red line," which, never attempting even to "form four deep," stopped and turned the Russian cavalry in its full career. He was present on the memorable 14th November, when the *Prince* was wrecked, and the stores on board all lost; present at the capture of Kinburn, also with the fleet in the Sea of Azof; in short, wherever there was honour to be gained or danger to

---

* The name generally given to Marines, originating in the popular song of Dibdin's "Joe the Marine."

be met, when possible Sergeant Drake was to be found in the thickest of it. Blessed with good health, a robust frame, a strong constitution, and, above all, a stout heart, he never looked upon duty, however hard, as being irksome, while danger had for him no terror.

The *Sphinx* was paid off on May 2nd, 1857; but true to his former character, we find him the following year on board the *Urgent*, on a voyage to a foreign station. With her he remained until June 19th, 1862; he was present at the taking of the Taku Forts, and wherever anything of note was performed, either in China or in Japan, during that period. On completing his twenty-one years' service he claimed his discharge, and on the piece of parchment, opposite to the printed word "Character," there is written *Exemplary*; below that are stated his services, and the medals and clasps which he has in his possession. The Commandant likewise gives him this certificate of character:

<blockquote>
Royal Marine Barracks, Forton,
October 31*st*, 1864.

Sergeant John Drake served in the Portsmouth Division R.M. for twenty-one years and eleven days: of this time he was fifteen years and 237 days colour-sergeant. *During his long service he never had an offence recorded against him.* He was specially promoted for distinguished gallantry after receiving two wounds. He is decorated with four war medals and three clasps, and he is an excellent soldier and an upright man. I have great pleasure and perfect confidence in recommending him for any situation requiring intelligence and trust.

(Signed) F. Clyles,
Commanding Portsmouth Division, R.M.
</blockquote>

There is no need to give any testimonials from the various captains he served under; the words in italics in the foregoing render that unnecessary. As to his character prior to enlistment, the following will be sufficient testimony:

<blockquote>
I have known Colour-Sergeant John Drake, Royal Marines, ever since he was born, and I can testify to his meritorious conduct, which justifies the character he bore in the service. His family are amongst the most respectable of those who live on my estate in Dorsetshire.

(Signed) Portman.
</blockquote>

It is nearly useless to state that Sergeant Drake received a pension of two shillings per diem. Had he never stirred out of the barrack gate in all those twenty-one years, his good conduct would have entitled him to *that*. But what I venture to think a mistake is that no distinction was made between him and others. His case was no ordinary one, and should it not have been treated accordingly? If it was against the rule to give him a commission, there are plenty of snug appointments in the gift of the Admiralty, which cannot be better bestowed than on distinguished soldiers. He certainly was presented with a fifth medal "for long service and good conduct," three months after he was discharged; but with this medal there was neither annuity nor gratuity. I should explain, for the information of some, that it is customary when a soldier's term of service expires, provided he has never been tried by court-martial, to give him a medal of this description. It is customary also to give a gratuity with it, a private receiving £5, a corporal £10, and a sergeant £15. Deserving sergeants, who, like Drake, have never had an offence recorded against them, are specially recommended for an annuity of from £10 to £15. But Sergeant Drake had neither, although plenty of staff-sergeants before and since have had both; this must have been by some oversight. Had a French soldier so distinguished and conducted himself, he would doubtless have attained a high rank in the service of his country. And as I have already mentioned that there are other rewards besides a commission wherewith gallant and deserving soldiers might be recompensed, it appears a great pity that he should have been neglected. Surely such a deed as the first I have mentioned was deserving of the Victoria Cross, with its accompanying £10 per annum.

Independently of all these, however, there are other preferments peculiarly adapted for cases such as his. We have what are termed warderships in the Tower, £60 a year and little to do; situations about the Admiralty or Greenwich Hospital, which are quiet and easy berths for veterans; and, above all, messengers in public offices, hours from ten to four, with salaries in an inverse ratio of the work to be performed. Sergeant John Drake simply got a good conduct medal, a decoration that any scamp may claim who has managed during his service to rub through without being brought to a court-martial.*

Most people will, I think, allow that this was but a poor recompense to one who had served his country so well. Apparently the duty performed so faithfully and the wounds received on board the slave-ship were ignored, his subsequent narrow escape from shipwreck forgotten, his services in the Baltic, in the Crimea, in China, and in Japan all regarded as worthless, and no more thought of him than of a feather-bed soldier who had steadfastly kept away from active service all the time of his engagement. Surely there must be some great error in this, perhaps an oversight, which the Admiralty will only feel too happy in having it in its power to rectify. I am confident that the nation never intends merit to go thus unrewarded, nor its brave defenders to be used like a pair of boots when done with—that is, slightly polished on the heels only, which are visible, then placed on the shelf and left to rot if the weather permits it. Luckily there is plenty of time yet for this to be remedied.

Often it happens that a man's services to his country have not been recognised until the green grass has grown over his grave, when all recognition either of "storied urn or animated bust" came too late. But *he is* still available to receive the Victoria Cross; he is still able to accept a warder-ship in the Tower, or at any rate to have his name placed on the roster for such an appointment; he is still able, and doubtless willing, to fill one of the many Government appointments which fall vacant from time to time; an annuity could even now be attached to the medal he last received, which at the present time is only a mockery, telling him once a month, when he goes to the Pension Office and looks round, that his country places no value whatever upon valour, even when combined with long, good, and faithful services. I feel sure that Sergeant Drake's services have been in some manner overlooked, and that it will be rectified in course of time, which will be a guarantee that distinguished conduct is not

---

* I know more than one or two whose troop and regimental defaulters' sheets would astonish most people, and who yet, by managing to evade a court-martial, have been decorated with the medal for "good conduct."

designedly passed over, nor the interests of those who perform their duty well *purposely* forgotten. And certainly the good would not end here; the certainty that services are acknowledged, and that bravery is recompensed, must act as a stimulant to the whole corps, who would perceive that gallant actions brought consequent rewards.

In conclusion, I beg to state that I am very little acquainted with Sergeant Drake, and that the facts I have told were corroborated in every respect by those well qualified to do so, and my only motive in writing this account is to endeavour to procure a more comfortable provision for a brave and upright man, who has now upon him the cares of a large and increasing family.

This ends the sketch of the veteran Drake, which is reproduced with its original footnotes. It is better given entire. The latter portion is somewhat of a curiosity now. The writer appears to have felt greater dissatisfaction at what he considered the neglect of Drake than was ever evinced by the gallant sergeant himself. It must be remembered that promotion was much slower in his early service days than it became in later years, and his rapid advancement to the post of colour-sergeant was a distinction of which any young soldier would be proud, while he retained that rank with its advantages for nearly sixteen years. John Drake's services were always highly appreciated. We do not say that he did not deserve more recognition than he received. Nothing that it was possible to bestow on him would have been too good for such a man. But Sergeant Drake was proud, and justly so, of his honours and his service, and of the esteem and admiration they brought him, and we never heard of him complaining. On the contrary, he seemed grateful, as well he might be, for having passed in safety through so many dangers by sea and land, and been spared to reach a grand and honourable old age.

That he was not forgotten by the Admiralty is shown by the fact, recorded in an earlier chapter of this book, that some years subsequent to his retirement the Lords of the Admiralty conferred on him a further medal for meritorious service accompanied by an additional pension of £10 a year, to both of which he was thoroughly well entitled. Had he stood in actual need of pecuniary help, it would no doubt have been granted him years before. But he was far from wanting it: he had a good pension, and for twenty-eight years he was an attendant at Westminster Abbey, a circumstance which proves that in civil no less than in Naval life his services were substantially recognised. The prominence given to his case by the Review, and the earnest and eloquent plea made for him by the writer of the notice,* may have influenced his appointment at the Abbey some few years later. The bestowal on the veteran of that post of trust was a timely and fitting step and a credit to all in any way concerned in it.

The account contained in the Review of the gallant Marine's adventure on board the *Romeo Primero*, when his courage and prowess unquestionably saved the ship and the lives of his officer and two seamen, is a passage of fine interest, equalling in its dramatic action the most stirring of tragic incidents of the sea, and surpassing many narratives of the kind in point of its strict truth.

Deeply interesting also and more directly concerning this work is the description of the wreck of the *Birkenhead* and the battle for life after, taken down from the lips of so notable a survivor. As to this, there are only one or two matters to which reference need be made. "Major Seton," as the name appears in the original, is, of course, intended for Lieut.-Colonel Seton. The steward of the *Birkenhead* was James Jeffery, not "Tom Jaffray." He signed himself James Jeffery in the letter he afterwards wrote to Major Wright which is included in the notice of that officer. Jeffery, it will have been seen, lived till after the 50th anniversary of the wreck, and died in London. Two statements attributed by the Review to Sergeant Drake are puzzling, not because of what they embody, which is plainly imagination, but because they are made at all. "The doctor was also sent away in a boat, as his services would in all likelihood be needed." That is one of them. The other is even more incomprehensible. "One,

* Anonymous. One of the staff of the Review, or a Service contributor.

I think an officer, leapt his horse overboard and got safe to shore." Neither of the doctors who escaped from the wreck was "sent away" in a boat. Nor did any officer leap a horse overboard. The second assertion must concern the legendary exploit of Dr. Bowen, which the apparent credulity of Sergeant Drake may have helped to foster.

The inventory of the wardrobe supplied to the sergeant after the wreck, on board the *Castor* frigate, is intensely amusing, and the memory of it would thereafter be a source of infinite merriment to himself and his comrades afloat. The spectacle of the staid and stalwart Marine arrayed in the expansive nether garments of jolly Jack Tar, which, while capable of receiving several reefs in their ample folds, scarcely reached longitudinally below the giant's knees; adorned also with a fancy frilled shirt and flowing tail-coat of blue, brass-bound, without doubt, if not otherwise ornamented; and with the whole curious costume crowned with the dazzling glory of a "long-sleeved hat," was surely one to make men laugh as they never laughed before, and the sea-gods envious for ever. It is astounding to read that poor Drake had to complete the voyage to England in this grotesque attire, and that when home at last he was compelled to report himself in it to his commanding officer, whose surprise must have been accounted one of the great jokes to which the proceeding gave rise. But even such a wardrobe had its advantages. It was better than no clothes at all. Had Sergeant Drake discarded his makeshift habiliments, they would have been thankfully appropriated by many a destitute *Birkenhead* survivor who returned with him in the *Amazon*.

As will have been noted in an earlier chapter, John Drake lived to a green old age, his death having occurred as late as April, 1905. The accompanying photograph shows the sturdy Marine as he appeared at the time of his discharge in 1864. A pathetic memory attaches to its appearance here. The portrait had always been a prized family possession, and Drake towards the close of his life promised it for this book. He died, poor fellow, on the very day he had it in readiness to hand over to us, a few minutes only before our appointed visit to him.

CHAPTER XXIV

RECOLLECTIONS OF A RAMBLING LIFE *

Of moving incidents by flood and field;
Of hair-breadth 'scapes.—SHAKESPEARE.

HAVING been born and brought up at Eydon, a village in Northamptonshire, and getting tired of a country life, I took it in my head to enter the Army in the year 1848. I accordingly joined the 12th or East Suffolk Regiment of Foot at Weedon Barracks, and being stationed there two years, I had the honour to be one of a guard formed for Her Majesty the Queen, who was then paying a visit to Birmingham. Our party was composed of two companies 12th Regiment, a squadron of the 5th Dragoon Guards, and a party of the 30th Foot. This being the time of the Chartist riots, my company was ordered to Wolverhampton, where we remained a few months, then returning to Weedon. In this year new colours were presented to the regiment, on which occasion the men had an advance of pay and three days' leave, and the gates were thrown open. The 87th Royal Irish Fusiliers, stationed there at the time, did all duties for the occasion. The gallant and tattered old standards, being replaced by the new, were sent to Ipswich with the object of being placed in the Cathedral, the 12th being a Suffolk Regiment. To this the Dean had an objection, as they were bloodstained banners. They were accordingly not admitted, but were permitted to stand outside at the corner of the building for some days, no one there knowing they were of any value, until fortunately an intelligent recruiting sergeant and party of the 6th Royal Lancers, stationed there, took notice of them, and conveyed them to the Tower of London; on which

* Written by Corporal William Smith, 12th Regiment, a *Birkenhead* survivor, and contributed by him to this book. Edited by the authors.

the officers and men of the old 12th contributed a day's pay each as a present, in gratitude to the sergeant and his men.

In 1850 the regiment was ordered to Chatham to relieve the 17th Leicestershire Regiment. We accordingly met them in London. The 12th being the senior corps, the 17th halted, formed line, and with flying colours, in accordance with Military etiquette, saluted us by presenting arms. We then proceeded to Waterloo Bridge, taking the boat for Chatham *via* Gravesend. On arrival we were quartered in the main barracks. At this time Chatham was the headquarters of the Royal Engineers, as now; also of a division of Marines and of the Provisional Battalion, composed of the depôts of about thirty regiments whose headquarters were serving abroad. The latter corps was commanded by Colonel Jarvis, of the Rifle Brigade. I served about two years in Chatham, doing garrison and dock duties. This place is on the Medway, about eight miles from Sheerness.

I cannot help mentioning an incident that happened here when I was on the main guard. It was customary for the men of the guard to what we called "board" a young officer mounting his first guard in the Army, to stand beer for the boys under his command. On the occasion in question I was deputed to "put a cheek on" and approach the officer in charge, in accordance with the rule. I went to his guard-room door and knocked. The usual "Come in!" was the response. I stated the case, after a stiff and formal Military salute. He stared at me first for a moment in astonishment, and then burst out laughing, saying, " I'll see you later on." I went back and informed my comrades-in-arms of the result of my mission. On the grand round taking the guard that night, the lieutenant in command, who we thought was a recruit, appeared with the Star of India and also the Sutlej medal on his breast, and when, on the guard being dismissed, he modestly explained that he had done guards years before, the very oldest soldier among us was "caught." He was too old for us—no beer out of him that night.

I might describe another incident which occurred while we were stationed at Chatham. Being on the main guard, I was placed on sentry before the quarters of the Commandant, in front of the building, and it being a very cold morning, I foolishly "ordered" arms from the "support," instead of first coming to the "carry," according to Military rule, this being the time of the old Brown Bess. Unfortunately for me, the old Commandant, who was standing comfortably in his drawing-room before a good fire with his hands behind him, saw me commit this breach of discipline. At the same moment his valet entered the room and announced that breakfast was ready.

"I've had my breakfast," exclaimed the Commandant decisively. "Look there!" he continued, pointing to your humble servant, and unfolding to the valet the tale of my delinquency. The flunkey being also a Military man, straightened out his fingers to their full extent, cast his eyes up to the ceiling in a manner that no sky-pilot could have excelled, and seemed horror-struck. This, of course, was natural, as the fellow was bound to be "shocked" at anything his master was. He was immediately despatched for the Brigade-Major, who came rushing past my post at the double, with his sword, scabbard, and spurs rattling terribly. The Brigade-Major at once went off for the garrison Adjutant. The Adjutant having been found, another hunt was made for the garrison bugler, who was discovered after some delay at the canteen fire warming his toes over a drop of "something short." The command given him was, "Sound morning garrison orders."

This done, repeating orders rang out from all the regimental buglers in the place. Such rushing to the garrison orderly-room by orderly sergeants, with order-books under their arms, was never seen; while I, the innocent cause of all this confusion, was quietly walking about on sentry, and could not make it out at all. It being an extraordinary thing in any garrison for morning orders to be sounded, I simply came to the conclusion that war had broken out, and began to think of getting off guard to pack my kit up, expecting to be ordered off to the seaside with my chums to help to repel the invaders. Presently up came the corporal of the guard with a file of men to relieve me of sentry—and place me a prisoner in the guardroom! And all this hubbub about a young

RECOLLECTIONS OF A RAMBLING LIFE

fellow's fingers getting cold, and his "ordering" arms from the "support." I was brought up with the other prisoners the following morning before our own Commanding Officer, who laughed at the whole affair and called them a "parcel of old fools." Be it known, the Commandant and his staff had seen about as much active service as I had myself, while my Commanding Officer had seen service in the Peninsular War under the Duke of Wellington. At any rate, I was ordered three days' sentry drill under the Sergeant-Major; but I gained a slight advantage here by missing a guard. This ended the adventure, and old England was not invaded after all.

In this year the Kaffir War broke out. Our 2nd Battalion was ordered to the Cape from India, with several other regiments, and as strong drafts as possible were sent out to reinforce them. I was detailed as one of our draft. We went by boat from Rochester Bridge, took train at Nine Elms Station for Portsmouth, and on January 1st, 1852, embarked at Spithead on board H.M.S. *Birkenhead* for South Africa. We took in drafts at Queenstown, Cove of Cork. On the passage out we touched at Madeira, Sierra Leone, and St. Helena. At Simon's Bay we coaled and watered, and we steamed out of the bay on the afternoon of February 25th. Early next morning the vessel ran on a sunken rock some two and a half miles out from the land, and became a total wreck, with the loss of nearly five hundred men, including Captain Salmond, in charge of the ship; also Colonel Seton, 74th Highlanders, commanding the troops on board. The ship struck at about 2 a.m., and was in pieces and under water in, I should say, about twenty minutes. The second cutter was launched, in which the women and children were placed as quickly as possible, this being the only boat that could be got to float.* An officer was placed in charge, and putting out to sea, the boat was fortunately sighted and picked up by a small coasting schooner named the *Lioness*, and taken into Mussel Bay.†

When the *Birkenhead* struck sixty men were at once told off to work the chain-pumps below, but the water coming

---

* The first cutter and the gig were also lowered and got away.
† It was the gig that landed, at Port D'Urban.

in with such a rush, the poor fellows were all drowned like rats in a hole. Some lost their lives by falling blocks and spars. When the vessel went to pieces I found myself in the water stark naked, having taken the precaution to tear off my shirt, as I could not swim. Some were drowned clinging to each other. I fortunately came in contact with a hencoop, to which I clung for a time; but not being able to get on top, owing to its turning round and my head bobbing under water, I found this would not do. Luckily for me, a spar from the ship washed up against me, to which I clung, and managing to get on top it bore me up. On this I contrived to keep the upper part of my body out of the water, but now and then a wave would pass over me entirely. I believe some of the poor fellows were pulled down by sharks, the water being tinged with blood in many places.

After being some time in the sea, day began to break, but the water became more rough. Fortunately the wind was blowing on shore, and towards mid-day I was nearing the land; but here I had another difficulty to encounter, this being the seaweed, which grew very strong in this part. With perseverance I at length got through, but having proceeded some distance further, I found the surf to be running tremendously high, and in this I was nearly washed off my spar. Not being able to swim, I believe, in part saved my life, for it caused me to cling more close to the little I had to hold me up. On looking back to where the ship was, I could see a portion of the mainmast out of the water. It seemed to be jambed into the rocks, and a few men were clinging to it; but the following morning this also disappeared. Having managed to get through the surf, I was close in to the shore, but here I was dashed about amongst the rocks to such an extent, that my limbs were bruised so badly I had to climb on all fours to "make a go" of it at all. I lay down on the sands quite exhausted, and slept soundly till daylight, having been about twenty-four hours in the water. I was as red as a lobster, what with the salt water and the hot sun in hobbling along the sandy beach.

Next day I came across some more men who were nearly, if not quite, in the same condition as myself. They had

General Viscount Hardinge, G.C.B., Commander-in-Chief 1852-56

(From an engraving specially presented by the Right Hon. Henry Charles, 3rd Viscount Hardinge, in honour of the *Birkenhead*)

succeeded in getting ashore on different parts of the beach. We were all glad to meet. As I was stark naked Ensign Lucas, of the 73rd Regiment, a survivor, kindly gave me a shirt, he having a flannel one on as an undershirt himself. This was serviceable on account of the hot sun. Being all strange and never from England before, we roamed along the beach, not knowing which direction was the best; but coming across some Dutchmen out on a fishing expedition, who had a waggon, they gave us some shellfish cooked on the fire, and this helped to sustain us a little. Our party by this time would number about thirty. Captain Wright, 91st Regiment, the oldest surviving officer, knew the coast. He started immediately on getting ashore and made his way to a place called Stanford Cove. There he procured a horse and rode to Mussel Bay, and from thence to Capetown, with the news of the disaster.* Simon's Bay was at once telegraphed to, and the Admiral despatched the *Rhadamanthus* sloop in search of us. During this time we managed to get to Stanford Cove, with the help of the Dutch fishermen's waggon and another sent by Captain Smales. Here we were helped with some clothes and food, after being about four days without. Then the *Rhadamanthus* arrived at the Cove and anchored outside, sent her boats and took us on board, and steamed into Simon's Bay, at which place we remained a few days to recruit our strength before proceeding to the Frontier to rejoin our different corps.

The headquarters of my regiment, the 12th, was then at Grahamstown, a frontier station some ninety-four miles from Port Elizabeth. It consisted of a lieutenant and about twenty men, and the regiment's baggage and spare arms and the band instruments were in the arsenal there. The remainder of the regiment was encamped in the field. Two companies, together with troops of the Rifle Brigade, 6th Royal Warwicks, 73rd Regiment, and irregulars, were ordered to storm the enemy's stronghold, the Waterkloof, a dense bush covering a large tract of country. After some hard campaigning and fighting the enemy were defeated, and that part of the country was cleared of them. Our men had another

* It was Dr. Culhane who rode with the news to Capetown.

small engagement on the banks of the Chumie River, where they also defeated the natives, but with some loss, including Colonel Fordyce, commanding the 74th Highlanders, the brigadier in command of the division, who was shot dead while leading the charge. The 74th Regiment were very unfortunate in losing two colonels within the period of three months. The enemy then retreated in the direction of Lower Albany.

I was next stationed at a frontier fort named Fort Brown, on the banks of the great Fish River. A convoy of waggons was being forwarded to Fort Beaufort, then the seat of war, from Port Elizabeth *via* Grahamstown, with provisions and a medicine chest and five hundred Enfield rifles. The escort, composed of the 9th Company, Royal Engineers, commanded by Captain Moody of that corps, was reinforced by twenty men of the 12th Regiment, and I had the honour to make one of the strengthening party. Colonel Ingoldsby, then Commandant of the garrison of Grahamstown, adopted the wise precaution of having the nipples taken out of the rifles and sent on by post. I may mention here that all posts and letters were conveyed by Military men, not less than twelve in number. At the Koonap Hill, a difficult and dangerous place to pass, the convoy was attacked by about four hundred natives. I was slightly wounded in the wrist. We lost thirty men of the Royal Engineers' company and six of the 12th Regiment; also two waggon-drivers (natives), and a woman assegaied and killed in the waggon. Being overwhelmed by weight of numbers, we had to retire to a farmhouse that had been burnt out and had only the bare walls standing. This place we held till morning. The enemy having decamped during the night, taking their dead and wounded with them, their loss was not known to us. A messenger was sent the following morning to Fort Brown, some ten miles distant, and from there reinforcements and help were sent us. Our dead and wounded were taken to the fort. It was only a small garrison, but we had a doctor, who looked after the wounded, and were able to bury the dead. Information was obtained by our scouts that the enemy had taken the direction of Burns' Hill, another of their strongholds. This part of the country was covered by dense bush, and accessible from it were the Amatola Mountains. A strong column was at once despatched to attack the enemy there, and an engagement ensued in which they were defeated, suffering heavy loss, while the plundered rifles were nearly all recaptured.

Some short time after this we had another brush with the natives, at a formidable kloof called the Booma Pass. Our force consisted of a portion of the 6th Royal Warwicks, 12th, 73rd, and 74th, a small number of Royal Artillery, and a troop of Cape Mounted Rifles. In this engagement Colonel Bissett, Cape Mounted Rifles, was carried out of the bush severely wounded. Major Wilmot and another officer, of the Royal Artillery, were at the same time shot dead. The number of men we lost was heavy, but of the enemy I should say six times as many fell. The natives bolted in great confusion. (This happened before the Snider or Martini-Henri rifles came into use in the Army.) On the next patrol the 2nd Queen's Regiment got a severe handling in the very dense Fish River bush, many of them being taken alive and tortured. Colonel Burns was then in command of this regiment. We could not get up in time to save the patrol, and on reaching the scene next day we found the dead and wounded lying in all directions, the enemy having made off. I was some time later stationed at another dangerous post, Driver's Bush, where our company of the Suffolks threw up a temporary mud fort. Here we had several brushes with the enemy by night, losing various men of our small detachment, also the gallant young officer in command of the party, Captain Hearn, who met his death by a spear-thrust. By this time the heart of the native war was pretty well broken, and the tribes in this part of South Africa were brought nearly under subjection. Then the Governor and Commander-in-Chief, Sir Harry Smith, was recalled, and Sir George Cathcart was sent out to relieve him.

Sir George found it necessary to make up a small army to proceed to Basutoland, to chastise the Basuto leader Mosheth, then the paramount chief. In that campaign I bore a part. It is not necessary here to mention the different corps in the command. All irregulars included, our force was divided into three small columns, but as it happened the centre division was the only one engaged. Our camp was formed in a large valley called the Beira, only a short distance from Thaba-Bosigo, the stronghold of the chief Mosheth, situate on a high mountain fortified with big guns, which had been mounted for the defence of the place. The Basutos, in my opinion, are the most powerful tribe in South Africa. They were the only natives who possessed heavy ordnance at this time. They also made their own powder and ammunition for war and hunting purposes, which I proved on my second visit to the country in 1880. General Cathcart engaged the enemy in the morning, and most regiments of the centre division lost a certain number of men. I don't clearly remember what the casualties were. I know that the 12th Royal Lancers lost twenty-eight killed, one of whom was a personal friend of mine, and the only man of the Lancers' draft who survived the wreck of the ill-fated *Birkenhead*.* After one day's hard fighting, in which I must honestly say we got the worst of it, this warfare came to an end. On the morning following that night's bivouac the chief Mosheth came into our camp under a flag of truce, desiring peace. He said that he and his tribe knew the power of the British, and although they had gained a small victory for the time being, they would have to succumb in the end to the superior arms of the English. An armistice was accordingly agreed to, and peace proclaimed, the General fining the tribe three thousand head of cattle and a thousand horses, to be handed over to the British Government. After this the expedition returned to Cape Colony, and peace was restored once more through South Africa. It had taken three years to bring the native tribes into subjection. I can recall scores of skirmishes and incidents by flood and field during that period.

I then proceeded once more to Grahamstown with the headquarters of my regiment. The Cape Mounted Rifles was at that time almost composed of natives, who could not be relied on for their loyalty, and the War Office decided to fill up the ranks partly with Europeans and volunteers from the different corps at the Cape. Myself and others accordingly

* Trooper J. Dodd. Wm. Butler, of the Lancers' draft, also survived.

volunteered to serve with the Mounted Rifles in the Cape of Good Hope and its dependencies. On joining I first went to King William's Town, where I was stationed for a time. The Indian Mutiny breaking out in 1857, we became temporarily dismounted, as our horses, and those of the Royal Artillery and as many remounts as could be procured from South Africa, were needed for the Indian cavalry. Colonels Appleby and Gould established for this purpose a depôt at Capetown. I was one of the party engaged to accompany these remounts to India on board the steamship *Himalaya*. We touched at Mauritius and Ceylon for coal and water, and landed our horses at Fort William, Calcutta, after which we returned to Table Bay. For this service we got double pay. In 1860, on Captains Speke and Grant starting on an expedition to explore Central Africa, thirty volunteers from the Cape Mounted Rifles were asked for, and I joined the party. We proceeded up the Mozambique Channel and arrived at Zanzibar. Fever raging there at the time, I got a touch of it, and had to be left behind, so that I could not continue with the expedition. Fifty pounds and a grant of land was the inducement held out to our fellows on their return, whenever they wished to leave Her Majesty's service. Later in the same year my troop was ordered to the colony of Natal, owing to a war scare there. Taking our horses, baggage, and all our gear on board the *Narcissus* frigate, we sailed at a day's notice to reinforce the troops in Natal, as the Zulu chief was thought to be meditating a descent on the Colony. Disembarking at Durban, we marched to Pietermaritzburg, the headquarters of the troops being at Fort Napier. Some time after this, things having become quiet again, our troop was divided into small detachments. My party was stationed at Nottingham Post, near the Mooi River. We formed patrols as far as the Drakensberg Mountains with the object of keeping the bushmen in check. This was a dangerous duty, as the little pigmies, although so small, used poisoned arrows, and made night raids on the border farmers, carrying off their cattle actually from under their very noses. These bushmen gave us a great deal of trouble. We could not light a fire at night, although it was very cold in the mountains. One particular night they stole on us, firing their arrows into us; but fortunately we were lying down with our heads in our saddles. Our horses escaped by a miracle. One man was hit in the knee and died the next day, although the slight wound inflicted was cut out and burned with powder, the only remedy we had. I should explain that, having no tents, we had to sleep in the open. In the morning we found several of their small arrows sticking in our saddle-flaps. It was impossible to catch the pigmies at the time, as they crept along the ground like snakes and were very active.

I must mention here an incident that occurred after our return to Fort Napier. Captain Harvey, in command of our detachment at the fort, died, and was buried in the cemetery at Pietermaritzburg. The following day his grief-stricken widow changed her mind as to his resting-place. She was not content to leave the body there, and, having arranged with the captain of a coasting vessel at Durban to convey it to East London, on the Cape Coast, the nearest point to Fort Peddie, the family burial-place, desired myself and four others to disinter the coffin by night. This we did. To our astonishment a few days afterwards, by an order of the Resident Magistrate, instigated by Dr. Colenso, then Bishop of Natal, the five of us were waited upon by the Chief Constable and a posse of police, arrested, and marched off to prison charged with body-snatching—a most serious offence in the eye of the law! We expected nothing less than penal servitude. However, on the intercession of the Commandant, coupled with the threatening attitude of the garrison, we eventually managed to get free again on our promising not to go body-snatching any more.

I was then ordered to a station on the Lower Tugela, the largest river in the Colony, dividing Zululand from Natal. At this place we had plenty of sport, as the hippopotamus, rhinoceros, and alligator abounded in plenty; also the boa-constrictor and all kinds of snakes—the black and green imamba * were considered the most dangerous. This was near

* Of the imamba, most dreaded by the natives, there are eight different kinds. These snakes elevate and throw themselves forward, and have been known to pursue a horseman.

the sea-coast, where trees and flowers are tropical to about forty miles inland; the weather then becomes cooler. Having lost nearly all our horses by sickness, we were removed to a post called Fort Buckingham, about a hundred miles more inland still on the Tugela River, at Kranz Kop, considered the highest land in that part of the Colony, twelve miles from the river. The post was under the command of Major Currie, Cape Mounted Rifles. Here we also had good sport, as there was plenty of large game, and the Major, being a keen sportsman, often formed hunting parties. On one occasion we started to hunt buffalo in the wilds of the river; but instead of us hunting them they hunted us, and the Major was carried some twenty yards on one of their horns, when a member of our party, a Hottentot, took steady aim and shot the beast through the eye. On our returning to camp a portion of the detachment was ordered to be stationed at Greytown, on the Umvoti River; but things having become quiet again, we soon returned to Pietermaritzburg, and from thence proceeded to Cape Colony once more.

Our station was then King William's Town, the headquarters of the Cape Mounted Rifles. Here another little adventure befell me. The groom of the Colonel in command, an old chum of mine, had a bit of a job on hand—namely, the building of a fowlhouse. One particular afternoon I was assisting him in the business, and he having occasion to leave for a short time, I was left to attend to the formation myself, when a heavy "swell" appeared on the scene, dressed in scarlet and tinsel. Calling out at some yards' distance, he said, "Hi, you fellow, where does your master live?" I being in my shirt sleeves, he evidently took me for the Colonel's servant. I paid no heed to him, but kept hammering away at the nails. He repeated the question in an arrogant tone. I could tell by his manner that he had not been long in the service. I made answer that I had not got a master, but only a mistress. He then asked, "Where does your mistress live, sirrah?" I said if he took the trouble to inquire at Windsor Castle or Balmoral, he would probably find her at one or the other. He then got into a bit of a rage, and demanded, "Why don't you stand to attention, and salute me?" I replied, "I don't know you." He said, "I would make you aware that I am Lieutenant Bazalgette, of the Ordnance Staff Corps." "Well," I innocently remarked, "Lieutenant Leathergate, had I known you I should have saluted you." Correcting me, he said, " Not Leathergate, but Bazalgette, sirrah." "Well," said I, "basel's leather, anyhow." "I demand your name," he fumed. " I shall report you to your commanding officer." I informed him that " my name was Norval."* This he did not " tumble to," but off he went, and I got hauled over the coals about it at orderly-room time next morning, when I was charged with " being impertinent to an officer in uniform" —and, as the commanding officer remarked, a personal friend of his also. I told the Colonel that it was quite the reverse— that the officer was impertinent to me, calling me a "fellow" and " sirrah." Said I, " You would not wish to have one of your non-commissioned officers addressed in this manner." (Be it known that I held the exalted rank of lance-corporal!) The officers in the orderly-room at the time were highly amused at the affair, which all ended in a reprimand, so far as I was concerned.

From King William's Town two squadrons of the Cape Mounted Rifles were now ordered to Fort Beaufort. There was a convict station at Katberg, some sixty miles farther in British Kaffraria, the superintendent of which had caused to be apprehended a deserter belonging to our regiment. I was detailed as corporal, with two men and a spare horse, to receive over the prisoner and bring him back to headquarters. On our return march to Fort Beaufort we had to halt for the night at half-distance, at an hotel. The fellow having plenty of money, managed to make the escort drunk (myself as well as the rest), and during the night took the liberty to bolt and leave us in the lurch. Next morning we found ourselves in a fix—we did not know how to go on. At any rate we saddled up and resumed our homeward march—without the

---

* My name is Norval ; on the Grampian hills
My father feeds his flocks ; a frugal swain,
Whose constant cares were to increase his store
And keep his only son, myself, at home.

John Home, in *Douglas*, Act ii., Scene 1.

prisoner. We knew the hotel-keeper, who was sorry for us, but we also knew that a court-martial was staring us in the face. I told the boys we must trust to providence, as something might turn up to get us out of the scrape. And so it did, for we fortunately overtook a man who had been discharged from the Army, hard up on the road. I accosted him, and telling him of the mess we were in, invited him to mount the spare horse and personate the deserter, saying we would make it all right with him after. To this he willingly agreed, so we marched him into the garrison guardroom and provided him with rations. In the morning he was brought up, but of course no one could identify him. Charged with being a deserter, he denied being anything of the sort, and said he should lose his situation through being detained! Every one was sorry for him, and we made him up a small collection and started him on the road again rejoicing. (I was much gratified by our old Colonel remarking that my duty had been satisfactorily carried out!) We never heard any more of our deserter.

The corps was at this time not fully mounted, owing to the departure of horses for service in India. While we were in this condition it was notified to the Admiral at Simon's Town, the Naval station of South Africa, that slavery was carried on to some extent along the west coast. An expedition was therefore formed to put this down. A small steamer, the *Waldensian*, was chartered, commanded by Captain Stadts, a German who knew the coast well. The vessel was flat-bottomed, to enable her to run up the mouths of rivers, and mounted four small guns and a brass swivel on the forecastle. The party was made of bluejackets from the Admiral's ship and twenty-five men of the Cape Mounted Rifles, myself included, acting as marines, with a few Lascars as interpreters.

Steaming down the coast, we passed Port Nolloth, and a dense fog coming on we anchored in Walfish Bay. Sailing again next day, we came in sight of a suspicious-looking craft, brig-rigged, which we chased on and off for several days. We lost sight of her for a time at the mouth of the Nourse River. Our skipper, being in a great hurry to overtake her, hugged the shore too closely, and in rounding Negro Point we struck on a rock, which knocked a hole in the steamer's bottom, and she became a wreck; but we managed to run her ashore at the mouth of the Nourse, and landed without losing any of our party and with our ammunition and arms all dry. We got our provisions ashore the next day. We made out the slaver by her spars about a mile and a half up the river, and on moving to the spot discovered that her crew had abandoned her and bolted inland. On searching the vessel we found eighty-four slaves on board in a deplorable state. We immediately released them, and they gave us great assistance in getting our remaining stores ashore from the steamer. The water we found to be poisonous through two of the slaves dying from the effects of drinking it, so we threw the casks overboard. The slave-ship proving sound, an officer was placed in charge of her with a small party of our men; the slaves were put on board, and she was despatched to Simon's Town to report the stranding of our steamer.

Thinking this a good opportunity to explore the country, our skipper made up two parties, taking one himself direct inland, and sending the other forward nearer the shore. I went with the captain. Carrying six days' rations and our arms, we made an advance into the interior, where we met with birds of the most beautiful plumage. Finding a sort of track through the bush, we knew from this and the absence of wild animals that there must be people of some kind inhabiting the country, and we were not surprised, after a few days' march, to observe some huts on a slight eminence. Towards these habitations we directed our steps, and on arriving at the place we found the natives in great commotion. Within the circle of the palm-leaf huts the chief was surrounded by a ring of his warriors, and armed with spears and looking very formidable. The old chief, Chaka by name, was terribly ugly, as were the rest of the tribe. We advanced with a white flag displayed, making known our condition and that we were friendly. We were conducted to the front of the chief's kama, or royal hut, and our captain rubbed noses with the old chap (this being their mode of salutation), a performance the enjoyment of which I did not at all envy him! We being so well armed, I thought they seemed a bit afraid of us. We were then invited to eat, and they brought out some food in an earthen vessel baked in the sun. Our rations having begun to run short, we partook of this dish, but we did not eat much of it. I thought it tasted something like wild pig. One of our Lascars had been making friends with members of the tribe, picking up what information he could, and he now told us that the old chief and his people were cannibals, and had made an attack on another tribe inland, killing nearly the whole village—men, women and children. I thought this might perhaps account for the peculiar taste of the meat they had regaled us with. The old chief said he was sorry we did not catch some of the slavers, but we all thought that he most likely had some hand in the business. Although these natives seemed friendly, we thought they were a little threatening, and I kept my hand pretty near my revolver most of the time, as one or two of my chums were somewhat fleshy and I thought Chaka eyed them rather affectionately!

Our skipper was a little nervous, and contrived to give orders to "back out" and prepare to retreat to our camp. I did not see any of the women; the men of the tribe were all but naked. On our march back to camp we had plenty of water, but could obtain shots at only a few of the wild animals we saw. We arrived in camp all right, and found our friends much as we had left them, except that they had experienced a hurricane, which had blown the mainsail covering our provisions into the sea, and at the same time received a visit from an enormous python, which had swallowed about a dozen pairs of our gauntlets and several pairs of the navy men's sea-boots! After being fired at by some of the party, the creature got clean away. The rascal must have had a strong appetite for leather! As we now found ourselves rather lonely, certain choice spirits of the party suggested making a raid on old Chaka's kraal, with the object of carrying off some of his dusky beauties; but the proposal was overruled.

Our captain began to feel a little anxious for the safety of the second party, who had not returned; and as a vessel might come any day to relieve us, he made up his mind to send in search of them. Half-a-dozen men volunteered to go, I myself being one of the number. We took our arms and three days' rations and started at daybreak, our route this time being more coastwise than the previous one. Tumbling along the rough bush and brake, on the fourth day we descried some bamboo huts in the distance, which proved to be a native village. For this we made, and on approaching were delighted to notice some white men, who, seeing us, came to meet us. We shouted to them, and they proved to be our own people. They told us they were among friendly natives, including females, with whom some of them had contracted matrimony! My chum, young Jack Riley, of the admiral's ship, being rather a "toff" in his way, had managed to captivate the old king's daughter, to whom he said he was married. (He did not inform me if it was the Princess Royal, or only one of the minor princesses.) I always knew Jack to be ambitious, but to marry into royalty was going a little beyond me. Still, matrimony, I knew, was not exactly the same form and ceremony out there as it is in Europe. After shaking hands with Jack, he invited me to his place. When I had rested a bit and made myself a little more presentable, I accordingly went to the entrance.

Jack met me and said he was sorry that "Mrs. Riley" had gone over to her pa's place on a foraging expedition, but he would introduce me to his "sister-in-law," the princess who was keeping house for him till his wife returned. Let me describe his "furniture." He had an old sea-chest, inverted, for a table, and three or four ancient tea-chests, richly ornamented with Chinese characters, as seats. On my entering the establishment Jack called the lady, by name Amarintha, who advanced to the centre of the apartment and bowed most politely. I also bowed, she making use of some jargon which Jack interpreted as meaning that I was welcome. I am forced to describe the get-up of the princess as not being quite *à la mode de Paris*, but more in the style of Adam and Eve in the Garden of Eden, with one or two slight exceptions. At any rate, we did very well. The lady produced a jar of "johalla," a native drink which was very tart and pleasant—of course, adapted to hot climates. Eventually out came a bottle of "Cape smoke," or brandy; also a "square face," by some vulgarly call "old Tom." The only way I could account for such good stuff being here, was that probably some pious missionaries had been about these parts! We "kept it up" till the small hours of the morning —when, I'm sorry to say, I could not walk exactly straight. The drinking vessels we used on this auspicious occasion were a couple of old sailor's pannikins, and one or two soldiers' rusty messtins, glassware and china not being much known in this region. I returned to my chums, who were all asleep and snoring in their leafy bower. The following morning the officer in charge assembled the party and read the despatch we had brought from the captain, informing the men that they were at once to proceed to the headquarters camp at the mouth of the Nourse River. The command was gently broken to the "married" ladies, who were one and all disconsolate, and about 9 a.m. we paraded and marched off, amid the tears and hand-waving of the "wedded" portion of the community, the men promising to return faithfully in a year and a day, and settle down and make their "spouses" happy ever after.

We arrived at the Nourse once more without any mishap. There we remained a few days amusing ourselves, principally by fishing and bathing. The only trouble we had to encounter was the swarms of mosquitoes which assailed us by night. On Sunday morning our skipper, in the absence of a "sky-pilot," conducted divine worship. The same day, in the afternoon, our look-out man reported a vessel in the offing, which proved to be H.M. steam sloop-of-war *Hermes*, arrived to relieve us and take us off. She fired a gun and cast anchor as near the mouth of the river as possible, and at once sent off a boat in which we embarked, getting our stores on board the same evening and bidding a long adieu to our "bowers of Arcadia." Once more we found ourselves on the blue waters of the ocean, *en route* for the Cape of Good Hope, where we disembarked at Simon's Town, where the Naval men rejoined their ship, the *Boscawen*, and the Lascars were discharged. We of the Cape Mounted Rifles marched twenty-one miles to Capetown, through Kalk Bay, Wynberg, Newlands and Rose Bank. We were paid up in Capetown, where we had a month's leave to spend the money in. Then we proceeded to the frontier once more and joined our regiment. This was in 1870, and my term of Military service having expired, I got the "kick out" of the old Corps and was pensioned off, after being seventeen years in the Cape Mounted Rifles and six in the Suffolks.

I then secured an appointment in the Mauritius Police, which I joined for two years, an officer coming to the Cape recruiting. The strength of the force was then five hundred, armed for the defence of the island, to act in conjunction with the Army and Navy forces stationed there. Mauritius, or Isle of France, as it was formerly named, is rightly called the gem of the Indian Ocean. It is surrounded by a coral reef, except at the entrance to Port Louis harbour. There is another small harbour on the opposite side thirty-one miles away, called Mahébourg. The island is situated within the tropics. The Isle of Bourbon can be seen with the naked eye from a small mountain called Cannonier's Point. This is the signal station. Another attraction is Pieter Botte, or Thumb Mountain,* shaped like a human thumb. I visited the graves of Paul and Virginia at Pample Moose, a short distance from Port Louis, which has become a resort for picnic parties and holiday-makers generally. Paul and Virginia, it may be remembered, were two French lovers † who fled from France to this island; but the ship was wrecked near Port Louis harbour and the lovers were found dead, locked in each other's arms. So goes the story.

We got nearly all salt rations at Mauritius, as no cattle are bred on the island, the meat being buffalo beef from Madagascar and Navy salt pork. We drilled on the Champ-de-

* In the Pouce Range, district of Port Louis, are the singular peaks of Pouce (2,650 feet), so called from its supposed resemblance to the human thumb. This is the "attraction" referred to. The still loftier Pieter Botte (2,676 feet) is a tall obelisk of bare rock crowned with a globular mass of stone. Lighthouses have been erected on Cannonier's Point and also on Flat Island.

† The child lovers in Bernardin de St. Pierre's popular romance, *Paul et Virginie* (1788).

Mars, a splendid parade-ground, along with the troops. We had particularly easy times during my stay on the island, having literally nothing to do; but I did not enjoy good health, as the yellow fever is very prevalent there in some seasons, so I managed to get invalided from the force after serving twelve months, and returned once more to the Cape by mail-steamer in 1871. During the same year I was able to get enrolled in the Cape Mounted Police, commanded by Sir Walter Currie, and proceeded to the Namaqualand district for a time, Port Nolloth being the seaport, and the inland capital in those days Springbokfontein, famed for its copper mines—the inhabitants being all Hottentots, except for a few European miners. Next I went to Damaraland, and from thence to Korannaland. This was a very wild country, and while there we had several encounters with lions and tigers and other animals, which abounded. We subdued the Koranna tribe,* taking several prisoners and conveying them in chains over a large tract of country to labour on the Table Bay breakwater harbour works.

Having completed my three years' police duties in 1874, I was employed by the Cape Government as convict overseer at Port Alfred, in the Kowie River district of Bathurst. This place is distant from Grahamstown 36 miles, and is the seaport for that city, which is noted as the home of the 1820 settlers. Here I remained until the Transkei War broke out in 1877. I then joined Major Nesbitt's Horse† as a volunteer, and served in Gaikaland, Galekaland, and Tembuland. The object of this campaign was to disarm the native tribes. Here we co-operated with the 24th Regiment, commanded by Colonel Glyn, who lost so heavily in Zululand. We defeated and shot the troublesome paramount rebel chief Sandili on the Bashee River, but this took nearly two years to accomplish. In 1879, the Zulu War breaking out, I again volunteered and got the rank of sergeant in the Frontier Light Horse, a corps

* The operations against the Korannas, Lower Orange River, were in 1869.
† Major, afterwards Colonel Nesbitt, also a *Birkenhead* survivor. Colonel Nesbitt has told us when, and under what circumstances, his Light Horse was raised.

raised by Colonel Redvers Buller, and commanded by Captain Cecil D'Arcy, V.C. Going by sea from East London, the most easterly port of Cape Colony, we landed at Durban harbour, and I marched once more to the Tugela River. There we concentrated with other troops, and crossing the border under General Thesiger, afterwards Lord Chelmsford, we joined Colonel Buller's division, engaged the enemy at Isandhlwana Mountain, and were victorious. Marching to Kwamagwasa, we met the flying column under Sir Evelyn Wood, and 20,000 Zulus were defeated. We then crossed the Umvolosi River and marched in three squares to Ulundi, where the Zulus were again defeated with great slaughter, their king being followed and taken at an old mission station named St. Paul's. The war being now virtually at an end, we retraced our steps once more to Durban, where we gave up our horses and Military appointments, and all the irregular corps were disbanded. Thinking to make my fortune, I next proceeded to Griqualand West, or Kimberley, to do a little diamond digging on the banks of the Vaal River—there was no charge for a claim on the Vaal, as in other parts of the compound. Not being very prosperous in this undertaking, and the Transvaal War breaking out, I joined Sir Owen Lanyon's corps of Kimberley Horse. It was our commander's intention to meet and co-operate with Sir George Colley, but owing to Sir George displaying too much haste in engaging the enemy at Laing's Nek and Majuba Hill, he was defeated and lost his life also. We were not, therefore, in time to assist him, and a hurried peace being prolaimed, the corps was disbanded. So I was again "out of collar."

I then went to Capetown, and from thence to East London. There are two East Londons, one on each side of the Buffalo River. East London East is called Panmure, and has of late years become a large town. At this time the Basuto War was in progress, and I joined Commandant Landry's Light Horse. We concentrated at Kei Road, got mounted at Queenstown, marched through Jamestown and Penhock, crossed the Orange River at Aliwal North, the boundary of the Orange Free State and Cape Colony, and crossed through the Free

State of the Boers. The Cape Government had arranged for this with President Brandt, as by the law of nations an armed party is not allowed to march through a neutral state without its previous sanction. Be it remembered that the Orange Free State did not join in the Transvaal War of 1881.

After passing the Orange State border, we proceeded through Rouxville and Wepener and crossed the Caledon River at Ficksburg. The Caledon, I may explain, is the boundary dividing the Free State from Basutoland. We joined Colonel Brabant's force and had a skirmish at Kallahama, where Brabant lost twelve men and twenty horses. We then pushed through Mafeteng to Bolika Heights, the headquarters of Colonel Carrington, the Brigadier in command, afterwards Sir F. Carrington, and made a reconnaissance in force, when we lost a few men and Colonel Carrington himself was severely wounded.

We were next ordered to Thlotsi Heights, where we engaged the enemy with some loss, including Major Lawrence and Captain Hanson of the Kimberley Horse, left dead on the field. Here we held the Basutos in check for some months. They were all mounted and well armed, and also carried a peculiar kind of battle-axe, and were the most intelligent tribe in that part of Africa, all speaking Dutch, although having a language of their own. The place we were at was well into the heart of Basutoland.

This little war was carried through entirely by the Cape Government, without the aid of the British troops. But the Cape Government became tired of the expense of the long-protracted war, Parliament dissolved, and a "pitso," or assembly of native chiefs, being formed by order of the then paramount chief, Masupha, an armistice was decided on and eventually peace was proclaimed, without any advantage accruing to the Cape Government. The tribe agreed to live under British rule, the General officer in command, Sir Mansfield Clarke (afterwards Q.M.G. at the War Office), to remain as Governor and Administrator for the British Government independent of the Cape. After this the Colonial troops returned to Cape Colony by another route, delivered up their horses at Queenstown, and disbanded at Kei Road.

Finding myself then, in 1882, once more "on my own hook," I proceeded to Capetown again and secured an appointment on the convict service at Table Bay breakwater, in which service I remained six years. Some time after joining I was sent to the Great Zworte Bergen to assist in cutting a road through that mountain, extending from the Prince Albert to the Oudtshoorn districts. On this work being completed I returned to Table Bay, and was employed on the cutting of a road from Sea Point to Houts Bay, at the back of Table Mountain.

Let me, before leaving it, describe Capetown in a few words. Viewed from the outer harbour, on the extreme left is the Blue Berg; next comes the Devil's Peak, and in the centre is Table Mountain looming over Capetown; then the Lion's Rump, and farther to the right, the Lion's Head, the resemblance being that of a lion couchant. The Dutch language is principally spoken at the Cape, where one meets people of all nations, not seafaring men but settlers in the town.

Having been a long time in these parts, I thought I should like to have a look at old England again. Accordingly I applied for and procured a passage in the s.s. *Orontes*, embarked at Table Bay, and touched once more at St. Helena, the Isle of Ascension, and Madeira, arriving at Portsmouth harbour in March, 1888, thus finishing my forty years' rambles and scrambles with all their adventures on land and sea under the British flag.

THE END

INDEX
compiled by S Monick

INTRODUCTORY NOTES

1 As will become apparent, the index is structured under the following headings: AWARDS; BATTLES, CAMPAIGNS, WARS; LOCATIONS (*ie* places); PERSONALITIES; SHIPS AND OTHER SEA-GOING VESSELS; UNITS AND FORMATIONS; WEAPONS AND AMMUNITION.

2 Often, the reader will find a term sub-divided into a number of further headings. This practice is a recurrent feature of terms appearing under the structured headings noted in (1) above. For example, under LOCATIONS the terms 'Great Britain' and 'Cape of Good Hope' are broken down into a number of sub-headings, each often being further sub-divided. This approach is especially noticeable in the section, SHIPS, in which the term 'Birkenhead' is subject to numerous sub-divisions. It is a further marked feature of the terms grouped under UNITS AND FORMATIONS. The object of this technique is to ensure specificity.

3 To a certain extent, it is intended that the index serves as a self-contained reference source. This objective has shaped the section headed PERSONALITIES. The individuals grouped under this heading relate solely to the persons who were passengers/crew of the *Birkenhead*. The key further delineates survivors or fatalities. The reader is thus furnished with a comprehensive muster roll of the *Birkenhead*. Those passengers who are not members of the crew or passengers are assigned to the general section. Thus, for example, Richard Athol Nesbitt, who was a child survivor of the wreck, is indexed under the heading PERSONALITIES; whilst his father, Qmr Nesbitt, who was not on board, is to be found in the general section, under N. Similarly, those who played an important role in the subsequent history of the wreck (*eg* naval

commanders such as Cdre Wyvill or Capt Ramsden), political and social figures (such as Lt Gen Sir William Napier), and those who provided important succour to the survivors (such as Mrs Kaye, Capt and Mrs Smales) are indexed in the general section.

4   The reader will note the presence of extensive cross references within the index. A major reason for this approach is the authors' practice of referring to an individual in terms of both his name and the rank/position held (*eg* Archbold is variously referred to as both the 'Gunner' and his name, Brodie is denoted by the terms 'Master' and by name, whilst Salmond is variously referred to as 'Captain', 'Commander' and by name).

5   The term 'illus - fp...' denotes 'illustration - facing page...'

6   The presence of square brackets indicates that the indexer has completed the full Christian names/initials of a personality; in those circumstances where the authors have omitted such information.

7   The reader will note that numerous terms are included which are only of marginal importance - and, indeed, often of no significance whatsoever - to the central theme of the work. This feature derives from the indexer's practice of citing the key terms appearing on each page. The keyword method of indexing must, inevitably, involve the inclusion of numerous extraneous terms in relation to the book's central theme. However, it is important to bear in mind that the essential purpose of a comprehensive index is not to furnish a reference guide to the work's core subject but should relate to the overall text in its entirety. Editing of such terms is potentially damaging to the integrity of the writer(s). In any event, the alphabetical ordering of terms enables the reader to locate the sought terms and bypass unwanted entries.

INDEX

A

Adams, Mr, 117
Adams, Cdr John, 162
Addison, A C, 211
  A deathless story, v
  The story of the Birkenhead, v, 174,242
Addison, D, 121
Addison, Daniel, viii
Addison, Sgt Maj J, 121
Admiralty House (Great Britain), 155
Admiralty House (South Africa - Simonstown), 159
Aeacus, 124
Aeneas, 166
Albert, Prince, 91
Alexander, Capt, 228
Alexandria, Queen, 188
Annual Register, 14
Argonauts, 121
Army List, 101,148

AWARDS
  Baltic Medal 1854-1855, 176,209,226,229
  Bath, Most Honourable Order of the
    [*see*: Most Honourable Order of the Bath]
  Cape of Good Hope General Service Medal 1880-1897, 222,241,258
  Clasps:
    Basutoland 1881, 222
    1877-8, 241
  China Medal (1857-1860), 209,229,254
    Clasps
      Pekin, 254
      Taku Forts, 209,254
  Crimea Medal 1854-1856, 177
    Clasps
      Azov, 209
      Sebastapol, 209
  Distinguished Service Pension, 148,157
  Indian Mutiny Medal, 217
  Long Service and Good Conduct Medal, 174,209,211,249,254,291,292
  Meritorious Service Medal (MSM), 209,214,294
  Most Excellent Order of the Star of India, 297

Most Honourable Order of the Bath
　　　　Companion (CB), 90,148,156,242,244
　　Order of the Bath [*see*: Most Honourable Order of the Bath]
　　Order of the Star of India
　　　　[*see*: Most Excellent Order of the Star of India]
　　Queen's South Africa Medal, 241
　　South Africa Medal 1834-1853, 143,174,177,201,211,217,241,249,254
　　South Africa Medal for the Zulu and Basuto Wars 1877-1879, 258
　　Star of India [*see*: Most Excellent Order of the Star of India]
　　Sutlej Medal, 297
　　Turkish Crimea Medal, 177,208
　　Victoria Cross (VC), 228,244,291,292
Academy, 192
Aylmer, Capt the Hon F W, 122
Aylmer, Lord, 92

B

Babbage, Dr, 89
Baines, Messrs, 95
Baines, G D, 110
Bandmann, Mr, 117,118
Barber, Mrs, 165
Barker, Capt, 102
Barrett, Dr J F, 163
Basutos, 233,234,317
　　Chief, 233,234,317 [*see also*: Masupha]

BATTLES, CAMPAIGNS, WARS
　　Acre (1840), 121 [*see also*: LOCATIONS: Syria]
　　　　Casualties
　　　　　　British, 121
　　　　　　Egyptian, 121
　　Afghanistan (1842)
　　　　Cabul (retreat), 23
　　Alma (1854), 177
　　American War of Independence (1776-1783), 160
　　Anglo-Boer War (1880-1881), 316,317
　　　　Laing's Nek (1881), 316
　　　　Majuba (1881), 316
　　Anglo-Boer War (1899-1902), 67,235,236,239,240,244,245
　　　　Bloemfontein (1900), 244

INDEX 323

Johannesburg (1900), 244
Kimberley (siege) (1899-1900), 236,238,239,240
Pretoria (1900), 244
China (1860), 209
   Taku Forts, 209,228,229,
Copenhagen (1801), 160
Crimean War (1854-1856), vii,123,142,151,166,176,177,203,
    227,229,289,292
   [see also: individual battles/campaigns; ie Alma;
    see also: LOCATIONS: Balaclava, Baltic, Crimea]
   Balaclava (1854), 130,154,289
    Charge of the Heavy Brigade, 153
   Baltic (1854-1855)
    Bomarsund, 289
    Kinburn, 289
    Sweaborg, 225
   Sebastapol
    Redan (1855), 194
Corunna (1809), 91
Franco-Austrian War (1859), 203
   Dybol (1859), 203
Indian Mutiny (1857-1858), 95,152,214,305
   [see also: individual battles/campaigns; ie Lucknow]
Japan (1863), 228
   Kagoshima forts, 228
   Simonosaki (Straits), 228
Lucknow (1857), 96 [see also under: LOCATIONS]
Minden (1759), 91
Peninsular War (1808-1814), 70,82,85
   [see also: individual battles/campaigns; eg Cuidad Rodrigo]
Rhodesia
   Mashonaland (1896), 244
Roleia (1808), 76
Rolica [see: Roleia]
Sebastapol (1854), 164
South Africa
   [see also: Anglo-Boer War (1880-1881)/Anglo-Boer War (1899-1902)]
   Frontier Wars, 144,217,239,240
    1846-1847,143,157
    1850-1853, 12,99,143,151,157,177,196,198,199,201,203,204,
     214,210,216,220,223,224,238,241,242,245,248,303
     Berea expedition, 144,214

    Booma Pass, 303
    Burns' Hill, 302
    Chumie River, 302
    Koonkap, 220,302
        Casualties
            12th Lancers, 220
        Orange River expedition, 196
            Waterkloof Pass, 128,301
    1877-1878, 221,241,315
        Bashee River, 315
    Basutoland
        1851-1853, 303
            Thaba Bosigo, 304
                Casualties
                    12th Lancers, 304
        1880-1881, 67,221,233,244,316
            Kallahama, 317
                Casualties
                    Brabant's force, 317
            Tholotsi Heights, 317
    Gaika war [*see*: 1877-1878]
    Galeka war [*see*: 1877-1878]
    Griqua war [*see*: 1877-1878]
    Tembu rebellion [*see*: 1880-1882]
    Transkei [*see*: 1877]
  Bechuanaland [*see*: Warren expedition]
  Koranna tribe (1869), 315
  Natal (operations against Boers) (1840s), 210
  Sekukuni war (1876), 240
  Stellaland [*see*: Warren expedition]
  Transvaal War [*see*: Anglo-Boer War (1880-1881)
  Warren expedition (1884), 234
  Zulu War (1879), 221,315,316
    Isandhlwana, 316
    [*Note*: This reference contains a serious error. The authors state that the Zulus were defeated in this battle whereas, as is well known, the British encampment was massacred.]
        Ulundi, 316
South America (1840s)
    Obligade, 164
    Parama, 164
    Uruguay, 164

INDEX

St Jean d'Acre [*see*: Acre]
Thermopylae (480 BC), 130
Torres Vedras (Peninsular War), 91
Trafalgar (1805)
   Centenary Day, vii
Waterloo (1815), 73,91,99,193
   French attacks, 99
   Squares, 99

Battles and sieges of the Peninsular War (Sir William Napier), 85
Baines, Capt Robert L, 162
Bazaglette, Lt, 308
Bechuanaland News, The, 235
Beard, H R, 260
Beatty, Detective Sgt, 262,263
Bedford School, 192
Belam, Cdr John, 60,123
Belgrave, Master Cdr, 82
Bennett, Capt W H W, 165
Bentley, Richard
   Remarkable passages in the life of John Drake, Marine, 281-295
Beresford, Maj William, 81,84,85,90,131,133
Biographical dictionary of eminent Scotsmen, 32,126,128,141
Birch, Capt, 282
Bird, T, 238
'Birkenhead drill', 4,10,280
'Birkenhead rock', 255,256
Birkenhead, The (Dr John A Goodchild), 277-279
Bisset, Andrew
   On the strength of nations, 174
Bissett, Col, 303
Black Ball (shipping line), 95
Blackbeard, Capt C A, 239
Blackbeard, Mrs, 239
Boers, 210,233,240,242,301,317
   Cape rebels, 304
Bond, Joshua Walter MacGeough, 203
Bond, Mrs Maria, 197
Boston School, 211
Bot (River), 51
'Bottleweed' [*see*: Kelpweed]
Bowen, Mrs, 178

Boyes, Mdmn Duncan G, 228
Boys, 102,175,226
Brabant, Col, 317
Bradshaw, Master Cdr Mauser, 162
Brandt, President [J H], 317
Breton, Maj Gen, 151,152,153
Briggs, Admiral Sir T, 90
Britannia's bulwarks, 35
British, 190 [*see also*: English]
British Army and Navy Review, The, 209,281,294
British Home for Incurables, 188
British Museum, vii,178
Broke, Capt, 161
Bromby, Capt C, 164
Brooks, Police Constable, 267
Brougham, Lord, 10
Brown, Sir George, 127
Bruce, H A, 86,87
   Life of General Sir William Napier, 86,89,141
Brydon, Dr, 23
Buffalo, 307
Buller, Col (later Gen Sir Redvers), 12,125,221,316
Bunce, Cdr Benjamin Holland, 24,28,36,41,48,49,57,116,119, 122,123
Bunce, Mrs Susan Henrietta, 123
Burghers [*see*: Boers]
Burgoyne, Capt Hugh (VC), 124
Burns, Col, 303
Bushmen, 305,306

C

Camberley Staff College
   [*see*: Royal Military College - Senior Department]
Cambridge, Duke of, vii, illus - fp 106,127,152
Cambridge University, 191
Campbell, Sir Colin, 96,289
Cannibals, 170,171
Cape Screw Steam Navigation Company, 115
Cape Times, The, 259
Carey, Lt, 128
Carlos I (King of Portugal, 1899-1908), viii, illus - fp 10
Carnegie, Hon John, 165

INDEX

Carrington, Col, 317
Carter, Thomas, 141
    Curiosities of war and military studies, 141
    Medals of the British Army and how they were won, 141
Cashman, Lt William, 168
Castle, G, 238
Castor, 121
Cathcart, Maj Gen the Hon George, 82,143,144,196,220,223, 303,304
Cattle, 304,305,314
Cave, Mrs Bridget, 188
Chads, Capt, 107
Chaka (Zulu chief), 310,311
Chamberlain, Mr, 221
Chamberlain, Joseph, 258,259
Chamberlain, Gen Sir Neville Bowles, 201
Chambers, Robert, 126
Chambers, Capt Samuel, 122
Chartists
    Riots, 296
Chelmsford, Lord, 316
Chelsea Hospital, 6,93,230
    Commissioner, vi,221,223,230
    Memorial [*see under*: PERSONALITIES: Girardot - Monument; Wright - Monument; SHIPS - *Birkenhead* - Monuments]
Children, 1,4,5,9,13,16,18,19,20,22,25,31,32,34,37,38,41,42,43,44,47,49, 50,51,53,55,56,60,65,70,71,74,75,79,83,85,88,92,98,108,125,131, 134,135,137,162,165,168,176,180,188,191,193,202,204,207,210, 211,212,213,214,216,219,226,229,230,240,246,249,252,253,254, 275,276,280,287,288,299
    [*see also under*: PERSONALITIES: Darkin, Miss Marian; Kelly, Master James; Kelly, Master Thomas; Nesbitt, Master Henry; Nesbitt, Master Richard Athol; Nesbitt, Master H; Zwyker, Miss]
Christian Knight, A (Hubert Handley), 276
Clanricarde, Lord, 231
Clare, Octavius Leigh- [*see*: Leigh-Clare, O]
Clarence, Duke of, 173
Clarke, Gen Sir Mansfield, 221
Cloete, Col, 13
Clyles, F, 290
Cocker, John R, 242,255,256,258
Coffin, Mr (Thomas Coffin's father), 225
Colenso, Dr, 306

Colley, Maj Gen Sir George Pomeroy-
    [*see*: Pomeroy-Colley, Maj Gen Sir George]
Compass, 107,115
Comprehensive history of England, 142
Connaught, Duke of, vii, illus - fp 132
Convicts, 172
Cook, John, 31,139
Cornhill Magazine, 7,190,197,199
Corry, Capt (later Rear Adml) Armor L, 123
Count Montalembert [*see*: Montalembert, Count]
Courts Martial, 10,291,292,308
    Birkenhead survivors, 58,59,104,105,106,109,108,115,149,198
        Judge-Advocate, 108,109,224
            [*see also*: Greetham, Sir G L]
        President, 106,107
            [*see also*: Prescott, Rear Adml H]
Cowieson, Inspector D, 238
Culhane, Dr F W S, 163
Culhane, Miss Kate, 163
Culhane, Dr Morgan, 56,163
Culhane, Rev Stephen, 162
Curiosities of war and military studies (Thomas Carter), 141
Currie, Maj Sir Walter, 315,317
Cyclopes, 110

D

Dalgety, Lt Col, 151
Daly, Mrs Charles (nee Roesch), 233,235
Darkin, Staff Sgt Alfred John, 249,251,254
Darkin, Catherine, 249
Darkin, Edward Charles, 259
Darkin, Drum Major John Robert, 203,248,249,250,254
Darkin, Robert Christopher, 249
Deathless story, A (A C Addison & W H Matthews), 244
De Beers Consolidated Mines, 236,237,241,261
De Lango, Hans [*see*: Lango, Hans de]
De St Pierre, Bernardin [*see*: St Pierre, Bernardin de]
De Villiers, Field Cornet, 27,52,255
Diamond Fields Advertiser, The, 261
Dillon, Mrs, 163
Divers, 117

INDEX

Dixon, Charles (*The wreck of the Birkenhead*), fp 30,35
Dobbie, Capt William Hugh, 122
Donohoe, WO Phil, 215
Donop, Cdr P B Van, 162
Douglas, 308
Doyle, Sir Francis Hastings, 6,31,191,270,272,277
   Loss of the Birkenhead, The, 270-274
Drackford, Joseph, 177
Drake, Sir Francis, 281
Drake, Harry, 288
Dreyer, Hans, 265
Drum, 31
Drummond, Henry, 64,87
Dryden, John, 124
Duchy of Lancaster
   Vice-Chancellor, vi,143
Duke of Cambridge [*see*: Cambridge, Duke of]
Duke of Clarence [*see*: Clarence, Duke of]
Duke of Connaught [*see*: Connaught, Duke of]
Duke of Marlborough [*see*: Marlborough, Duke of]
Duke of Northumberland [*see*: Northumberland, Duke of]
Duke of Ormond [*see*: Ormond, Duke of]
Duke of Sutherland [*see*: Sutherland, Duke of]
Duke of Wellington [*see*: Wellington, Duke of]
Duke of York [*see*: York, Duke of]
Dundas, Capt (later Adml J[ames] W[hitely] D[eans]), 122,225
Dutch (language), 317,318
Dutchmen [*see*: Boers]

E

Earl of Hardwicke [*see*: Hardwicke, Rt Hon the Earl]
Earl of Ossory [*see*: Ossory, Earl of]
Eden, Cdr Henry, 161
Edge, Capt W H, 165
Edgell, Cdre Harry E, 162
Edward VII (King of England 1901-1910), vii, illus - fp 2,95,186, 187,214
   [*see also*: Wales, Prince of]
Ellenborough, Lord, 83
Ellis, Gen, 147
Ellis, Mrs, 147
Emperor of France [*see*: Napoleon III]

Emperor of Japan [*see*: Japan, Emperor of]
Empress of France [*see*: Eugenie]
England, King of [*see*: Edward VII]
English, 73,76,129,180,192,194,202,212,228,245,258,283
Eton College, 10
Eugenie (Empress of France, consort to Napoleon III), 156
Europa, 124
Evans, James, 196
Examiner, The, 58
Express (Dublin newspaper), 72

F

Fairclough, Lt (later Capt), 12,13,60,244
Falkiner, Dr, 197
Farmers, 305
Faro, David, 255,illus - fp 258
Fearon, Col, 78
Fire drill, 9,10
Foggi, Prof Ferdinando, 126
Forbes, Maj D, 148
Fordyce Hope, Lt Col [*see*: Hope, Lt Col Fordyce]
Franks, Brig Gen, 96
Freeland, Lt Cdr John D, 162
French, 119,238

G

Gane, Maj W H, 211
Germans, 258
Gilly, [William Stephen] (*Narrative of the shipwrecks in the Royal Navy between 1793 and 1857*), 30,31,33
Girardot, Rev John Chaucourt, 196
Girardot, Mrs Mary, 196
Girls, 202
Gladstone, William Ewart, 229
Glascock, Capt W N, 123
Globe, 70
Glyn, Col, 315
Godlonton, R, 146
Gofton (family) (Eland Hall), 188
 [*see also*: Gofton-Salmond]

Gofton-Salmond, Robert, 185,188
Golden Fleece, 121
Goodchild, Dr John A, 6,277,279
   Birkenhead, The, 277-279
Goodliff, H, 209
Gordon, Lt, 128
Gordon, Capt Bertie, 77
Gordon, Sir Willoughby, 128
Goschen, Lt Col George, 190
Gould, Col, 305
Gower, Lady Elizabeth Levison - [*see*: Levison-Gower, Lady Elizabeth]
Grace Darling (Algernon Charles Swinburne), 2
Grant, Mr, 167
Grant, Capt [James Augustus], 305
Great Eastern Railway Company, 223
Greenwich Hospital, 291
Greetham, Sir G L, 105
Greville, Hon Sidney, 186
Grey, Sir George, 150,151
Griffiths, William, ix

H

Handley, Hubert
   A Christian Knight, 276
Hardinge, Viscount, vii, 83, illus - fp 300
Hardwicke, Rt Hon the Earl, 160,194,195
   Our naval position and policy, 160
Hare, Maj Gen, 66,143
Harries, E L, 262
Harris, Capt, 105
Harris, Col D, 238,239
Hartog, Mr, 238
Hartz (River), 234
Harvey, Mrs, 306
Harvey, Capt, 306
Havelock, Sir Henry, 88
   Biography of the Duke of Wellington, 88
Hayward, [Abraham] (*Selected essays*), 193
Hearn, Capt, 303
Heath, Cdr A J, 164
Hemy, C Napier, 35

Hemy, Thomas M, 35,80,202
Henderson, Capt, 105
Henry Castle & Sons, Messrs, 121
Herd, Richard Jeffery, 124
Herd, Robert, 124
Hill and valley (Catherine Strickland), 130
Hippopotamus, 306
Hodges, C J, 123
Home, John (character in *Douglas*), 308
Hope, Lt Col Fordyce, 128,136,302
Hope, Rear Adml Sir James, 162,228
Hope, Hon William, 31,137,139,140
Hopley, Mr Justice, 265,266,268,269
Horse Guards (administrative centre of Commander-in-Chief of British Army), 59,128,152
Horses, 13,18,21,27,51,54,55,129,134,136,151,153,158,167,168,178,180, 183,202,220,245,246,265,287,295,301,304,305,306,307,309,316, 317,318
Hoskyns, Dr, 251,252
Hospitals
   Haslar, 285
Hospitals Association
   Committee, 188
Hotham, Capt Sir Charles, 164
Hottentots, 128,144,307,315
Howe, Lord, 119,120
Howlden, H L, 251,252
Hutton, Capt Frederick, 123

I

Illustrated London News, 73,95,103
Ingleby, Lt Col, 37
Inglefield, Cdr Edward A, 163,164
Ingoldsby, Col, 302
Ingram, Capt, 112
Ingram, Lt Col, 96
Innes, Capt S T, 105
Irish, 73,129,163
Italie (farm), 234
Italy, King of [*see*: Victor Emmanuel III]

INDEX

J

Jackson, Lt Cdr G M, 176
Jackson, Sir James, 143,144,146
Jacobs, David, 268
Japan, Emperor of, viii
Japanese, 228
Jarvis, Col, 297
Jason, 121
Jenkins, Robert, 123
Johnson, Capt, 107
Johnstone, Capt W J H, 122
Jones Noytada, 264,267
Jones, Lt, 125
Jones, Cdre W, 160
Joslin, Flag Capt J, 228
Jove, 110,111
Jupiter, 111,121,124

K

'Kaffirs', 12,128,211,240
Kaye, Mrs, 254,260
Kaye, Erick Malcolm, 260
Kelly, Vet Sgn, 94
Kelly, Thomas, 187
Kelpweed, 20,21,26,37,39,49,52,54,74,176,191,193,200, 212,254,300
King ... [*see under* name of King; eg Edward VII (King of England)/
  name of country; eg Italy, King of]
Kingsley,-
  Life and letters, 193
Kipling, Rudyard, 4,280
Klyne River (farm), 49
Knight, Austin, 239
Kreli (African chief), 177
Kuper, Adml, 228
Kyanston, Capt A, 164

L

Laforey, Capt Francis, 120
Laird, Messrs, 110,111,114

Lango, Hans de, 205
Lanyon, Sir Owen, 316
Lascars, 309,313
Lawrence, Maj, 317
Leigh-Clare, Octavius, vi,143
Levison-Gower, Lady Elizabeth [*see*: Westminster, Marchioness of]
L'Huillier, 120
Life and letters (Kingsley, Charles), 193
Life belt, 219
Life of General Sir William Napier, KCB (H A Bruce), 86,141
Livingstone, Dr David, 170
Lloyd's (underwriters), 116

LOCATIONS
  Aberdeeshire
    Deputy Lieutenant, 126
    Justice of the Peace, 126
  Africa, 257 [*see also*: South Africa]
    Central, 305
    East coast, 120,170
    West coast, 120,121,144,160,162,170
  Albany [*see*: Lower Albany]
  Alexandria, 121
  Algoa Bay, 13,14,24,60,68,129,144,158,179,224,257
  Aliwal North, 316
  Amatola (Mtns), 197,303
  America, 231
  Antigua, 92
  Arctic seas, 163
  Armagh, 203,204,239
  Ascension Island, 102,167,224,318
  Atlantic Ocean, 92,257
  Australia, 124,125,129,231
    Colonies, 126
      [*see also*: specific locations; eg Van Diemen's Land]
  Azof (Sea), 289
  Balaclava, 289
    [*see also*: BATTLES, CAMPAIGNS, WARS - Crimean War]
    Harbour, 289
    Hospital, 289
  Baltic, 123,176,209,225,227,289,292
    [*see also*: BATTLES, CAMPAIGNS, WARS - Crimean War]

INDEX

Balmoral, 307
Banbury, 187,218
Bangalore, 196
Barkly East, 243
Barkly West, 242
Bashee (River), 220
Basutoland, 214,242
  Beira, 304
  Governor & Administrator, 317
    [*see also*: Clarke, Gen Sir Mansfield]
Bath, 277
Bathurst, 315
Bay of Biscay, 13,218
Beaconsfield, 236,237,238,239,261,262,268
  Mayor, 238,239 [*see also*: Blackbeard, Capt C A]
  Police, 237,262,264,267,269
Bechuanaland, 231
Beckingham, 187,248,250
  Church, 250
  Clergy, 251
  Vicar, 249,251 [*see also*: Round, Rev C R]
Bellisle (Straits), 92
Benin, 171
Berlin, 193
Bermuda, 92,122,169,172
Birkenhead, 110,123
Birmingham, 258,296
Blackguard Chine, 172
Black Sea, 150,209,214
Bloemfontein, 233
Bloemhof, 234
Bolika Heights, 317
Bordighiera, 277
Boshof, 267
Boston (Lincolnshire), 185,209
Bot (River), 184
Bridlington-on-Sea
  Borough Engineer, 174
Brighton, ix
Bristol, 186,187,223
British Kaffraria [*see*: Kaffraria]
Brixton, 172

Brockhurst, 186,226
Buckinghamshire, 218
Buckland, 207
Buffalo (River), 14,158,159,179,197,257,316
Bultfontein, 237,261,263
   Mine, 236,239,241,261,263,265
     Mining Board, 238
        Searching Department, 240
   United Mine, 238
Caiffa, 121
Calcutta, 95,96
   Fort William, 305
Caledon, 225,255
   Civil Commissioner, 27,54, [see also: Mackay, Mr]
   Postmaster
     Daughters, 224
Caledon (River), 317
Canada, 92,177,224 [see also: specific locations; eg Quebec]
Canton, 289
Cape Agulhas, 213,218,257
   Lighthouse, 29,50,204,257
   Reefs, 257
Cape Colony [see: Cape of Good Hope]
Cape Danger, 80
Cape Finisterre,124
Cape Hangklip, 14,43
Cape Horn, 171
Cape Mudge, 50
Cape of Good Hope, v,viii,12,13,45,68,70,77,78,82,84,94,108,112,115,
     116,117,119,120,122,123,124,128,129,147,149,150,151,167,170,
     184,192,214,217,220,224,242,244,245,249,254,256,257,259,260,
     276,286,299,304, 305,307,313,314,315,316,317
   [see also: specific locations; eg Cape Town, Simon's Bay]
   Auditor-General, 31,139 [see also: Hope, Hon William]
   Chief Justice, 269
   Coast, 218,306
   Commander-in-Chief, 23,59,81,143,303
     [see also: Cathcart, Maj Gen the Hon George; Jackson, Sir James;
     Maitland, Maj Gen Sir Peregrine; Smith, Maj Gen Sir Harry]
   Commissioner for Frontier Affairs, 144
     [see also under: PERSONALITIES: Wright]
   Customs, 117,139

Eastern Province, 240
Frontier
   Eastern frontier, 2,12,133,144,145,198,199,218,232,301,314
      Botha's Hill, 133,146
      Cathcart's Hill, 177
      Driver's Bush, 303
      Eilands Post, 144,147
      Fort Beaufort, 143,144,145,302,308
      Fort Brown, 302
      Fort Fordyce, 148
      Keis Kama Hoek, 136,198
      Old Fort, 177
   Government, 244,317
   Governor, 23,81,82,118,143,269,303
      [*see also*: Cathcart, Maj Gen the Hon George; Grey, Sir George; Jackson, Sir James; Loch, Lord; Smith, Maj Gen Sir Harry]
   Legislative Council, 93,146
   Lighthouse Service, 256,258
   Naval Commander, 14 [*see also*: Wyvill, Cdre Christoper]
   Observatory
      Assistant Astronomer, 101 [*see also*: Mann, Mr]
   Parliament, 317
   Signal station, 256
   Supreme Court, 268
   Tribes, 304,315
Cape Point, 50,102
Cape Town, 13,22,28,48,57,58,48,57,58,168,176,178,213,230,235,258, 260,301,305,313,314,316,318
   Barracks, 25
   Commandant, 37 [*see also*: Ingleby, Lt Col]
   General Post Office (GPO), 124
   Memorial to *Birkenhead*, 258
   Navy League, 60,259
      Secretary, 60,245 [*see also*: Penny, Herbert]
   Port Book, 60
   Table Mountain, 318
      Blue Berg, 318
      Devil's Peak, 318
      Lion's Rump, 318
Cardiff
   Lansdowne Road School, 10
Ceylon, 305

Channel, 92
  Islands, 112
Chatham, 119,127,163,171,297
  Barracks, 297
  Dockyard, 110
    Superintendent, 122 [*see also*: Wyvill, Cdre Christoper]
Cheltenham
  Orphan School, 93
Chichester, 226
China, 166
China Seas, 114,195
Chislehurst
  Postmaster, 174
Continent [*see*: Europe]
Cork, 12,60,122,128,197,213,245,288
  Cove, 299
  Harbour, 179
Crimea, 144,147,151,225
  [*see also under*: BATTLES, CAMPAIGNS, WARS - Crimean War]
Damaraland, 315
Danger Point, 15,24,26,37,39,40,47,48,49,52,60,65,70,101,114,117,123, 204,210,213,224,232,255,256,257,260
  Lighthouse, illus - fp 254,255,illus - 255,illus - fp 256,257,260
    Keeper, 242,255,256 [*see also*: Cocker, John R]
    Memorial tablet to *Birkenhead*, 258
Diamond Fields [*see under*: Kimberley]
Dinapore, 127
Dorsetshire, 187,286,290
Dover, 12,120,124
Drakensberg (Mtns), 305
Drumsill, 203
Dublin, 72,73,128,235,245
Duitospan [*see*: Beaconsfield]
Dundas (bridge), 146
Dundruin Bay, 112
Dungannon, 213,215
  Castle Hill, 215
Durban, 22,48,57,232,235,244,299,306,316
  Chief Magistrate, 204 [*see also under*: PERSONALITIES: Lucas]
  Harbour, 316
  Dyer Islands, 25,26,27,28
Eastbourne, 173

INDEX

East Caicos, 168
East Ham
  Shaftsbury Road School, 9
East Indies, 217
East London, 14,218,257,306,316
  East London East, 316
Eastville, 223
Edinburgh, 31,139,140
  St Giles Cathedal
    Memorial
      [*see*: SHIPS - *Birkenhead*; Monuments - 74th Regiment]
Eilands (Mtns), 144
England, 8,41,58,59,60,82,92,112,115,124,127,159,150,151,158,167,
    168,169,170,175,176,177,187,189,190,191,198,199,204,218,223,
    224,227,228,231,251,252,285,288,289,295, 299,301,318
  [*see also*: specific locations; eg Sheffield]
  Public schools, 192 [*see also*: individual schools; eg Rugby]
English Channel [*see*: Channel]
Europe, 190,235
Eydon, 218,296
Eyrie (Lake) [*see*: Lake Eyrie]
False Bay, 14
Ficksburg, 317
Fish Bay, 224,225
Fish (River), 302,303
Fishbourne, 166
Forest Gate, 249
Fort Peddie, 306
  Commandant, 306
Fort Hare, 249,254
France, 119
Fratton, 229
Gaikaland, 315
Gainsborough, 187
Galekaland, 315
Germany, 79,127,190,193
Gibraltar, 177
Glasgow
  School, 9
Gort (County Galway), 231
Gosport, 186,226
Grahamstown, 145,146,301,302,304,315

Commandant, 302 [*see also*: Ingoldsby, Col]
Drostdy Ground, 146
Gravesend, 297
Great Britain, 76,81,163,191
  [*see also*: specific locations; eg England, Scotland]
  Government, 77,81,87,110,153,197,234,292,304
    Cabinet, 81,91
      Ministers, 82,83
        Colonial Secretary, 81,258
          [*see also*: Chamberlain, Joseph; Grey, Lord; Parkington, Sir J S]
        Foreign Secretary, 81 [*see also*: Malmsbury, Lord]
        Home Secretary, 86 [*see also*: Bruce, H A]
        Paymaster General, 199
        Secretary-at-War, 83,84,86,88,98,132,136,148
          [*see also*: Drummond, Henry]
        Secretary for War, 81 [*see also* : Beresford, Maj William]
        Secretary of State for the Colonies, 144
      Treasury, 118
      War Office, vi,84,86,88,132,199,304,317
Greenhithe, 107
Green Point, 102,236
  Location, 262,264,265
    Headman, 267 [*see also*: Jones Notyoda]
Greytown, 307
Griqualand West, 316
Guadaloupe, 92
Guildford, 253
Halifax, 92,112,167,175
Hampshire, 186,222
Hastings, 174
  Lloyd's Bank, 174
  Marine Parade
    Government House, 173,174
  Wesleyan Church, 174
Higher Broughton, 256
Hout Bay, 318
Howison's Poort, 146
Hucknall Torkard, 245
Hydra Bay, 257
India, 81,96,127,129,220,251,299,305,309
  [*see also*: specific locations; eg Lucknow]
Indian Ocean, 125,257,314

Ipswich, 296
  Cathedral, 296
    Dean, 296
Ireland, vii,72,112,128,129,214,222,231,232,233,235,239
  [*see also*: specific locations; eg Cork]
  Famine, 163
Isle de Bourbon, 314
Isle de France [*see*: Mauritius]
Isle of Wight, 166,172 [*see also*: individual locations; ie Fishbourne]
Italy, 126,277 [*see also*: specific locations; eg Pisa]
Jamaica, 68,177
  Port Royal, 168
Jamestown, 316
Japan, 289
Jellalabad, 23
Kaffraria, 220,308
Kalk Bay, 314
Kamptee, 127
Katberg, 308
Kei (Road), 316,318
Kildare, 229
Kimberley, 237,265,266,269,316
  Diamond fields, 240,261
    Kimberley Mine, 240
  Jail, 265
Kings County, 214
King Williams Town, 82,134,246,257,305,307,308
Knaresborough, 249
Korannaland, 315
Kowie (River), 315
Kronstadt, 227
  Forts, 227
  Hang's Head, 228
Kwamagwasa, 316
Labrador, 92
Ladysmith, 204,205
Lake Eyrie, 78
Lambeth, 186
Landport, 177
Leeds, 187,229,249,254
Leith, 122
Lincoln

County Hospital, 250
Lincolnshire, 185
Lisbon, 112, 120
Liverpool, 95,111,112,164,165
London, 39,67,68,70,159,188,198,202,235,249,254,297
   St Katherine's Docks, 124
   Waterloo Bridge, 297
Long Green Key Island, 168
Lower Albany, 302
Lucknow, 96 [see also under: BATTLES, CAMPAIGNS, WARS]
Lydenburg, 240
   Goldfields
      Diggers, 240
Madagascar, 235,314
   St Augustine's Bay, ix
Madeira, 13,60,129,218,299,318
Madras, 196
   Fort St George, 216
Mafeteng, 317
Mahebourg (Indian Ocean), 314
Malacca, 125
   Straits, 166
Malta, 149,172,173,210
   General Officer Commanding (GOC), 147 [see also: Ellis, Gen]
   Military Secretary, 147 [see also: Pakenham, Col]
Manchester, 256
Marseilles, 235
Mauritius, 305,314,315
   Flat Island
      Lighthouses, 314
   Port Louis
      Cannonier's Point (signal station), 314
         Lighthouse, 314
      Champ de Mars (parade ground), 314,315
      Harbour, 314
      Pample Moose, 314
   Pieter Botte [see: Thumb Mountain]
   Pouce (mtn range), 314
   Thumb Mountain, 314
Mazoe (Rhodesia)
   Refugees, 244
Mediterranean, 120,122,123,125,162,194,280

Medway, 297
Mersey, 111
Middleton Cheney, 187,218
Mooi (River), 305
Molopo, 234
Monaghan, 204
Monte Video, 164
Mosita, 231,234
Mozambique
  Channel, 305
Mussell Bay, 301
Nagpore, 127
Namaqualand, 315
Natal, 136,150,204,205,240,257
  [*see also*: specific locations; eg Pietermaritzburg]
  Bishop,306 [*see also*: Colenso, Dr]
  Chief Constable, 306
  Coast, 307
  Krantz Kop, 307
  Police, 306
Needles, 172
Negro Point, 310
Newfoundland, 119
Newlands, 314
Nore (River)
  Mouse Lighthouse, 166
North America (British) [*see*: Canada]
Northamptonshire, 218,296
North Shields, 121
Nottinghamshire, 196,245,245,248
Nottingham Post, 307
Nourse (River), 309,313
Orange (River), 316
Orange Free State, 232,316,317
Osborne, 35,93,156,202
Oudtshoorn, 318
Oxfordshire, 218
Paris, 203,235
Panmure [*see*: East London - East London East]
Parkhurst
  Barracks, 172
  Prison, 172

Parsonstown, 214
Penhock, 316
Penkridge, 186,204
Pevensey, 173
  Pevensey Sluice, 174
    Mission Hall, 174
Pisa, 121
Pietermaritzburg, 136,305,307
  Fort Napier, 305,306
Plymouth, 12,82,91,94,112,161
Pokwani, 267
Port Alfred, 315
Port D'Urban [see: Durban]
Port Elizabeth, 14,210,218,242,244,257,301,302
Port Nolloth, 309,315
Portsmouth, 10,90,91,92,95,104,113,122,166,177,186,188,207,208,229, 289,299,318
  Commander-in-Chief, 155,286 [see also: Seymour, Adml Sir George]
  Dockyard, 225
  Harbour, 228
  Royal Naval College, 90
  Workhouse
    Royal Infirmary, 188
Portugal, 85 [see also: specific locations; ie Lisbon]
  Coast, 123
Prince Albert (district of Cape Province), 318
Prince Edward's Island, 92
Prussia, 199
Pudimoe, 234
Quebec, 92,167
Queenstown (Ireland), 299
Queenstown (South Africa), 245,257,316,318
  Whittlesea district, 245
Quillimane, 170
Robben Island, 13,210
  Lighthouse
    Keeper, 258 [see also: Cocker, John R]
Romford, 222
Rouxville, 317
Saint [see: St...]
Saldhana Bay, 257
Scotland, 112,130

INDEX

  [*see also*: specific locations; eg Edinburgh]
  Coast, 68
Sea of Azof [*see*: Azof (Sea)]
Sea Point, 318
Sheerness, 91,121,297
Sheffield, 251
  Cutlers Hall, 8
  Lord Mayor, 8,9
Sierra Leone, 13,125,129,218,245
Simon's Bay, 13,14,22,24,28,29,37,38,41,43,45,47,48,50,56,57,60,67,
    70,102,115,116,124,129,158,159,169,171,176,179,188,196,207,
    210,214,218,219,220,223,227, 230,241,245,246,260,287,288,301
  Naval hospital, 28,47
Simons Town, 244,309,310
  Naval Commander, 309
Solent, 10
South Africa, v,vi,115,144,147,150,177,205,210,217,222,231,235,236,
    237,239,245,256,259,260,261,299,305,304,309
  [*see also*: specific regions; eg Cape of Good Hope]
  1820 settlers, 315
  Coast, 255
Southampton, 197,201
Southsea
  Common, 225,228
Southwell
  Bishop, 251,252 [*see also*: Hoskyns, Dr]
Spithead, 102,113,153,218,299
Springbokfontein, 315
  Copper mines, 315
    Miners, 315
Staffordshire, 186,204
Stanford, 255
Stanford Bay [*see*: Stanford Cove]
Stanford Cove, 26,28,41,48,49,183,206,256,301
St Helena, 13,102,129,218,232,245,299,318
St Ives, 186,222
St Lucia, 92
St Paul's Isle, 125
Stoughton
  Barracks, 253
Streatham, 188
Sudbury, 216,217

Suez Canal, 235
Suffolk, 216
Syria
  Coast, 121,225
Table Bay, 78,102,116,305,318
  Harbour, 315
Taungs, 234
Tembuland, 242,315
Thaba Bosigo, 233
Toronto, 9
Transvaal
  Goldfields, 240 [*see also under*: Lydenburg]
    Diggers, 240
  Government, 240
Tricomalee, 102
Tugela (River), 307,306
  Lower Tugela, 306
Turk's Island, 169
Tyrone, 202,213
Umvolosi (River), 316
Umvoti (River), 307
United Kingdom, v [*see also*: specific locations; eg England]
United States [*see*: America]
Vaal (River), 316
Vryburg, 230
Walfisch Bay, 309
Walker's Bay, 41
Waterkloof (Mtns), 144
Weedon, 218
  Barracks, 296
Wepener, 317
West Indies, 168,173,177 [*see also*: specific locations; eg Jamaica]
Westminster
  Office of Works
    Surveyor's Department, 174
Wiltshire, 203
Windsor
  Castle, 307
Wolverhampton, 296
Woolwich, 91,112,119,121,123,161,164,167,175
Wynberg, 314
Winchester, 249

INDEX

Yana Masibe (camp), 235
Zambezi, 170
Zanzibar, 170,305
Zululand, 306,315

Loch, Capt, 105
Loch, Lord, 118
Lombardi
    Duke of Wellington (portrait), fp 96
London Gazette, 156
Longford, Lord [*see*: Pakenham, Col]
Lord Aylmer [*see*:Aylmer, Lord]
Lord Brougham [*see*: Brougham, Lord]
Lord Chelmsford [*see*: Chelmsford, Lord]
Lord Clanricarde [*see*: Clanricarde, Lord]
Lord Ellenborough [*see*: Ellenborough, Lord]
Lord Longford [*see*: Longford, Lord]
Lord Malmsbury [*see*: Malmsbury, Lord]
Lord Pitmedon [*see*: Pitmedon, Lord]
Lord Portman [*see*: Portman, Lord]
Lord Wolseley [*see*: Wolseley, Field Marshal Lord]
Loss of the Birkenhead (Sir Francis Hastings Doyle), 270-274
Lucas, Rt Hon Edward, 204
Lyster, Capt Henry, 170,171
Lushington, Capt Stephen, 160

M

Macdonnell, Capt, 95
MacGregor, Col, 78
Mackay, Mr, 27,49,52,54
Mackenzie, Lt Col, 221
Mackie, Lt Col, 203,204,221,223,248,249,251,252,253,254
Mackintosh (life belt), 53
Mackintosh, David, 265
Macomo (African chief), 128
Madge, William Robert, 107
Magistrates, 24
Magnetic observations (Dr Scoresby), 115
Malahleve, John, 236,262,266
Mail (Dublin newspaper), 72
Maitland, Maj Gen Sir Peregrine, 143

Malmsbury, Lord, 81
Mann, Gen, 101
Mann, Mr, 101
Mansfield, Cdr, 208
Mansfield, Lt, 282,283,284,285
Marchioness of Westminster [*see*: Westminster, Marchioness of]
Mariners, 172
    [*see also*: UNITS AND FORMATIONS - Great Britain - Navy - Seamen]
Marlborough, Duke of, 88
Martin, Capt G B, 104
Mason, Cdr Thomas, 161
Masupho (Basuto chief), 233,317 [referred to as Masupha on this page]
Matson, Capt, 105
Matthews, Joseph, 166
Matthews, Richard, 166
Matthews, W H
    A deathless story (jt author), v,174
Maurice, Maj Gen, 7,190,191,197,272
Mauser Bradshaw, Master Cdr [*see*: Bradshaw, Master Cdr Mauser]
Maxe, Capt A F, 164
Medals of the British Army and how they were won (Thomas Carter), 141
Mehemet Ali, 121
Memorials [*see*: Monuments]
Mends, Capt R W, 164
Metford, Mrs, 60
Miles, Sgt W E, 260
Military and Naval Exhibition (1890-1891), 35,80,202
Milne, Capt David, 178
Milne, W J, 178
Milward, Cdr Anthony W, 160
Mining Board, 238
    Sanitary Constable, 238 [*see also under*: PERSONALITIES: McClusky]
Minos, 124
Mongale, Michael, 236,237,261,262,263,264,265,266,267,268,269
    Trial for murder of William McClusky, 265-269
Monkey, ix
Montalembert, Count
    The political future of England, 192
Monuments [*see under*: SHIPS - Birkenhead; LOCATIONS - Edinburgh -
    St Giles Cathedral/Danger Point - Lighthouse - Memorial tablet;
    PERSONALITIES - Darkin; Girardot; Wright]
Moodie, Capt, 220

INDEX

Moody, Capt, 302
Moore, Lt Col Willoughby, 94
Morning Herald, The, 69,70,79
Mosheth (Basuto chief), 220,303,304
Mosquitos, 313
Murphy, Mrs Bridget [*see*: Cave, Mrs Bridget]

N

Napier, Sir Charles, 89,99,225
Napier, Lt Gen Sir William, vii,82,83,85,86,87,88,89,90,93,99,147,155
    Battles and sieges of the Peninsular War, 85
Napoleon III (Emperor of France 1852-1870), 156
Narrative of a Non-Commissioned Officer, 20
Narrative of the shipwrecks in the Royal Navy between 1793 and 1857
    (William Stephen Gilly), 30,31
National Zeitung, 193
Naval and Fisheries Exhibition (1905), 35
Naval and Military Gazette, 75,77
Navy and Army Illustrated, 35
Neilly, M, 119,120
Nelson, Adml Lord Horatio, 160
Nesbitt, Capt/Quartermaster, 13,66,67,241
Nesbitt, Capt C W, 244
Nesbitt, Capt N, 244
Nesbitt, Ralph, 244-245
Nesbitt, Lt W W, 244
Newspapers [*see*: Press]
New Testament, 121
    Acts, 121
Nightingale, Mr, 245
Northumberland, Duke of, 81
Nourse, Col, 223

O

O'Mahoney, Dr, 162
O'Neill, Frederick George, 212
O'Reilly, Lt, 101,102
On the strength of nations (Andrew Bisset), 194
Orient Steamship line, 177
Ormond, Duke of, 130

Orphans, 93
Ossory, Earl, 130
Our naval position and policy (Rt Hon the Earl of Hardwicke), 160,194
Owen, J, 286
Oxford University
　Professor of Poetry, 270 [*see also*: Doyle, Sir Francis Hastings]

P

Pakenham, Col, 147
Palmer, Mr, 232
Palmerston, Lord, 83
Parkingham, Sir J S, 81
Parkinson, George, 249
Parkinson, Rose, 249,252
Parliament, 68,97,90,203
　House of Commons, 81,83,109,114,133
　　Members, 83
　House of Lords, 81,83,97,98
Patton, Lt Col, 133
Paul (Apostle), 121
Paul (character in French romance)
　Grave, 314
Paul et Virginie (Bernardin de St Pierre), 314
Penny, Herbert, 60,245,259
Percival, Lt Col J M, 218

PERSONALITIES (CREW/PASSENGERS OF *BIRKENHEAD*)
Key: † fatality; * survivor
Note: Where neither symbol is attached to an individual, this denotes:
– A cross reference to another name.
– Original member of crew not on board at time of wreck.

　* Allan, Pte P, 65
　* Ambrose, Pte Edward, 64
　† Anderson, Pte George, 63
　† Anderson, Pte John, 63
　* Andrews, Sgt (later Staff Sgt Maj) David, 31,65,134
　* Archbold, John Thomas, 14,17,20,21,33,36,52,66,105,109,118,139,
　　161,164,186,187,205,206,207,226,227
　† Archer, Pte Thomas, 62
　† Armstrong, Pte J, 62

INDEX

* Ashbolt, Stoker John, 65,104,108
* Auther, Pte A, 65
* Babb, Pte W, 65
† Bank, Pte William de, 63
* Barber, Benjamin, 46,65,66,106,164,illus - fp 164
† Bark, Pte Abraham, 62
† Barrett, Pte J, 62
† Barton, Pte William, 63
† Baxter, Pte Archibald, 63
† Bellingham, Pte T, 62
† Bennie, Pte John, 63
† Bernard, Pte James, 63
* Bewhill, AB Henry, 66,108
† Biggam, Pte James, 63
† Birmingham, Pte H, 63
† Birt, Pte Joseph, 64
† Blackie, Pte Robert, 63
* Bond, Cornet (later Capt Bond-Shelton), vii,5,6,18,20,21,26,27,32,33, 35,36,52,53,54,55,60,63,65,80,134,139,183,186,189,197,201,202, illus - fp 202,203,214,220,244,247,254
  Sketch of *Birkenhead*, illus - fp 80,202,250
Bond-Shelton, Capt [*see*: Bond, Cornet]
† Booth, Lt A H, 12,19,27,60,63,94,167,180
† Boswell, Pte W, 62
* Bowen, Staff Sgn (later Sgn Gen) Dr John, 21,22,42,43,45,60,90, 108,133,134,160,176,244,246, illus - fp 176,177,178,181,295
  Photograph, 178
* Bowen, AB John, 65,104
* Boyce, Pte William, 64
* Boyden, Pte (later Col Sgt) John, 65,253,254
† Boylan, Ensign, 12,62,94,200,204,253,254
* Brachley, Pte G, 65
† Bradley, Pte George, 62
† Brennan, Pte Daniel, 63
† Brennan, Pte William, 63
† Brian, Pte James, 64
* Bridges, Pte G, 65
† Brodie, William, 14,20,29,44,51,53,56,64,159,161,206,246,287
† Bromley, Pte Joseph, 62
† Brookland, Pte James, 63
† Brown, Pte James, 63
† Brown, Pte William, 62

† Bruce, Pte, 63
† Bryan, Pte E, 63
† Bryan, Pte John, 62
† Bryan, Pte Patrick, 62
† Bryan, Pte William, 62
† Buckingham, Pte James, 64
† Buckley, Pte Daniel, 63
† Buckley, Pte W, 63
† Burke, Pte H, 62
* Burlow, Pte William, 64
* Bush, Pte W, 64
* Bushe, Pte William, 64
† Butler, Pte John, 63,247
† Butler, Cpl (later Sgt) William, 64,94,187,220,244,247,304
* Butler, Pte W, 65
† Byrne, Pte J, 62
† Byrne, Pte John, 63
† Caffrey, Pte Michael, 63
† Callaghan, Pte James, 63
* Carey, Pte David, 65
† Carrigan, Pte Patrick, 62
† Carrington, Pte M, 63
* Cash, Pte Thomas, 64
† Cateneech, Pte John, 63
† Caulfield, Pte Dennis, 62
† Cavanagh, Pte James, 64
† Cave, Pte Thomas, 63,188
† Cellars, Pte M, 63
* Chadwick, Pte Thomas, 64
† Chapman, Pte William, 63
* Chase, Stoker William, 66
* Cheeseman, AB H, 66
† Clark, Pte William, 64
* Clark, Pte William, 64
† Clay, Pte William, 62
† Clements, Pte John, 63
† Clifford, Pte Alfred, 62
† Clince, Pte M, 63
* Coa, Pte Thomas, 64
† Coalborn, Pte, 62
† Cocker, Pte G, 63
† Coe, Pte James, 62

INDEX

* Coffin (Ord Smn, later Qmr), Thomas, 15,66,105,186, illus - fp 224,225
† Coleman, Pte Richard, 62
† Collins, Pte Matthew, 63
† Connel, Pte William, 63
† Cooney, Pte Patrick, 63
* Cooper, Pte John, 56,66,208
* Cordey, Pte J, 65
† Cornell, Pte Charles, 62
† Cosgrove, Pte John, 63
† Costello, Pte J, 63
* Cougham, Pte John, 65
† Cousin, Pte David, 63
† Cousins, Cpl Benjamin, 63,94
† Cowan, Pte John, 63
† Cragg, Pte J, 63
* Croker, AB E, 66
† Croker, Pte John, 62
* Crosser, AB Edward, 66
* Culhane, Dr William, 14,22,23,28,46,47,48,51,57,58,59,65,74,75, 105,108,109,149,161,162, illus - fp 162,163,198,301
† Cull, Pte H, 62
† Cummins, Pte B, 63
* Cunnynham, Pte P, 65
† Curtis, Cpl Francis, 63
† Daley, Pte Daniel, 64
* Daley, AB Thomas, 65,105,187
* Daly, Charles, 187,229
* Daniels, Pte Thomas, 66
* Darkin, Mrs, 65,248,260
* Darkin, Miss Marian, 248, illus - fp 248,249,250,252,254,260
   Memorial tablet, 250-251
† Darsey, Pte George, 63
† Davis, Jeremiah O D, 14,15,50,64,159
† Dawson, Pte Charles, 63
† Day, Pte William, 62
De Bank, Pte William [see: Bank, Pte William de]
† Deegan, Pte Hugh, 63
† Deeley, Mr, 64
† Delaney, Pte James, 64
† Demmack, Pte W, 63
† Dews, Pte Thomas, 63

† Dickson, Pte Hugh, 62
* Dobson, J, 66,205
† Dockery, Pte M, 63
* Dodd, Pte J, 65,220,247,304
* Dolan, Pte Robert, 64
† Donald, Pte William, 63
† Donaldson, Pte David, 63
† Donnel, Pte William, 62
* Dopson, Pte W, 65
* Double, Pte Henry, 64
† Doyle, Pte Patrick, 63
* Drackford, Smn (later Ldng Smn) Thomas, 66,167,
    illus - fp 174,175,176,177
* Drake, Col Sgt John, 17,30,56,66,105,108,135,137,186,189,207,208,
    illus - fp 208,214, illus - fp 282,284,285,286,287,
    289,290,292,293,294,295
* Drew, Stoker Thomas, 65
† Drury, Pte James, 64
† Dudley, Pte J, 63
* Dunn, AB Thomas, 65,104,108
† Durkin, Pte J, 63
* Dyke, A B John, 66
† Elliot, Pte Eli, 63
† England, Pte J, 63
† Englison, Pte I, 62
† Evans, Pte James, 64
† Feeley, Pte Hugh, 63
* Ferguson, Pte C, 64
† Field, Pte J, 63
† Finn, Pte R, 62
* Fitzpatrick, Pte James, 64
† Fitzpatrick, Pte Matthew, 63
† Fitzgerald, Pte T, 63
† Flanagaan, Pte Patrick, 63
† Flanagan, Pte P, 63
† Flanley, Pte T, 63
† Fletcher, Pte William, 62
* Flynn, Pte P, 65
† Flynn, Pte William, 63
† Flynn, Pte W, 63
* Forbes, AB Thomas, 66
† Forbes, Pte William, 62

INDEX   355

† Ford, Pte Hugh, 64
† Foster, Pte William, 64
† Freeman, Pte O, 63
† French, Pte Michael, 63
Freshfield, Mr, 13,41,45,60,115,149,150,158,159,287
† Frost, Pte Thomas, 63
† Gaffey, Pte Patrick, 64
* Gale, Boy 1st Class William, 66
* Gardner, Stoker Edward, 66
† Gavin, Pte Malachi, 63
† Gavin, Pte Michael, 63
† Gibson, Pte James, 63
† Gildea, Pte James, 64
† Giles, Pte L, 63
† Gilham, Pte George, 63
* Ginn, Pte Francis, 65,187
* Girardot, Lt (later Col) J F, 12,18,21,26,30,31,37,39,51,54,60,64,65, 79,83,84,85,87,89,90,99,147,163,180,183,186,187,191,196, illus- fp 196,198,199,200,204,205,206,213,218,272
    Monument, 201
* Goldin, Pte James, 64
† Goman, Pte D R, 63
† Gowan, Pte Charles, 63
† Grady, Pte John, 62
† Graham, Pte J H, 63
† Grant, Pte John, 63
† Grant, Pte Joseph, 64
† Green, Pte J, 62
† Greenleaf, Pte John, 62
† Grimshaw, Pte A, 63
† Hackenley, Pte Francis, 64
† Haggan, Pte Patrick, 64
† Haggan, Pte Stephen, 64
* Haggard, Pte J, 65
† Haher, Pte John, 63
* Halfpenny, Pte William, 64
* Haines, AB John, 14,65
† Hall, Pte William, 63
† Hamilton, Pte Arthur, 63
† Hamilton, Pte Peter, 64
† Handley, Pte James, 62
* Handrain, Leading Stoker, 66

† Hanley, Pte Patrick, 63
* Hanlon, Pte J, 65
† Hannen, Pte John, 63
† Hare, C W, 14,21,64
* Harold, Sgt, 64
† Harpey, Pte John, 64
† Harris, Pte Joseph, 62
* Harris, AB Samuel, 66
* Harris, AB Thomas, 66
† Harris, Boatswain T, 64
† Harrison, Cpl Joseph, 63,94
† Harrison, Pte Thomas, 63
† Hart, Pte F, 63
* Hartey, Pte M, 65
* Hartle, Pte R, 65
† Hayward, Pte Henry, 64
† Hayward, Pte S, 63
† Hendry, Pte Alexander, 63
* Herin, Pte John, 64
* Herrick, Pte John, 64
† Hicks, Sgt William, 63,94
* Higgins, Pte L, 65
* Hire, Mr G W S, 21,45,46,47,56,65
* Hobdy, Pte J, 65
* Holden, Pte J, 65
† Holmes, Pte H, 63
* Hornett, Pte J, 65
* Hoskins, Stoker Edward, 66
† Houchin, Pte Robert, 63
† Houghton, Pte J, 63
† Howard, Pte John, 62
* Howard, J R, 66
† Hudson, Pte Joseph, 62
* Hudson, Mrs, 65
* Hunt, Pte R, 65
† Hunter, Pte David, 63
† Hurley, Pte Michael, 63
† Hussey, Pte Patrick, 64
† Hutchings, Pte G, 62
* Irvin, Pte John, 64
† Jacobs, Pte Henry, 62
† Jacobs, Pte Simon, 63

INDEX

† Jays, Pte Thomas, 64
* Jeffery, James (Paymaster/Purser's Steward), 26,52,66,149,150,159, 188,189,214,287,289,294
* Johnson, Pte James, 64
† Johnston, Pte Samuel, 63
† Justice, Pte George, 64
† Keane, Pte Henry, 62
* Kearns, Pte Thomas, 66
† Kearns, Pte William, 63
* Keath, Pte J, 65
* Keating, Pte Adam, 64
† Kelcher, Pte Michael, 63
† Kelcher, Pte T, 63
* Kelly, Stoker George, 66
† Kelly, Pte J (12th Regt), 63
† Kelly, Pte J (43rd Light Infantry Regt), 63
† Kelly, Pte M, 62
* Kelly, Mrs, 229,230
* Kelly, Master Thomas, 229,230,illus - fp 230
† Kelly, Pte Patrick, 64
† Kelly, Pte Timothy, 63,187,229
† Kelly, Pte William, 63
† Kemp, Pte George, 64
* Kilkeary, Sgt Bernard, 64,18,134,135,150,186,199,213,214, illus - fp 214,215
* King, Stoker John, 56,65
* Kirkford, Pte D, 64
† Kirkwood, Pte James, 63
† Kitching, Pte William, 62
† Kitchingham, Mr, 46,64,106
* Kitson, Pte J, 65
† Knight, Pte George, 62
* Lacey, James, 66,206
* Lackie, Pte A, 65
† Ladd, Pte Joseph, 63
† Laing, Dr (Staff Sgn), 27,64,94,117
† Laird, Cpl William, 63,94
* Lamb, Pte John, 65
† Lambden, Pte C, 63
* Langmaid, AB William, 65
† Larkin, Pte Thomas, 63
* Laucey, Pte J, 65

† Lavery, Pte Patrick, 62
* Law, Pte (later Col Sgt) 254
† Lawler, Pte M, 63
† Lawrence, Pte George, 63
† Lee, Pte E, 63
† Lee, Pte M, 63
* Lewis, AB John, 66,106
† Lewis, Pte John, 62
† Lombrest, Pte Henry, 62
† Lowrie, Pte John, 63
† Lucas, Pte Charles, 63
* Lucas, Ensign (later Capt), Gould Arthur, 4,12,18,19,20,21,28,29,33, 36,60,65,136,137,139,178,illus - fp 180,181,184, 188,189,204, illus- fp 204,205,210,213,223,244,272,301
* Lynch, Pte Patrick, 64
* Lyons, Pte G, 65
† Maber, Pte Michael, 63
† Mackinnon, Pte James, 63
† Maher, Pte James, 63
* Maley, Pte Michael, 64
† Maloney, Pte Cornelius, 62
† Maloney, Pte Patrick, 62
† Maloney, Pte Thomas, 62
* Maltier, Pte H, 65
† Marsh, Pte, 62
† Martin, Pte John, 62
† Matravis, Pte W, 63
* Matthews, Boy 2nd Class William Henry, v,viii,ix,66,165, illus - fp 165,166,167,168,169,170,171, 172,173,175,176
† Matthieson, Pte William, 64
† Matthison, Pte Alexander, 63
† Matthison, Cpl M, 63,94
* Maxwell, Quartermaster Henry, 21,66,182,183
† Maxwell, Pte Thomas, 63
* May, Pte Patrick, 64
† Mayn, Pte John, 62
* McCabe, Stoker John, 66
† McCacy, Pte John, 63
† McAnley, Pte William, 63
† McCann, Pte Patrick, 62
* McCarthy, A B James, 66
* McClusky, Sgt William Henry, 187,235, illus - fp 236,237,238,239,

INDEX

261,265,269
Funeral, 238
† McClymont, James, 64
* McCreary, Pte Patrick, 64
† McDermott, Pte J, 63
† McDonnel, Pte J, 63
* McDonnell, Pte J, 65
† McElarney, Pte John, 63
† McFudden, Pte Alexander, 64
* McGregor, Pte J, 65
* McGregor, Pte W, 65
* McKay, Pte A, 65
* McKee, Pte J, 65
† McKenzie, Pte T, 62
† McLeod, Pte Edward, 63
† McManus, Cpl, 62,94
† McMorrow, Pte T, 63
* McMullins, Pte J, 65
† McMurray, Pte James, 63
* McNeal, James, 66
† McQuade, Pte Daniel, 63
† McQuade, Pte John, 63
† Meally, Pte A, 63
† Meara, Pte Hugh, 62
† Measures, Pte William, 64
† Metford, Ensign, 12,62,94,159,197
† Milham, Pte James, 62
† Miller, Pte Alexander, 63
† Miller, Pte A, 62
† Miller, Pte David, 63
† Miller, Pte George, 63
† Montgomery, Pte A, 64
* Montgomery, Mrs, 65
† Moon, Pte James, 64
† Mooney, Pte Charles, 62
† Moore, Pte James, 63
† Moore, Pte John, 64
* Moore, Pte John, 64
† Moran, Pte T, 63
† Morgan, Pte Michael, 62
† Morrison, Pte R, 63
† Morton, Pte James, 63

† Mullany, Pte J, 63
* Mullins, Pte P, 65
* Mullins, Mrs, 65
† Munns, Pte R, 63
* Munroe, Pte D, 65
† Murphy, Pte John, 63
† Murdock, Pte Alexander, 63
† Murray, Pte Thomas, 63
† Nason, Pte James, 62
* Neale, William, 66,227
† Nelson, Pte John, 64
* Nesbitt, Mrs, 13,65,66,241
* Nesbitt, Master (later Capt) Henry, 66,241,242
* Nesbitt, Master (later Col) Richard Athol, 66,187,241-242,243,
    illus - fp 244,245,315
* Noble, AB Charles, 65
* Northover, Pte William, 66
* Nuttall, Pte Thomas, 64
* O'Brien, Pte Michael, 64
† O'Brien, Pte Patrick (60th Rifles), 63
† O'Brien, Pte Patrick (73rd Regiment), 63
† O'Connel, Pte William, 63
† O'Connell, Pte Michael, 62
† O'Connor, Pte D, 63
* O'Neill, Cpl (later Col Sgt) John, 13,34,38,65,185,189,197,198,209,
    210, illus - fp 210,211,212
† Oolrenshaw, Pte John, 62
* O'Reilly, Pte J, 65,240
† Owen, Pte J, 63
† Oxley, Pte James, 62
* Page, Pte Robert, 64,253
† Palmer, Pte J, 63
† Parklin, Pte Michael M, 63
† Parkinson, Mrs Marian [*see*: Darkin, Mrs Marian]
† Peacock, Pte Thomas, 63
† Penning, Pte Joseph, 63
* Peters, Pte G, 65
* Peters, Pte John, 64
* Peters, Pte P, 64
† Pettifer, Pte J, 63
* Phinn, AB Robert, 66
† Pratt, Pte David, 64

INDEX

† Price, Pte Charles, 62
† Pride, Pte Thomas, 64
† Prince, Pte Charles, 62
† Purcell, Pte T, 63
† Quin, Pte Edward, 63
† Quinn, Pte John, 62
† Randall, Pte George, 63
* Randall, Stoker George, 65
† Ranshaw, Pte Charles, 63
† Rees, Pte John, 63
† Rennington, Pte John, 62
* Renwick, Charles Kerr, 20,22,33,42,44,45,46,65,106,107,113,136,137, 138,139,161,162-164
† Reynolds, Pte C, 63
* Richards, Rowland Bevan, 14,18,22,43,44,45,46,47,49,51,55,65,104, 108,161,176,213,219,240,286
† Rider, Pte John, 62
† Riddelsden, Pte John, 63
† Riorden, Pte D, 63
† Roberts, Carpenter James, 64,179
† Robertson, Dr (Asst Sgn), 60,64,111
† Robertson, Pte Thomas, 64
† Robinson, Lt G W, 60,63,94
† Roche, Pte J, 63
† Rolt, Cornet J, 17,53,56,60,62,67,94,138,158,207,247,288
† Ronen, Pte Michael, 63
† Rowley, Pte James, 62
* Rush, AB Martin, 66
† Russell, Ensign Alexander Cumine, 3,12,60,63,94
† Russell, Pte William, 63
† Rutherford, Pte Ebenezer, 64
† Ryan, Pte Patrick, 62
† Salmond, Capt Robert, 14,16,17,18,20,28,30,33,39,40,42,50,55,56, 60,64,68,69,79,86, 112,115,134,138,144,150,158, illus - fp 158, 159,160,164,168, 188,194,208,213,218,219,272,287,288
* Sangaw, Pte Thomas, 64
† Scott, Pte Phillip, 63
† Scutts, Pte H, 63
† Sedgwood, Pte William, 64
† Seton, Lt Col Alexander, vi,viii,12,16,18,19,20,27,30,31,32,33,34, 37,39,50,53,60,63,79,82,83,85,94,117,126, illus - fp 126,127,129, 130,131,132,133,134,135,136,137,138,140,141,142,167,180,181,

191,194,203,204,210,214,299
† Sharp, Pte John, 64
† Shaughnessy, Pte G, 62
* Shaw, Pte Daniel, 64
† Shaw, Pte Duncan, 64
† Shea, Pte Daniel, 63
† Sheeham, Pte Timothy, 63
† Sheehan, Pte P, 63
Shelton, Capt Bond- [*see*: Bond-Shelton, Capt]
† Shephard, Pte Robert, 63
† Sheppard, Pte G, 63
† Sheppard, Pte R, 63
† Simmons, Pte Timothy, 62
* Simon, Pte John, 64
† Smith, Cpl, 64
† Smith, Pte George, 63
* Smith, AB John, 65
† Smith, Pte John, 64
* Smith, Pte John (2nd Regt), 65,205,221,illus - fp 222,223
* Smith, Pte John (74th Regt), 64
† Smith, Pte Patrick, 64
† Smith, Pte Robert, 64
† Smith, Pte Thomas, 62
* Smith, Pte Thomas, 64
* Smith, Cpl William, 4,25,34,187,205,217,218, illus - fp 218,220,221
  Recollections of a rambling life, 296-318
† Smith, Pte William, 64
* Smith, Pte W, 65
† Smith, Cpl W S, 64,94
† Smith, Pte W, 63
* Sooter, Pte William, 64
† Speer, R D, 14,23,50,64,159
† Spicer, Pte Thomas, 62
† Spriggs, Pte W, 63
* Spruce, Mrs, 65
* Stanfield, Pte J, 65
* Stanley, Pte John, 65
† Starr, Pte Michael, 62
† Steward, Pte Robert, 64
† Stokes, Pte Patrick, 63
* Stone, Ord Smn Abel, 15,66,104,108
† Story, Pte James, 63

INDEX

† Straw, Sgt John, 62,94,247
* Sullivan, Pte D, 65
† Sullivan, Pte James, 63
* Sullivan, Pte John, 64
† Sullivan, Pte T, 63
† Summerton, Pte Mark, 62
† Sweeney, Pte John, 64
† Tarney, Pte James, 64
* Taylor, Pte G, 65
* Taylor, Pte P, 65
* Taylor, Pte Walter, 64
* Teile, Sgt, 64
* Thalen, AB John, 66
† Thomas, Pte Nathaniel, 62
† Thompson, Pte Adam, 64
† Thompson, Pte James, 63
† Thompson, Pte John, 64
† Thompson, Pte J, 63
† Tierney, Pte John, 62
* Tiggle, AB Richard, 66
† Tigne, Pte W, 63
* Till, AB George, 65,106
† Torpy, Pte Edward, 62
* Tuck, Pte William, 66,186,187,226,illus - fp 226
† Tucker, Pte H, 63
† Tully, Pte Edward, 62
* Turner, Boy 2nd Class Benjamin, 66,186,226,227, illus - fp 228
† Turner, Pte Francis, 64
* Vernon, Pte Henry, 64
† Vesse, Pte Samuel, 62
† Vickery, Pte, 63
* Voss, Pte J, 65
* Wade, Pte James, 64
* Ward, Pte P, 64
† Wales, Pte T, 63
† Walker, Pte J, 62
† Walker, Pte Robert, 64
† Wallis, Pte John, 63
* Walmsley, Pte John, 65
† Walsh, Pte T, 64
* Waters, Pte Daniel, 64
† Watson, Pte George, 64

† Webber, Cpl Alexander, 64,94
† Webster, Pte B, 62
† Weller, Pte George, 62
† Wells, Pte C, 63
* Wells, Pte G, 65
† Welsh, Pte Maurice, 63
* Welsh, Pte William, 64
* West, Pte James, 64
* Wessum, James, 66
† West, Pte J, 62
† Wheeler, Pte W H, 62
† White, Andrew (Servant), 13,64
* White, Pte J, 65
† White, Pte Thomas, 62
† Whyham, W, 46,64,106,159
† Wilkins, Pte William, 63
† Wilkinson, Pte William, 63
* Wilson, Edward (Boatswain's Mate), 66,106
† Wilson, Pte James (60th Rifles), 63
† Wilson, Pte James (73rd Regiment), 63
† Wilson, Pte W, 63
* Windsor, AB George, 66
† Winnington, Pte Alexander, 64
* Winterbottom, Pte Frederick, 65
* Wood, Pte William, 64
† Woodman, Pte William, 64
* Woods, Stoker Thomas, 66
* Woodward, Pte J, 65
† Woodward, Pte William, 63
* Woodward, Smn William, 66
† Woolfall, Pte Thomas, 62
† Wootton, Pte J, 63
† Worill, Pte Henry, 64
† Worth, Pte George, 62
* Wright, Capt (later Col) Edward William Carlyle, vi,vii,4,12,16,19, 21,25,26,27,28,29,30,34,36,37,38,39,40,46,47,65,68,72,73,75,76, 78,79,83,85,87,89,90,91,93,95,98,113,117,133,135,136,137, 139, illus - fp 142,143,144,145,146,147,148,149,150,151,152,153,155, 156,188,189,191,192,198,206,207,210,211,214,220,244,246,251, 272,276,294,301
 Monument, 156-157
 Record of service (ms), fp 148,154-155

INDEX   365

† Wybrow, Pte William, 64
† Wyer, Pte Christopher, 64
* Wyndham, Boy 2nd Class George, 66
* Yale, Pte John, 64
† Zwyker, Bandsman, 62,203,205,213,254
* Zwyker, Mrs, 65

Philip, Rev Josiah, 262,263,266
Phillips, Maj Gen H P, 250,254
Phillipson, Mr, 22
Phillott, Capt, 78
Pitmedon, Lord [*see*: Seton, Sir Alexander]
Political future of England, The (Count Montalembert), 192
Pollux, 121
Pomeroy-Colley, Maj Gen Sir George, 316
Pork, 314
Portman, Lord, 208
Portugal, King of [*see*: Carlos I]
Powell, J M, 238
Prescott, Rear Adml H, 104
Press, 87,89,185,192,198,212
    [*see also*: individual publications; eg *Times, The*]
Pretorius, Miss B, 239
Pretorius, Miss M, 239
Pretorius, P, 238
Pride, Thomas, 228
Prince of Wales, viii,95,185 [*see also*: Edward VII]
Princess of Wales, 188,203 [*see also*: Alexandra, Queen]
Prussia, King of, 6,8,190,221,252

Q

Queen Alexandria [*see*: Alexandria, Queen]
Queen Victoria [*see*: Victoria, Queen of England]
Queens of England, The (Agnes Strickland), 130

R

Ramsay, Mrs, 56 [probably misprint for Ramsden, Mrs]
Ramsden, Mrs, 39,43,46,56,242
Ramsden, Capt Thomas, 24,36,39,41,43,47,56,124,176,242
Recollections of a rambling life (William Smith), 296-318

Remarkable passages in the life of John Drake, Marine
   (Richard Bentley), 281-295
Rhadamanthus, 124
Riley, Jack, 312
Roberts, Miss, 124
Roberts, Field Marshal Earl, vii,185,190, illus - fp 190,198,212,244
Roberts, Mr T, 124
Robertson, Lt,12
Robinson, Capt, 105
Robinson, Charles, 35
Roesch, Miss [*see*: Daly, Mrs Charles]
Rolph, Dr, 91,92,114
Rolt, Peter, 67
Rolt, Triscott, Lt Col J [*see*: Triscott, Lt Col J Rolt]
Round, Rev C R, 251
Rowley, Cdr Richard F, 161
Royal Academy
   Banquet (1 May 1852), 88,98
   Secretary, 98
Royal Acquarium, 175
Royal College of Surgeons
   Fellow (FRCS), 177
Royal family, 93,95,156 [*see also*: individual Sovereigns; eg. Victoria]
Royal Magazine, The, 4
Royal Military College
   Sandhurst, 143
   Senior Department, 127,156
Royal Naval College (New Cross), 188 [*see also*: Eltham College]
Royal Naval Exhibition (1891), 160
Royal United Service Institution, 124
   Council, 124
Rugby School, 192
Russell, Lord Alexander, 125
Russell, Lord John, 125
   Administration, 81
Russians, 227
   Prisoners-of-War, 289

S

Saddler, Sub-Inspector, 238
Sadlier, Dr, 197

INDEX 367

Salaman, Capt S, 238
Salmond, Mrs, 150,159
Salmond, Miss F S, 93
Salmond, Gofton - [*see*: Gofton-Salmond]
Salmond, John, 160
Salmond, Peter, 160
Salmond, Robert Gofton - [*see*: Gofton-Salmond, Robert]
Salmond, William, 160
Sandhurst [*see*: Royal Military College]
Sandili (African chief), 315
Scarlett, Sir [John] Yorke, 153
Scobell, Capt, 114
Scoresby, Dr (*Magnetic investigations*), 115
Scotch Press, 70,71
Scots, 129
Scotsman, The, 71
Scott, Capt, 104
'Sea bamboo' [*see*: Kelpweed]
Seaweed [*see*: Kelpweed]
Seeley, Ord Smn William, 228
Selected essays [Abraham Hayward], 193
Seppings, Sir Robert, 119
Seton, Mrs (mother of Lt Col Alexander Seton), 128
Seton, Mr Alexander, 126
Seton, Sir Alexander, 126
Seton, Maj Alexander David, vi,117,126,129,132,139
Seton, David, 32,37,79,85,86,87,94,118,132,133,134,135,137,139,140,
    204,213
    Wreck of the Birkenhead, 87,140
Seton, Maj George, 132
Seymour, Capt F B P, 164
Seymour, Adml Sir George, 152,155
Sharks, ix,10,20,21,53,54,58,74,139,168,182,191,193,197,199,211,212,
    213,219,227,253,254,274,287,300

SHIPS AND OTHER SEA GOING VESSELS, 18,153
   By name
     Amazon, 41,68,71,74,102,103,159,168,176,224,227,288,295
     Amphion, 119
     Anne and Sarah, 177
     Arab, 122
     Arctic, 275

Arethusa, 105
Ariel, 164
  Chief Engineer, 164 [*see also under*: PERSONALITIES: Barber]
Argo, 121
Argus, 228
Arrogant, 105
Asia, 122,160
Avenger, 113
Baron Osy, 166
  Officers, 166
Barossa, 228
Bellerophon, 162,227
Belvedere, 223
Bermuda, 168
  Crew, 168
  Officers, 168
Birkenhead, vi,vii,viii,1,2,4,5,6,7,8,9,10,12,14,15, illus - 15,18,illus - 19,19,20,26,illus-27,28,30, illus - fp 30,31,34,37,41,43,45,47,52,55, 59, 60,61,66,67,68,70,71,72,73,74,75,79,80, illus - fp 80,81,82,83, 84,85,86,88,89,90,91,92,93,94,95,97,98,99,100,101,102,103,106, 112,113,114,115,116,117,118,121,124,126,128,130,133,136,141, 142,144,145,147,152,156,158,159,160,162,163,164,165,166,167, 168,169,174,175,176,177,178,179,184,185,186,187,188,189,190, 191,192,193,194,195,197,198,199,200,201,202,203,204,205,207, 208,209,210,211,212,213,214,216,218,219,220,221,223,224,225, 226,230,231,232,233,235,236,237,238,239,241,242,243,245,246, 248,250,251,252,257,258,259,261,270,271,275,276,277,279,280, 286,294,295,299,304
Armament [*see under*: WEAPONS AND AMMUNITION]
Artillery [*see*: Armament]
Boats, 1,4,16,17,18,19,21,22,24,31,32,34,38,39,40,41,42,43,44,45, 46,47,48,49,51,53,55,57,59,60,62,65,70,73,74,78,79,85,86,92,105, 107,109,114,132,134,136,139,162,163,165,167,168,175,176,180, 181,182,184,191,193,197,199,202,203,204,207,210,211,212,213, 214,216,219,221,222,224,225,226,229,231,233,235,236,237,238, 239,240,241,242,243,245,246,247,248,251,252,253,257,272,274, 275,276,280,287,288,294,295,299
  [*see also*: Gig, Paddle Box boat]
Boatswain, 149,167 [*see also under*: PERSONALITIES: Harris, T]
Boatswain's mate, 106
  [*see also under*: PERSONALITIES: Wilson, Edward]
Bulk heads, 107,113

INDEX 369

Bulwarks, 180
Cabin boy, 246,248
Captain [*see*: Commander]
Carpenter, 179 [*see also under*: PERSONALITIES: Roberts]
Carpenter's Mate, 227
  [*see also under*: PERSONALITIES: Neale, William]
Casualties, 22
Chain pumps [*see*: Pumps]
Clerk, 14,21,41,45,46,47,56,60,150,159
  [*see also under*: PERSONALITIES: Freshfield; Hire]
Coal bunkers, 113
Commander, 14,15,16,18,19,20,29,39,44,45,46,51,52,53,55,57,
  106,108,134,160,185,206,210,224,246,253,271,276
  [*see also under*: PERSONALITIES: Salmond]
Crew, 3,14,37,38,41,42,76,165,168,175,176,182,210,224
  [*see also*: Death Roll; Muster Roll; Officers;
  see also under: PERSONALITIES]
Cutters [*see*: Boats]
Death Roll, 62-64,214 [*see also under*: PERSONALITIES]
Doctor [*see*: Surgeon]
Decks, 17,21,30,40,44,134,136,137,175,179,181,199,202,210,211,
  213,217,218,219,222,226
  After-deck, 16
  Forecastle deck, 55,160
  Lower deck, 33,167,180,218
  Main deck, 46,245,247
  Poop-deck, 16,19,20,31,33,34,37,42,44,45,46,47,50,51,53,55,
    56,57,105,106,112,133,134,136,138,140,147,148,159,160,
    178,180,181,191,199,219,226,227,246,247,272
  Quarter-deck, 30,135,181,226,227
  Troop-deck, 16,53,69,180
  Upper deck, 17,24,275,276
Engineers, 149,150
  Assistant Engineers, 106,107,137,163,164,206
    [*see also under:* PERSONALITIES: Barber, Deeley,
    Kitchingham, McClymont]
  Boatswain's Mate, 206,227
    [*see also under*: PERSONALITIES: Lacey]
  Chief Assistant Engineer, 22,40,106,113
    [*see also under*: PERSONALITIES: Renwick]
  Chief Engineer, 106
    [*see also under*: PERSONALITIES: Whyham]

Engine room, 17,37,46,106,107,113,164,214
Engines, 14,16,17,46,55,106
Figurehead, 110
Forecastle, 112,207,287
Funnel, 18,19,37,51,168,180,222,245
Gig, 17,18,22,38,43,44,45,46,47,48,49,50,51,53,55,57,58,
   108,162,163,219,224,299
Gunner [*see*: Master Gunner]
Hold, 18
Life boats [*see*: Boats]
Long boats [*see*: Boats]
Master, 14,15,20,29,40,41,44,53,56,161,206,246
   [*see also under*: PERSONALITIES: Brodie]
   2nd Masters, 14,21
      [*see also under*: PERSONALITIES: Davis; Speer]
   Assistants, 14,18,21,22,40,49,104,108,160,161,213,219
      [*see also under*: PERSONALITIES: Hare; Richards]
Master Gunner, 14,33,52,105,108,149,164,205,226,227
   [*see also under*: PERSONALITIES: Archbold]
Masts, 15,17,18,20,21,33,34,37,41,42,45,46,47,48,49,51,55,56,62,
   167,168,176,180,181,182,184,208,219,226,246, 287,254,288,300
Monuments, vii,6,8,89,93,94,156
   74th Regiment, illus - fp 138
Muster Roll, 64-66 [*see also under*: PERSONALITIES]
Officers, 161,165,167,176,186,210,218,220,245
   [*see also under*: PERSONALITIES]
Paddle box boats, 16,17,18,20,21,24,42,44,49,51,53,54,55,56,106,
   134,161,180,197,206,210,226,227,246,280,287
Pumps, 4,5,16,18,19,37,39,43,51,53,55,167,180,193,198,217,218,
   287,299
Purser's Steward, 149,150,188,214,287,289,294
   [*see also under*: PERSONALITIES: Jeffery]
Quartermaster, 54,182
   [*see also under*: PERSONALITIES: Maxwell]
Regimental drafts on board, 12,62-65,70,79,85,191,
   193,194,195,198
   [*see also under*: UNITS AND FORMATIONS - Great Britain -
      Army - Regiments]
Rigging, 49,57,132,134,181,182,213,217,246,254
Sailors [*see*: Crew]
Sketches, 34
Stokers, 40

INDEX

Surgeon, 13,38,105,108,162,224,287,294
  [*see also under*: PERSONALITIES: Culhane]
Survivors [*see*: Muster Roll; *see also under*: PERSONALITIES]
  'Roll call', illus - fp 186,186,187,201
Blenheim, 105
Boscawen, 313
Bouncer, 228
Brisk, 164
  Assistant Engineer, 164
  [*see also under*: PERSONALITIES: Barber]
Britannia, 122,167
Calypso, 169,170
Cambrian, 78
Cameleon, 120,122
Captain, 124
Carysfort, 120
Castor, viii,ix,14,24,25,28,39,41,47,48,102, illus - fp 118,119,120,
  121,123,149,214,246,288,289,295
  Armament, 171
  Coxwain, 171
  Crew, 170,171
  Figurehead, 121,122,illus - fp 122,159
  Launch, illus - fp 100,101
  Master, 123 [*see also*: Hodges, C J]
Castor (18th Century ship), 119,120
Champion of the Seas, 95
Chesapeake, 162,163,227
  Chief Engineer, 162,163
  [*see also under*: PERSONALITIES: Renwick]
Chesapeake (sailing ship), 161,228
Cleopatra, 122
Commerce, 78
Conqueror, 228
Constitution, 160
Coquette, 228
Crocodile, 227
Curlew, 166
  Captain, 166 [*see also*: Shepherd, William]
Cyclops, 112
Cydnus, 122
Dart, 170
Doris, 165

Dover, 122
Europa, 94
Euryalus, 227,228
Excellent, 104
Fortuna, 173
Frolic, 170,208,286
Fury, 164
Gladiator, 82,101
Gorgon, 164
   Assistant Engineer, 164
     [*see also under*: PERSONALITIES: Barber]
Great Liverpool, 66,74
Guardian, 78
Hermes, 313
Highflyer, 105
Himalaya, 305
Hydra, 82,160
Illustrious, 166
Imperieuse, 166,227
Implacable, 227
James Baines, illus - fp 92,95,156
Java, 160
Kent, 78
Lady Jocelyn, 95,156
Lee, 228
Lightning, 95
Lioness, 21,22,24,39,43,45,47,52,56,60,123,124,168,176,178,184,
   208,213,219,223,242,288,299
   Master, 24,36,46 [*see also*: Ramsden, Capt Thomas]
Majestic, 119
   Chief Engineer, 164
     [*see also under*: PERSONALITIES: Renwick]
Malabar, 92
Marabetta, 172
   Captain, 172
   Mate, 172
Medea, 161
   Chief Engineer, 161
     [*see also under*: PERSONALITIES: Renwick]
   Surgeon, 161 [*see also under*: PERSONALITIES: Culhane]
Megaera, 12,124,125
Minx, 162

Monarch, 176
Montagu, 209
Narcissus, 305
Neptune, 105,123
Oberon, 125,162
Oneida, 95
Orion, 68,71,74,113
Orontes, 318
Pasha, 114
Patriote, 119
Patroclus, 122
Pegasus, 74
Penelope, 144,160
Perseus, 228
Phoenix
  Chief Engineer, 163 [*see also under*: PERSONALITIES: Renwick]
Pique, 92,121
Pitt, 225
Plover, 228
Porcupine, 176
Prince, 289
Prince Regent, 105,123
Propontis, 60,115,119
Racehorse, 195
Resistance, 162
Retribution, 105,112,160
Rhadamanthus, 24,25,27,28,36,41,42,43,45,46,47,48,49,50,52,55,
  60,65,102,206,213,214,220,227,246,301
  Armament, 123
  Boats, 25
  Boatswain's Mate, 226
  Figurehead,123
  Model, illus - fp 124
Rio, 78
Rodney, 164
Romeo Primero, 208,282,285,294
Rover, 123
Royal Albert, 164
Royal George, 74
Salamander, 165
Sans Pareil, 119,120
Sappho, 171

Scourge, 162
Shannon, 161
   Armament, 161
Shannon (American frigate), 161
Sidon, 112
Simpson, 105
Sphinx, 289,290
Spiteful, 164
Styx, 82,102,218
St Vincent, 161
   2nd Master, 161 [*see also under*: PERSONALITIES: Brodie]
Superb, 123
Tagus, 122
Tamar, 288,289
Tartar, 228
Terrible, 165
Thunderbolt, 150,214
Tiger, 149
   Boatswain, 149 [*see also under*: PERSONALITIES: Jeffery]
Torch, 225,226
Towey, 122
Tribune
   Chief Engineer, 164 [*see also under*: PERSONALITIES: Barber]
Tyne, 123
Urgent, 305
Vengeance, 160,194
Vestal, 168
Victoria, 280
Victory, 104,171,228
   Master, 107 [*see also*: Madge, William Robert]
Vulcan, 112,149,162
Waldensian, 309
Warren Hastings, 8
Warspite, 175
Wasp, 26
Waterwitch, 208,282,285
   Crew, 282
Wellesley, 122
Winchester, 105
Wolverene, 169
By type/function
   Brig, 120,170

INDEX 375

Brigantine, 92,170,282,283
Clipper, 95
Collier, 175
Convict ship, 171
Corvett, 168
East Indiaman, 78
Frigate, viii,ix,28,39,48,111,112,119,120,123,165,166,213,288,
    295,305 [*see also*: *Castor*; *Lioness*; Screw steamer frigate]
Gunboat, 26,175,228
Iron, 92,110,111,112,113
Lifeboat, 172
Mail steamer, 60,135,315
Paddle sloop, 123
Paddle wheel steamer, 12,13,162,176
Paddle wheel steamer sloop, 164
Revenue cutter, 166
Schooner, 21,22,24,25,38,39,40,41,43,44,45,47,48,49,52,56,57,60,
    105,109,122,169,172,176,177,178,185,206,208,214,219,246,242,
    288,299 [*see also*: *Lioness*]
Screw steam gunboat, 162
Screw steamer, 12,17,124,162
Screw steamer frigate, 161,162,163
Slave ships, 121,171,208,282,292,310
    Brazilian, 282
Sloop, 122,123,165,171,220,310
    [*see also*: *Rhadamanthus*; Paddle sloop, Paddle wheel steamer
    sloop, Steam sloop]
Steamers, 110,123,160,173,177,184,309
    [*see also*: Mail steamer,Paddle wheel steamer, Steam frigate]
Steam frigate, 149,160
Steam sloop, 161,163,313
Steamships [*see*: Steamers]
Submarine A4, 10
Troopship, 12,18,38,39,92,95,112,113,149,156,159,162,167,185,
    186,188,196,202,207,216,217,226,232,229,241,250,252,259,276
    [*see also*: *Birkenhead*]
West Indiaman, 177
Whaleboat, 25,26,28,41
Wooden, 92,113

Shipwrecks, 71
    [*see also*: SHIPS - *Arctic, Bermuda, Birkenhead, Captain, Cedarine,*

Curlew, Great Liverpool, Marabetta, Megaera, Orion, Pegasus, Prince, Racehorse, Royal George, Thunderbolt, Torch, Victoria]
Sidwell, Miss, 249,250,251,252
Simeon, Capt Charles, 122
Short, Capt F, 164
Sinclair, Miss Catherine, 130
   Hill and valley, 130
Slavery/slave trade, 121,309 [*see also*: SHIPS - Slave ships]
Slaves, 310
   Children, 171
   Women, 171 [*see also*: SHIPS - Slave ships]
Smales, Capt, 26,39,41,51,54,60,136,184,197,206,220,223,227,255,301
Smith, Gen Sir Harry, 12,14,23,59,81,82,99,143,210,220,223,238,303
Smugglers, 166
Snakes
   Boa constrictor, 306
   Mamba, 306
   Python, 311
Society for the Propagation of Christian Knowledge [*see*: SPCK]
Somerset, Capt, 125
Somma Medici, 277
Spaniards, 283,284
Spectator, The, 75,275
SPCK, 276
Speke, John Hanning, 305
Spratt, William Robert, 265,268
Staff College [*see*: Royal Military College - Senior Department]
Stafford, Sir Augustus, 81,91,114
Standard, The, 186
Staniland, Lt Col R W, 211
Stephenson, Capt, 93
Steuart, Sir Hew, 122
Stillwell, Thomas, 123
Stillwell, William, 123
Stoney, William Walter, 267,268
Stopford, Sir Robert, 121
Story of the Birkenhead, (A C Addison), v,174,192,242,252
Strickland, Miss Agnes, 130
   The Queens of England, 130
Strong, Mrs, 130
Strong, Rev Linwood, 130
St Andrews School, 235

INDEX 377

St Paul's (mission station), 316
St Pierre, Bernadin de, 314
    Paul et Virginie, 314
Sultan of Turkey, 121
Sutherland, Duke of, 110
Swinburne, Algernon Charles (*Grace Darling*), 2
Symonds, Capt, 105
Symonds, Cdr T W C, 123

T

Tamplin, H T, 265
Tatham, Mr, 9
Teachers, 9,10
Thackeray, William Makepeace, 66
Thesiger, Gen [*see*: Chelmsford, Lord]
Thompson, Mr, 107
Thompson, Rev Thomas, 126,141
Times, The, 14,68,69,82,83,86,89,98,108,113,114,195
Tower of London, 296
    Yeoman Warders, 291,292
Trained Nurses Annuity Fund, 188
Transportation, 172
Trinity College, Dublin
    Provost, 197 [*see also*: Sadlier, Dr]
Triscott, Lt Col J Rolt, 67
Trojans, 163
Trotter, Cdre, 170
Troutbridge, Capt Thomas, 119,120
Tyson, Capt, 239

U

Uithaalder (Hottentot leader), 144
United Services Gazette, 76,77
United Service Magazine and Naval and Military Journal, 127
United Service Fund, 91,93
United Services Institution
    Council, vii

UNITS AND FORMATIONS
    Austria

Navy
  Fleet, 121
Denmark
  Army, 203
France
  Army
    Cuirassiers, 76
    Imperial Guard, 76
    Lancers, 76
  Navy
    Fleet, 119
      Squadrons, 119
Great Britain, 74
  Army, viii,76,86,87,91,92,98,127,141,143,147,156,157,189,192, 193,196,200,203,204,214,215,217,223,227,248,258,259,296, 297,303,309
    Army of the East (Crimean War 1854-1856), 151
    Artillery, 14,175,224 [*see also*: Regiments - Royal Artillery]
    Adjutant General's Office, 141
      Deputy Adjutant General, 127 [*see also*: Brown, Sir George]
    Brigades
      Eyre's Brigade (South African Frontier War 1850-1853), 204
    Cavalry, 143
    Commander-in-Chief, vii,77,81,84,87,97,98,189,190
      [*see also*: Cambridge, Duke of; Roberts, Field Marshal Earl; Wellington, Duke of]
        Private Secretary, 190 [*see also*: Goschen, Lt Col George]
    Commands
      South Western District, 151,153,156
    Corps
      Ordnance Corps, 308
      Royal Engineers, 101,297
        9th Company, 220,302
    Dragoons, 26
    Garrisons
      Malta, 147
      Mauritius, 314
    Infantry, 143
    Inspector General of the Forces, vii
      Deputy Inspector General, 156
        [*see also under*: PERSONALITIES: Wright]
    Inspector General of Reserve Forces, 156,157

INDEX 379

[*see also under*: PERSONALITIES: Wright]
Jounopore Field Force
(Indian Mutiny 1857-1858), 96
Non-Commissioned Officers/Warrant Officers, 6,12,13,16,30,
  93,94,134,135 [*see also*: specific ranks; eg Sergeants]
  Annuities, 291
Officers, 1,2,4,6,8,13,14,16,18,21,24,30,31,32,34,37,38,39,40,
  41,42,44,47,48,49,50,51,53,59,60,69,70,71,72,74,79,82,84,85,
  86,90,93,94,96,98,109,129,133,135,138,144,148,149,157,179,
  184,191,1 92,194,197,198,199,200,201,202,204,205,223,226,
  244,248,249,250,252,259,274,276,287,297,301,303,308
  Survivors of *Birkenhead*, 21,41
    [*see also under*: PERSONALITIES: Bond; Bowen;
      Girardot; Lucas; Wright]
  Quartermaster General, 128,152
    [*see also*: Clarke, Gen Sir Mansfield; Gordon, Sir Willoughby]
    Assistant Quartermaster General, vii,151,156
    [*see also under*: PERSONALITIES: Seton; Wright]
  Regiments, 84,192,276,286,299,304
    Argyll and Sutherland Highlanders,
      (Princess Louise's), 132,210 [*see also*: 91st Regiment]
    Black Watch, The [*see*: Royal Highlanders]
    Coldstream Guards, 249,251,254,258
    Derbyshire Regiment (Sherwood Foresters)
      1st Battalion, 195 [*see also*: 45th Regiment]
    East Suffolk Regiment, 220
    Grenadier Guards, 203
    Highland Light Infantry, 3
      Colonel-in-Chief, viii
      2nd Bn, viii,195 [*see also*: 74th Regiment]
    King's Royal Rifle Corps, 195 [*see also*: 60th Regiment]
    Leicestershire Regiment [*see*: 17th Regiment]
    Leinster Regiment, 215
    Oxfordshire Light Infantry, viii,201
      1st Battalion, 195 [*see also*: 43rd Regiment]
    Princess Louise's Regiment
      [*see*: Argyll and Sutherland Highlanders]
    Queen's Own Royal West Kent Regiment, 95
      [*see also*: 97th Regiment]
    Queen's Regiment
      [*see*: Royal West Surrey Regiment/2nd Regiment]
    Rifle Brigade, 133,178,297,301

1st Battalion, 125,178
Service companies, 12
Royal Artillery, 144,303,305
Royal Highlanders (The Black Watch)
  2nd Battalion, 195 [*see also*: 73rd Regiment]
Royal Irish Fusiliers [*see*: 87th Regiment]
Royal Marines, 135,149,170,186,199,200,204,205,207,208, 212,213,225,226,228,282,285,288,289,293,297
  Assistant Adjutant General, 285
  Deputy Adjutant General, 285,286 [*see also*: Owen, J]
  Divisions
    Portsmouth Division, 208,281,286,288,290
      Commanding Officer, 285,290 [*see also*: Clyles, F]
Royal Warwickshire Regiment [*see*: 6th Regiment]
Royal West Surrey Regiment (The Queen's), 195,221
  [*see also*: 2nd Regiment]
  1st Battalion, 250,251,260
  2nd Battalion, 250,251
Royal Warwickshire Regiment, 195 [*see also*: 6th Regiment]
Sherwood Foresters
  [*see*: Derbyshire Regiment; *see also under*: Militia]
Suffolk Regiment, 195 [*see also*: 12th Regiment]
  1st Bn, 221
West Surrey Regiment, 222
York and Lancaster Regiment
  2nd Bn, 8
2nd (Queen's) Regiment,12,60,64,65,94,112,149,167,175,186, 195,199,200,203,204,205,222,223,224,248,249,250,252, 253,254,260,303
  Bandmaster, 253
    [*see also under*: PERSONALITIES: Zwyker]
5th Dragoon Guards, 296
6th Dragoons, 95
6th Lancers, 296
6th Regiment, 12,60,62,64,65,94,159,180,195,197,301,303
7th Dragoon Guards, 184,197
7th Light Dragoons (later 7th Hussars), 210
11th Hussars, 245,247
12th Lancers, vii,4,12,13,17,18,21,26,32,52,53,56,60,62,65,67, 80,94,116,139,186,187,189,195,197,202,207,213,220, 244,247,288,304
  [*see also*: 12th (Prince of Wales) Royal Lancers]

INDEX

12th (Prince of Wales's) Royal Lancers, 195,201
   [*see also*: 12th Lancers]
12th Regiment, 25,60,62,64,65,66,94,146,187,205,217,218,
   220,297,301,302,303,314 [*see also*: Suffolk Regiment]
   Colours, 296
   2nd Battalion, 299
14th Regiment, 92
17th Regiment, 297
   Colours, 297
21st Royal North British Fusiliers, 126,127
23rd Regiment, 78
24th Regiment, 315
30th Regiment, 296
31st Regiment, 78
33rd Regiment, 101
43rd Light Infantry Regiment, 12,18,21,54,60,63,64,65,
   79,94,147,180,187,188, 195,196,201,204,247
   [*see also*: Oxfordshire Light Infantry - 1st Battalion]
45th Regiment, 63,64,94,195
   [*see also*: Derbyshire Regiment - 1st Battalion]
49th Regiment, 132
60th Regiment, 31,63,64,65,134,137,140,195
   [*see also*: King's Royal Rifle Corps]
   2nd Bn, 12
73rd Regiment, 12,18,19,21,26,27,60,63,64,65,94,101,134,136,
   179,180,186,187,195,204,213,215,216,223,229,230,301,303
   [*see also*: Royal Highlanders (The Black Watch) - 2nd
      Battalion]
74th Regiment, viii,3,12,16,63,64,65,82,92,94,127,128,133,
   136,180,194,195,213,303
   Paymaster, 136
   [*see also*: Highland Light Infantry - 2nd Bn]
87th Regiment, 296
91st Regiment, 12,13,16,21,36,38,50,60,64,65,75,77,94,
   135,137,143,145,146,150,157,185,195,206,207,209,210,
   212,219,246,247,276,301
   [*see also*: Argyll and Sutherland Highlanders]
   Reserve Battalion, 144
93rd Highland Regiment, 132
97th Regiment, 95
   [*see also*: Queen's Own Royal West Kent Regiment]
   Colours, 96

Sergeants, 12,13,31,56,137,140,149
    [*see also*: Non-Commissioned Officers/Warrant Officers]
  Soldiers, 1,2,3,6,8,11,17,25,31,32,37,38,42,43,44,50,56,59,
    60,65,66,68,69,70,71,75,76,84,86,94,95,98,129,130,133,135,
    139,144,145,163,165,166,167,172,179,182,184,189,191,192,
    193,194,195,199,202,204,210,211,213,214,216,218,221,224,
    240,246,247,251,252,257,259,272,274,275,281,287,297
  Surgeons, 13,74,117,133,224,295
    [*see also under*: PERSONALITIES: Bowen; Laing; Robertson]
  Transport, 220
  Troops [*see*: Soldiers]
  Warrant Officers [*see*: Non-Commissioned Officers]
Coastguards
  Atherfield Station, 173
  Chief Officer, viii [*see also under*: PERSONALTIES: Matthews]
  Hastings Division
    St Leonard's, 173
  Langley Station, 173
Mercantile Marine, 175
Militia
  Forfar and Kincardine Artillery Militia, 132
  Sherwood Foresters, 196,201
Navy, viii,18,59,69,98,112,114,119,122,123,124,160,161,162,166,
  170,175,177,186,219,229,259
  Admiral of the Fleet, 90 [*see also*: Briggs, Sir T]
  Admiralty, vi,36,39,41,69,78,90,108,110,111,113,116,117,149,
    206,208,285,286,291,293
    First Lord, 81,98
    Secretary, 81,114,140 [*see also*: Stafford, Sir Augustus]
  Deputy Judge Advocate, 105,108 [*see also*: Greetham, Sir G L]
  Fleets, 289
    Channel Fleet, 209
    Home Fleet, 176
  in: Mauritius
  Naval Brigade, 225
  Non-Commissioned Officers, 55,56
  Petty Officer, 55
  Officers, 24,90,91,92,104,139,186,259
    Midshipman, 74
  Rear Admiral, 81
  Sailors [*see*: Seamen]
  Seamen, 1,11,14,17,26,42,50,60,66,69,76,91,102,259,282,288,309

INDEX

    Squadrons
      Channel, 160
      North America, 123
      Western, 123
      West Indies, 123
    Stations
      Africa, 282
      Australia, 165
      China, 102,162,163,227,228
      East Indies, 120,161,162,163
      North America, 122,123,160
      South Africa, 193
      West Indies, 122,123,160
   Volunteers
    Mid-Ulster Royal Garrison Artillery
      Paymaster Sergeant, 214
        [*see also under*: PERSONALITIES: Kilkeary]
      Rifle Volunteers, 209,210
India
  Cavalry, 305
Italy
  Army, 203
Mauritius
  Police, 314
Prussia, 203
  Army
    Regiments, 6,193,199,221
    Soldiers, 193
Rhodesia
  British South Africa Company Police, 244
  Mashonaland Mounted Rifles, 244
Russia
  Cavalry, 289
  Navy
    Fleet, 227
South Africa
  Boers
    Commandos, 233
      Field Cornets,24,54
    Transvaal forces, 233
  Colonial forces,310,303,316,317
    Beaconsfield Town Guard, 236,239,241

Cape Corps, 146
Cape Mounted Riflemen, 142,146,151,187,204,205,217,220,238, 239,240,244,303,304,305,307,308,309,314
Diamond Fields Horse, 238,239,240
   C Troop, 238
Cape Police, 238
   Cape Mounted Police, 315
Frontier Armed and Mounted Police, 243
Frontier Light Horse, 221,315
Kimberley Light Horse, 316,317
Kimberley Regiment, 238
Landry's Light Horse, 316
Mounted Police
[*see*: Cape Police - Mounted Police/Cape Mounted Riflemen/Frontier Armed and Mounted Police]
Natal Frontier Guard, 204
Nesbitt's Horse/Nesbitt's Light Horse, 67,242,244,315
Police [*see*: Cape Police; *see also*: Mounted Police]

V

Van Donop, Cdr P B [*see*: Donop, Cdr P B van]
Victor Emmanual III (King of Italy, 1906-1946), viii, illus - fp 6
Victoria (Queen of England, 1837-1901), 6,35,59,83,85,93,94,144,156, 202,225,229,296
Victoria and Albert Museum, vii,178
Villaret, M, 119
Villiers, Field Cornet de [*see*: De Villiers, Field Cornet]
Vincent, Mdm, 74
Virginie (character in French romance), 314
   Grave, 314
Viscount Hardinge [*see*: Hardinge, Viscount]
Vulcan, 110

W

Waggon drivers, 302
Wakenham, David, 283,284
Walker, Capt E W M, 146
Wallach, Advocate, 265,267,268
Walsh, A, 60
Warden, Capt, 105

INDEX

Warren, Sir Charles, 238,240
Wavell, Gen, 221

WEAPONS AND AMMUNITION
    Ammunition, 304
        Powder, 304
        Round shot, 228
    Assegai, 240
    Congreve rockets [*see*: Rockets]
    Guns, 33,212,218,228,246,304,309,313
        Swivel, 309
        32 pr, 111,161,227
        68 pr, 111
        96 pr, 111
    Muskets
        'Brown Bess', 298
    Rifles
        Carbines, 116
        Enfield, 302,303
        Martini Henry, 303
        Snider, 303
    Rockets, 33,172,173,206,218,227

Wellesley, Sir Arthur [*see*: Wellington, Duke of]
Wellington, Duke of, vii,73,76,81,82,85,88,89, illus - fp 96,97,98,99,100,
    144,199,299
Wesley (family) [*see*: Wellington, Duke of]
Wesley, S R, 285
West, J, 124
Westminster Abbey, 209,294
Westminster, Marchioness of, 110
White, William, 211
Widows, 93
Willes, Flag Capt George O, 228
Willoughby Moore, Lt Col [*see*: Moore, Lt Col Willoughby]
Wilmot, Maj, 303
Windsor Magazine, 2
Wines, 116
Winter, Mrs, 188
Wives [*see*: Women]
Wolseley, Field Marshal Lord, vii,185,illus - fp 188,202,212
Women, 1,4,13,16,18,19,20,22,25,31,32,34,37,38,39,41,42,43,44,47,49,

50,51,53,55,56,60,70,71,74,75,79,83,85,87,88,92,98,108,125,131,
135,136,137,139,145,162,165,168,176,180,191,193,199,203,204,
207,210,211,212,213,216,219,222,226,229,230,240,246,249,252,
253,272,275,276,280,287,288,299
[*see also under*: PERSONALITIES: Darkin, Mrs; Hudson,
Mrs; Montgomery, Mrs; Mullins, Mrs; Nesbitt, Mrs; Spruce, Mrs;
Zwyker, Mrs]
Wood, Sir Evelyn, 316
Wood, G, 146
Woodward, J D, 124
Wotherspoon, John, 188
Wotherspoon, Lucy, 188
Wreck of the Birkenhead (David Seton), 87,140
Wreck of the Birkenhead, The (Charles Dixon), fp 30,35
Writer to the Signet, 31,139
Wyvill, Mrs, 122
Wyvill, Cdre Christoper,14,23,24,25,28,29,36,39,40,41,43,45,48,50,52,57,
58,116,119,122, illus - fp 122,123,158,159,206
  Despatch, 37,39,40-41,60
Wyvill, Marmaduke, 122
Wyvill, Marmaduke d'Arcy, 122

Y

Yarborough, Lt Col, 146
Yates, Mr, 239
Yates, Mrs, 129
Yellow fever, 315
York, Duke of, 173

Z

Zinn, C, 235
Zwyker, Miss, 254
Zulus, 316

Lightning Source UK Ltd.
Milton Keynes UK
UKHW020739180521
383915UK00003B/93